NARRATIVES OF AFRICAN AMERICAN ART AND IDENTITY

THE DAVID C. DRISKELL COLLECTION

The Art Gallery and the
Department of Art History and Archaeology
University of Maryland
College Park, Maryland

Pomegranate
San Francisco, California

Published in conjunction with the exhibition of the same title,
Narratives of African American Art and Identity: The David C. Driskell Collection

Juanita Marie Holland, *Principal Essayist and Editor*

EXHIBITION TRAVELING SCHEDULE

The Art Gallery
College Park, Maryland
October 22–December 19, 1998

Colby College Museum of Art
Waterville, Maine
July 21–October 17, 1999

The Fine Arts Museums of San Francisco
San Francisco, California
November 20, 1999–February 12, 2000

High Museum of Art
Atlanta, Georgia
June 20–September 10, 2000

The Newark Museum
Newark, New Jersey
October 25, 2000–February 25, 2001

Published by Pomegranate Communications, Inc.
Box 6099, Rohnert Park, California 94927

Pomegranate Europe Ltd.
Fullbridge House, Fullbridge
Maldon, Essex CM9 4LE, England

Front cover: Romare Bearden, *Morning,* 1975 (catalogue no. 29)
© Romare Bearden Foundation Licensed by VAGA, New York, NY
Back cover: William H. Johnson, *Children Playing London Bridge,* c. 1942 (catalogue no. 39)
Frontispiece: Aaron Douglas, *Go Down Death,* 1934 (catalogue no. 14)
Pomegranate Catalog No. A504

Library of Congress Cataloging-in-Publication Data
Narratives of African American art and identity : the David C. Driskell collection.
    p. cm.
       Catalog of a traveling exhibition first held at the Art Gallery of the University of Maryland,
    College Park, Maryland, Oct. 22–Dec. 19, 1998.
       Written by Terry Gips and others.
       Includes bibliographical references and index.
       ISBN 0-7649-0722-0 (hc. : alk. paper). — ISBN 0-7649-0689-5 (pb. : alk. paper)
       1. Afro-American art—Exhibitions.   2. Art, Modern—20th century—United States—
    Exhibitions.   3. Driskell, David C.—Art collections—Exhibitions.   4. Art—Private collections—
    United States—Exhibitions.   I. Gips, Terry, 1945–   .   II. University of Maryland, College Park.
    Art Gallery.
    N6538.N5N27   1998
    704.03'96073'007475251—dc21   98-21510
                                                                          CIP

Cover and interior design by Poulson/Gluck Design, Richmond, California

Printed in China
07 06 05 04 03 02   10 9 8 7 6 5 4 3 2

First Edition

CONTENTS

Foreword
Terry Gips

7

David C. Driskell
Terry Gips

10

Tribute
Stephanie E. Pogue

12

Acknowledgments
M. Colleen Chapman

13

Introduction: Driskell the Collector
Keith Morrison

16

*The Color of Art: African American
Artistic Identities in the Twentieth Century*
Juanita M. Holland

23

A History of Collecting African American Art
Sharon F. Patton

45

In the Archive and the Garden
Richard J. Powell

55

The David Driskell Motives
Allan M. Gordon

59

The David C. Driskell Collection: Object Entries
Adrienne L. Childs, Tuliza Fleming,
Kim Kindelsperger, Jennifer Strychasz

65

Artists' Chronologies
Adrienne L. Childs
and Tuliza Fleming

169

Notes

177

Selected Bibliography

179

Exhibition Checklist

183

Photography Credits

186

Notes on the Contributors

187

Index

188

Foreword

In both real and metaphorical terms, this exhibition and catalogue have been in the making for more than twenty years. When David Driskell arrived at the University of Maryland in 1977, he carried with him much of the legacy that is now unveiled to the public and celebrated through *Narratives of African American Art and Identity: The David C. Driskell Collection*. *Legacy* is a fitting term in that it implies a heritage or tradition, a history or culture carried forward. The legacy here is both that grand cultural narrative and its many distinct components, each possessing its own significance: the art collected; the stories and histories of those objects told, retold, and recorded; the books, news clippings, articles, letters, photographs, slides, and other primary sources of African American cultural history archived for the future; the extensive body of artwork produced by the artist; and the man himself: teacher, scholar, public servant, as well as collector and artist.

This multifaceted legacy has grown and attained international distinction during Driskell's tenure at the University of Maryland. It was four decades earlier, though, during his years as a student at Howard University, that he first became acquainted with many leading African American artists, teachers, and scholars, and built relationships that formed the basis of lasting collegiality and friendship. From 1955 to 1976, while he was teaching at Talladega College, Howard University, and Fisk University, his reputation grew as one of the most dedicated scholars and practitioners in the arts. Driskell's long career as a collector and his assistance to other collectors —especially black colleges and universities—in creating holdings of African American art also began well before coming to

Maryland. He acquired his first work, a print by James L. Wells, in 1954 and worked with Talladega College as early as 1955. Essays in the catalogue chronicle this story and record David Driskell's many contributions in the broad arena of American art. A distinctive perspective permeates many of the texts, however, on how Driskell, through his own experiences and development, embodies much of the complex history of African American art. By investigating and articulating David Driskell's story, we can better understand the story of African American art—its production, its reception and collection by both black and white societies, its African roots and its American roots, and its role in reflecting and shaping culture. We hope and expect that thefresh insights offered here will become valuable additions to the discourse on the art of African Americans and on the African Diaspora.

During Professor Driskell's twenty-one years at Maryland, his colleagues in art and art history and elsewhere on campus have developed an enormous respect for his knowledge, commitment, and contributions to the field of art. However, true to his unassuming character, Driskell did not flaunt the prized objects in his collection—even though he generously lent individual items for exhibitions throughout the U.S. He also invited students to work with his collection, carrying on the mentoring tradition that had been so invaluable to him in his student years. But over time, Driskell's friends from the university became more aware of the art collection and cultural archives that he was steadily assembling. Even though most of the university community had little idea of the remarkable resources so close at hand, a few colleagues dreamt quietly of a time when Driskell

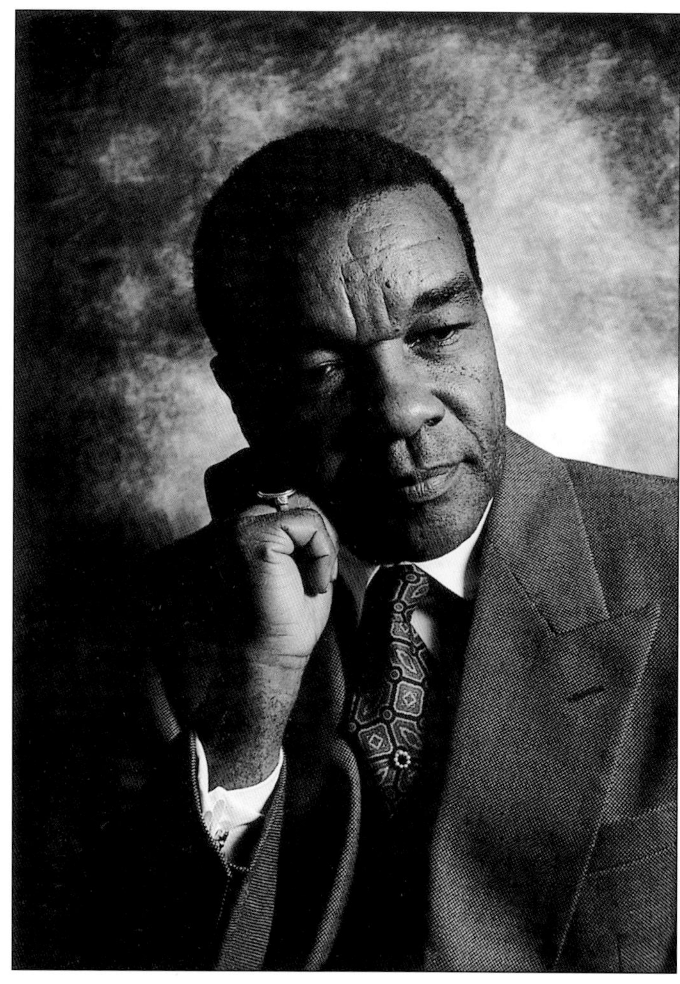

David C. Driskell, 1995 (Michael Parish, photographer)

the public. Some harbored the idea of a magnificent exhibition at the University of Maryland, with a scholarly catalogue, an opportunity to view the works and to learn from them, and an opportunity to honor the individual responsible for creating the collection.

As David Driskell's time for retiring from teaching moved closer and closer, various ideas for an exhibition at The Art Gallery were floated. Eventually, the subject was broached with Driskell. But which exhibition? There were many possibilities. To his colleagues at the University, Driskell was first and foremost a teacher and an artist. Thus, a major retrospective of his painting and collage work would be a splendid conclusion to his years at Maryland. But why pass up the extraordinary opportunity to bring works from his collection into a museum setting and give them the public exposure they deserved? Perhaps Driskell himself could be foregrounded, inviting a curatorial perspective that told of his various contributions as artist, collector, scholar, teacher, and mentor to the next generation of African American artists and art historians, thereby including both his own art and his collection of works by others. Since his collection was both large and diverse, comprising not only works by the vast majority of recognized African American artists from the nineteenth century to the present but also numerous African objects, prints from Europe and Japan, and pieces by Anglo Americans, there also was the question of *which* work to include and how to structure the exhibition.

Throughout 1996, the shape of the exhibition was molded and remolded many times. In brief, the outcome that materialized from the lively discussions among project participants at the University of Maryland as well as with colleagues from elsewhere integrated several ideas. One of our goals would be to present the story of African American art of the twentieth century through the lens of Driskell's role as mentor to artists, collectors, and historians and as quiet catalyst to its evolution. However, a larger theoretical framework emerged to surround this perspective: Curator Juanita Holland organized a structure for both the exhibition and catalogue that traces the unfolding of racial and artistic identities as they are revealed in Driskell's rich collection of African American art and that places the narrative of Driskell's contributions front and center with regard to current diaspora theorizing. Her lead essay presents scholarly analysis and provocative discussion that serves to challenge simple art-historical thinking about African American art and cultural identity.

To solve the remaining dilemma of how we could simultaneously present Driskell *the artist*, we decided to prepare a separate companion exhibition of his work. In some ways, *Echoes: The Art of David C. Driskell 1955–1997* is only a tiny glimpse of Driskell's prolific career as an artist. Curated by Adrienne L. Childs, this mini-retrospective highlights the evolution of Driskell's style and examines the important themes that reverberate throughout his more than forty years of artistic production.

Like many other exhibitions, especially those originating within an educational setting, *Narratives of African American Art and Identity: The David C. Driskell Collection* has expanded beyond the confines of exhibition and catalogue. The project, as it is being played out, also encompasses educational programs for all ages, an extensive website with links to an array of databases on African American art and culture, and a symposium of the arts of the African Diaspora. After its debut at the University of Maryland in the fall of 1998, the exhibition travels during 1999 to the Colby College Museum of Art in Maine and The Fine Arts Museums of San Francisco, and in 2000 to the High Museum of Art in Atlanta and The Newark Museum. The resource materials, the educational programs, and the scholarly research that evolve from the exhibition will continue and, in fact, have a life of their own, generating more exhibitions, more collectors, scholars, artists, teachers, mentors—taking cues from the singular contributions of David C. Driskell as a model for nurturing the future of African American art.

The Art Gallery is very honored to have overseen the production of this catalogue and exhibition. We join the departments of Art and Art History and Archaeology, the College of Arts and Humanities, and the President's office in congratulating David Driskell on his extraordinary achievements. We will treasure his legacy and trust that this catalogue will be one document among many that will partially preserve some of the riches that David Driskell has given to us.

—Terry Gips
Director
The Art Gallery
University of Maryland

David C. Driskell

David C. Driskell's roots are southern and infused with art. Born in 1931 in Eatonton, Georgia, David moved with his family when he was five to the Appalachian Mountains in western North Carolina. His paternal grandparents came originally from the Georgia Sea Islands, where they spoke Gullah, a patois of African dialects, French, and English. Driskell's grandfather was an artist in the African tradition, making ornaments from bark for the household and for the harnesses of horses. David's father worked as a blacksmith, a furniture maker, and a Baptist minister. He also occasionally made small sketches and gouache paintings of religious subjects. His mother made quilts and wove baskets from bullrush and pine needles.

David Driskell has been both a practicing artist and a dedicated champion of African American art since 1951, when he was an undergraduate student at Howard University in Washington, D.C. His primary mentor at that time was James A. Porter, who was—as Driskell would come to be—a teacher, artist, and art historian. Driskell received his B.A. from Howard in 1955 and his M.F.A. from Catholic University of America in 1962. He also attended Skowhegan School of Painting and Sculpture in Maine in 1953 and studied art history in The Hague, Netherlands, in 1964. Driskell had hardly completed his undergraduate degree when he took his first teaching position in 1955 at Talladega College in Alabama at age twenty-four. After teaching there for six years, he returned to Washington, D.C., to complete his M.F.A. and accept a position as associate professor at Howard, where he taught until 1966. He then became a professor and chair of the department of art at Fisk University in Nashville. Twelve years later, he once again returned to the nation's capital, this time to become chair of the depart-

ment of art at the University of Maryland. Twenty-one years and many awards later, David Driskell received the President's Medal, the highest university award bestowed on a member of the faculty and staff.

Driskell was named Distinguished Professor at Maryland in 1995 and between 1977 and 1994 received seven honorary doctorates. In the forty-five years since he enrolled in college, he has been the recipient of scores of scholarly awards, as well as numerous travel grants, prizes for his art, citations for service, and other honors. He also has served on more than twenty prestigious boards of directors and maintains a full schedule of lecturing and guest appearances throughout the U.S., Europe, and Africa.

In his numerous publications, Driskell evidences his commitment to enhancing the study of the art of the United States by emphasizing the multicultural contributions made to it by Native American, black, Asian, and European artists. His *Two Centuries of Black American Art*, published in 1976 for the Los Angeles County Museum of Art, is considered a standard survey in art-historical scholarship. Driskell also has edited, authored, or collaborated on numerous other publications, including *African American Visual Aesthetics*, which investigates notions of the postmodern as they pertain to African American art. Driskell has curated more than thirty-five exhibitions on African American art including, most recently, an exhibition of the work of the contemporary artist Claude Clark. Currently, he is finishing a book on the private collection of Dr. and Mrs. William Cosby, for whom he has served as collection consultant over the past twenty years: *The Other Side of Color: The African American Collection of Camille O. and William H. Cosby, Jr.*

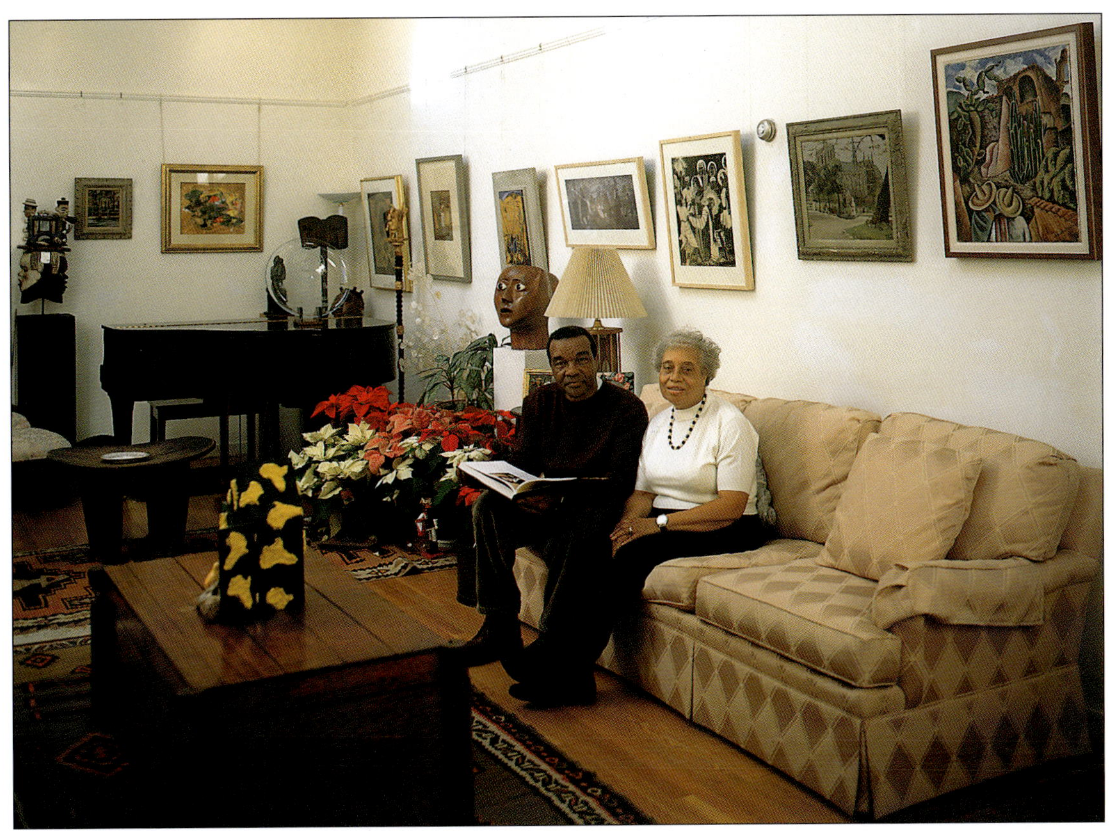

David Driskell and Thelma Driskell in their home in Hyattsville, Maryland, 1998 (Greg Staley, photographer)

Driskell's own artwork, primarily painting and collage, has been described as colorist and reflects his southern heritage and racial and social identities. While sometimes working in typical genres such as landscape, portraiture, and still life, Driskell's paintings often employ vigorous brushwork that allows them to function also as formal studies of color, shape, and texture. He has had solo shows at Midtown Payson Galleries (New York) and numerous other private and university galleries. He has also completed several major commissions, including stained-glass windows for two churches. His work is included in various public and private collections, including the Baltimore Museum of Art, the Corcoran Gallery of Art, Talledega College, and the Birmingham Museum of Art.

David Driskell lives in Hyattsville, Maryland, with his wife, Thelma G. DeLoatch, whom he married in 1952. They have two children and five grandchildren. The inside of his Victorian house is replete with the smells of food, the lively voices of friends and family, antiques, and works of art from his collection, which blanket the walls and populate most every corner and tabletop. One sees, of course, the full sweep of African American artists from the nineteenth century to the present, but also the Rembrandt and Hiroshige prints; masks, staffs, and a variety of objects from Africa; and historically important photographs. Behind the house is Driskell's two-story studio, overflowing with his own works and smelling of fresh paint on work in progress. In the large front yard is Driskell's profuse garden of vegetables, flowers, shrubs, trees, meandering paths, and wooden benches. Nature is an even more salient element at the Driskell summer residence in Falmouth, Maine, where he retreats every summer to paint. As David Driskell moves from kitchen to studio, from garden to classroom, from lecture circuit to family gathering, he is always a quiet and persistent nurturer of art and human values; his lifelong role as catalyst and mentor is beyond easy measure, but it is made tangible through his collection.

— Terry Gips
Director
The Art Gallery
University of Maryland

Tribute

There are rare occasions when one is privileged to work with an exceptional individual. David Driskell is just such a person. Complex and multitalented, he is appropriately referred to as a twentieth-century Renaissance man. Our association spans thirty-two years, including the last seventeen with the Department of Art at the University of Maryland. During that time I have had the good fortune to experience at times, and at other times to observe, David's outstanding strengths as teacher and mentor, artist, researcher and scholar, art historian, art theorist, collector, and philanthropist. To excel in any of these areas is desirable. But to reach the highest standards in all of them, and indeed to redefine some, speaks to the genius and "completeness" of David Driskell.

Society benefits when there are those in its midst who, through their hard work and insight, help make it grow in positive ways. That there are both reflection and revelation of David's work in so many areas in the exhibition at The Art Gallery at the University of Maryland is significant in and of itself. The insight to be gained from David's research, his own creative images, and those from his collection afford his students, associates, and the art community and larger community an opportunity for a unique and insightful sharing of some of the essence that is David Driskell.

David has always continuously created his paintings and drawings, his works on paper, and his sculpture during his forty-three years of professional activity. His sheer joy of nature and his embrace of the large and small of the human experience have made him one of the country's finest artists.

An especially meaningful and important aspect of David's work has been as a teacher and mentor. His commitment is to share and communicate his knowledge on many levels with succeeding generations. He has helped those in art and art-related fields to become the best and the most knowledgeable they can be, encouraging them to embrace education, creativity, and the sharing of knowledge as a way of life. It is David who has given to so many young scholars the "key" to the mysteries of education: the joy and sense of personal identity in *knowing*.

His has been a steady voice for the recognition and excellence of African American art as an integral and significant part of American art. His research in this area has led to many associations that have been helpful in his life's work. He has largely defined the field of African American art history and brought recognition of a vast body of artwork by African American artists to the world community. Through early association with Ms. Brady at the Harmon Foundation, luminaries such as Georgia O'Keeffe and Aaron Douglas, artists such as William T. Williams and Jacob Lawrence, and educators such as Professors James A. Porter and James V. Herring, David has listened, learned, and mentored. He eventually eclipsed them all in his gathering, digestion, and dissemination of knowledge. His sum is more than the sum total of the parts.

— Stephanie E. Pogue
Professor and Chair
Department of Art
University of Maryland

Acknowledgments

Like the medium of collage in which David Driskell works so powerfully, this exhibition has taken its shape from the blending of many contributors. Without the help of these dedicated individuals, we surely would not have succeeded in bringing the influential David C. Driskell Collection to the nation and to the world through this catalogue and exhibition. However, not only do we have this volume and the traveling exhibition as the products of several years of work, but we also have a circle of friends. We are honored and grateful to have worked with so many warm, generous, and knowledgeable individuals.

First and foremost, we extend abundant thanks to the Driskell family—David's wife, Thelma; his children and grandchildren—who endured many different people invading their home and office to access the collection and archives. Few others would have been as gracious and accommodating as they, welcoming us into their kitchen and nourishing us with coffee, homebaked goods, and many warm stories. The stories were not only entertaining; many enriched our understanding of Driskell's life and work, and they often related directly to artists featured in this exhibition who were also the collector's friends and colleagues: Elizabeth Catlett, Loïs Mailou Jones, James Porter, and others. David's wisdom and graciousness provided calm and optimism throughout the challenging journey from conceptualization to completion. The opportunity to work with him and the many others who contributed to this project at all its layered stages renewed our faith in art and artists as the soul of society.

The overall product of catalogue and exhibition was crafted under the direction of Juanita Holland, Curator of the exhibition and faculty member in art history at the University of Maryland, and Terry Gips, Director of The Art Gallery. Their combined vision, expertise, and tenacity in the midst of many complicated tasks have made this catalogue and exhibition, and the companion exhibition of Driskell's own artwork, a reality.

Juanita Holland oversaw the editorial conception of the catalogue, wrote the principal essay, which provides the theoretical framework for the project, and worked with the essayists to bring their texts to final form. Among the individuals responsible for much of the content of this catalogue, special thanks and profound appreciation go to Adrienne Childs, Catalogue Production Manager, who juggled many hats with great dexterity, including those of author, curator, researcher, photography administrator, and archivist. Her unfailing attention to detail was invaluable. A veritable mountain of research was done by Tuliza Fleming, who authored close to half of the object entries and chronologies. As the publisher's deadline approached, two undergraduate students, Kim Kindelsperger and Jen Strychasz, lent a generous hand to complete entries and chronologies. Gallery staff and student interns also played instrumental roles in coordinating the preparation of the catalogue; several individuals helped with final editing, proofreading, and assembly of various textual components of the catalogue. Others organized and labeled the photographic reproductions used to illustrate this catalogue and assisted with the day-to-day tasks of copying, mailing, faxing, and phoning. Most of the photographs included in this volume were taken by Greg Staley, whose flexibility and good nature enabled us to meet tight deadlines with little anxiety.

Coordinating the national exhibition schedule has

been a particularly rewarding task. We are grateful for the opportunity to work with several distinguished museum professionals who are dedicated to bringing significant exhibitions to economically and ethnically diverse audiences: Hugh Gourley III, Director, and Lynn Marsden-Atlass, Assistant Director and Registrar, at the Colby College Museum of Art; Kathy Hodgson, Coordinator of Exhibitions, and Harry S. Parker III, Director of Museums, for The Fine Arts Museums of San Francisco; Ned Rifken, Director, Michael E. Shapiro, Deputy Director and Chief Curator, and Marjorie Harvey, Manager of Exhibitions, at the High Museum of Art; and Joseph Jacobs, Curator of American Art, at The Newark Museum. A special thank-you goes to Edward Brown, former trustee at the High Museum and longtime friend of David Driskell, for his insight and understanding of the unique value of this project.

We have had the great fortune to assemble this catalogue and exhibition under the umbrella of a campus with several top administrators who believe in the cultural value of the art as well as the academic contributions of artists and art historians. In fact, in 1997, the University of Maryland awarded David C. Driskell the President's Distinguished Medal of Service. The campus president from 1988 to 1998, William E. (Brit) Kirwan, was especially fond of David and worked enthusiastically to support this project, knowing that Driskell's collection and life work stand as models of scholarship and service. James Harris, Dean of the College of Arts and Humanities at the time of the exhibition, and Ira Berlin, Acting Dean when the project was initiated, have provided both personal and administrative support. Thanks are also given to William Pressly, Chair of the Department of Art History and Archaeology; Stephanie Pogue, Chair of the Department of Art; and Wendy Jacobs for her support as Acting Gallery Director during the summer and fall of 1997.

We have also had a wonderful partner on the Pacific Coast: our publisher, Zoe Katherine Burke of Pomegranate Communications. It seems that direct phone and fax lines have been established and that Federal Express knows by heart the route from College Park, Maryland, to Rohnert Park, California. We will be eternally grateful for the vital role that Pomegranate has played in producing this catalogue.

We are indebted to Keith Morrison, former Dean of the College of Arts and Humanities, as well as Chair of the Department of Art at the University of Maryland, and one of the first supporters of the project in its infant stages. He has continued to champion the project while serving as Dean of the College of Creative Arts at San Francisco State University.

The exhausting task of coordinating contracts under the constraints of state institution guidelines was deftly executed by Elena Paul, Counsel to the President of the University of Maryland. Her wit and wisdom, and that of Martina Grunwald, Director of Corporate and Foundation Relations, render both of them valuable advocates of the arts at Maryland.

Educational and public programming were made possible by numerous collaborative efforts. The university's Center for Renaissance and Baroque Studies, under the leadership of Executive Director Adele Seeff and Associate Director Susan Jensen; other academic departments; and many other individuals and organizations extended the reach and interpretive value of this project. Robert Hall, Director of the Educational Department of the Smithsonian Institution's Anacostia Museum in Southeast D.C., helped coordinate a uniquely valuable series of educational workshops for middle school students.

Those who supported this project as my gallery staff colleagues receive my heartfelt thanks. The professionalism and high standards of Terry Gips, Kimberly Gladfelter, Karen Werth, Rob Blitz, and Wendy Grossman provided the backbone for this enormous undertaking. It was they who taught me the art of improvisation inherent to exhibition work, the determination needed in the endless struggle to secure funding, and the choreography necessary to perform seemingly herculean tasks under great constraints, all of which combined to bring this project to fruition. Their problem-solving acumen, humor, and insight have provided both foundation and inspiration to me and ensured both my success as Project Coordinator and the success of the entire project.

Finally, sincere appreciation is extended to the individual artists and their families who permitted the publication of their work in this catalogue. Without the great web of support that exists throughout the African American art community, this exhibition would never have been possible. It is in recognition of this interwoven web of influence in the creation of art and identity that this catalogue and exhibition are presented to you.

> — M. Colleen Chapman
> Project Coordinator
> for the David C. Driskell
> Exhibition

Introduction: Driskell the Collector

David Driskell's full collection spans almost four decades and includes African art, nineteenth-century African American art, European art, and Euro-American art. This exhibition, curated by Juanita Holland, represents a selection from the twentieth-century African American portion of his collection. It is not intended that the works in this exhibition represent a comprehensive overview of African American art, although they are an outstanding collection of art by some of the best-known African American artists of more than the last hundred years. And, very significantly, much of it is art the collector acquired from personal experience with the artists, as colleague, teacher, mentor, or friend. David has acquired his collection mostly through purchase and through exchange with other artists. As I will describe later, his own art demonstrates, in the final analysis, that his collection is a dimension of his personal aesthetics as an artist and helped shape his approach to African American art history.

I first met David Driskell in 1965, when I visited Howard University, where he was a professor of art, teaching painting and drawing. Two years later, one year after he was appointed Chair of the Art Department at Fisk University, he invited me to teach there. My indelible memory of my early experiences with David is how committed he was to exhibiting African American art and to preserving its legacy. In those days, having studied at predominantly white art schools, where nothing was taught about any African American artist, I was completely ignorant of the field and amazed at its revelations in the exhibition program David developed at Fisk. David had learned about collecting from two kinds of

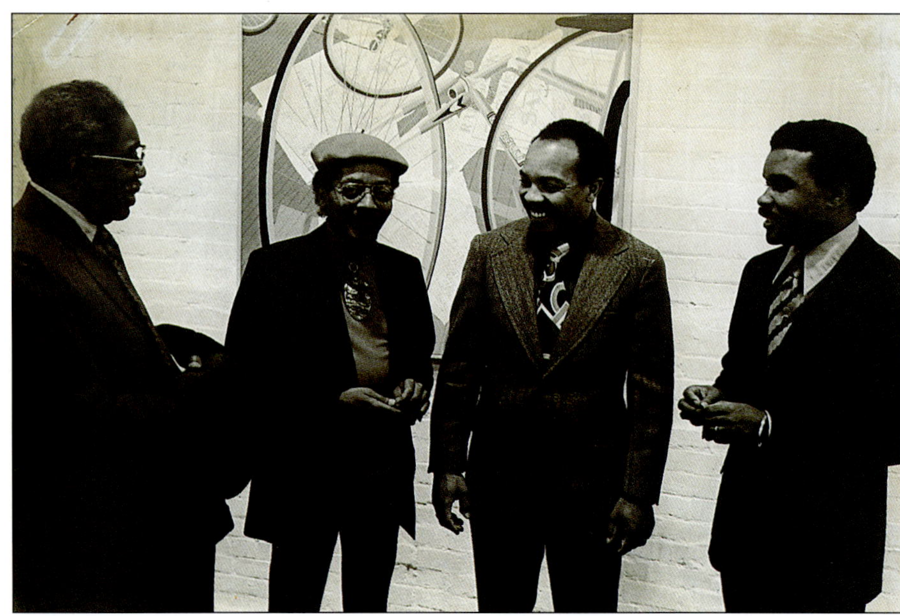

Left to right: Aaron Douglas, Earl Hooks, Keith Morrison, and David Driskell; Carl Van Vechten Gallery, Fisk University, Nashville, 1974 (David C. Driskell Archives)

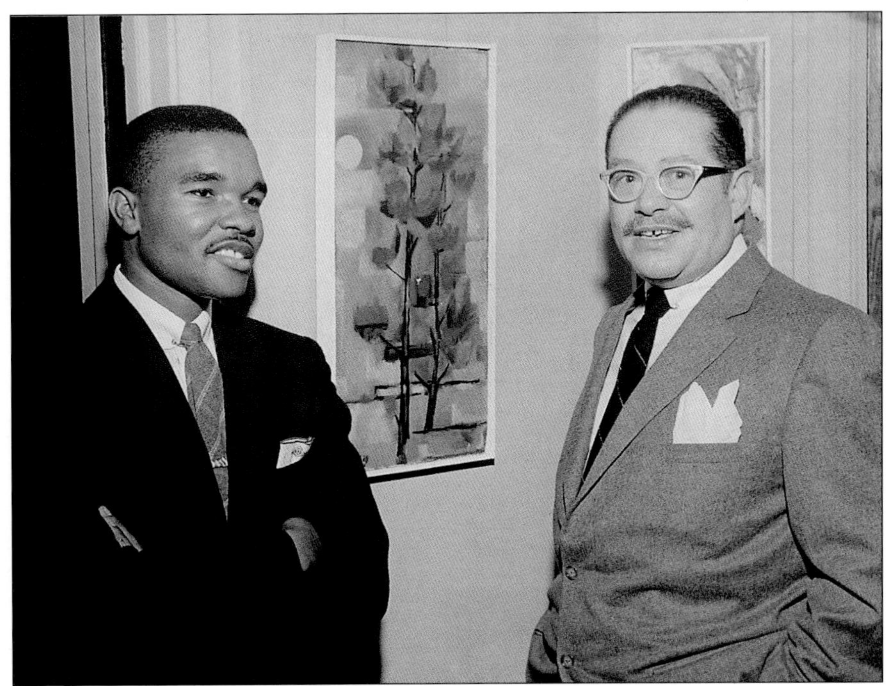

David Driskell and Alonzo J. Aden;
Barnett-Aden Gallery, Washington, D.C.,
1957 (David C. Driskell Archives)

sources: professors such as Alain Locke, James Porter, and James Herring, at Howard University; and private collectors such as Duncan Phillips, Albert Barnes, William E. Harmon, and Carl Van Vechten.

At Howard in the late forties, Driskell learned the lessons of philosopher/aesthetician Alain Locke, the author of many publications on the African legacy of African American art and the most distinguished national spokesman on the subject. Locke, the first black Rhodes scholar and a Harvard Ph.D., had fueled the imagination of African Americans in the Harlem Renaissance with his writings about what characterized the uniqueness of African American art. His life's work, verified by travel throughout the world, especially to Europe, and by the art objects he collected, left a lifelong impression on Driskell. Even more fundamental to Driskell's early education was his study with Professor James A. Porter, who assumed the Chair of the Art Department at Howard University in 1953 and who was one of the great scholars of African American art history. Porter's example taught Driskell detailed knowledge of the field and the methodology of scholarly research to further that knowledge. The foundation Driskell learned from Porter has been the basis for his own venerable scholarship and a guiding principle for the historical emphasis

for the selections in his collection. But the love of collecting art is a passion he gained from another of his teachers, Howard University Art Gallery founder Professor James V. Herring. Driskell not only studied art with Herring but worked in the Art Gallery as an apprentice. In the evenings and on weekends, Driskell often worked for Herring and his partner, Alonzo Aden, in the Barnett-Aden Gallery, a private gallery they owned in Washington, D.C. As a result, Driskell came to learn about curating, the operation of art galleries, and the complexities of the art world. Through Herring, even while a young student, Driskell came to meet important international artists of many colors and races, since both the Howard University and Barnett-Aden galleries were at the national forefront of creating interracial and international exhibitions. Driskell was a student when Eleanor Roosevelt visited the Barnett-Aden Gallery, as did the artists Irene Rice Periera, Theodoros Stamos, Romare Bearden, Wifredo Lam, and Candido Portinari; and collectors such as Albert Barnes and Duncan Phillips, a close friend of Herring and founder of the Phillips Collection.

Through the help of Herring and Loïs Mailou Jones (also his teacher at Howard), Driskell went to study at the Skowhegan School of Painting and Sculpture in the summer of 1953. There he studied with Jack Levine,

Henry Varnum Poor, Sidney Simon, and paint manufac-
turer Leonard Bocour. The experience at Skowhegan
broadened his scope and connected him to the central
core of the art world even as a very young man. His relationship with Skowhegan and the professional affiliations
he developed there beginning in 1953 have remained a
strong part of his relationships in the art world until
now. After teaching at Skowhegan and serving for more
than ten years on its Board of Governors with distinguished artists such as Sidney Simon, Jacob Lawrence,
William T. Williams, Lois Dodd, Janet Fish, and Robert
Indiana, Driskell is now a member of the school's Board
of Trustees. Indeed, to this day he still maintains the
home he purchased in Maine, sixty-five miles from Skowhegan, in the early sixties.

Driskell also studied art history and curating in Holland at Rinksbureau voor Kunsthistorisches Documental
den Haag in 1964. He learned all these lessons well and
soon came to apply them with his own singular vision.
By the time I went to work with him at Fisk in 1967, he
was creating the new wave of African American art exhibitions at a level that had not been realized anywhere in
this country since the heyday of Herring's work at the
Howard University Art Gallery in the 1930s and 1940s.

It has always seemed to me that there were four
curatorial models that inspired Driskell during the time
he was at Fisk: (1) the 1953 exhibition of African art
assembled by his mentors, James A. Porter and James
V. Herring, at the Howard University Art Gallery; (2)
the 1966 exhibition *One Hundred Fifty Years of Afro-
American Art,* also curated by Porter but this time for the
UCLA Art Gallery; (3) the Carl Van Vechten and Alfred
Stieglitz Collections at Fisk University; and (4) the Harmon Foundation's documentation and preservation of
African American art. In 1953, Driskell saw the exhibition *Contemporary African Art,* which included works by
every major artist from non-apartheid African countries
of the day. Assembled originally with a catalogue of
many photographs and a text written by Evelyn S.
Brown, this show served to broaden African perspectives
showcasing current trends in art. It created for Driskell,
as it did for others, a global perspective of an African Diaspora. Porter's 1966 exhibition *One Hundred Fifty Years*

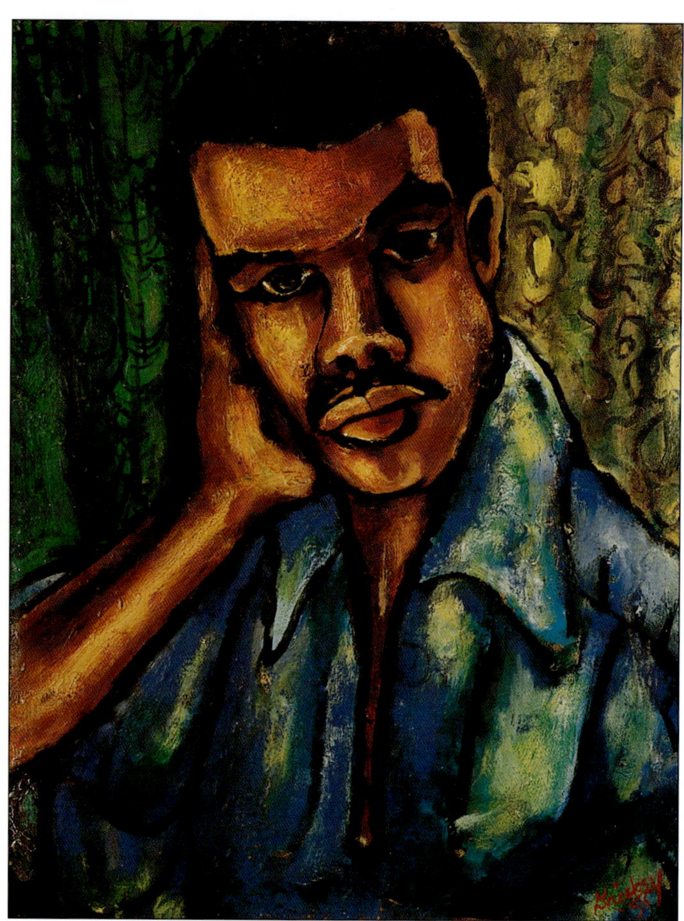

Self Portrait, *David C. Driskell, 1955, oil on board
(Greg Staley, photographer; David C. Driskell Collection)*

of Afro-American Art described and framed as never before
a period of the legacy in relation to world art.

When I first visited him at Fisk, Driskell was armed
with the catalogues of both of those exhibitions. I vividly
remember how well he articulated their worth, how he
put them in perspective with the art he was beginning
to curate, and how impressed I was that his own budding
collection was guided by many of the principles of those
exhibitions, especially the commonality of the African
Diaspora and the ideological relationships of African
American art. When he got to Fisk, Driskell added the
other two sources as working models for his own endeavor: the Carl Van Vechten Collection of books and
photography, given to Fisk University by Van Vechten,
and the Stieglitz Collection.

The Alfred Stieglitz Collection was donated to Fisk
in 1949 by artist Georgia O'Keeffe in memory of her
husband, modern art collector and photographer Alfred
Stieglitz. The chief custodian of the Stieglitz Collection

during that time, O'Keeffe took an active role in working with Driskell to preserve this famous collection of works by many artists of different races and cultures. Driskell met O'Keeffe after coming to the chair of the Department of Art and served as director of the Van Vechten Gallery from 1966 until 1976. They corresponded from time to time about the more than 100 works of art by Picasso, Cézanne, Renoir, Marin, Hartley, Stieglitz, O'Keeffe, Nadelman, Maurer, Sheeler, Demuth, and many other European and American artists that comprise the Stieglitz Collection. Driskell did much to preserve the collection, re-cataloguing and re-preparing many of the works in it. The collection served as a source of research and inspiration for him and became a working example of a great collector's legacy.

The Harmon Foundation provided Driskell an example of how to document art by African Americans. He had worked with Ms. Mary Beattie Brady, director of the Harmon Foundation from its inception in 1922. Founded by William E. Harmon as a student loan foundation for youths attending college, the Foundation, in cooperation with the Federal Council of Churches, established awards for distinguished achievements by African Americans in literature, music, the visual arts, science, industry, education, religion, and race relations. Between 1928 and 1934 the Foundation helped fund the work of more than 125 artists in exhibitions that traveled to twenty-seven states and some fifty cities and were seen by thousands of people. The Harmon Foundation continued to help African American artists through the 1960s.

We African American artists owe the Harmon Foundation a great debt, and Driskell has never forgotten the debt nor the lessons he learned from the members of the Foundation, who worked tirelessly to collect, preserve, and house more than 4,000 original works by African and African American artists. I am certain that Driskell patterned many of his Fisk exhibitions after the style of the Harmon Foundation catalogues, most (if not all) of which he had on hand when we were at Fisk. The Harmon Foundation catalogues and those Driskell created were about the same size and manner of layout, and they contained the same kind of information:

introductory essay, a few black-and-white photographs, a list of the artists' exhibitions, and a checklist of works in the show. I also remember that the Driskell catalogues (funded in large part by foundation grants), like the ones produced by the Harmon Foundation, were free.

Over a ten-year period, from 1967 to 1977, Driskell curated and wrote catalogue essays for some forty exhibitions of many prominent artists of the day, including Walter Williams, Vincent Smith, Earl Hooks, Jacob Lawrence, Romare Bearden, Richard Hunt, Aaron Douglas, William T. Williams, Palmer Hayden, Claude Clark, Loïs Jones, Elizabeth Catlett, Martin Puryear, Ellis Wilson, Sam Middleton, Stephanie Pogue, and me. There were also Caucasian artists, including ceramicist Eleanor Landreau, printmaker Tom Cornell, and Father Vincent from Pittsburgh, called "the Painting Priest."

Most important, Driskell showed a landmark exhibition of art by William H. Johnson, with the help of the Harmon Foundation, which had preserved his work. It was the first time many of my generation had seen the artist's work. The exhibition served to resurrect the

Letter from Georgia O'Keeffe to David Driskell, 1968 (Greg Staley, photographer; David C. Driskell Archives)

prominence of William H. Johnson, inspiring future, better-known exhibitions of his work and ultimately reestablishing the reputation of this great artist. Today, the National Museum of American Art holds a collection of more than 1,000 works by William H. Johnson, thanks in part to the early curatorial work of David Driskell. It was he who suggested to Ms. Brady that the National Collection of Fine Arts (now the National Museum of American Art, Smithsonian Institution, under the direction of Adelyn Breeskin) become the chief repository of Johnson's work at the Foundation.

Driskell has also been an exceptionally important teacher. And in his role as teacher/mentor, he has nurtured the talents of many artists and scholars whose ideas and insights have expanded his perception of art and augmented his approach to global thinking and hence to collecting. These include filmmaker Johnny Simmons; art historians Guy McElroy, Richard Powell, Tritobia Benjamin, Juanita Holland, and Jacqueline Bontemps; activist Stokely Carmichael; singer Jessye Norman; collector Walter Evans; sculptor Terry Adkins; printmaker Stephanie Pogue; and painter Mary Lovelace O'Neal. The scholars with whom he associated, many serving as guest lecturers to his students, have furthered and reinforced this perspective. In addition to the aforementioned people such as James A. Porter, James V. Herring, Carlton Moss, Albert Barnes, and Sam Hunter, others with whom Driskell interacted over the years include Edmund Barry Gaither, Director of the Museum of African American Art and Culture, Boston; Margaret Burroughs, Director Emeritus of the DuSable Museum, Chicago; Howard Dodson, Director of the Arthur Schomburg Library, New York City; E.J. Montgomery, art promoter and researcher; Dr. Samella Lewis, African American art historian; Arna Alexander Bontemps, former literary critic for the *New York Times*; art historian Leslie King-Hammond; Dr. Mary Schmidt Campbell, former Director of the Studio Museum of Harlem and currently Dean of the Tish College of Art at NYU; entertainer/activist/collector Bill Cosby; and college president/collector William (Bill) Harvey.

The dimension that association with a wide array of students and scholars brought to Driskell was a wider consciousness, from the eyes of younger people, of global thinking in a changing world. This perspective is an important part of the Driskell Collection, which is largely characterized by a diverse range of socio-aesthetic thought as much as it is by stylistic harmony. Put another way, the collection reveals as much about the social history of the collector's time as it does about an aesthetic progression in art. It shows some of the range of choices by African American artists over the last 200 years and exemplifies that their ideas were from their own cultural point of view.

Driskell's own work as an artist is similar to the ideology·reflected in the works he collects, but it includes a couple of other things as well; these are the land and Christianity. Driskell is a dedicated gardener and farmer, a tradition he gained from his Southern forefathers. I believe that a kind of Southern respect for nature, its beauty and the evolution from birth to decay, permeates Driskell's work as artist and collector. In his art, as in his collection, one sees earth, plants, stones, wood, and rustic objects that characterized rural African American life, all of which come together to form a timeless aesthetic that is personal to David Driskell.

Driskell's collection has been selected with profound knowledge of art history but especially with the collector-artist's perspective of that discipline. He documents not only art of the past but art that expresses his own view of life. His collection reveals much of what has interested him about African American art, especially in painting and sculpture: traditional aesthetics through the lens of the African American social experience. His collection reflects his own private interests, as revealed in his lifestyle. There are few high-tech multimedia images in the Driskell Collection; there are no themes of cyberspace, nor is there cutting-edge experimental art or conceptual art. The reason is not that he is oblivious to these things. Far from being oblivious, David Driskell has been a champion and supporter of new art and of many young artists of both sexes and different races. In 1971, he hired sculptor Martin Puryear to teach sculpture and photography at Fisk University. It was Puryear's first teaching job on the college level. Driskell also has been a strong advocate for women artists, writing rebuttals in the national press to the opinions expressed by Hilton Kramer and other conservative critics who do not support institutions such as the National Museum for Women in the Arts and the National Center for Afro-American Art.

However, like any good curator, Driskell hones his own point of view. Thus, consistently among the works collected are themes of African art, African American history, and culture, as exemplified by Jacob Lawrence's *Confrontation at the Bridge* or, in this exhibition, the works of Augusta Savage, such as her *Gamin* (catalogue no. 21), Elizabeth Catlett's *Seated Mother and Child* (catalogue no. 69), or Romare Bearden's collage *Morning* (catalogue no. 29). Christianity, a central part of the life of the collector, is to be found in many of the works in Driskell's collection, such as Walter Williams's *Black Madonna* or, in this exhibition, William H. Johnson's *I Baptize Thee* (catalogue no. 16). Nature, the earth, and soil—so beloved to Driskell—also are themes in the collection. An avid gardener, Driskell, in the tradition of his Southern forefathers, venerates the land. See how various forms of nature are revealed in works featured in this exhibition, such as Alma Thomas's *Falling Leaves Love Wind Orchestra* (catalogue no. 95), Ellis Wilson's *Untitled* (Fish in Net, catalogue no. 48), or Edward M. Bannister's *Landscape with Pond* (catalogue no. 2). Long fascinated with African craftsmanship and its relationship to African American art, Driskell has documented it in art history as well as in his own collection, as in the meticulously beaded "Yoruba Crown" or the "Gelede (Yoruba) Mask" and, in this exhibition, the montage technique of Sam Gilliam's *The D Series* (catalogue no. 78).

In this collection one sees not only African American art but the values of the collector himself in the relationships with other artists that he has cultivated and in the personal values that he has nurtured. It is here that the life, art, education, and passion of David C. Driskell come together to create one of the singular African American collections of our time in a narrative of African American art.

— Keith Morrison
Dean, College of Creative Arts
San Francisco State University

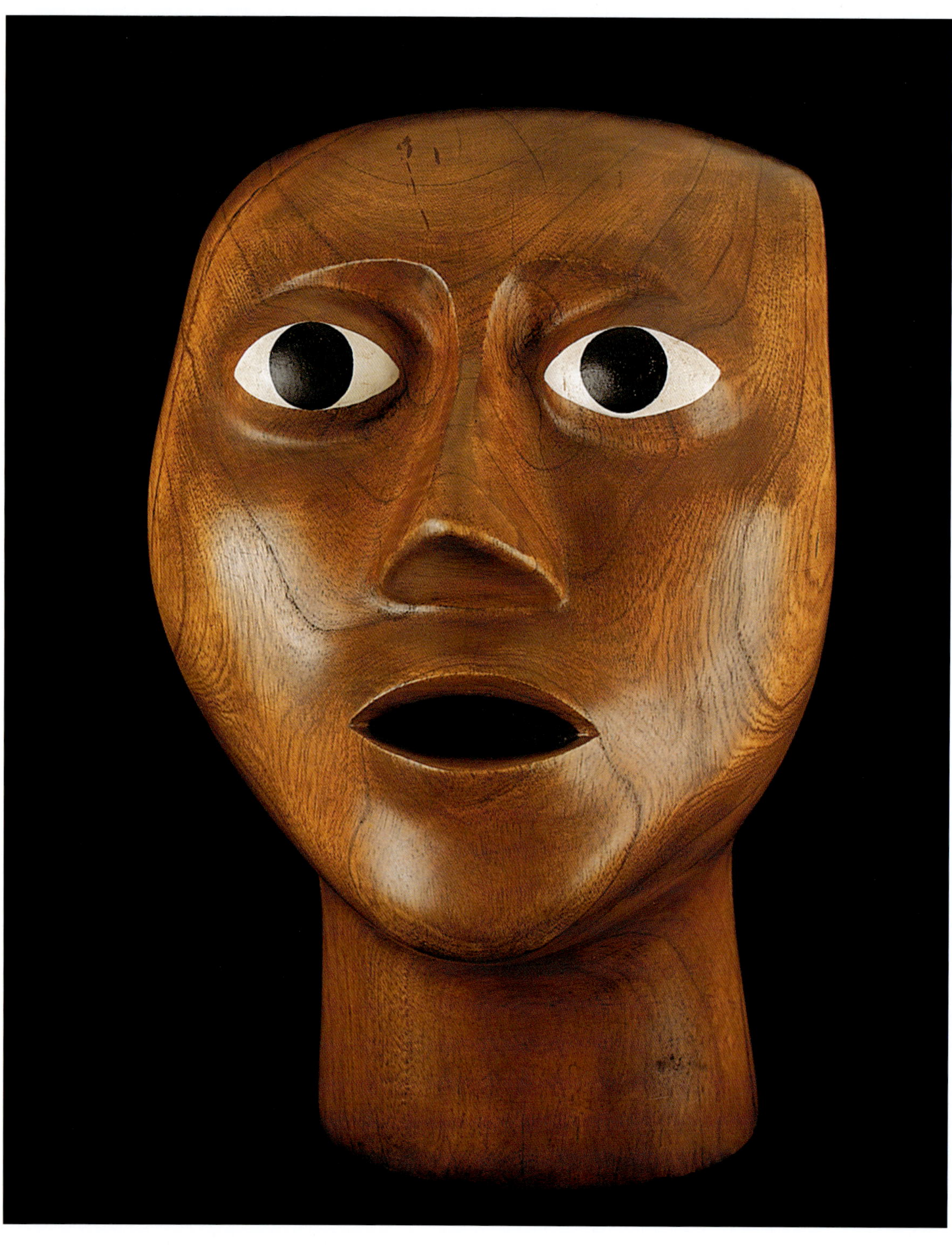

Elizabeth Catlett, The Black Woman Speaks, *1970 (catalogue no. 53)*

The Color of Art:
African American Artistic
Identities in the Twentieth Century Juanita Marie Holland

INTRODUCTION

The works in this show are by American artists. They are all artists of African descent, but their works do not necessarily share stylistic affinities, or common evolution or purpose. What they all express are the overriding concerns about how to construct self, how to be black in white America, how to be an artist, and how to arrange all of these selves within one body and one lifetime.

As disciplines of art-historical study go, African American art history is still quite young. It has been only in the last thirty years that universities began to offer courses about the developments in African American art and to hire specialists to teach those courses. After the initial decades spent celebrating the existence of this wondrous child, we are now confronted with a difficult and contrary adolescent. Like that of a teenage child, the growth of this field defies our expectations: It will not fit into the categories we have complacently reserved for it. It does not follow geographic, stylistic, or nationalistic boundaries. It has adopted a new name: diaspora art history; this is a wonderfully inclusive and global term, but it still defines the artistic production of a group we separate out only by race, and segregation for any reason is always problematic.

If we cannot group artists of African descent together for reasons of stylistic cohesion and development, geography, or time, is there any reason to segregate them by race, aside from the very proper revisionist notion that we must all re-discover and re-insert the histories of minorities into our official canon?

This exhibition is an affirmative answer, structured around the conviction that the study of artists of African descent—as a separate entity—is indeed appropriate and necessary. We are studying the communities resulting from a common cultural experience so vast that it redistributed many millions of people, redesigning the demography of several continents. What these communities have in common is an agenda of cultural survival: the construction of identities—complex, creolized, and constantly changing—that mapped out strategies not just for survival but for creative growth.

Narratives of African American Art and Identity: The David C. Driskell Collection guides the viewer through a thematic journey that documents the complex unfolding of racial and artistic identities as expressed in African American art and the various strategies employed by twentieth-century African American artists to pursue their aesthetic and expressive concerns, to establish their place in the world of art, and to further various social and political agendas with which they were aligned.

We focus as well on the reception of those strategies by white and black America as expressed through patronage and collection. Especially relevant to our understanding are the complex and little-explored relationships that have existed among African American artists, art historians, institutions, and collectors in the twentieth century. These relationships illustrate the importance of the cultural support network that existed—and still exists—between student and mentor, artist and collector, scholar and material in the African American community.

Indeed, the works in this show demand such an approach. Although other significant collections of African American art have enjoyed well-deserved attention and visibility in recent years, this exhibition represents a truly singular creation: a collection of objects both visually and historically rich, assembled by a successful black artist with an equal dedication to the preservation and promotion of the history of African American art.[1] Working since the 1950s, David Driskell has shared in the black artist's struggle to define artistic identity. His training in European and African American traditions, his study and travels in Africa, and his dedicated search to understand the struggles of his artistic predecessors all reflect his intimate acquaintance with the unique perspective of the artist of the African Diaspora.

This exhibition of objects from the Driskell collection can therefore serve as a larger paradigm, a nexus by which we may understand the objects in it: objects chosen with the connoisseurship of an artist, the historical agenda of an archivist, and the critical perspective of an art historian who shares the challenges of racial and artistic identity construction with those whose work he collects and chronicles.

To better highlight and understand these strategies toward identity, we will explore, in five thematic categories, the variety of choices made by African American artists as they navigated the experience of being black artists in white America. The sections frame groups of choices, and various artists and artworks pass easily through the membranes of these divisions. One artist is quite often represented in more than one section, and a work that illustrates the theme of one section could sometimes just as easily have been placed in another. These themes are not meant to create new, static, or rigid art-historical categories. Instead, I hope they will help provide new ways to think about artistic production and identity.

The search for identity in the Americas has always been complex, often confusing and contradictory, never monolithic, and more vital and organic than the hybridizing that our hyphenated names, whether "Italian-American" or "African-American," would suggest. The choice for those of African descent in the Americas has never been simply between African or American, and we are constantly shifting into some newer and more useful model of cultural identity.

What is suggested here is a way to think about not the evolution of style or movement but the evolution of racial and artistic identities in nineteenth- and twentieth-century America. This evolutionary model can provide us with a useful paradigm for other black diaspora communities. While their geographical and historical particulars may be wildly different from those in the U.S., most share the necessity of creating identities out of an initial condition of enslavement, responding to identities created for them by dominant and colonizing cultures and the need to synthesize the cultural imperatives that were operative in their original African cultures with the realities of their new lives.

The construction of a public identity in a diaspora setting has been a central imperative for persons of African descent since slavery began. The institution of slavery, as practiced in the United States, required the enslaved to accept a public presentation of self fashioned by their captors. Expression or remembrance of past cultures was forbidden, and the enslaved were required to imitate in their appearance, language, and interests, on an appropriately subordinate level, those of white America. Before and after slavery, the public presentation of free blacks was also regulated by pressure from the white community. In popular culture, vicious stereotypes of Jim Crow, Zip Coon, mammies, bucks, and pickaninnies gave most white Americans, especially in the North, their only image of black behavioral and visual norms. As so-called free blacks in the North struggled to expand their limited rights and to fight slavery and racism, they also felt compelled to answer these white constructions of black identity.

This exhibition focuses in particular on the legacy of identity construction that began in the free black community, with African American artists working primarily in European aesthetic traditions. The strategies toward identity building by enslaved Africans are no less integral to this discussion, but, in this instance, our examination is framed by a collection that focuses on the work of free blacks and their inquiry into identity. This exploration should complement past and future studies of identity construction in enslaved communities, as we work toward a more thorough understanding of the vast cultural experience in the African Diaspora.

Section One of the exhibition, "Strategic Subversions: Cultural Emancipation, Assimilation, and African American Identity," looks at how the artworks created by African American artists in the nineteenth and early twentieth centuries expressed some of the ways free blacks chose to respond to these white constructions and to investigate their own agendas of public identity construction. Seeking to subvert the degrading and ubiquitous stereotypes of black people on songsheets and in newspaper cartoons, minstrel shows, etc., many black men and women sought to build an image of themselves that mimicked the mores of white civilization they saw expressed everyday. They chose landscapes or still lifes that provided a neutral haven for artistic expression or depictions of black men and women who were identical in dress, lifestyle, and daily concerns to the white American everyman/woman.

Section Two, "Emergence: The New Negro Movement and Definitions of Race," explores choices blacks made out of the legacy of the nineteenth-century explorations of cultural assimilation. As the backlash to Reconstruction through the Red Summer of 1919 made clear, merely absorbing and expressing an identity identical to that of white Americans was an ineffective tool against racism, or toward building a place in American society. The intellectual and creative forces that drew America's attention to Harlem in the early decades of the century moved toward building images that, although still expressing the dream of the American everyman/woman, cast its figures and concerns in specifically and visually outspoken black terms. Rather than humbly and invisibly inserting themselves into white America, blacks publicly embraced black moments in history, black depictions of traditional Christian figures, blacks arrogantly displaying wealth and success as they aggressively participated in the American Dream. Although initially the white fascination with the Harlem Renaissance provided patronage and support for creative African Americans who were expressing these new definitions of blackness, black artists, writers, and intellectuals found that the expectations of white patronage also implied control; the onset of the Depression and then the next World War also diverted white American attention away from the Renaissance, and many forums for black crea-

tivity withered away without that economic support.

Section Three, "The Black Academy: Teachers, Mentors, and Institutional Patronage," helps illustrate how African American individuals and institutions continued to provide support, patronage, and exhibition forums for black artists who were originally nurtured through Harlem Renaissance patrons and the Harmon Foundation. Support provided by the African American community allows us also to gauge what kinds of identity construction were favored by African Americans, individual community leaders, and community institutions.

Section Four, "Radical Politics, Protest, and Art," highlights the ways in which African American artists expressed the increasingly aggressive political means that African Americans began to use in those mid-twentieth-century years of what is commonly called the *civil rights movement*. This period of identity construction represented profound rebellions against the cultural mores that blacks and whites had accepted as the norm. Sit-ins, boycotts, natural hairdos, raised fists—all these provided images of African American discontent that sought to tear down accepted norms and create completely new ones. These images also implied that black Americans were no longer willing to wait for the slow and resistant wheels of justice and public opinion to change in their favor. They intended to force movement toward securing their rights to the full.

The final section, "Diaspora Identities/Global Arts," represents the contemporary interest in a global definition of what it means to be of African descent. With current scholarly and cultural interest in the African Diaspora, African American artists are able to mine a larger and more complex set of choices about how to define their identities. African artists who chose European abstraction demanded to be considered as African artists producing African art. Black artists in the United States utilized African and Caribbean imagery as part of the repertoire available to them as cultural legacy. Rather than choosing between the two poles of a hyphenated identity, African American artists find a more resonant kind of identity construction in the ability to choose it all.

In 1853, Frederick Douglass wrote, "The most telling, the most killing refutation of slavery, is the presentation of an industrious, enterprising, thrifty and intelligent free black population."[2]

To understand the paths toward identity taken by twentieth-century African American artists, we need to understand the legacy they were given by black artists of the preceding century. Nineteenth-century artists of color who were able to achieve some measure of success and recognition as American painters, sculptors, and photographers were frequently nurtured in Northern black communities that placed a premium on education, success, and excellence. Free African American communities in the North found in achievement an important key to the struggle against slavery and racism.[3] The pursuit of excellence became a weapon with which to hold back the deluge of racial stereotypes in literature and art. Every successful black businessperson, doctor, lawyer, writer, or artist was irrefutable proof that blacks could excel in any area of white American society, and they believed that such proof struck an effective blow against the beliefs that fostered slavery and racism. African American and anti-slavery newspapers throughout the country took special care to publicize any noteworthy accomplishment by free blacks or former slaves. Achievement was not only a matter of personal pride, it was a duty to the race.

The nineteenth-century African American artists who pursued European-American academic art traditions represent a particularly class-driven aspect of artistic production. Nineteenth-century art was, by definition, hierarchically structured, where painting and sculpture represented "fine art" and American artists were most often judged by their ability to assimilate European traditions in those media. Middle-class African Americans shared white America's belief that the European-derived arts such as painting, sculpture, or opera represented the height of human achievement. They wished to show that African Americans were indeed capable of what sculptor and writer Horatio Greenough described as "the susceptibility, the tastes, and the genius which enable a people to enjoy the Fine Arts, and to excel in them...."[4] Thus, while the first aspect of their public identity must validate their membership in the human race, equally important was their need to establish a place in that class of Western society that was considered able to appreciate and participate in "high culture."

Three of the most successful black landscape painters of the nineteenth century—Edward Mitchell Bannister (c.1826–1901), Grafton Tyler Brown (1841–1918), and Robert S. Duncanson (1821–1872)—are represented in the Driskell Collection. For these artists, their artistic success depended on how well they upheld the popular aesthetic conventions. Their possibilities for financial success in their chosen profession, precariously dependent on a quite limited patronage pool, forbade any significant challenge to artistic norms.

Scottish Landscape, c.1870 (catalogue no. 4), is an unsigned work attributed to Duncanson that certainly reflects Duncanson's reputation as a Midwestern proponent of the Hudson River landscape style. Much of Bannister's work reflected the Barbizon landscape aesthetic that won over many young New England landscape artists in the 1860s and was favored by many American collectors by the fourth quarter of the nineteenth century. *Untitled* (Landscape with Cows, catalogue no. 1), and the 1876 *Untitled* (Landscape with Pond, catalogue no. 2) reveal Bannister's lifelong interest in the tactile exploration of the effects of weather and light in nature. Grafton Tyler Brown's landscape style, illustrated here in the spectacular *Mt. Hood from John Day's Station* (catalogue no. 3), grew out of his first profession as lithographer, surveyor, and documentor of the American West.

For the most part, nineteenth-century African American painters worked in portraiture, landscape, and still life, and understanding why they primarily limited themselves to these areas is important to our developing knowledge of how they shaped artistic identity.

European and American art of the nineteenth century had delineated a clear hierarchy of genres from which painters could choose. History painting, especially in Europe, had traditionally been held as the highest form of painting to which one could aspire. Without the long historical past of which Europe could boast, America grew to hold landscape painting in high regard. Portraiture had a highly respected mid-level place in this hierarchy, and genre scenes, still lifes, "conceits," and "fancy pieces" all occupied respectable but lower places than history and landscape.

History and genre, conspicuously absent from the oeuvres of most black artists during the nineteenth century, brought with them the tensions of representing the history and social fabric of a society that did not include or welcome those artists. Aspects of American history that a black artist could have most sympathetically approached would have been too controversial for most of white America. Genre scenes—the intimate portrayal of everyday lives and people—required black artists to portray lifestyles from which they were excluded.

Landscape and still life—types of painting in which nature took primacy over the human figure and often eliminated it outright—were the only choices in which African American artists could unreservedly assert a subject authority, free of the shadows of a racially divided society. Well into the twentieth century, African American artists such as Charles Ethan Porter explored the possibilities of still life (*Untitled* [Still Life: Mums in a Bowl], n. d., catalogue no. 7), and continued to paint aspects of the American landscape (see James Herring's *Newport Scene*, n. d., catalogue no. 6).

In the 1910s and 1920s, the construction of an idealized "New Negro" continued to define excellence and success by European cultural standards. The 1900 book by Booker T. Washington, Fannie Barrier Williams, and N. B. Wood proclaimed in its title that there would be *A New Negro for a New Century*.[6] Like the images and biographical sketches of ideal New Negro men and women compiled by these turn-of-the-century black leaders, early photographs by James VanDerZee, later known for his portraits of Harlem celebrities, intellectuals, and fashionable upper- and middle-class blacks, place his subjects (in this case, members of his family) firmly within the mold of white American life. The *Portrait of First Wife and Daughter* (catalogue no. 10) establishes the genteel associations of mother-and-child images such as those promulgated by American artist Mary Cassatt. The photo of the *VanDerZee Boys*, c.1900 (catalogue no. 9), projects the informal familial intimacy of a genre scene while asserting blacks' ability to access pursuits, such as skiing, with which they were not normally associated in popular visual culture. These are African Americans firmly entrenched in a nostalgic myth of Americana, in ways no white-created images of the time would depict.

Our consideration of the works in this exhibition by Henry Ossawa Tanner (*Gate at Tangier*, 1910, catalogue no. 8) and Meta Warrick Fuller (*Pietà*, c.1930, catalogue no. 5) serves as a useful transition from Section One to Section Two. Tanner and Fuller began their careers with a firm academic background in Euro-American painting and sculptural traditions. Both had formative training experiences in Paris—experiences that highlighted how different a European perception of black artistic identity could be. Although these artists used their academic training as part of their aesthetic expression, each also went on to employ that academic training in the service of profoundly felt subject matter.

While Fuller returned to America permanently, Tanner embraced the possibilities that European identity brought him as an artist. Adopting France as his new home, Tanner demanded the right to construct an artistic and racial identity that he perceived would allow him the greatest freedom as an artist. Within that freedom, he was able to pursue the painting of religious subjects with an emphasis on archaeological and ethnographic authenticity that had generally been lacking in other artistic depictions. Although he refused to become symbolic propaganda as "the greatest Negro painter," he mentored and supported the African American artists who made pilgrimages to France to simultaneously enjoy European culture's legacy and visit this eminent painter of color.

Fuller, who benefited from Tanner's support while in Paris, returned to live in the United States. She fought the burdens of racism and sexism that constrained her options as a practicing sculptor: the racism of white American society, which narrowed her exhibition opportunities and limited her patronage, and the sexism embedded in white and black communities, which demanded that her role as mother, wife, and hostess override any artistic ambitions she entertained. Fuller is best known as the forerunner of the Harlem Renaissance, with works such as *Ethiopia Awakening* (1914) and *Mary Turner: A Silent Protest Against Mob Violence* (1919). Aside from her groundbreaking role as the sculptor whose works celebrated the African physique and African and African American folk culture and spoke to the national and international concerns of the diaspora, she also created many religious works.

Fuller's religious subjects, like Tanner's, reflect strong personal convictions, but they also reflect aspects of her reality as a black woman sculptor, discouraged both by her husband and by American art institutions. The church provided an acceptable outlet for Fuller's need for community as well as a way for her to express her artistic talents that probably seemed more appropriate to her husband and her society.

In fact, the Harlem Renaissance's explorations of black identity are grounded in the history of survival strategies, as defined by nineteenth-century free blacks. Nineteenth-century black American society, traveling through slavery, emancipation, Reconstruction, and Redemption, concerned itself with the immediate necessity of establishing humanity by the yardstick of the only cultural norms available. In the first decades of the twentieth century, the Great Migration of blacks into Northern urban landscapes, along with industrial growth, Southern stagnation, and the powder keg issues of black soldiers fighting for freedom abroad—all these factors combined to change the impetus of black identity construction.

African American intellectuals and artists—men and women such as Charles Johnson, Jessie Fauset, W. E. B. Du Bois, and Alain Locke—continued to support Du Bois's idea that a "Talented Tenth" would, by virtue of cultural accomplishment, lead black Americans in the twentieth century. The realities of Redemption, Jim Crow laws in the North and South, the growth of the Ku Klux Klan and lynching, and the Red Summer of 1919 showed black Americans that cultural assimilation would not deliver the true emancipation and integration into American society that had been hoped for.

But unlike their nineteenth-century counterparts, black Americans did begin to build black identities during this time that would openly glory in a measure of difference from white American cultural norms. They also began to define notions of twentieth-century African American identity—"The New Negro"—to include and embrace aspects of African heritage and to react against models of black identity that were being created in white popular culture of the 1920s.[7] The interplay of these co-existing, and sometimes colliding, deliberate constructs of the public "negro"—a collision of two very different agendas about the nature of black identity—produced a discourse about race, class, patronage, and reception that is key to our understanding of subsequent developments in African American art in the twentieth century.

As with any aspect of the African American experience, various public identities created by white Americans elicited a wide range of responses from members of black communities. Although Marcus Garvey and Du Bois both promoted the prestige of African connections, they stood on different sides of the ideological fence in how they wished to use that African connection. Alain Locke and Du Bois might praise the creativity and classical beauty of African arts and urge black artists and writers to mine Africa's cultures for inspiration, but they also wished to use that heritage as part of an assimilation into mainstream American life. Some black intellectuals were more comfortable with classically performed Negro spirituals than with the down-home sexuality of Bessie Smith.

As whites flocked to Harlem's Cotton Club and looked to Carl Van Vechten's *Nigger Heaven* as a guide to the steamy, lush jungle of tropical rhythms and sinuous black bodies, African American artists envisaged very different versions of black identity.

In the midst of enormous creative activity by black writers, artists, and intellectuals, white Americans began writing and producing plays with black casts, music, and subject matter. While the 1921 production of *Shuffle Along* or Eugene O'Neill plays such as *Emperor Jones* provided precious exposure and opportunities for black musicians and actors, black intellectuals such as George Schuyler complained of these white efforts that, "even when he appears to be civilized, it is only necessary to beat a tom tom or wave a rabbit's foot and he is ready to strip off his Hart Schaffner & Marx suit, grab a spear and ride off wild-eyed on the back of a crocodile."[8]

Photographer James VanDerZee is best known for his images of tony and celebrity residents of Harlem, exemplified by his 1932 *Couple in Raccoon Coats* (catalogue no. 25). These were Harlemites as they wished to be portrayed—in no danger of shedding their coats and riding off on a crocodile's back.

By and large, African American artists tended to produce images of black men and women that challenged the degrading stereotypes still so popular in American culture and also responded to the imperatives of intellectuals such as Alain Locke and W. E. B. Du Bois. Like the free black communities of the nineteenth century, these African Americans still posited a class-associated image of dignified demeanor, conservative dress, and association with professional occupations. Sculptor Richmond Barthé (*Untitled* [Head of a Man], catalogue no. 11) and photographer P. H. Polk (*Portrait of Aaron Douglas*, catalogue no. 20) were both known for eloquent and intelligent portrayals of black men and women. Like Barthé's head of an unidentified man, Polk's portrait of well-known African American artist Aaron Douglas does not define the sitter by what he does but rather concentrates on the interior man. Like their nineteenth-century counterparts, these

images continue to address the central issue of humanity by emphasizing the intelligence, sensitivity, and aesthetic sophistication of the sitter. Even William H. Johnson's 1939 *Seated Woman* (catalogue no. 15), animated by his self-styled Primitivist palette and brushstroke, still depicts a well-dressed woman seated erect, with hands demurely folded in her lap.

Along with asserting the existence of this black American middle class, the first three decades of the twentieth century witnessed a growing awareness of the importance of African heritage in understanding and defining African American identity. As the Great Migration established significant black communities in Northern cities, leading intellectuals such as W. E. B. Du Bois and Alain Locke urged black artists to look toward African arts for inspiration and to choose African and African American subject matter. Although these black intellectuals shared an affinity with Euro-American conservative respectability, these twentieth-century definers of black identity took the somewhat radical step of embracing what had once been considered the primitive and uncivilized African past. Alain Locke helped sponsor exhibitions of African art in New York City, and black artists, exposed to African works of art, began to incorporate images and design principles in their artistic journey toward self.

While James Lesesne Wells's 1929 linocut *Sisters* (catalogue no. 27) showcases the same fashionable currency as VanDerZee's couple, it also reflects Locke's plea that black artists mine African cultures for visual inspiration. Aaron Douglas earned early recognition as the premier black artist of the Harlem Renaissance, as he combined Egyptian and West and Central African motifs, art deco elements, and stylized but easily identified black features into a signature style that defined much of his work through the 1940s. He combined these stylistic elements with the African American intelligentsia's interest in African and African American history, eloquently expressed in works such as the 1934 mural series *Aspects of Negro Life*, commissioned for the 135th Street Branch of the New York Public Library, now known as the Schomburg Center for Research in Black Culture. The Loïs Mailou Jones painting *Ethiopian Boy* (catalogue no. 17) in the Driskell collection attests to the continued depiction of Africans by African American artists in portraiture as well.

African Americans' interest in African and African American history had existed throughout their years in the Americas but in visual culture had up until now been confined to portraits of black heroes of the past and present. Led by pioneers such as sculptor Meta Warrick Fuller, black artists began inserting aspects of black history into the canon of history painting. *Aspects of Negro Life* was among a number of mural and painting series in the 1930s and 1940s by artists such as Hale Woodruff, Jacob Lawrence, and Charles Alston, that dealt with specific aspects of black history and culture.

Douglas's *Aspects of Negro Life* chronicled the history of African Americans from their African origins through the years of the Great Depression. The Driskell collection includes a study for one panel in that mural, *An Idyll of the Deep South* (catalogue no. 13), which functions both as historical narrative and pungent political commentary.

Likewise, both Jacob Lawrence and James VanDerZee pay homage to black courage and heroism, but they are also positing definitions of black manhood that are clearly outside the comfort zone of white America's definitions. Rather than celebrate the humble and less-threatening accomplishments of scholarship or community service, both artists celebrate the capacity of black men to bear arms in service to a cause, in heroic events that were usually overlooked in the standard historical canon.

Lawrence celebrates in forty-one panels the first successful self-emancipation achieved through organized aggression, leading to the first nation established by previously enslaved blacks. Jacob Lawrence's series documented how Haitian blacks won their freedom and established the first black republic in the Americas, led by the remarkable military leader Toussaint L'Ouverture. *General Toussaint* (catalogue no. 19), like the rest of the series, paid homage to a man and event that had always been revered by black Americans[9] and reminded 1939 America that African Americans were capable of effective and aggressive actions to secure the rights due them.

VanDerZee, in his 1932 photograph *Roberts and Johnson* (catalogue no. 22) celebrates the courage and sacrifice of black soldiers during World War I; rather than their being welcomed home by all Americans as conquering heroes, they found that many white Americans were infuriated by blacks' expectations that they would enjoy at home the rights for which they had fought and died. The Red Summer of 1919 provided bloody confirmation to black Americans that white America was not ready to allow black men and women to stand up assertively for their rights as citizens.

African American artists and writers created versions of the black American everyman to stand in all the important niches of American culture: in representations of man, woman, and family; in adding black history to American history; and in translating the tenets of Christianity, a crucial institution for black solidarity, self-help, resistance, and hope, by casting the central figures of Christianity's narrative in black. Wells's 1932 *Escape of the Spies from Canaan* (catalogue no. 26) not only depicts a specific Old Testament moment, but in it Wells also carries on the black tradition of identification with Moses and the Israelites. Slaves sang spirituals about their journey as a metaphor for black hopes for freedom, either by earthly escape or heavenly reward. The Israelites, blacks chased by a white giant, continue to stand in for black aspirations against the obstacles of the dominant culture.

Works such as Douglas's 1934 *Go Down Death* (catalogue no. 14) and William H. Johnson's *I Baptize Thee* (catalogue no. 16) take the further step of adding African American traditions to the vocabulary of religious imagery. Johnson's baptism scene shows the religious rite in a black community, and Douglas's painting was one of the works meant to accompany James Weldon Johnson's book of black sermons. One of VanDerZee's most unusual photographs, *Barefoot Prophet,* 1929 (catalogue no. 23), shows a black street preacher not wildly gesticulating on a street-corner soapbox but engaged in literate study; although barefoot, his dress is conservative, his demeanor sober and dignified.

Humorous and light-hearted depictions of African Americans had too often, in the hands of white artists, been occasions for racist and demeaning commentary on blacks' appearances, demeanors, and customs. Although the initial response by many African Americans was to emphasize a serious and sober identity, works such as Hale Woodruff's *Trusty on a Mule* (catalogue no. 28) and Augusta Savage's *Gamin* (catalogue no. 21), as well as photographic treatments such as P. H. Polk's *The Boss* and James VanDerZee's *Undeclared War* (catalogue no. 24), all illustrate an aspect of visual identity for African Americans that also claimed the humbler, sometimes humorous sides of life that were as much a part of the black public identity as portraits of glamorous celebrities, revered historical figures, and dignified scholars and professionals.

All of these works served notice that blacks would participate in and appropriate all the hallowed aspects of American culture. Visual images of African Americans by African American artists asserted in no uncertain terms that "we are part of America; we claim our places in history, our ability to interpret a common religion, our place in the everyday issues of life that universalize us all."

To have these visual images work as purveyors of public identity, however, it was necessary for them to be seen. The opportunities for African American artists to hone their skills, take advantage of support networks and the community of artists, and finally exhibit and sell their work were much more limited than for Euro-American artists. Part of artistic identity requires the validation of a like community, and African American artists utilized every strategy they could to succeed in their ambitions. Whether training in Europe, as Loïs Mailou Jones did in preparation to create works such as her *Notre-Dame de Paris* (1936, catalogue no. 18), or in the United States, African American artists found their best resources in a web of individual, institutional, and community resources we might call *the black academy*.

THE BLACK ACADEMY:
TEACHERS, MENTORS, AND
INSTITUTIONAL PATRONAGE

Perhaps the least explored area of African American art history is the role of black institutions and individuals in nurturing the development of black artists. Featured in this section are some of the many African American artists who nurtured future generations and whose works appear in the Driskell collection. Scholarly studies have often tended to appraise the works and careers of black artists only to the extent that they have been recognized by influential white individuals and institutions in Europe and America. Certainly there were a few white-run private and governmental institutions, such as the Harmon Foundation and later the WPA Federal Arts Project program, which were important support mechanisms for black artists.[10] In 1933, the Harmon Foundation awarded its George E. Haynes prize to James Lesesne Wells's *Escape of the Spies From Canaan* (catalogue no. 26) and to Ellis Wilson's *Untitled* (Fish in Net, catalogue no. 48). African American artists such as Wells who worked for the WPA arts program also had the invaluable experience of meeting and working with other New York artists, both black and white, sometimes for the first time; it was while working on such a project that Wells met artists and brothers Beauford and Joseph Delaney. But these institutions provided opportunities for black artists that were limited, like the WPA, to a specific time period and a mandate for a particular kind of public art, or by well-intentioned but misguided attempts to "help the Negro." White patrons, whether institutional or individual, often offered their support according to racial constructs that identified them as "benevolent benefactors" helping to foster the "wonderfully primitive and visceral talents of an exotic race."

The black artistic community's sensitivity to this problem is illustrated in a 1934 article written by a young Romare Bearden and published in *Opportunity* magazine. Bearden identified the misguided efforts of white philanthropic organizations as one of the major obstacles to the development of African American artists. He criticized the Harmon Foundation, in particular, for its "coddling and patronizing" attitude. He used the example of a California exhibition that combined the work of Negro and blind artists to illustrate the accepted practices of white institutions that reflected a racist condescension to African American endeavors.[11] Leading African American artist Aaron Douglas criticized individual white benefactors such as Charlotte Mason, who attempted to influence his work, as well as that of writers Langston Hughes and Zora Neale Hurston, in order to bring out what she and others believed were the essential primitive elements of African American artistry.[12]

But there also existed what can be called the black academy, a continuous flow of encouragement, patronage, instruction, and mentoring that black artists received from other African American individuals and institutions. Artists who gained prominence during the Harlem Renaissance became devoted teachers to the next generation of artists. Historically black colleges and institutions developed some of the most impressive collections of African American art. Throughout black communities, libraries, schools, YMCAs and YWCAs, and fraternal and civic organizations provided patronage and forums for exhibitions and competitions when such opportunities were rare or nonexistent for black artists in white mainstream institutions. Black patronage offered the invaluable support of a community that shared the same range of aspirations and obstacles as the artists themselves. Records of the black community's public recognition, exhibition, and support often provide rare documentation of African American artists whose works and histories would be lost to us.

Local exhibitions in African American northern art communities have provided important resources for public presentation of African American art since the nineteenth century. In the first three decades of the twentieth century, the "colored branches" of the YWCA and YMCA sponsored lectures, social events, and art exhibitions for a black community excluded from most of white America's cultural life. In 1905 and 1919, exhibitions of paintings by William E. Braxton, Samuel O. Collins, Clinton J. De Villis, and W. O. Thompson were held at two sites of the Colored Men's Branch of the Brooklyn YMCA. African American artists from New York, Philadelphia, Washington, D. C., Chicago, and Boston presented their works at exhibitions sponsored by the 135th Street Library and the 135th Street YMCA in 1921, 1922, and 1923.[13]

Prominent black individuals provided much-needed exhibition opportunities. Writer Wallace Thurman held "An Exhibition by Young Negro Artists" at his home in 1927, which included works by a number of rising black artists.[14] In 1911, Arthur Schomburg, historian and archivist of African and African American cultural history, founded the Negro Society for Historic Research, appointing the artist Braxton as its art director. Schomburg later helped found the Negro Library Association, and by 1918 the group was sponsoring its first annual "Exhibition of Books, Manuscripts, Paintings, Engravings, and Sculptures, et cetera," accompanied by a catalogue that listed numerous works of African art, as well as those by African Americans Braxton, Collins, De Villis, Robert H. Lewis, Smith, Ella Spencer, and Laura Wheeler. These annual exhibitions eventually moved to the 135th Street Branch of the New York Public Library, which today is known as the Schomburg Center for Research in Black Culture.

Community groups, artists' clubs, and African American secondary schools also provided additional exhibition opportunities and patronage. In 1917, Chicago's black artists were first exhibited by the Arts and Letters Society of Chicago. The Tanner Art Students Society in Washington, D. C., held exhibitions of African American art from 1919 on. Artists' groups exhibited at New York's 135th Street Library throughout the 1920s. In 1919, Dunbar High School in Washington, D. C., commissioned May Howard Jackson to sculpt a bust of Paul Lawrence Dunbar. In 1926 the Baltimore Federation of Parent-Teacher Clubs sponsored an exhibition at Douglas High School, featuring works by Henry O. Tanner, Meta Warrick Fuller, and more than twenty-two works by Augusta Savage.[15]

Black political organizations supported African American cultural aspirations as another aspect of the struggle for full rights and privileges in American society. The NAACP held an art exhibition at its annual meeting of 1913 that included works by Richard Lonsdale Brown

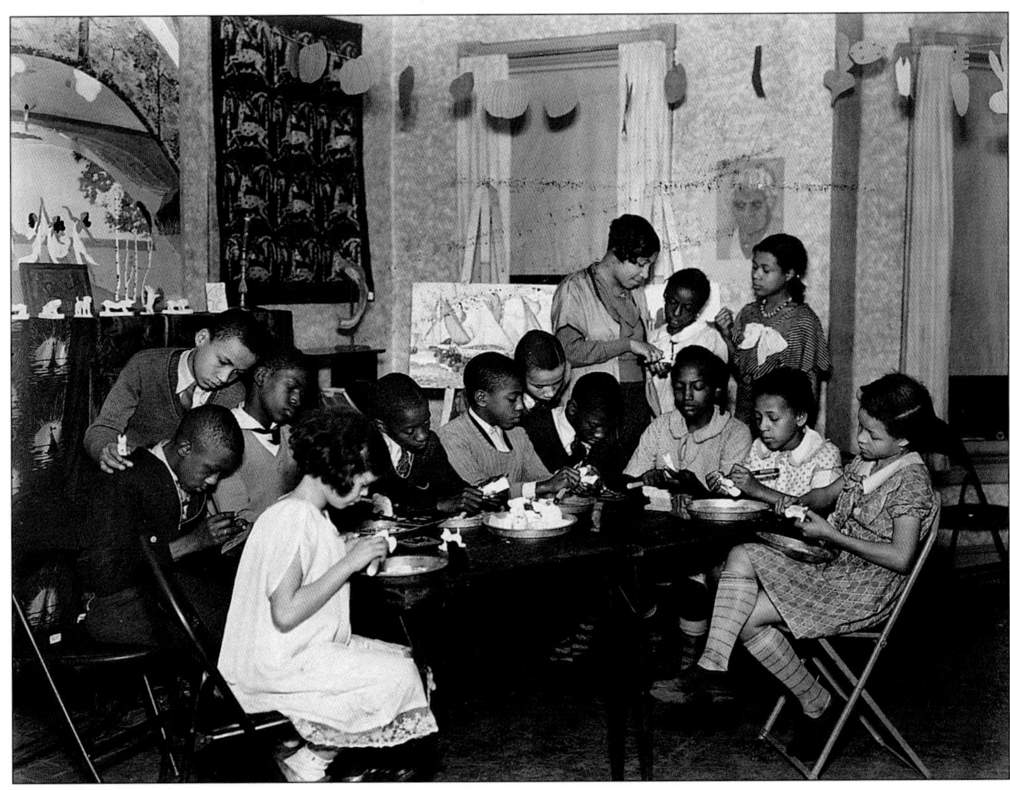

Loïs Mailou Jones and Junior Crafts Club students; Howard University, Washington, D.C., c. 1933 (David C. Driskell Archives)

and sculptor May Howard Jackson. Some of the most influential periodicals in black America—*The Crisis* (published by the NAACP), *Opal Magazine* in Philadelphia, and *Opportunity* (a publication for the National Urban League)—provided significant exposure for African American artists as early as 1923. In the 1920s and 1930s, these periodicals published reproductions of artworks and inside and cover illustrations by artists including William E. Braxton, Aaron Douglas, Meta Warrick Fuller, Edwin Harleston, Loïs Mailou Jones, William E. Scott, Albert A. Smith, and James Lesesne Wells, as well as articles about artists and announcements of exhibitions.[16]

Certain individual artists combined their artistic endeavors with teaching careers dedicated to the next generation of African American artists. Perhaps the most significant factor in the development of these young artists was the existence of trained, professional black artists who provided excellent role models and evidence that their artistic aspirations were not an impossibility in America. During the years of the Harlem Renaissance, artists such as Augusta Savage, James Lesesne Wells, and Charles Alston established and taught in Harlem art schools, and their studios often served as salons where artists, writers, and intellectuals could find a common community.

Savage was, by many accounts, one of the most influential teachers and mentors for African American artists in New York during the 1930s and 1940s. During the 1930s, when Savage sculpted works such as *Boy on a Stump* (catalogue no. 42), she mentored a generation of young black artists, including William Artis, Norman Lewis, Morgan and Marvin Smith, and Ernest Crichlow. She was often able to secure scholarship or apprenticeship opportunities for her students in the Savage Studio of Arts and Crafts, established in 1932. Savage subsidized these classes with her own funds, often lending space and materials and even providing work for her students in financial need. In 1935 she combined her private art classes with the adult education project of the State University of New York, forming one of the largest free art classes in New York. In that same year she organized an exhibition of her students' work, *Artists and Models Exhibition,* which was held at the 138th Street YWCA and sponsored by the New York Urban League. At this and other exhibitions her students won favorable reviews. Among the exhibitors were Savage, instructors from the various programs she had established, and students Norman Lewis, Marvin Smith, Gwendolyn Knight, and others. In 1936 Savage became an assistant supervisor on the WPA Federal Art Projects and worked tirelessly to increase the number of African American artists employed by the FAP.

Augusta Savage's own works, while clearly situated within a Euro-American aesthetic, reflect her political and artistic activism. Her many images of African Americans served to enhance a visual identity of powerful physique and noble countenance. Savage was, in fact, such an outspoken advocate for the recognition and rights of black artists that she may well have short-changed her personal artistic ambitions. The considerable time and energy she expended teaching and mentoring her students left less time for her own work and career. She also probably alienated much of the network of influential white patronage of Harlem Renaissance artists and writers by her aggressive advocacy for her own career and the careers of her students and by her alignment with communist ideas and organizations.[17]

Among the African American community of artists and intellectuals working in Harlem, Savage was recognized as one of its guiding lights. James Weldon Johnson was a frequent visitor to her studio, which was the site of weekly gatherings by Harlem intellectuals and artists. Acknowledging her special role as mentor to so many African American artists, collector and archivist Arthur Schomburg honored Savage at a Phi Delta Kappa ceremony for her teaching achievements. In 1939, in a remarkable effort by the black community to further institutionalize its support of black artists, Savage was named Director of the Salon of Contemporary Negro Art in Harlem, a gallery devoted solely to the works of black artists and owned and operated by blacks. Although the gallery closed after a few months due to lack of funding, the list of more than thirty African American artists whose works were featured in the first show remains a testament to this community's support of its artists and to Savage's place as a recognized and respected leader and teacher/mentor extraordinaire to the next generation of African American artists.[18]

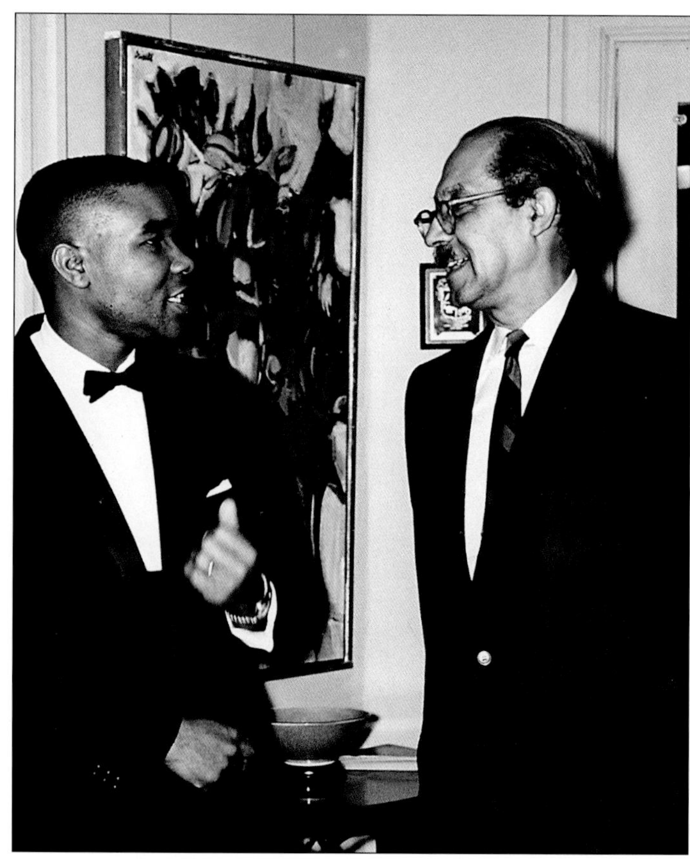

David Driskell and James Lesesne Wells;
Barnett-Aden Gallery, Washington, D.C., 1962
(David C. Driskell Archives)

James Lesesne Wells (*Primitive Girl*, catalogue no. 46) was another artist who early on devoted himself to a distinguished career of teaching and mentoring, beginning in his early years in New York City. In the early 1930s, Wells, primarily known as a printmaker, along with the director of the 135th Street Library, secured a Carnegie Grant and established a summer art workshop in an old Harlem nightclub. Wells was the workshop's director, and he was assisted by fellow artists Palmer Hayden and Georgette Seabrooke. This summer workshop, whose students included Charles Alston and Jacob Lawrence, taught classes in carving, printmaking, textile design, drawing, and painting.[19]

Like the weekly salons at the studio of Augusta Savage, artist Charles Alston's studio became an important gathering place for many black artists.[20] In 1936 Alston was appointed supervisor of mural painters for the WPA Federal Arts Project; he established his Harlem art workshop as the site where artists would come to his studio and sign onto the project. These artists became known as the "306 group." Jacob Lawrence studied there, and he remembered that

> at "306" I came in contact with so many older people in other fields of art…like Claude McKay, Countee Cullen, dancers, musicians…It was like a school.…Socially that was my whole life at that time, the "306" studio.[21]

At 306, one could have discussed politics and/or the arts with other black musicians, poets, playwrights, musicologists, historians, intellectuals, and artists from New York, Philadelphia, Chicago, and Washington, D.C. The list of those one might meet—which could include Langston Hughes, actor Canada Lee, Ralph Ellison, Richard Wright, Claude McKay, or artists Selma Burke, Aaron Douglas, Ernest Crichlow, Robert Savon Pious, Gwendolyn Knight, Robert Blackburn, Charles White, Norman Lewis, Romare Bearden, and many, many others—indicated the richness of Harlem's creative community. This sense of community was a priceless resource to artists, both established and just beginning, and an essential component of the black academy.

In 1935, Augusta Savage, Elba Lightfoot, and Charles Alston established the Harlem Artists Guild, which counted among its membership Ernest Crichlow, Jacob Lawrence, and Henry W. Bannard. Formed to serve the interests of black artists, the guild "was instrumental in increasing the number of Black artists hired by the WPA."[22] Douglas was elected its first president and, like Savage, worked hard to win recognition and greater participation for black artists on WPA projects. When Savage was named Director of the Harlem Community Art Center in 1937, its first exhibition featured FAP works by the Harlem Artists Guild.

HISTORICALLY BLACK COLLEGES AND UNIVERSITIES

Historically black colleges and universities, often the only institutions of higher learning to hire African Americans, provided a remarkable resource, not only in training and employing artists but also by developing collections of African and African American art that are now priceless repositories of a black cultural legacy. Many prominent contributions include not only the art they created but also the generations of younger aspiring artists for whom they provided training and role models.

Painter Laura Wheeler Waring, represented in this section by her still life *Rose of Sharon* (catalogue no. 45), is one who dedicated herself to teaching the next generation. In 1907, Waring began teaching part-time at Cheyney State Teacher's College, the only historically black state college above the Mason-Dixon line. Thereafter, having traveled abroad to study art in Europe and North Africa and at the Pennsylvania Academy of Fine Arts, she began teaching at Cheyney full-time, eventually heading the art department.

While a student at Hampton University, John Biggers (*Quilting Party,* catalogue no. 51) studied under Elizabeth Catlett (*Harriet,* catalogue no. 32) and Charles White (*Awaiting His Return,* catalogue no. 47). As their works in this section illustrate, Catlett and White, both well known for their dedication to social and political commentary on African American lives and experiences, surely helped to solidify Biggers's lifelong interest in the depiction of African and African American life.

Hale Woodruff (*Two Figures in a Mexican Landscape,* catalogue no. 49) used his tenure as professor at a historically black college to effect some remarkably far-reaching support systems for African American artists. In 1931, Woodruff began teaching art at Spelman and at Atlanta University in Georgia. He worked tirelessly to make art resources, especially the High Museum where black visitors were not yet welcome, available to his students. With very limited resources, he found materials and space for his students, held solo shows of African American artists, secured art slides, and convinced traveling exhibitions to come. He taught artists such as Wilmer Jennings (*Still*

Life, catalogue no. 38), who noted Woodruff's dedication to his students. Woodruff organized his students into a "Painters Guild" and took them on field trips so that they might paint the local landscapes and people, thereby participating in the national interest in Regionalism in American art.

In 1941, after the Harmon Foundation ended its New York exhibitions, Woodruff managed to convince Atlanta University administrators to institute an annual exhibition that would provide a forum for black artists to show their work and to award purchase prizes that would also establish an institutional collection of African American art. These annual shows, which continued until 1970, provided a remarkable opportunity for black artists, and each year, hundreds of black artists from around the nation exhibited in the Atlanta University juried exhibitions.

Aaron Douglas (*The Junk Man*, catalogue no. 35) headed the art department at Fisk University from 1939 to 1966. He first came to Fisk in 1931, at the urging of sociologist Charles S. Johnson, to paint a series of murals in the new Cravath Library. When he retired, Douglas was succeeded by David Driskell, who became the new department chair.

Howard University was another remarkable resource for African Americans wishing to study art and art history. Artist James Herring (*Campus Landscape*, catalogue no. 37) founded the art department there, and along with James A. Porter (*Playground*, catalogue no. 41) helped mentor a generation of African American artists. In addition to his teaching and creative contributions, Porter published *Modern Negro Art* in 1943, considered by many the first thorough survey of African American art history and a work so valuable that it continues to serve as an important index and reference tool for historians today.

Herring brought James Lesesne Wells to Howard in 1929, and Wells taught graphic arts there for many years. Loïs Mailou Jones (*Notre-Dame de Paris*, catalogue no. 18) headed the art department of Palmer Memorial Institute, a private black boarding school for girls in Sedalia, North Carolina, from 1928 to 1930. From 1930 until her retirement in 1977, Jones taught design and watercolor painting at Howard University.

These were some of the remarkable faculty who taught and mentored younger artists. Exceptional students such as David Driskell (*Boy with Birds,* catalogue no. 36) then taught the succeeding generation of students. He was first on the faculty at Talladega College, Fisk and Howard Universities, and later at the University of Maryland. Driskell has won national and international recognition for his artistic career. Since his student days, he has patronized the work of his colleagues, building both a remarkable collection of works by African and African American artists and a priceless archive of African American art history. He has curated numerous exhibitions, nationally and internationally, that stand as significant contributions to both the scholarship and public awareness of the gifts of black artists, historic and contemporary. Driskell is today one of the leading and most influential scholars in the field, and he represents the unbroken link between the black academy in the first half of this century and the growing scholarly and commercial appreciation of the work of African American artists today.

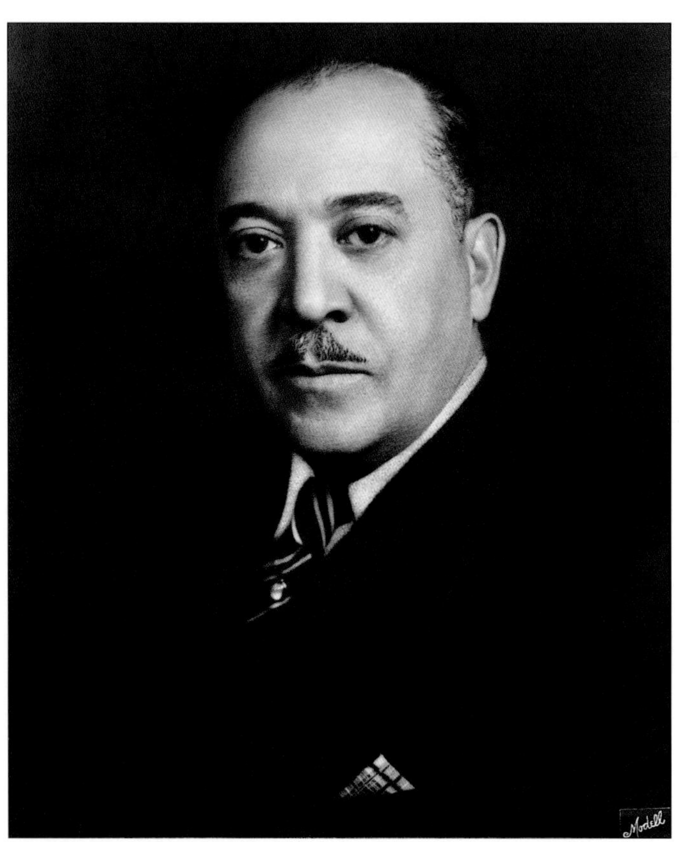

James V. Herring, c. 1950
(Addison N. Scurlock, photographer; David C. Driskell Archives)

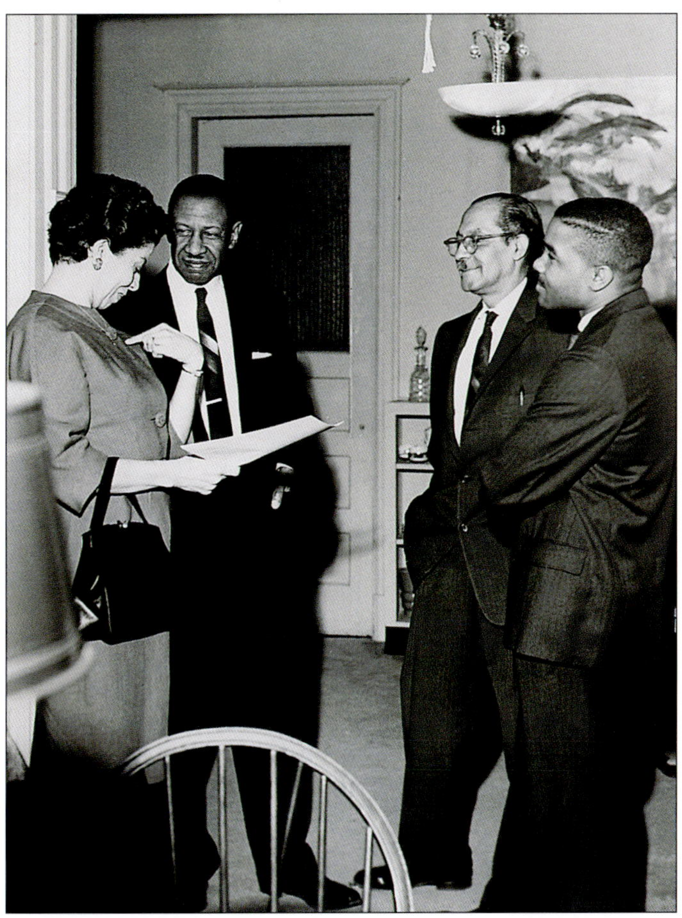

Left to right: Ann Burwell, James Porter, James Lesesne Wells, and David Driskell; Barnett-Aden Gallery, Washington, D.C., 1961 (David C. Driskell Archives)

Continuing, expanding, and enriching the artist/teacher model he learned from his mentors, Driskell in turn has mentored a succeeding generation of African American academic scholars, museum curators and administrators, dedicated collectors, and artists too numerous to list here. Stephanie Pogue, a Driskell mentee, was Chair of the Department of Art at the University of Maryland in College Park from 1992 to 1998. Pogue's 1977 work *Aaron's Meadow* (catalogue no. 40) specifically references both the name and stylistic vocabulary of another African American artist, Aaron Douglas, who has served as an inspiration to so many black artists from the 1920s to the present.

COMMUNITIES OF ARTISTS AND INTELLECTUALS

Contact with other African American artists, as well as achievers in other areas, must be properly understood as an essential part of the black academy. A sense of community, shared opportunities, shared obstacles, and the ability to establish networks was crucial for black artists who were usually excluded from mainstream networks.

James Lesesne Wells met Alain Locke in New York City after Locke's publication of *The New Negro* in 1925. Wells and Locke later were neighbors in their Washington, D.C., neighborhood, and had frequent contact with one another. Locke gave high praise to Wells's *African Series* in his 1936 *Negro Art: Past and Present*. This series included *African Phantasy* and *Primitive Girl* (1929, catalogue no. 46). Locke described Wells and his work "as a force in the sane non-melodramatic use of African motives and rhythms in design."[23]

Although the Harlem community in New York City is often the focus when studying black artists and arts of the twentieth century, the young artist Ellis Wilson (*Untitled* [Fish in Net], catalogue no. 48) found mentors, role models, and colleagues when he moved to Chicago to study art. At Chicago's Art Institute, Wilson met artist William McKnight Farrow, the first black instructor to teach at the Institute. Farrow introduced Wilson to a community of black artists that included sculptor Richmond Barthé. Farrow and another prominent Chicago black artist, Charles C. Dawson, established the Chicago Art League. The League not only worked to research African American art history, it also helped create an Art Institute exhibition of historic and contemporary African and African American art. Wilson remembered fondly the sense of artistic identity fostered by the Art League's frequent exhibitions and discussions, saying, "…oh, they were good times! I had never before been in a group of artists—you know, creative black people."[24] When Wilson moved to New York in 1928, he reveled in the community of black artists he met there; his greater exposure to known black artists, including Aaron Douglas and Horace Pippin, helped shape the direction of his work.[25]

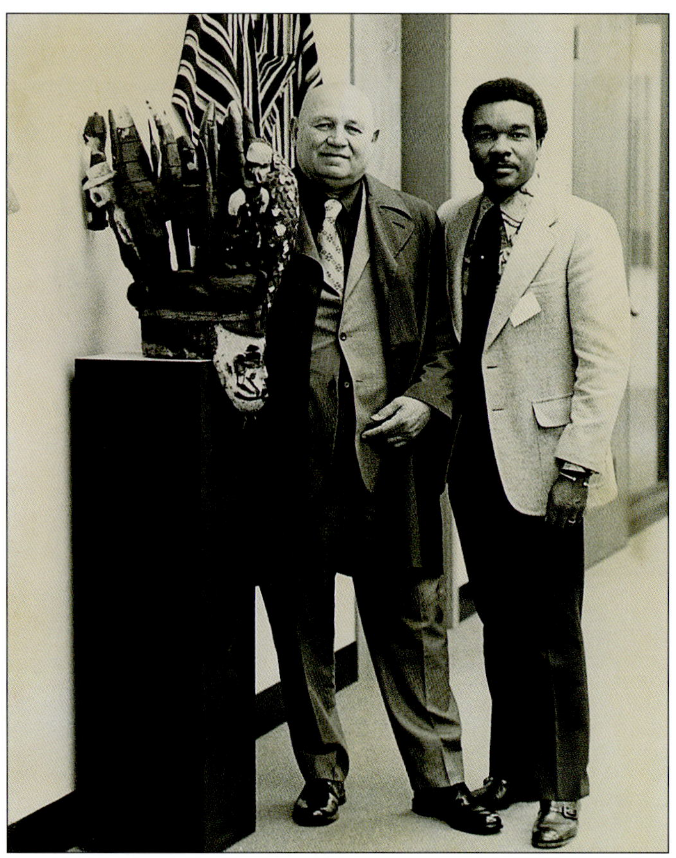

David Driskell and Romare Bearden; Fisk University, Nashville, 1975 (David C. Driskell Archives)

Unlike the experiences of those Chicago and New York artists in the 1920s and 1930s, Allan Crite (*Last Station*, catalogue no. 33) remembered a feeling of isolation in his early years, unaware of other black role models that would affirm his aspirations to become an artist. With efforts that have included his projects for schoolchildren and his formation of the Artist's Collective, an institution devoted to young African American artists, Crite has used his own artistic successes and recognition to make sure the next generation does not experience a similar sense of isolation.

Romare Bearden (*Morning*, catalogue no. 29; *Woman and Child Reading* and *Untitled* [Verso], catalogue nos. 30 and 31) both benefited from and contributed to the informal institutions of the black academy. Raised in a circle of Harlem intellectuals, community leaders, artists, and musicians, Bearden grew up in the midst of an activist, thoughtful, and creative black community.

As a young artist in the 1930s, Bearden's colleagues were the black artists of Charles Alston's "306 group" and those who later helped organize and run the Harlem Artists Guild. Bearden continued to promote the activism and artistic communalism he had gleaned from these associations, lending his active support to community organizations and helping to form the group "Spiral" in 1963. This organization sought to blend artistic and racial identity by creating works that spoke to the issues of the civil rights movement. Like other artist/scholars, Bearden helped to provide a framework for discourse on the nature and development of black artistic contributions in the exhibitions he helped curate and the articles and texts he contributed to the field of African American art history.[26]

RADICAL POLITICS,
PROTEST, AND ART

While African American artists engaged issues of identity and racism in their art throughout the twentieth century, the 1950s and 1960s witnessed a heightened politicization. The increasingly radical and aggressive push for civil rights in black communities across the nation was mirrored in the art of these decades, as artists explored themes of the black urban experience, black labor, confrontation and resistance, and racial violence. Images directly related to the civil rights and black power movements, depictions of important black leaders, and documentation of racism's effect on black America characterized the work of many African American artists of this period. These artists vigorously participated in the discourse on identity and racism.

Visual conventions that aggressively embraced diasporan elements were an important element in black constructions of identity during these years. Works such as Eldzier Cortor's *Cuban Souvenir* and John Biggers's *Third Ward* clearly reference Afro-Caribbean cultural legacies as valid to the expression of black American identity. Eldzier Cortor's *Cuban Souvenir* (catalogue no. 55) combines the artist's lifelong interest in depicting the African American woman within the framework of his equally compelling interest in African aspects of Caribbean cultures.

Although by the early fifties many American artists were beginning to embrace principles of abstraction in their work, many black artists continued to work in the Social Realist traditions they had used in the 1930s and 1940s, out of a strong conviction that the political realities of racism in America demanded visual narratives that emphatically stated black Americans' concerns.

Responses to racism were crucially important aspects of black public identity throughout the nineteenth and twentieth centuries. African Americans with access to public forums—writers, artists, intellectuals, etc.—frequently felt a responsibility to express the often-ignored plight of the black community.

Many African American artists have incorporated political commentary into their works. They reflected the political concerns of black Americans, and they also helped to document, express, and shape a new visual vocabulary for the black American experience.

Claude Clark depicted the historical narrative of the punishment of an enslaved African American in his 1946 *Slave Lynching* (catalogue no. 54). Purposefully including the word *lynching* in the title, he drew attention to another horrific practice of Southern racism that was not safely removed into a historical past.

When artist Charles White drew *Awaiting His Return* (catalogue no. 47), his depiction of a patiently heroic woman awaiting the return of her soldier son or husband, he reminded America not only of the black servicemen who fought so valiantly in World War II but also of the poignant sacrifices of black families at home. Indeed, issues of family—particularly the education of black children—were used to argue legislative civil rights efforts in the 1950s, culminating in the *Brown v. Board of Education* decision.

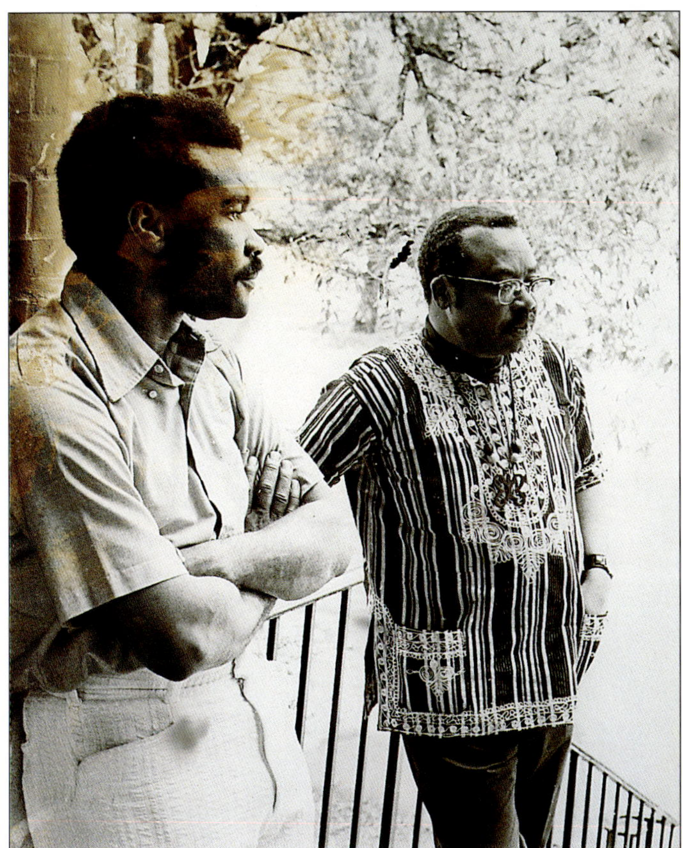

David Driskell and Claude Clark; Van Vechten Gallery, Fisk University, Nashville, 1975 (Susan Carter, photographer; David C. Driskell Archives)

Roy DeCarava's photograph of Paul Robeson (catalogue no. 34), unlike the familiar glossy celebrity shots by Harlem Renaissance photographers such as James VanDerZee or Carl Van Vechten, is a dark and moody portrait of the singer and socialist. It anticipates the difficulties that African American leftists such as Robeson and Du Bois would face in the anti-Communist hysteria of that decade. This photo was taken in the year Robeson's passport was revoked because he would not sign an affidavit swearing he had never been a member of the Communist party.

Lawrence's 1961 *The Travelers* (catalogue no. 60) subtly comments on issues of segregation simply by portraying a family traveling; this act, which seems a fairly benign and common practice, was normally fraught with dangers and humiliations for black Americans. Romare Bearden's *Urban Street Scene* (catalogue no. 50) is a jarring collage that aptly portrays the jagged edges of much of black urban life. Both artists use compositional and media choices to state sharp-edged commentaries about black life. Like the most effective tactics of civil rights activism, these artists speak to those universal sentiments that sought to bring white awareness beyond the limitations of a racist past.

James Phillips's *The Dealer* from the *Junkie in the Twilight Zone Series* (catalogue no. 63) was completed in 1966. Pairing organic shapes with jagged linear patterns and jarring colors, this work seems to reflect the growing impulse to black radicalism and a response to the violence of those years. In 1965 Malcolm X was assassinated. That summer saw the Watts riots, and school segregation was still entrenched in many parts of the nation.

Some African American artists began to display the public identity so eloquently expressed by the image of the raised black fist, which quickly became an icon of more aggressive visual and verbal expressions of black frustration and anger. Phrases such as "black power" and "by any means necessary" were heard by the media and a frightened white America as "burn, baby, burn."

Elizabeth Catlett, in works such as *Malcolm X Speaks for Us, Target Practice,* and *The Black Woman Speaks* (catalogue no. 53), created some of the most visually compelling expressions of black political sentiments of that period. *The Black Woman Speaks* also expresses the concerns of black feminism, as black women activists were often counseled by their male colleagues to subordinate issues of black women's rights in favor of the larger struggle. Charles White's *Wanted Poster Series* (catalogue

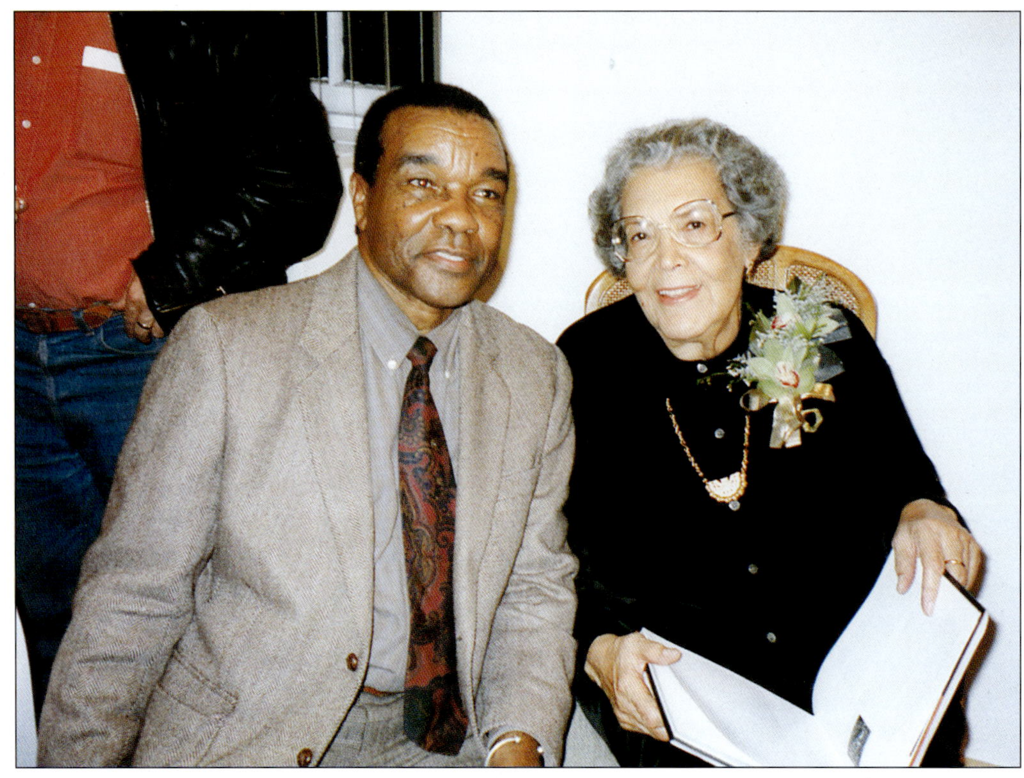

David Driskell and Elizabeth Catlett; June Kelly Gallery, New York, 1998 (David C. Driskell Archives)

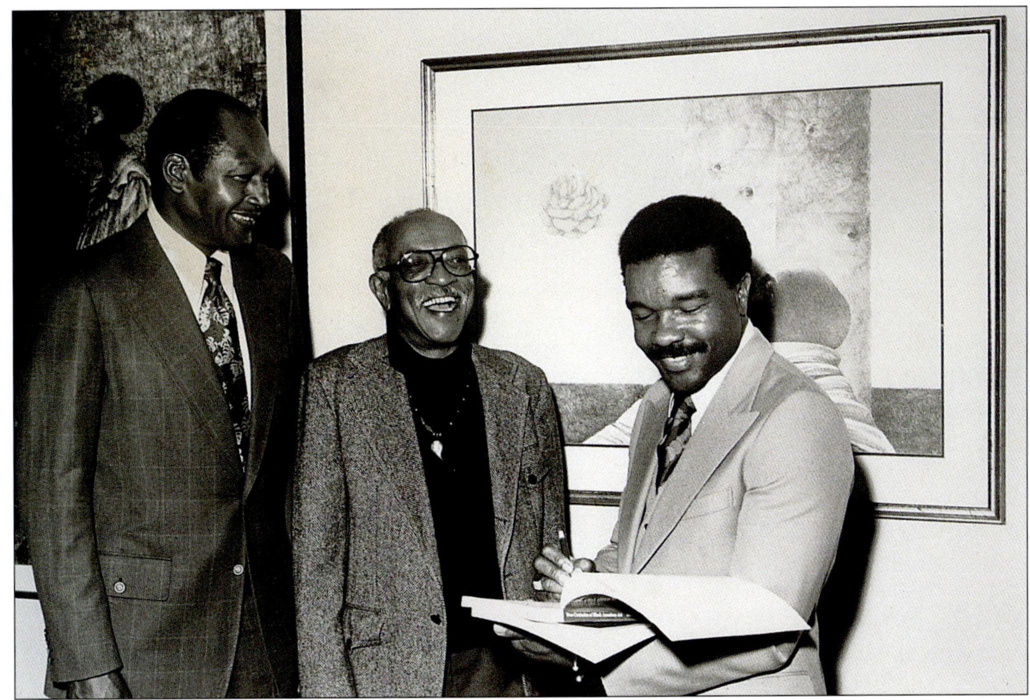

*Left to right: Mayor of Los Angeles
Tom Bradley, Charles White,
and David Driskell; Los Angeles
County Museum of Art, 1976
(David C. Driskell Archives)*

no. 64) layers the present over the most persistent aspect of America's racial past, insisting that the problems begun in 1619 were still very much part of black and white America in 1970.

White's 1975–1976 work, *The Prophet* (catalogue no. 65), speaks to the role of black leadership, decimated by the murders of Martin Luther King, Jr. and Malcolm X, but it also affirms the power and nobility of the African American leader, clothed in voluminous robes that suggest the Greek or African scholar and evoke associations with wisdom and peace. Against a pillar pockmarked with the bullet holes of the previous decades of violence, this undaunted prophet looks optimistically skyward, to a rose unfolding with the as yet unrealized promise of equality and peace in America.

DIASPORA IDENTITIES/GLOBAL ARTS

This final and largest section defies easy categorization, expressly because it does not represent a category. It represents, rather, a range of choices that explore how racial and artistic identities intersect in works by artists of the African diaspora living in America. After the more radical years of the sixties and seventies, ideas about what constituted "black art" began to enlarge, to embrace a growing interest in a broader consideration of cultures of African descent. The term *diaspora studies* began to appear, suggesting the possibilities of cultural commonalities and perspectives among black people in varying geographical locations. An increasing interest in African art, both traditional and contemporary, brought more international attention to the careers of artists of color and also contributed to discussions about racial identity and presumptions about artistic expression. Did an African American artist need to produce something that was recognizably "black"? Was a contemporary African artist who utilized European aesthetic traditions therefore betraying his or her heritage and identity?

A central issue in the dialogue among black artists, their work, and the public has been the conflict inherent in appropriating European-American aesthetic and art-historical traditions, especially when juxtaposed with the diversity of black experience that was often not well served by those traditions. Some black artists consciously rejected the growing popularity of abstraction in 1950s America, feeling that narrative and figurative conventions suited their message-oriented agenda much more than did subject-neutral expression.

The issue of abstraction, in particular, required from African American artists a particular discourse on how race must/should/would/could inflect artistic practice. One of the most powerful ways that African American artists had combined their artistic ambitions and their racial identities was found within the mostly narrative structure of the visual arts. If one could tell a story, one could illuminate some aspect of the drama of African American life. No matter what part of the spectrum that story fell in, from humorous drama to poignant family scenes to strident militancy, the artist was still filling an enormous vacuum in American visual culture, as well as altering the damaging stereotypes of the past.

But with narrative removed, how would the African American abstract painter continue to tell that story? As abstraction began to overtake realism's popularity in American art, this became more and more a pressing question for black artists. Success in the art world would increasingly depend on dealers and critics who classified realism and narrative as passé. But at the same time that the art world deepened its love affair with abstraction, the black political consciousness of the 1950s through the 1970s began to develop dogmatic definitions of what constituted properly political "black art."

Where would works such as Aaron Douglas's 1956 *City Scape* (catalogue no. 73) lie on this landscape? Neither fashionably abstract nor sufficiently political, Douglas's creation of this work affirms a belief that the artist should not be bound by dogma or fashion. At the same moment, Beauford Delaney in Paris (*Untitled*, catalogue no. 72) and Norman Lewis (*Good Morning* and *The Red Umbrella*, catalogue nos. 80 and 81) embraced principles of abstraction that allowed them to explore issues of color, texture, and form with little or no textual framework. African American artists represented in this col-

lection diligently pursued abstraction in their work, expanding beyond the boundaries of any particular movement. Rather than becoming mired in a particular ideology or system of abstract aesthetics, they utilized instead the liberating aspects of an artistic creation no longer tied to the representational.

Just as Norman Lewis had done in his work, Alma Thomas (*Falling Leaves Love Wind Orchestra*, catalogue no. 95), Richard Mayhew (*Landscape*, catalogue no. 82), William McNeil (*Elegy*, catalogue no. 83), and Gilda Snowden (*Tornado*, catalogue no. 92) retained some reference to subject that expressed their very personal relationships with nature. Stephanie Pogue's *India Pattern—Pattern of India* (catalogue no. 88) and Terry Adkins's *Budo* (catalogue no. 66) freely appropriated other non-Western cultures, owning these experiences and legacies as much as any other artist might. Mary Lovelace O'Neal used color and form, allied to a title that conjured up conversational black proverbs, to continue African American artists' traditions of political commentary (*Racism is Like Rain, Either It's Raining or It's Gathering Somewhere*, catalogue no. 87). Works by Sam Middleton (*Untitled*, catalogue no. 84) and William T. Williams (*Untitled*, catalogue no. 99), like their predecessor Beauford Delaney's untitled exploration of color and form, leave subject behind in both composition and title.

The freedoms inherent in the use and stylistic vocabularies of abstraction were also mined in works which combined representational elements with abstract ones. Sam Gilliam (*The D Series*, catalogue no. 78) draws his canvas into a three-dimensional conversation with paint, adding an enigmatic hint of subject with the inclusion of a single letter. Walter Williams's *Butterflies #2* (catalogue no. 98), close to Douglas's *City Scape* in its recognizable subject, uses decorative elements and expressive colors outside the range of realism. Margo Humphrey employs similar decorative and expressive touches in *The Last Bar-B-Que* (catalogue no. 76), a continuation of the long-standing tradition of black artistic discourse on African Americans' relationship to Christianity. Ray Saunders disarms the viewer with the sketchlike quality and penciled text of *Untitled* (catalogue no.

89), a gentle commentary on Christian practice by black American families.

WHO WE ARE/WHAT WE DO

African American artists have been utilizing diasporan themes from African and Caribbean cultures throughout the twentieth century. As artists of African descent continued to explore the many threads of diasporan cultural history, works such as Keith Morrison's *Night Food* (catalogue no. 86) explore the syncretic nature of personal experience. Rather than choosing between polarizing terms such as *Afro-Caribbean* or *African American*, neither of which completely describes this artist's own life's experience, Morrison mines the aesthetic and subjective landscape that includes Eurocentric as well as African-derived sources and arrives at a more complex definition of artistic/racial identity than was possible with the old labels. Vincent Smith's portrayal of *Arthur Rimbaud's House in Harar* (catalogue no. 91) addresses Beat poetry and Beat culture's problematic association of Africa with the idealized primitive, with white citizens of Africa, and with the heritage and sense of place of a particular locale in an East African country.

Diasporan visual identity continues to react to, and be inflected by, contemporary ideas about men and women of color. Eldzier Cortor maintains a lifelong fascination with the black female nude (*Jewels/Theme V*, catalogue no. 71), at the same time that our response to the appropriations of black male and female bodies evolves. Images of these bodies appear today in ostensibly benign advertisements to sell clothes, perfume, and recordings but often are laced with troubling associations with the allure of an ethnic other. Robert Colescott's *I Love You Forever* (catalogue no. 70) challenges our myths about an interracial society, addressing not only our past hopes for integration and harmony but also our current concern with interracial adoption, biracial census categories, and the complexities of both black and white responses to these issues. Archibald Motley, Jr. addressed some of these same concerns in his 1920s studies of African American

women so light-skinned that they might pass as white. If we adopt the polar definitions of black and white, like Colescott's two figures, where do we place the many shades between black and white that fall on both sides of that arbitrary color line?

What we do—one of the major ways through which we identify ourselves in social interactions—steadfastly serves as an essential signifier of visual identity. Images of African Americans in various contexts today, from popular television shows to aggressive music videos, challenge historic notions that have typically limited African American identity. While Frank Stewart's *Wynton Marsalis* from the *Sweet Swing Series* (catalogue no. 93) documents and celebrates the contributions of black jazz musicians, it also reflects a changing perception of those individuals. In a society once content to celebrate these great artists as long as their genius could be confined to a kind of visceral affinity for music, a "natural rhythm," artists such as Marsalis and those who document them are now foregrounding the particular aspects of jazz production that defy the stereotype.

In *The Potter's House* (catalogue no. 97), Yvonne Tucker affirms many facets of the African American artist's creative process, inflecting as well issues of partnership, family, communal creation, and the appropriation of legacies not normally considered part of the black cultural experience. Just as Wynton Marsalis excels in classical music as well as jazz, Yvonne Tucker claims and draws upon Asian heritage as well as African.

Another group of artists once (and often still) called *folk* or *primitive* has acquired the new label *outsider*. Clementine Hunter (*Baptism*, catalogue no. 77) and Minnie Evans (*Face of a Man*, catalogue no. 74) are artists who have been affected by this shift in name. Their reception as artists and the reception of the objects they produced have been modified by changing ideas of how to deal with art outside the academy. This art, once celebrated, like jazz, for the received notion of its mysterious and mythic connection to the "primitive," is now gradually being reassessed: *self-taught* begins to replace *untaught* as these artists' unconventional training gains validity in the art world. The term *outsider* (a label these artists never used to describe themselves) continues to impose troubling imperatives from an art establishment whose power remains primarily in the hands of white culture brokers.

Jacob Lawrence has documented, throughout his career, the trials of African Americans under the yoke of slavery and racism and helped promote a collective public identity of pride, place, and dignity in his depictions of historical figures and moments. In works such as *Lawyers and Clients* (catalogue no. 79), Lawrence affirms an image in which African American professionals provide support for the black community. This work, which places African Americans in relationship to each other rather than in reactive opposition to the agendas of the dominant culture, reflects a fuller participation by persons of color in all aspects of society.

Similarly, black faces appear today in popular media in ways previously unthinkable. The family relationships in "Amos 'n' Andy" are replaced by the Huxtables; black lawyers represent black clients in high-profile cases; amid the stories told in films about black gang members or civil rights leaders, black filmmakers begin also to present works in which race is the framework but not the sole impetus for black interaction.

African American artists have embraced a wide range of media and practices from European painting and sculpture to Caribbean religious artifacts and installations. All the varied combinations, whether based in African, European, or other cultures, or consisting of complex syntheses of myriad elements—*all* are expressions of contemporary African American identity.

As the context for making, exhibiting, and selling art becomes more global, identity for artists of color crosses boundaries of nationhood, gender, and color. Perhaps the most valuable aspect of this continual reworking of African American identity is its refusal to settle in one place. As African Americans changed themselves from *colored* to *Negro* to *black* to *African American*, these labels are no longer seen as sufficient in themselves. As West Indians assert themselves in Toronto and Africans emigrate to Vienna, their identity is more easily named *diasporan* or, simply described, of African descent. No matter that global dispersion frees people from identities wedded to single nations and undercuts nationalistic loyalties;

defining oneself as a member of a diasporan community is a valid assertion, one of association and shared identity.

Many have rightly argued during recent decades that the grand image of the melting pot no longer works as an appropriate metaphor. Unfortunately, the sometimes-used image of a mosaic of distinct and different parts is not satisfactory either, since it requires each unit to exist in static relationship to the others. The demographics of global travel create societies of "others" and also shift like tectonic plates against the effects of the global media that seem to make certain cultural norms universal. African American artists explore this constantly shifting landscape and pay particular attention to its outer edges and separating wedges, the areas so often pictured by mainstream institutions as marginal. These transnational explorations of diasporan identity mark both the beginning of fresh perspectives and the continuation of a dialogue that has been going on since Africans were first brought to the Americas.

A History of Collecting African American Art

Sharon F. Patton

If we, as individuals and institutions, don't buy the artifacts and reminders of our culture, someone else will, and then they won't belong to us. If they get away from us, we'll have no tools with which to teach our children, no evidence of the depths of our cultural identity.

— Mary Schmidt Campbell, 1986

In this century, institutions and individuals have assumed the arduous task of locating and preserving African American cultural patrimony. It has been understood as essentially an effort that prevents, if not delays, the erasure of any record that there existed a minority culture in the United States. Among other things, art represents that presence. If the literature on collecting is any indication, important American art collections are secondary to European ones. In addition, the history of collecting American art has traditionally excluded African American art. Consequently African American art may be construed as having no value. Collectors are complicit in a practice that implicitly addresses issues of ethnic and racial identity, consumerism, and consumption. Collecting fine art and owning certain types of fine art are important signs about class and wealth; to function as such, groups of paintings, sculpture, prints, etc., must not be accessible or must be only minimally accessible to certain groups of people. Owning art gives a collector prerogative to interpret and determine what and subsequently what does not have cultural significance. Collecting as a political enterprise denotes an exercise of power and the capacity to negotiate change.

Museum curators and collectors, by the act of assembling objects, reinforce notions of cultural identity—often to the disadvantage of other cultures. For collecting automatically establishes, according to anthropologist Ivan Karp, "a hierarchy of cultures" in which "those worth examining are separate from those that deserve to be ignored."[1] In the late nineteenth century, the collecting of art and artifacts from Africa occurred simultaneously with colonial expansion in Africa. Collections of African art displayed in European and American museums conveyed a representation of the "other" (the non-European or non-white American) as being in a state of arrested cultural, social, and political development. The assumptions that black art and artifacts represent primitivism were fueled by racial theories, eugenics, and popular stereotypes. As a result, the artistic efforts of black people were typed as artifacts or folk art, which further removed their art from a priority list of acquisitions by individuals or institutions. Not surprising is that the collecting of African art preceded that of African American art by approximately seventy years in the United States. Ironically, the earliest-known collected African American artifact is a virtual replica of an African object: a mid- to late-seventeenth-century drum from Virginia that Sir Hans Sloane acquired in the eighteenth century (and that is now in the British Museum).

Because the majority of American museums are based on one or several individual private collections, institutions perpetuate a vision of a selected few. Museum exhibits and programs reflect an institutional point of view, which is often understood as a consensual perspective by society about art and culture. Concerted acquisitions of black art by institutions lagged behind the efforts of individuals. Beginning in the late nineteenth century and continuing into the twentieth century, collectors of black art—white or black—have attempted for various reasons to ensure that there exists a legacy of black cultural achievements and inevitably have shaped our understanding about black Americans.

In the 1850s, Americans who chose careers in the arts were eagerly greeted as patriots and heroes whose careers proved that the new nation was rising above merely material and commercial endeavors. Art was a means of social legitimization among all Americans, a way of transcending lower-middle-class origins, and for blacks, race. The goal of the African American artist was then seen in a broader cultural context, the same as for any American artist. African American Edward M. Thomas commented in 1862, "Where the Fine Arts are not reflected, there exists some great fault in construction of a nation, and the individual."[2] Free blacks who became professional artists were considered a "credit to the race," and the black press and books by black authors extolled the achievements of their black brethren. Only when black art imitated European-derived aesthetics and styles of fine arts could African Americans hope to garner the attention of American collectors.

Where then would a collector see art that conveyed the grand historical stories represented in landscape painting, so popular in the 1850s, that portrayed the ideology of American territorial expansion and reflected European-derived high culture? There were few art institutions at the time. The flowering of art museums did not begin until the 1870s and 1880s. Only a few black American artists—Robert Douglass, Jr., Henry Ossawa Tanner, and Edward Bannister—had exhibited their works in museums or art clubs, all of which were in the Northeast. Several types of venues for viewing African American fine art were targeted at established and potential collectors (as opposed to the promotion of nationalism in exposition fairs of the late nineteenth century). One was the public exhibition space. African American photographer James P. Ball's Great Daguerrean Gallery of the West opened in 1847 in Cincinnati, Ohio, where Robert S. Duncanson (1821–1872) displayed his paintings. Presumably affluent middle-class and wealthy citizens purchased Duncanson's works, which were among the best of American landscape paintings of the

period. His works were praised by critics and connoisseurs nationally and internationally. Undoubtedly, sizable numbers of middle-class black Americans in Cincinnati saw his works, and whether they bought any of his works is conjectural; possibly they purchased his or Ball's less expensive photographs. Wealthy whites, on the other hand, could and did buy Duncanson's paintings. One was Cincinnati philanthropist and abolitionist Henry Longworth, who commissioned Duncanson to paint his portrait and in 1850 commissioned him to paint eight murals for his mansion, Belmont (now the Taft Museum).

As a status symbol, art was and remains today cultural capital. By the mid-nineteenth century, newly wealthy Americans had become interested in collecting art and displayed decorative arts and fine arts in the same room. In this context, the display of art in private homes functioned as both spectacle and possession (as in Duncanson's case). Consequently, the collector laid claim to and also defined taste, or culture. African American fine artists effectively won patronage from whites, most of whom were abolitionists who could express their cultural sensibilities and aspirations as seen to be comparable to those of their European counterparts and royalty, at the same time showing their support for the plight of the black American by acquiring and praising works by African American artists. Essays about their work in abolitionist newspapers focused on the content and meaning of images, subject matter, and race. Black artists were promoted as being representative of an alternative, more civilized image of the black man and woman. Both whites and black abolitionists wanted to demonstrate the humanity of blacks, that they were capable of full citizenship: mostly white Americans such as James Francis Conover, who commissioned Duncanson's *Uncle Tom and Little Eva* (1853, Detroit Institute of Arts); or John Duff, who bought Bannister's acclaimed *Under the Oaks* (untraced), which won the prestigious 1876 Philadelphia Centennial Prize; and Europeans such as the British Duchess of Sutherland; but also blacks such as Dr. John V. DeGrasse, who was a collector of Edward M. Bannister's (1826/1827–1901) works and who purchased paintings, prints, and sculptures of artists such as Robert S. Duncanson, Edward M. Bannister, Edmonia M. Lewis, Patrick H.

Reason, and Henry Ossawa Tanner. During the antebellum period, subject matter appealed to the sentimentalism favored by white collectors. Images taken from literature such as Harriet Beecher Stowe's *Uncle Tom's Cabin* (1852) portrayed abolitionists' portraits, grandiose or romantic landscapes, and, later, sentimental genre scenes. Black collectors too preferred the same type of art, especially those works whose narratives were understood as metaphors for freedom and that showed dignified images of black people. Singularly, the biblical paintings of Tanner universally appealed to whites and blacks; for blacks their meaning recalled Sunday sermons in the black community. On rare occasions, an individual's efforts created a sizable collection of a single black artist's works. Joseph Crane Hartzell, a white Methodist Episcopal bishop, and his wife purchased an entire exhibition of Tanner's paintings in the 1890s so that Tanner could travel to Europe to study. Although documentation about other nineteenth-century collections of black art is incomplete, research by Juanita Holland and Steven Jones have shown that African Americans also were avid collectors of black American art in Boston and Philadelphia, respectively.[3]

The history of collecting of folk art is virtually nonexistent. If we understand collecting to mean the acquisition of a work by someone outside the artist's immediate family or community, there is one notable exception: Jennie Smith, a white woman, purchased in 1891 Harriet Powers's first Bible Quilt (1886, Smithsonian Institution) when extreme poverty forced Powers to relinquish what she called "the offspring of my brain."[4] If, on the other hand, we understand collecting as merely the accumulation and preservation of objects, then nineteenth-century folk art collections of quilts and walking sticks can be found among the descendants of slaveowners.

Between 1913 and 1945, African Americans seized the opportunity to promote political, economic, and social agendas that would benefit the black community. Between 1924 and 1935, educated African Americans, whom philosopher and political activist W. E. B. Du Bois (1868–1963) called the "Talented Tenth" (approximately 10 percent were educated and middle class), were called upon to act as role models for less fortunate black Americans and to lead this "New Negro" to social and economic empowerment, to realize the value of their African American culture, and to appreciate their African heritage. This Negro Renaissance marked a time when blacks decided to define for themselves who they were and when, as cultural historian Nathan Huggins noted, there was a struggle to show an African American cultural "coming of age," mostly in northern cities. The visual arts were seen as a means to define racial identity and provide self-esteem. Throughout the 1920s and 1930 periodicals such as the NAACP's *Crisis* and the Urban League's *Opportunity* often had articles about the visual arts. There was a call for writers and artists to lead as the cultural vanguard. Cities such as Harlem, New York, Chicago, Detroit, Cleveland, and Los Angeles became places for a "dramatic flowering of a new race spirit." Alain Locke (1885–1954), professor of philosophy at Howard University and a Rhodes scholar, spearheaded the movement, calling for an identifiable racial art style and aesthetic. In his seminal essay "The Legacy of the Ancestral Arts" in *Survey Graphic* (1925), he urged visual artists to retrieve and appreciate the value of African art and culture, and to focus on black subjects as they developed a black modern art. African Americans such as W. E. B. Du Bois and Alain Locke lobbied for collectors to buy African American art. To some degree they succeeded, although Du Bois would lament the weak efforts by black Americans to collect African American art. Wealthy African Americans held events in their houses at which artists and writers and cultural dilettantes gathered for discussions about the arts. For example, A'Lelia Walker (daughter of multimillionaire Madame C. J. Walker) held periodic cultural events during the afternoons in one of her townhouse rooms, popularly called "Dark Tower Salon." On such occasions were hung the art work of the major Negro Renaissance painter and graphic artist Aaron Douglas. Individual private collections consisted mostly of traditional media—oil paintings and prints—and subjects such as landscapes, and particularly portraits, and in a realistic style as shown in the works of William E. Scott, Laura Wheeler Waring, Archibald Motley; and the photographs of Addison N. Scurlock and James VanDerZee. Not all artists were collected by black Americans in the 1920s, but for those who were, their likelihood of success was dependent on publicity and accessibility by living in the major cities, primarily in the Midwest and Northeast. Alain Locke aggressively worked to promote the collecting of black American art. He co-organized exhibitions with commercial gallery directors such as Edith Halpert, whose Downtown Gallery (established 1926, New York City) was the first mainstream white gallery to exhibit more than one black American artist at one time.

The Harmon Foundation (1922–1967), established by a white American real-estate investor, William E. Harmon, and under the administration of Mary Beattie Brady, sought to encourage excellence in a variety of professional endeavors, including visual arts beginning in 1935. One activity was to sponsor local (within New York City) and traveling exhibitions in major cities and colleges in the South. Later in the mid-1930s, the Foundation was accused of promoting mediocrity; a popularly held opinion among black artists was that race was the only criterion for selecting artists to exhibit. Several artists' complaints, including those of Romare Bearden, suggest that this perception may have hindered their opportunity to be taken seriously by art critics and collectors. Nonetheless, one goal was to promote and encourage collectors to buy black art. In this the Foundation was relatively unsuccessful, acquiring works by several African American artists, particularly accumulating a sizable body of work by William H. Johnson, and eventually creating a major collection of modern black American art. In 1967, when the Foundation ceased operation, the entire collection was given to the National Collection of Fine Art (now the National Museum of American Art), forming the cornerstone of that institution's African American modern art collection. Pieces from the collection were given to the National Portrait Gallery and to various Historically Black Colleges and Universities; one was the Amistad Research Center at Tulane University, which received approximately 240 works and was renamed in 1982 in honor of artist Aaron Douglas.

The Great Depression in the 1930s mostly hindered the growth of strong private collections of black art. Instead, the Federal Arts Project (1935–1943) inadvertently

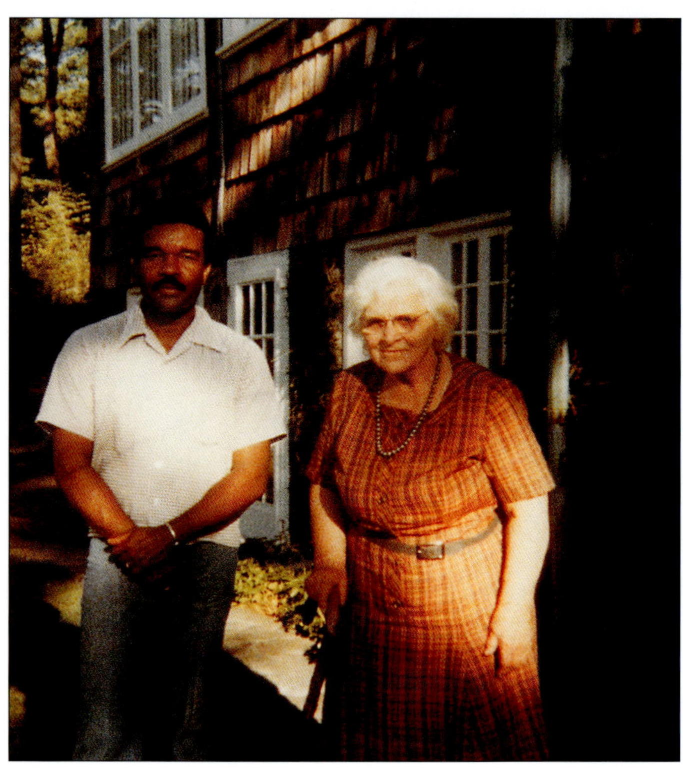

David Driskell and Mary Beattie Brady; Brady residence, Putnam County, New York, 1977 (David C. Driskell Archives)

created its own collection of black art when it bought works by black artists such as Dox Thrash, Charles Alston, and Archibald Motley, who were part of the WPA. Artists were paid on the average $20 per week, and their work became public property. Popular were American subjects and realism that accorded with the nationalistic fervor of President Franklin D. Roosevelt's New Deal administration. Fortunately, one couple have assembled works documenting the period: Reba and Dave Williams began collecting prints. A catalogue of their collection, *Alone in a Crowd: Prints of the 1930s–1940s by African-American Artists*, as with all the catalogues of private collections, has become an invaluable research tool for art historians. The WPA provided the opportunity to promote and develop black art in community art centers and in local art exhibitions that sustained a visibility in the black community, and for white artists and critics who later purchased these artists' works.

Galleries were very important in the development of black art collections beginning in the 1940s and continue to be so today. Edith Halpert's promotion of Jacob Lawrence's *Migration of the New Negro* series (1940–1941) made him popular among many of the major white American collectors, including Duncan Phillips, who bought half of the painting series; and Alfred H. Barr, Jr., director of the Museum of Modern Art, who bought the other remaining thirty paintings in the series (with money from Adele Rosenwald Levy, daughter of Julius Rosenwald and board of trustees member of the Museum). Halpert's plan in 1941 was to establish a Negro Art Fund to purchase art for public collections; in the exhibition brochure she urged clients to donate money or purchase paintings, sculpture, and graphics by contemporary black artists Jacob Lawrence, Eldzier Cortor, John H. Smith, Romare Bearden, and Sargent Johnson, whose works were on display in her gallery. Despite the efforts of Halpert, Caresse Crosby's G Place Gallery in Washington, D.C., and the McMillen Gallery in New York City, few white-owned galleries showed African American art, and few white Americans collected it. Two notable exceptions were Jacob Lawrence and Romare Bearden, who garnered a loyal cadre of collectors in the 1940s.

There were also black-directed and/or black-owned galleries supporting black artists in their respective communities that were successful in placing black art among black collectors. Some, such as South Side Community Art Center in Chicago and Karamu House in Cleveland, survived after WPA support ended. Two notable examples were Howard University Art Gallery (1930), founded by James Herring (1897–1969), and Barnett-Aden Gallery (1943–1969), cofounded by Herring and Alonzo Aden (1906–1961). Aden focused on modern African American art but included Caribbean and white American art for the sake of the gallery's sales. An important collection of modern African American art also developed under Aden's and Herring's direction. After Herring's death, a major portion of the collection was bequeathed to Adolphus Ealey (later sold to Florida Endowment Fund for Higher Education). According to a recent report in the *Washington Post*, the collection was slated for purchase by Robert Johnson, founder and chairman of Black Entertainment Television in Washington, D.C., thereby potentially catapulting Johnson into becoming a major collector of black art. Unlike their white counterparts who gave their black art to museums, black collectors of black art rarely were donors to major art museums such as the Art Institute of Chicago, Metropolitan Museum of Art, or Los Angeles County Museum, as was, for example, Gertrude Vanderbilt Whitney's purchase of Richmond Barthé's sculptures in 1933 for the Whitney Museum of American Art or later in the 1960s, when Joseph Hirshhorn's collection of Romare Bearden's collages became part of the Hirshhorn Museum and Sculpture Garden (Washington, D.C.) collection. Black collectors such as Morgan and Marvin Smith, Duke Ellington, Ralph Ellison, Billie Allen, and Albert Murray circulated among themselves and in their respective communities at galleries, the YMCA, and clubs and bought their friends' art—works by Jacob Lawrence, Romare Bearden, Charles Alston, and Hale Woodruff. Their efforts remained hidden from the mainstream, only to resurface when museums, especially African American museums, began building their collections of black art. The situation changed for the worse during the Cold War. African Americans lacked appreciable market value in an art community in which art was increasingly considered a speculative investment. The number of collectors presumably declined, especially among African Americans, although again, substantial research is needed in this particular historical period. Review of the literature does show entertainment personalities such as Harry Belafonte purchasing the works of black artists such as Charles White.

The flurry of activity among galleries during the first half of the twentieth century was matched by the establishment of approximately thirty African American museums and galleries, most of them at Historically Black Colleges and Universities: Hampton (established in 1867), Howard, Fisk, Spelman, and Atlanta University. Slowly yet systematically, these and other black institutions amassed collections of African American art. Hale A. Woodruff's *Annual Exhibition of Works by Negro Artists (1942–1970),* held at Atlanta University, resulted in the acquisition by Atlanta University (now Clark Atlanta University) of one of the largest collections of art by African Americans, rivaled only by those at Howard University and Hampton University.

In the late 1960s, as a result of the civil rights movement and black nationalism, mostly black culture and history museums and galleries were established in nearly every major city. Art, as in the 1920s, was seen as a significant aspect of culture, representing black pride and having palliative capabilities in the fight against racism. Art reflected the aspirations and desires of the community and was not only an aesthetic object. Museums were conceived as educational institutions to serve the community, but many became collecting institutions which, with educational programs, hoped to effect social change. In agreement with Edmund Barry Gaither, museums could be "crucibles for forging citizens who see themselves as part of civil society, as important members of a valid social order."[5] These new black museums were typically independent of any formal institutional support or individual philanthropy, and, unlike most of the major art museums in America, they did not develop around a private collection. In other words, communities established their own museums and determined the institution's mission and activities.

Artists' groups or artist/teachers such as Elma Lewis, who established the Museum of the National Center of Afro-American Art in Boston in 1968; Margaret Burroughs, who established the Du Sable Museum in Chicago in 1961; or artist groups such as Weusi (Swahili for "people"), who maintained the Weusi Yaa Sanaa Gallery in New York City from 1968 until 1978, spurred the interest in black American art and in turn promoted collecting. One example is the Studio Museum in Harlem, which holds as part of their regular activities seminars (begun in 1976) on collecting art. Black-owned galleries such as Cinque, Acts of Art Galleries, Kenkeleba, and June Kelly were in business to foster collecting of contemporary black art. After the 1950s, more than ninety African American museums were established in Detroit, Los Angeles, Philadelphia, Atlanta, and elsewhere, most of them after the 1970s. Initially, they had no or very small collections. Individual artists and collectors began donating to these community museums with the intention of educating people about black art, as a counter-strategy to the promotion of white artists. Edmund Barry Gaither praised the efforts of Rowena Stewart, formerly director of the Rhode Island Black Heritage Society and also the Afro-American Historical and Cultural Museum in Philadelphia, who has established an example of how to weave a closer relationship between a museum and its community through the activity of collecting. Having the people who owned the works of art or artifacts interpret their collection and specific works in them is pivotal.[6] Typically, curators interpret and contextualize a work without regard for how the work's original owner, the collector, understood the object's meaning. English museum historian Susan Pierce considers collecting an "aspect of individual and social practice which is important in public and private life as a means of constructing the way in which we relate to the material world and so build up our own lives."[7]

One artists' group, AfriCobra (African Commune of Bad Relevant Artists, established in 1968) promoted their art in the black communities. They made silk-screen posters of their paintings to make art affordable, creating images of black people, jazzy designs, interwoven with exhortative slogans and words that people could readily appreciate. Suddenly, less affluent people could become collectors. As a result of offset printing, a popular art market flourished (and continues today), undermining the notion of collecting as owning something unique. This undermining of class privilege is generally ignored by mainstream art critics and art historians; often considered too kitsch. A new class of black collector was developed.

But as artist Benny Andrews noted, artists in the 1970s "always talked about the potential role of African American collectors," and only recently have black Americans been among Andrews's most serious buyers. Continuing, he says, "the best thing in the world is seeing black people purchase your works. For a while I started getting paranoid. I was wondering if it was a case of whites buying from the natives."[8] Simultaneously, the traditional class of black collector continued to grow during the post–Vietnam War era.

White-owned and/or white-directed galleries also profited by the interest in black art of the late 1960s and 1970s. They renewed their earlier (i.e., early 1940s) enthusiasm for black art by sponsoring local and traveling exhibitions, as in *Thirty Contemporary Black Artists,* an exhibition organized by the Minneapolis Institute of Arts and underwritten by the public relations firm Ruder & Finn. The Whitney Museum of American Art and the Museum of Modern Art held exhibitions of contemporary black art. However, the art mostly belonged to the artists. David C. Driskell's curatorial efforts in the mid- to late 1970s are consequently important because he tapped into the private and public collections of black and white Americans, thereby revealing the existence and extent of black art collections in the United States. The overwhelming success of *Two Centuries of Black American Art* (Dallas Museum of Art, 1976) and subsequent shows was a catalyst for other white institutions to show large group exhibitions of black American art into the 1980s. Harmon and Harriet Kelley, after seeing *Hidden Heritage: Afro-American Art, 1800–1950* at the San Antonio Museum of Art (brought there through the effort of two other African American collectors, Joseph and Aaronetta Pierce) in 1986, became avid collectors. In 1979 the nineteenth-century collection of 200 works by African American artists (developed under the advice of art historian Carroll Greene and acquired by founder and director of the Museum of African Art Warren Robbins) was transferred to the National Museum of American Art when the African Art Museum became the National Museum of African Art (Washington, D.C.). This same collection was the foundation (with forty-two out of forty-nine exhibited works) for the exhibition *Sharing Traditions, Five Black Artists in Nineteenth-Century America* (National Museum of American Art, 1979), which showed the paintings and sculptures of Joshua Johnston, Robert S. Duncanson, Edward M. Bannister, Edmonia M. Lewis, and Henry Ossawa Tanner.

In the 1980s, the investor-collector dominated the art scene. Again, as a way to obviate the mainstream's avoidance of African American artists and promotion of a "star system" of artists (most of whom were part of the New York gallery scene), African American collectors spoke about their collections not only in culturally focused ways but as investments. *Black Enterprise* magazine began in 1980 to focus on collecting African American art. Tonya Bolden Davis writes in her essay "Collecting Black Art" in *Black Enterprise* (December 1986) that black art is the American art market's last frontier. Continuing, she writes, "Today there is an urgency to our patronage, a determination to get in on the ground floor, based on the very real fear that if we don't wake up with regard to contemporary black artists, history will repeat itself." Davis summarizes the percentage of return on initial investments, acknowledging that the return is moderate compared to that for white artists, and discusses the role of galleries and auction houses in the art market. In "Going Once…Going Twice…Sold!" (1988), she and Kevin D. Thompson cite several African American collectors, including Richard Clarke and Watson Hines, both in New York City, focusing on corporate CEOs and founders such as Thomas J. Burrell (Burrell Advertising, Chicago) who, along with the late Reginald F. Lewis (Beatrice Foods), have each established a substantial collection of modern and contemporary black art. Davis and Thompson candidly admit that "art is rarely purchased solely for its aesthetic beauty—but for its monetary value as well." Self-esteem prevails, however, as a motive for building a collection based on race and culture. As Burrell stated, he thought it was very important that black people vigorously support African American artists: "This is important because black artists are the agents of expression for our culture and it's important to keep that alive." The consensus in the 1980s was not unlike that of previous decades: The majority of black artists were ignored by art historians, excluded from the vanguard critics' circles, and locked out of commercial galleries. Major purchases by Camille and Bill Cosby of nineteenth-century artist Joshua Johnson and Henry Ossawa Tanner set auction records for African American art, making headline news in the black and white art communities. Continuing to collect nineteenth- and twentieth-century African American art, the Cosbys' very public personae have done much to encourage the buying of black art (in the "Bill Cosby Show," viewers saw works of black art by Varnette Honeywood and others in the Huxtables' home, and another episode showed a scene set at Sotheby's auction house, both conveying a clear message about the importance of black art collecting). Most black collectors initially started purchasing art of their own generation and soon shifted to art of the previous century, or they maintain an equal distribution of modern and contemporary. Many learned through art history, auctions, investment tips, seminars, and advice from consultants such as gallery directors George N'namdi and Sherry Washington, who in 1996 had a show titled *Collecting African American Art: A Detroit Tradition,* or Alitash Kedebe, Asake Bomani, Madeline Rabb, Peg Alston, Eric Robertson, and countless others.

In the 1990s, according to art critic Amei Wallach in a recent article in the *New York Times,* collectors began to see art more as "an agent for social change and wanted to play a role in the process" and now capitalize on an "expanded vision," which translates as a marketable interest in African American artists, particularly emerging younger artists. Wallach considers the collaborative exhibition *The Decade Show: Frameworks of Identity in the 1980s* as a benchmark show that introduced black artists to a wider public, and as a result, kindled by the popular interest in multiculturalism, more white collectors such as Peter and Eileen Norton are buying contemporary African American art (they now have 100 works). As Norton stated, he was interested in "artists who come out of that very interesting cultural milieu that is now called African American because it's given us some wonderfully interesting things, which I can summarize in one word: jazz."[9] Emblematic of the post-modern period, they have abandoned old cultural parameters and show a preference of idiosyncratic assem-blage of works, usually of young or "cutting-edge" artists such as Lorna Simpson, David Hammons, Kara Walker, Carrie Mae Weems, and Gary Simmons. Often mid-career or older artists are left behind in the stampede by collectors to acquire "new" art.

Numerous African American collectors have benefited black artists by showing a commitment to build black art collections. Several catalogues about individual collections have been published in the past decade, including *African American Artists 1880–1987, Selections from the Evans-Tibbs Collection* (Washington, D.C., 1989); *Walter O. Evans Collection of African American Art* (Detroit, 1991); and *The Harmon and Harriet Kelley Collection of African American Art* (San Antonio, 1994). Occasionally,

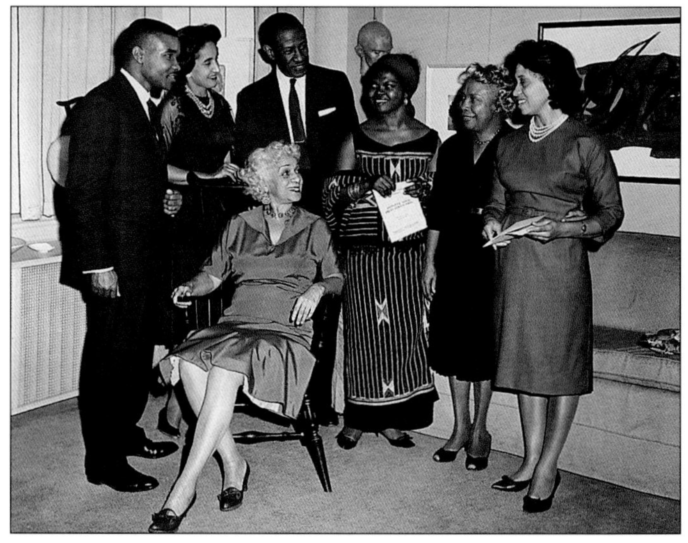

Left to right: David Driskell, unidentified woman, Lillian Evanti (seated), James A. Porter, unidentified woman, Dorothy Porter, and Thelma Driskell; Barnett-Aden Gallery, Washington, D.C., 1962 (David C. Driskell Collection)

collections were inherited and formed the foundation of a major body of work, as in the nineteenth-century master artists and twentieth-century master and emerging artists (with a focus on Washington, D.C.) collection of the late collector and art appraiser Thurlow Evans-Tibbs, the grandson of Lillian Evanti. Other collections are new, as is the case for Texans Harmon and Harriet Kelley. Theirs and other African American collectors' activity in museums and social status have provided leverage for scheduling black art shows at white museums, thereby providing another opportunity to seduce potential collectors.

A recent phenomenon is the collecting of folk art as a result of the immensely popular exhibition in 1980 at the Corcoran Gallery of Art, *Black Folk Art in America.* Before folk art became cachet, art historian Regenia Perry and, eventually, photographer Roland L. Freeman began collecting folk art. Perry's own collection, amassed over twenty years, totals approximately 3,000 pieces. She poignantly remarked, "It's been a very solitary and lonely journey…I haven't been able to interest other African Americans in collecting black folk art on a serious basis and I don't know why. It's sad that we've never appreciated this kind of work. Now it's too late for most people to start buying. It's impossible to build a good collection without a lot of money."[10] These two collectors and others have been pathfinders for folk art collecting in the African American community. African American folk art has always been popular among white collectors ever since the late 1930s and the 1940s. It was a time when William Edmundson and Horace Pippin belonged to the folk art craze of the inter-war period and when such art represented a nostalgia for pre-industrial America and a simpler culture. Folk art was the modern primitive art of the 1930s and 1940s, and being black reinforced the primitivist aura of naive painting or sculpture. Postmodernism's critical views about art now include folk and fine art; old hierarchies about "high" art and crafts are quickly eroding. Folk art now qualifies as investment art. Black folk art is again in vogue, as the dearth of exhibition catalogues recently have shown. Collectors, most of whom are white, perhaps are searching for another new art idiom—the "other" of the "Other." Folk art collections are increasingly used to promote collectors rather than the culture (or community) that produces it. African American collectors such as Regenia Perry consider aesthetics important, but the principal interest is cultural, which reflects a motive to retrieve black folk art as essentially an authentic form of art production. In some examples, the display of aspects of African concepts and aesthetics further motivates many black collectors and collectors (white and black) of African art. The Museum of African-American Life and Culture in Dallas now specializes in the collecting of black folk art from the South.

Singularly noteworthy is Derrick Beard, whom *Arts and Antiques* magazine touted as one of the top collectors in America. He has amassed a sizable collection of African American decorative arts, including rare early nineteenth-century furniture made by Dutreuil Barjon (New Orleans), Thomas Day (North Carolina), and others; and pottery by "Dave" (South Carolina). Beard has organized several traveling exhibitions, often adding pieces from local collectors and public collections, through the Center for African American Decorative Arts in Atlanta, which he founded circa 1984.

Collectors, regardless of race or ethnicity, sustain, however, the European tradition of defining themselves and their cultural relationships in material terms. Preservation is motivated by a desire to keep historical narratives that are based upon memory. Memory, either archival (specific details and sequences of events) or mythical (events selected for particular cultural or social significance), creates the heroic aspects of America's history and social order, varying in individual collections. Individuals collect objects for their intrinsic artistic qualities and for their accumulated histories, as mementos, and consequently they function as material autobiographies.[11] One's identity as an individual may depend on differences between one's personal collection and anyone else's. That identity has a value for African Americans. As John Elsner and Roger Cardinal noted, "As one becomes conscious of one's self, one becomes a conscious collector of identity, projecting one's being onto the objects one chooses to live with."[12] Taste is a mirror of self. Collecting can also attempt to challenge the norm. That is the case with the Nortons and in a sense with all black collectors, for they historically have not been perceived as "art collectors," i.e., the arbiters of high culture or culture generally. African American collectors within the past eighteen years have inverted the usual understanding of collecting, which is that a collector's identity is constructed and thrives only because he or she posits an "other" (by the absence of objects to mean non-white or non-European) that will never be perceived as "them."[13] Black collectors want their collections to be taken for themselves, for they want their art to reflect themselves as black people (at least partly). As Detroit physician and collector Walter O. Evans remarked in 1991, he wants to show that black people were and are very skilled artists, comparable to the best of the best.[14] African American collectors who have the capital to invest in art and who are educated in the art history of black art gather traditional and newer art forms and styles. Their numbers have increased considerably within the past ten years and have grown steadily throughout this century. However, if catalogues are any indication, current tastes are conservative, focusing on established artists before the 1970s, preferring the figurative, and overtly narrative content, or on younger, riskier artists. The artists of the 1950s through the 1970s such as Hughie Lee-Smith, Alvin Loving, William T. Williams, Richard Mayhew, and others are often overlooked. Many of them have not had the broader public visibility that other more successfully collected black artists such as Lorna Simpson or Sam Gilliam have had. African American museums that constantly solicit from collectors of African American art have a wide range of art forms and styles, from figurative to abstraction, fine to folk, established to emerging artists. Yet reliant on collectors who particularly now are asking that their collections remain intact after an institution's acquisition, art museums focus by default on fine and marketable artists. But the bottom line is the continued aggressive collecting of black American art by African Americans.

Theorist Jean Baudrillard noted, "Here, indeed, lies the whole miracle of collecting. For it is invariably *oneself* that one collects."[15] Collecting is not only self-referential but is a confirmation of and revelation about culture. Collecting African American art is not merely a pastime but for many African Americans a commitment.

In the Archive and the Garden

Richard J. Powell

I had *heard* about David C. Driskell before actually *meeting* him. As an undergraduate art major in the Atlanta University Center in the early 1970s, I (along with many other students) had been schooled in African American art history, past and present. The names of Henry Ossawa Tanner, Loïs Mailou Jones, and Romare Bearden were as central to *our* cultural canon as John Singer Sargent, Georgia O'Keeffe, and Andy Warhol were to the American art mainstream. In the middle of hearing and having to remember a lengthy roll call of African American art luminaries, the consonantal alliteration of "David C. Driskell" was both poetry to the ears and memorable in terms of who and what it represented

Yet "David C. Driskell" was not only a name to remember but one of those pivotal figures in "Afro-American art" that, increasingly, we began to see in our textbooks and in the "black art" publications that would appear from time to time. Looking back at circa 1970 art publications such as Samella Lewis and Ruth Waddy's multivolumed "yearbook," *Black Artists on Art*, I am reminded of how photographs of black artists were just as important in defining this cultural moment as the works of art that were created by them. Pictures of these artists —standing beside easels (or inside studios), wearing vibrant African printed fabrics and supporting huge crowns of woolly black hair, like living and breathing caryatids—subconsciously communicated to the world a new black aesthetic in the making, especially as expressed in one's art, possessions, and in one's life.

My earliest recollections of David C. Driskell are situated within these pre-postmodern era memories and were concretized and substantiated by actually meeting him, I believe, in the mid-1970s at the Washington, D.C., home of printmaker and painter James Lesesne Wells.

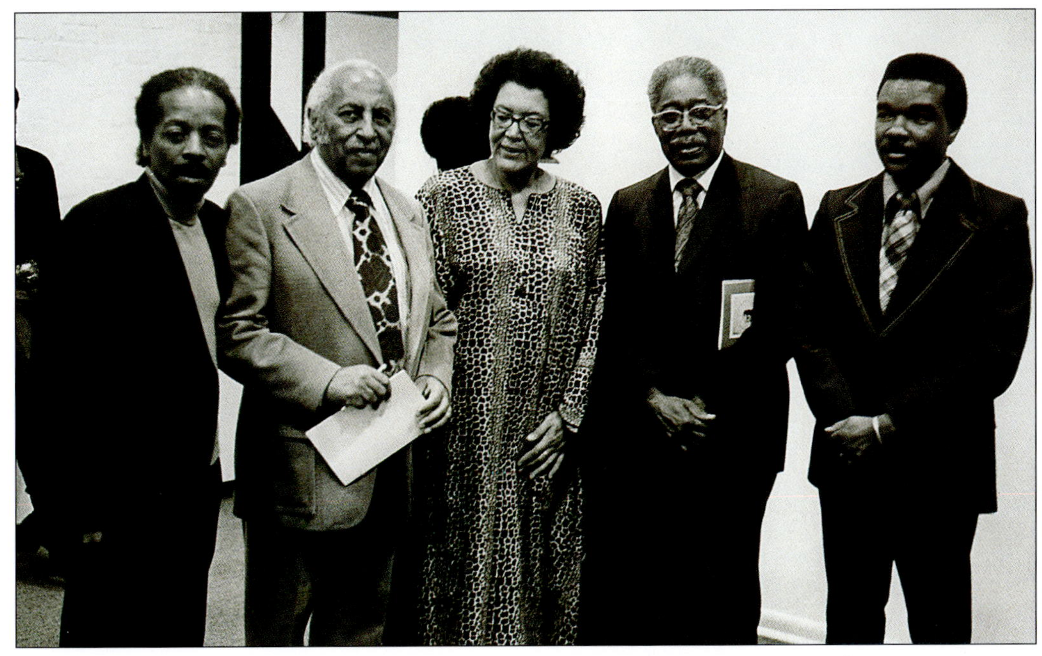

Earl Hooks, Arna Bontemps, Elizabeth Catlett, Aaron Douglas, and David Driskell; Fisk University, Nashville, 1973 (David C. Driskell Archives)

One of the reasons for his visit with Wells (who, coincidentally, had taught Driskell at Howard University in the early 1950s) was Driskell's curatorial activities surrounding *Two Centuries of Black American Art,* arguably the most important exhibition of African American art ever assembled. Presented to museum-going audiences in Los Angeles, Atlanta, Dallas, and Brooklyn during and immediately after this nation's bicentennial celebrations in 1976, *Two Centuries of Black American Art* introduced African American artists, their works, and their art historical canon to many people who were unfamiliar with this particular aspect of our nation's artistic heritage. Although *Two Centuries of Black American Art* was not the first exhibition to survey the artistic contributions of African Americans from colonial times to the present, it was the first art exhibition of its kind to arrest the public's attention and to capture the imagination of so many people in the art world, i.e., it was a kind of African American "Armory Show," presenting under one roof masterpieces by Tanner, Jones, and Bearden, as well as by the mid-nineteenth-century folk artist "Dave the Potter," the flamboyant neoclassicist Edmonia Lewis, the Harlem Renaissance icon Aaron Douglas, the mid-twentieth-century chronicler Jacob Lawrence, and others.

As the curator and art historian for *Two Centuries of Black American Art,* David C. Driskell continued a tradition of artist-generated scholarship in African American art history that was perhaps first pioneered in the early 1940s by painter and art historian James A. Porter (another former teacher of Driskell's) and, thirty years later, just prior to Driskell's efforts, by the collagist and amateur historian Romare Bearden. Of course, what made David C. Driskell's curatorial and art historical activities even more significant than either Porter's or Bearden's was *Two Centuries of Black American Art*'s comprehensive scope and its cultural reverberations throughout the mid- to late 1970s. Driskell, presenting this novel art historical narrative during a relatively rare, welcoming moment in American cultural life, forever transformed American art history from a largely white male bastion to a racially and ethnically diverse picture of art practitioners in the United States.

Commenting several years later on the challenges,

on the one hand, of re-educating the American populace about its heterogeneous cultural roots and, on the other hand, of re-educating African Americans about their special role in America's artistic past, Driskell stated that "it is so important that we recognize our full selves in every way, regardless of past assumptions and societal prejudices. American culture cannot stand alone as European-American culture. It includes the gifts of the Native American, blacks, Asians and Europeans alike. I want to help establish a picture of equity in American culture. My art and interest in scholarship should aid the process." Although it was attacked by a few critics who questioned Driskell's predetermined focus on black artists and artworks with an overwhelming social and political basis, the exhibition's corporate and governmental sponsorship by Philip Morris Inc. and the National Endowment for the Humanities, respectively, signaled an unprecedented statement of broad-based acceptance and cultural legitimacy, as well as a radical shift in African American cultural patronage that, to date, we're still engaged in and/or grappling with.

Two Centuries of Black American Art was not David C. Driskell's first endeavor that attempted to bridge the vast cultural gulf between African American art, European American influence, and mainstream expectations for black artists in the West. While still a very young man, Driskell met and worked closely with the influential yet often mercurial and testy administrators of the William E. Harmon Foundation, a New York City–based philanthropic organization that was legendary for its patronage of and power-wielding among black artists, especially during the period of the Harlem Renaissance and in the World War II years. Navigating the frequently treacherous waters of white liberal philanthropy, benevolence, and, at times, condescension, Driskell supplemented his early training in painting and drawing with something possibly far more valuable for a young African American artist to learn: the art of listening, looking, gentle persuasion, and (to paraphrase Ralph Ellison in his novel *Invisible Man*) "playing the game, but raising the ante." Driskell's relationship with the Harmon Foundation not only provided him with an element of support for his own career (he was a recipient of one of their prestigious

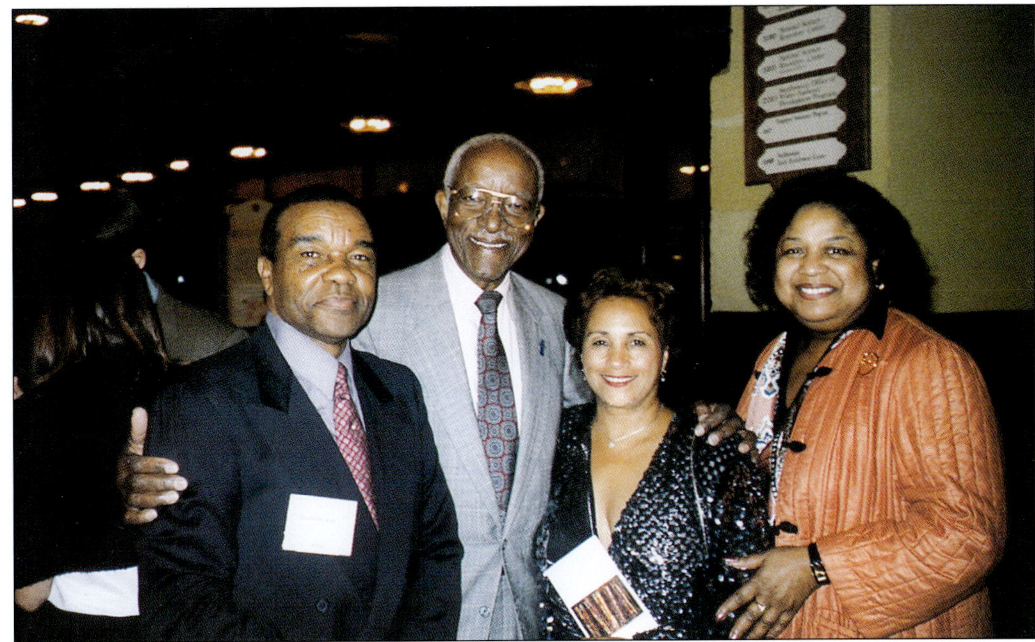

David Driskell, John Hope Franklin, Constance Porter Uzelac, and Tritobia Hayes Benjamin; Smithsonian Institution, Washington, D.C., 1997 (David C. Driskell Archives)

fellowships in 1964), but it helped the Foundation to increasingly change its long-standing ways of dealing with blacks from a paternalistic treatment of black artists and institutions to equal partnerships with these same artists and institutions in promoting African American art and culture. A witness to (and the cultural conscience for) the Harmon Foundation's circa 1960s de-accessioning of more than 1,000 paintings, sculptures, drawings, and prints by African American artists to assorted educational and art institutions nationwide, David C. Driskell is irrefutably positioned—intellectually as well as philosophically—in the midst of this historic cultural transferal and, in retrospect, can now be seen as primed and poised at that juncture to undertake the historical, curatorial, and entrepreneurial challenges of his *Two Centuries of Black American Art* exhibition a decade later.

David C. Driskell also had the distinct honor during these early years of spreading the message about African American art and artists to the interested and curious in Africa and Europe. He was part of a growing and diversified contingent of globe-trotting black Americans in the 1960s and 1970s who studied art, exhibited their art works, or lectured about African American culture in the relatively uncharted territories of an oil-rich Nigeria (where Driskell was a visiting professor at the University of Ife in 1970), an apartheid-dominated South Africa, a

socially tolerant Scandinavia, or a "swinging" England. Following art historical studies in the Netherlands in 1964 (and the requisite "grand tour" of European art museums that same year), Driskell would return in 1972 to Europe, where he lectured in museums, universities, and cultural centers in four countries. Under the auspices of the Rockefeller Foundation and the U.S. State Department, Driskell lectured on the lives and careers of countless black American artists to African audiences not only in Nigeria and South Africa but in Senegal, Sierra Leone, Liberia, Côte d'Ivoire, Ghana, Tunisia, Ethiopia, Kenya, and Tanzania. One of the purposes for a portion of this extensive African tour was Driskell's supervision of a Smithsonian Institution traveling exhibition of paintings by the colorful black American modernist William H. Johnson. First introduced to Johnson's paintings while a gallery assistant at the renowned Barnett-Aden Gallery in Washington, D.C. (and while an undergraduate art student at Howard University), Driskell brought special insights into William H. Johnson's art and life that African audiences immediately empathized with.

It is this rare quality—of being able to communicate to one and all the beauty, power, genius, and, above all, the *spirituality* in African American art—that has enabled David C. Driskell to take his message from Eatonton, Georgia (his birthplace) to the world's cultural centers, and from assorted college and university classrooms (in Alabama, Tennessee, Maine, Michigan, New York, Maryland, and the District of Columbia) to the far reaches of the globe. It is also this distinctive mixture of African American art connoisseurship, historiography, testimony, and a priest-like stewardship of the culture that has put David C. Driskell in the center of the African American art archive and garden, where his position as a gatherer and grower is indisputable.

Finally, not to mention David C. Driskell's many years of advice and counsel to fellow artists, educators, students, historians, curators, collectors, and just plain folks would be negligent. The legacy for these interactions will most certainly be his almost singular efforts toward the creation of a critical mass of African Ameri-

can art patrons: black, white, private, communal, and, above all, visually and culturally *literate*. Driskell's powerful presence in "the archive" and "the garden" speaks to a combination of missionary zeal (as pertaining to African American art matters) and a black cultural self-reliance that, in a sense, harkens back to the Tuskegee Institute model. "No one will culturally emancipate me," Driskell observed in 1979. "I must be big enough to do it myself. It may require my wearing three hats at the same time but perhaps I'm strong enough to do it." David C. Driskell's undeflected critical role for the past forty-odd years in helping to bring about this cultural, national, and spiritual self-discovery through the visual is solid evidence of that strength.

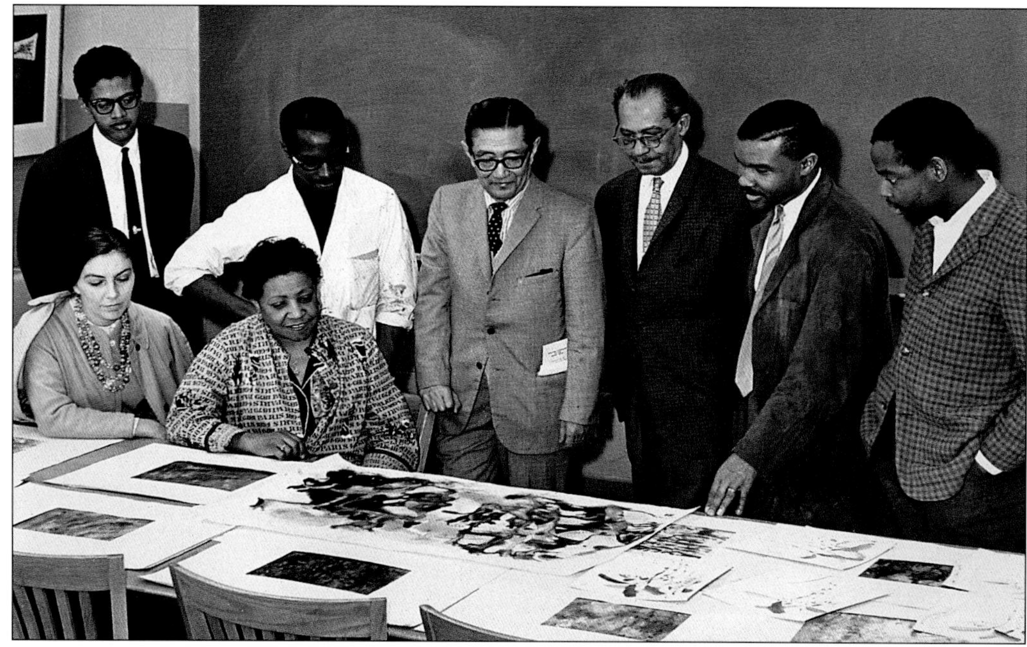

Left to right: Leo Robinson, unidentified woman (seated), Loïs Mailou Jones (seated), Lou Stovall, unidentified man, James Lesesne Wells, David Driskell, and David Stephens; Howard University, Washington, D.C., 1964 (David C. Driskell Archives)

The David Driskell Motives

Allan M. Gordon

Human kind / Cannot bear very much reality.
　　—T. S. Eliot

Life is short, the art long.
　　—Hippocrates

The works under consideration by Driskell were created from a set of core beliefs, attitudes, and an emotional foundation that make a statement about how he perceives himself and his environment. He states, "We are blessed to live in a world where the indomitable human spirit rises above the chaos of violence, hunger and pain and soars to a heightened relief through the making of art. In such a world, we are classless and raceless so long as we create the *spiritual vision* [italics added]. But then, we must all return to who we are in the real world."[1] If the "spiritual vision" does not produce the classless and raceless society that Driskell desires, he is prepared to forgo that and, instead, to retain the "refuge and…solace" that he creates in his "own beautiful world."

An analysis of a series of the most frequently recurring motifs in Driskell's works—The Chair, The Angel, and The Landscape—provide some insight into Driskell the artist.

THE CHAIR

Driskell is an artist who prefers the solace of the familiar and the accessible rather than the angst of the strange and spectacular. His choice of the chair as subject matter[2] is an example of this. The chair, of course, is a pretext. The real subject is his feeling about his immediate,

personal world around him. This is a world of order and re-order. There is balance, solace, complacency; a sense of ease and well-being. Not only does his art seem to reflect a satisfaction with an existence that he has constructed over a period of time from an Ideal gathered from diverse sources, but the choices made in the selection of theme and content suggest that frequently the art is also used as a shield against a world he never made and can hardly be asked to control. This is the world of chaos and disorder. The control he does exert lies in making art whose subject matter is carefully measured, and the emotion or feeling to be abstracted or conceptualized is carefully considered.

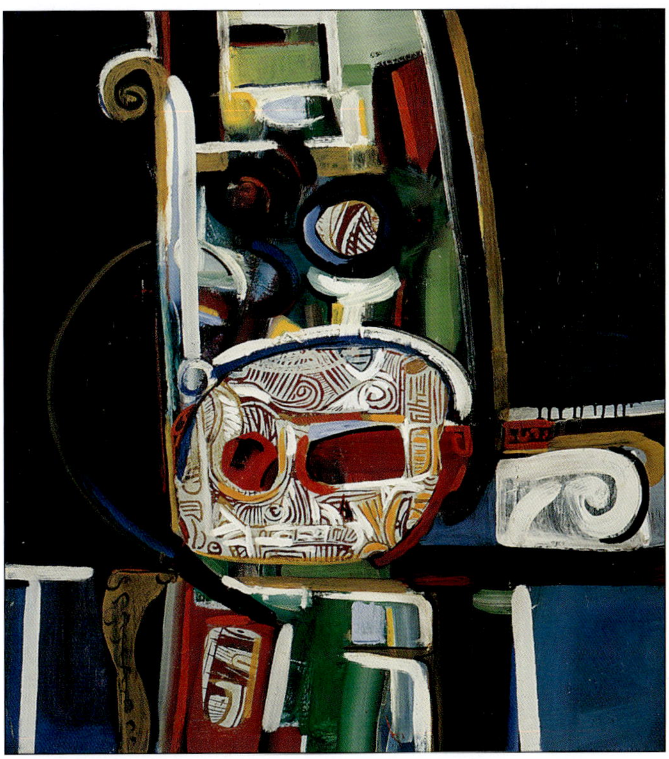

Chieftain's Chair, *1966, David C. Driskell; oil on canvas*
(Greg Staley, photographer; Howard University Gallery of Art)

The chair motif, alluding to the hearth, the well-appointed interior, allows the familiar to be embellished and expanded into compositions of minor tensions and resolutions that rarely become worrisome. The feelings expressed, in a symbolic manner, are real because they are imbedded in and buttressed by an accepted reality that has passed the test of time. It is a reality that places emphasis on continuity, perseverance, and triumph.

The chair, in another context, becomes a throne (*The Chieftain's Chair* hints at such). The Chair-Throne is frequently a prop for the aggrandizement of an incredible ego. The dark side of this symbolism of the Figure-Who-Sits-In-The-Chair-Throne carries with it implications of conflict, intrigue, and pretentiousness

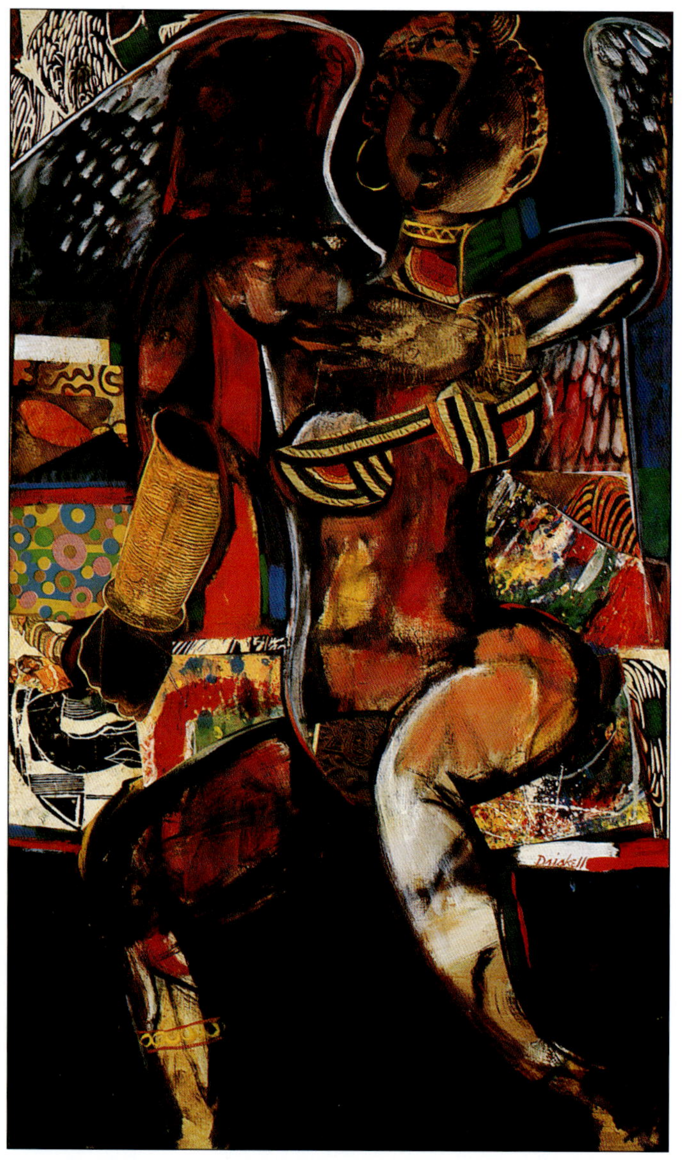

Dancing Angel, *1974, David C. Driskell; collage*
(Greg Staley, photographer; David C. Driskell Collection)

that, in the context of the other works, would be too acute for Driskell, and it does not appear to be the analogy that he seeks.

Instead, he shares with the viewer feelings and emotions that can be immediately recognized as having been experienced by them—unrestrained, intimate aspects of the world around them. The chair is an invitation and is to be pulled up to the fireplace or around the table, or among a circle of friends and family. The important Seated Figure in The Chair is not a monarch, but it is you and I. Thus, Driskell abstracts elements of this emotive world by using an ordinary chair, which enables the viewer to perceive more clearly qualities such as acceptance, harmony, stability, equilibrium, compensation. This is the portion of his reality that Driskell chooses to make into art.

Paramount to any understanding of Driskell's work is the realization that he attempts to seek, to establish, and to maintain a special, intimate relationship between himself and the viewer. This is seen repeatedly in the circumscribed format that he prefers. The small drawings, paintings, and photographs can be handled easily, approached readily, and taken in by a single gaze. The dimensions rarely aspire toward a pretension to the sublime, the heroic, or the misaligned historic. Rather, the intent is found in the soothing, personal, intense style that can be experienced in most of the works. You may call this "lyricism" if you choose.

THE ANGEL

The angel is a symbol of invisible forces that ascend and descend between Heaven and Earth, and, as such, communicates between God and humankind. The incorporeal angels, for Driskell, become all too human and are given titles to suggest as much: *Earth Angels, Dancing Angel, Angel with Trumpet, Guardian Angels (The Angel Watching Over and Carrying Ebenezer)*, etc. The angel as a symbol is representative of a personal belief in that which is held to be of ultimate importance. It is a motif that thrusts Driskell reluctantly toward the sublime, since he prefers the intimate to the awe-inspiring. The angel as a manifestation of the sublime is more acceptable because of its religious origins. Yet, he remains consistent in not straying too far from the familiar. Angels may be supernatural creatures, adhering to hierarchies of the nine choirs, but those created by Driskell are to be approached on a personal rather than an institutionalized level. No differentiation is made between Dominions, Principalities, and Archangels. Instead, it is the angel as a stand-in for a personal religious relationship that remains paramount.

THE LANDSCAPE

Kenneth Clark's landscapes of symbol, fact, and fantasy[3] are Driskell's domesticated landscapes culled from the garden or placid views seen from a studio window. Nature, at once filtered through the eyes of the artist, is further abstracted by Driskell into a series of vertical bars[4] that become a variation on a theme. In the 1960s, he experimented with heavy, dark, and brooding forms that suggested pine forests and rock outcroppings (*Nocturne*, 1961). These were to evolve into landscape as an abstracted vertical series with densely packed intervals. Some verticals are formed from collaged elements pasted on the surface, which allowed color to bleed from beneath or behind the vertical strips. Sometimes the dominant verticals are animated by the addition of glyphs, hieroglyphics, and cursive arabesques.

The spatial distance between the vertical strips are distinctive but arbitrary, and often the impact is found in the tension between the ground and figure, or in the suggested movement between the blanks (white) and lines (color). Or sometimes it is reversed: White becomes the color that obscures and hides other elements.

The verticals turned on their sides become horizontals and the variations continue: borders with elements working/existing within the border; confined, delimited; heavy, darker; smooth versus rough texture; cut paper versus torn paper, ad infinitum.

Thus, the landscape as a motif is not unlike the chair or angels or other motifs selected by the artist. All celebrate a love of life, with emphasis placed on the intimate: things placed on a table, dark woods in winter, a comfortable chair, a view from a window, a cultivated garden. These are subjects of everyday experiences and are non-heroic, non-threatening. Yet, there exists another overlaid quality of "visions and revisions" that is revealed when

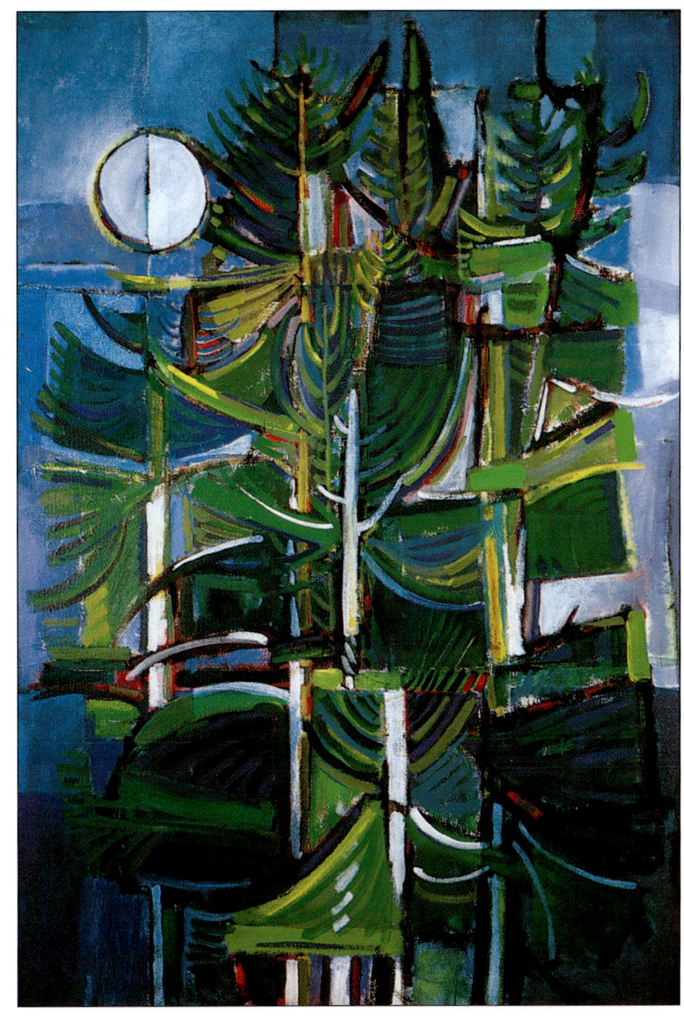

Pines at Falmouth, *1961, David C. Driskell; acrylic on canvas (Greg Staley, photographer; David C. Driskell Collection)*

several of the works are seen together. It is found in the exuberant lines that sometimes go astray and become nervous, broken and disjointed; a piecemeal, busy, mosaic effect obtains when emphasis is placed on minutia. The sense of spontaneity that is integral to the works is lost. Instead, a sense of the horror vacuii prevails.

If one is to understand more completely the works of Driskell, one question that remains to be considered is this: Is David Driskell an artist who happens to be "black," or is David Driskell a "black artist"? The most immediate response is that such a question is boring and irrelevant, especially in this context. Yet, this is a question that cuts to the core of the importance of the "black experience" as it relates to a "black aesthetic" or a "black art." Other but similar questions arise: What distinguishes black art from any other kind of art? Is the art "black" because the artist who produced it is black? Or do African Americans (black Americans) possess some qualities or share some experiences that make them different from other Americans? The political, social, and cultural history between the races in this country tend to get in the way and make these sorts of questions problematic. Any attempt to answer them is usually informed by consideration being given to factors other than art and aesthetics. The reason for this is that the politicians and human rights activists have long insisted that no significant differences existed among the races; to be told otherwise would seem to undermine their positions and programs. Perhaps one day it can be accepted that American artists are American but may also be Other and are not to be diminished by that fact.

Whatever your answer to the question, it will affect your experience and understanding of the works of Driskell. You will also, inevitably, find yourself on the slippery slope of an aesthetic incline that was posited during the halcyon days of the New Negro movement of the 1920s. The question, even in its embryonic state, was never as presumptuous as its detractors would suggest. Nevertheless, it must have been an intellectual leap of faith during the first couple of decades of this century by those with the temerity to assert that the black experience had value. The recognition of the uniqueness of this experience suggested that therein was contained the essential elements that could provide the foundation for the development of a new racial art, a black art. It followed that if a black art could be developed, then a black aesthetic would be the corollary (or vice versa).

Nevertheless, the initial idea of a black art made in America that would be different from art produced by white Americans was met with ridicule by some and defended by others.

George Schuyler, a journalist and one of the leading African American intellectuals of his era, labeled such an idea as being "The Negro-Art Hokum."[5] Schuyler's contention in that infamous 1926 essay by the same title was that "as far as the literature, painting, and sculpture of Afra-american [*sic*] —such as there is — it is identical in kind with the literature, painting and sculpture of white Americans: that is, it shows more or less evidence of European influence." His argument was that the black American was "merely a lampblacked American" since blacks were "subject to the same economic and social forces that mold the actions and thoughts of the white Americans."

In the same year Langston Hughes responded to Schuyler's article with the opposite position. Hughes's rebuttal, "The Negro and the Racial Mountain,"[6] insisted that black was beautiful. He directed the artist

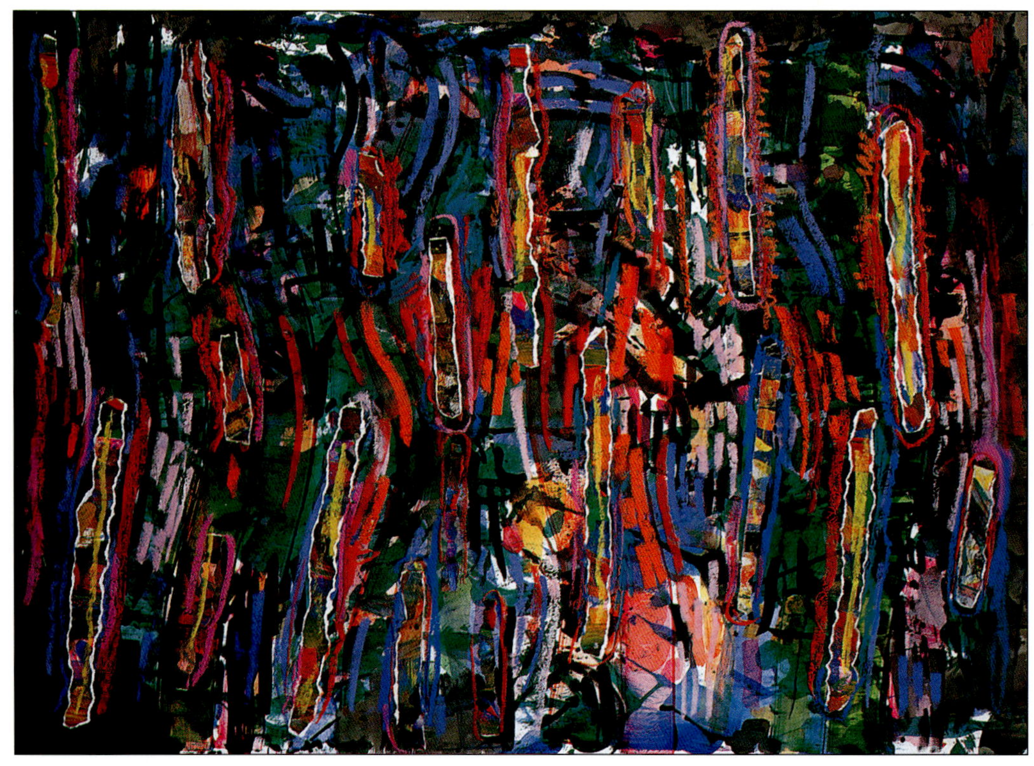

Flowing Like a River, 1996/1997, David C. Driskell; collage and gouache (Greg Staley, photographer; David C. Driskell Collection)

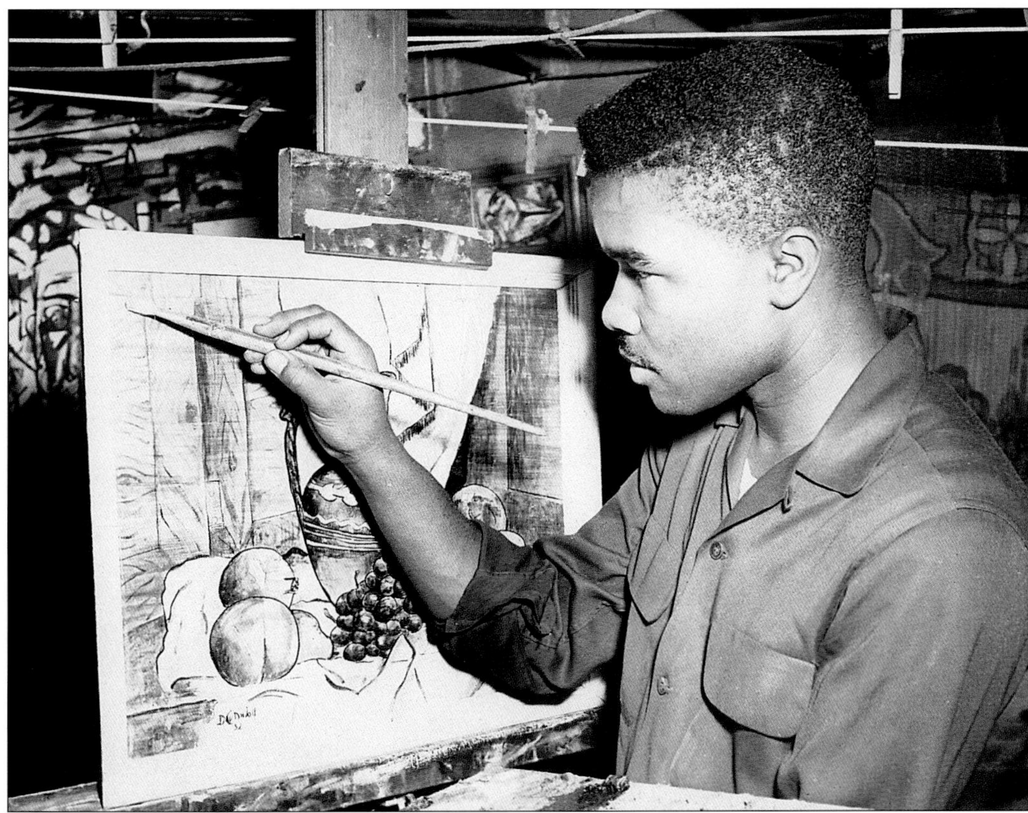

David Driskell, 1953
(David C. Driskell Archives)

to look inward and to plumb his own experiences, since these experiences contained the necessary ingredients to be used as valid subject matter and content for a legitimate black art. Hughes stated that it would be the uninhibited black masses who would ultimately provide the source material for those interested in developing a truly distinctive black art made in America.

These two essays, among certain others, especially the famous 1925 "Legacy of the Ancestral Arts,"[7] by Alain Locke, helped to establish what would become the central issues regarding a black aesthetic. The questions asked were these: (1) Is the existence of black Americans within the body politic sufficiently different on enough conceptual levels to justify the development of an aesthetic that could be identifiably different from that of the majority culture? and (2) If a black art can be developed, should it stem from an African source, since black Americans collectively share an African legacy; or should the experience in the New World hold sway, especially the experiences of the common folk? This debate continues, and it is this contextual environment from which the works of Driskell should be viewed.

Is David Driskell a black artist or an artist who happens to be black? Is his work black art? If one has to be an art maker in order to make something art, then it seems reasonable that to make black art, one has to be black. If one is to make Japanese art, does not one have to be Japanese?

Part of the difficulty lies in determining who has the authority to enfranchise the black art makers. Who bestows the "correct" aesthetic values upon the work of art? Are they (the works of art and/or the artists) to be appreciated or evaluated solely on the manifestation of the correct social/institutional properties? These are only a few of the philosophical, political, aesthetic, and other questions that remain open-ended. Yet, Driskell seems to posit a conceptual position that identifies (through personal experiences) and transcends (by rising above) race.

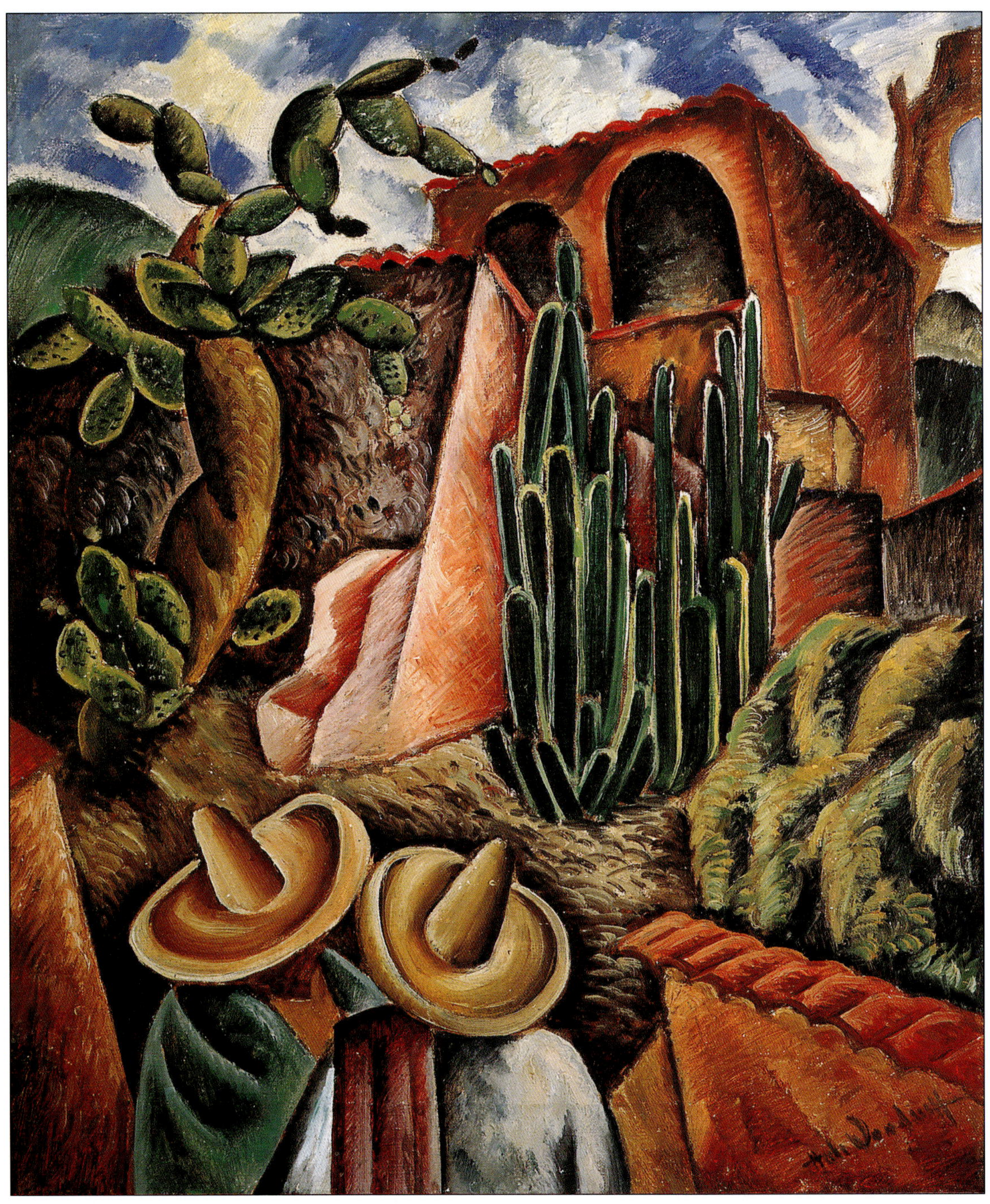

Hale Woodruff, Two Figures in a Mexican Landscape, *c. 1934 (catalogue no. 49)*

The David C. Driskell Collection

Perhaps the most satisfying aspect of a project with the scope of the David C. Driskell Collection exhibition is working with the objects themselves. When given the charge to research David Driskell's extensive collection of African American art, we were at once delighted and daunted, but ready to accept the challenge of documenting one of the finest collections of its kind in the country.

Curator Juanita Holland performed the difficult task of assembling 100 representative objects from a collection of hundreds of important pieces that range from the latter part of the nineteenth century to the present. Although a significant number of the objects have been exhibited and published, most are being introduced to the public for the first time. Few of these objects were accompanied by the traditional documentation that facilitates standard methodologies of art historical research. The small core of general texts on African American art, such as Romare Bearden's and Harry Henderson's *A History of African-American Artists from 1792 to the Present,* Samella Lewis's *African American Art and Artists,* David Driskell's *Two Centuries of Black American Art,* and the *St. James Guide to Black Artists,* among others, provided much of the background information on many of the artists featured in the exhibition who are otherwise severely underrepresented in mainstream texts and periodicals on American art. We also relied on non-traditional methods germane to the study of African American history and culture, such as archival research, contextual analysis, newspaper and magazine articles, primary materials, and oral histories that, for us, were graciously provided by raconteur par excellence David Driskell.

The following analysis of objects in the Driskell Collection represents our attempt to place each work in the context of the artist's life and/or the social and cultural milieu out of which it emerged. Despite uneven documentation and limited and sometimes conflicting sources, we attempted to assemble the most accurate information possible at this stage in hopes that the collection will inspire more in-depth inquiries. This is the initial phase of research on the David C. Driskell Collection, a dynamic body of work that enriches, expands, and will continue to add new dimensions to our understanding of African American material culture.

—Adrienne L. Childs
Tuliza Fleming

I. Strategic Subversions: Cultural Emancipation, Assimilation, and African American Identity

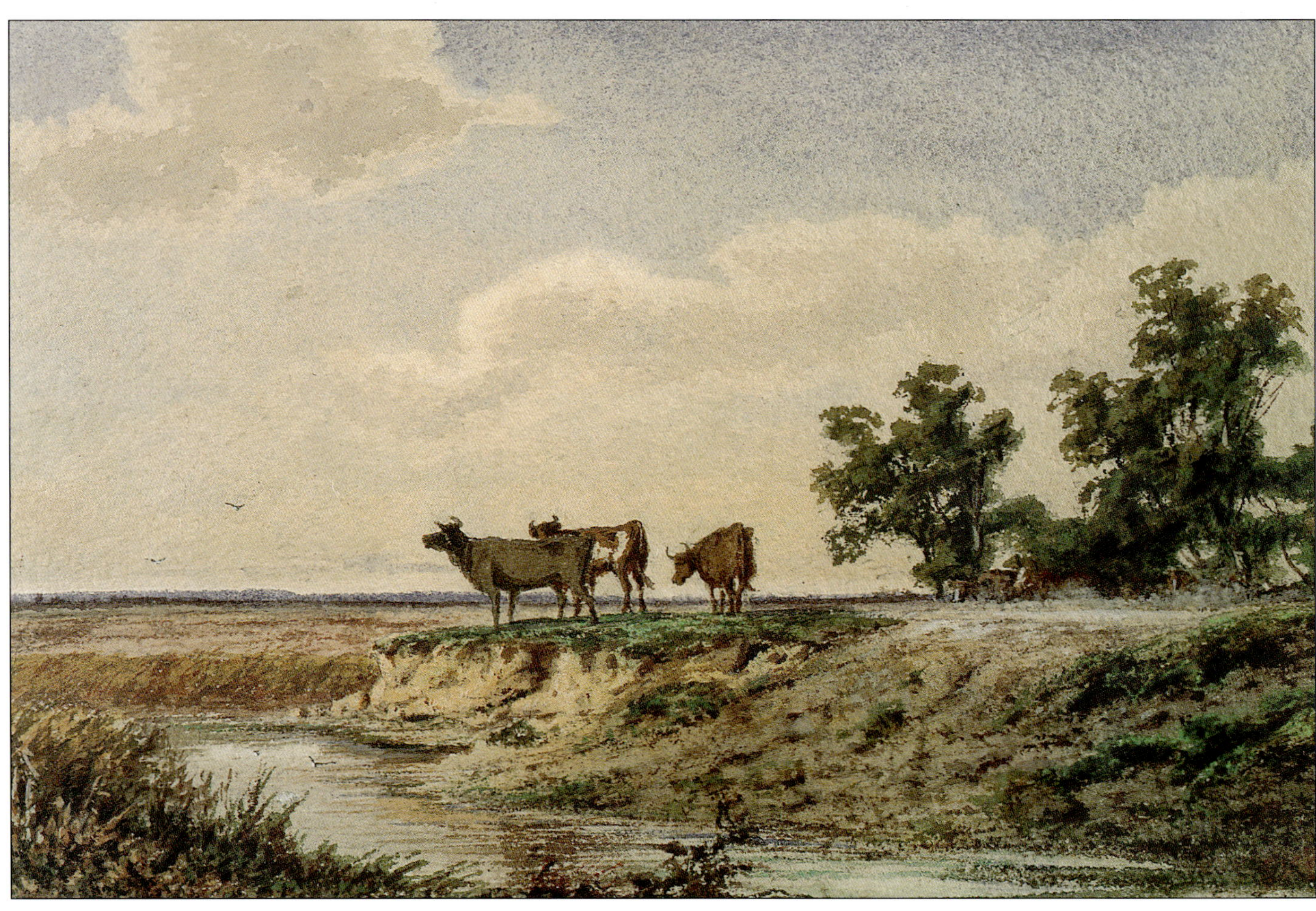

By the third quarter of the nineteenth century, African American painter Edward Mitchell Bannister had become a recognized and successful New England artist. Born in New Brunswick, Canada, Bannister emigrated to Boston as a young man. One of Bannister's earliest artistic influences was his exposure to the French Barbizon painters that were beginning to be exhibited in Boston in the late 1850s. Bucolic scenes of farm animals in tranquil landscape were a staple in this increasingly popular mode of landscape painting, and Bannister's earliest memories of Canadian farm life no doubt added to the nostalgic attraction of such scenes for him.

By the 1880s Bannister was successful enough to purchase a small sailboat. He spent summers sailing along the Narragansett Bay, creating the sketches and watercolors that provided the inspiration for the oil paintings he produced in his studio. Along with these sketches and studies, Bannister created many signed drawings and watercolors as finished works similar to the Driskell Collection's untitled landscape with cows.   A. L. C.

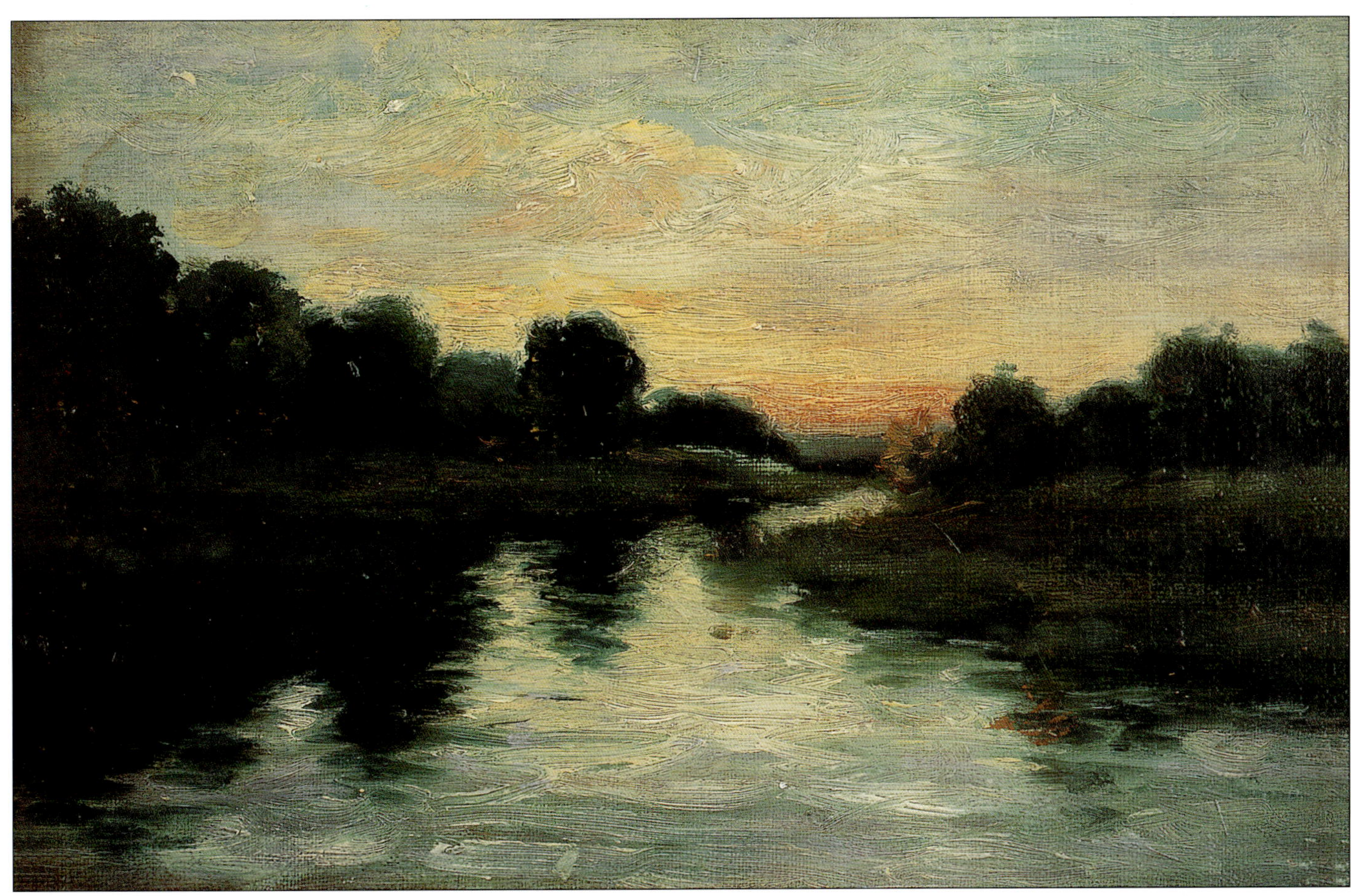

EDWARD MITCHELL
BANNISTER

2.

Untitled

(Landscape with Pond),

c. 1876

Oil on canvas

7.75" x 11.75"

Edward Mitchell Bannister won his first significant recognition when his large landscape *Under the Oaks* won a first-prize medal at the 1876 Philadelphia Centennial Exhibition. Bannister had by this time established himself in both Massachusetts and Rhode Island as an accomplished landscape painter. His works were favorably reviewed; *Under the Oaks* had been sold for a considerable amount of money even before it was hung at the Exposition. Although that work has been lost since the turn of the century, other works from this period survive to give us a sense of Bannister's artistic explorations of these years. Bannister is often described as a Barbizon painter and indeed created many works in that tradition. *Under the Oaks* was likened by one reviewer to the English painter John Constable's work; another 1876 landscape, *Oak Trees* (National Museum of American Art), is a meticulously painted static landscape quite unlike this *Untitled* (Landscape with Pond), which attests to another aspect of his work. A number of works in this style combine a tactile attention to thickly applied paint on canvas with a loose, Impressionistic brushstroke that begins to dissolve the forms. These works often study the resonant effects of light on water, a subject Bannister returns to again and again throughout his career. The cloud-filled sky glowing with color reflects as well the artist's lifelong fascination with the effects of weather and time of day in the New England landscape.   A. L. C.

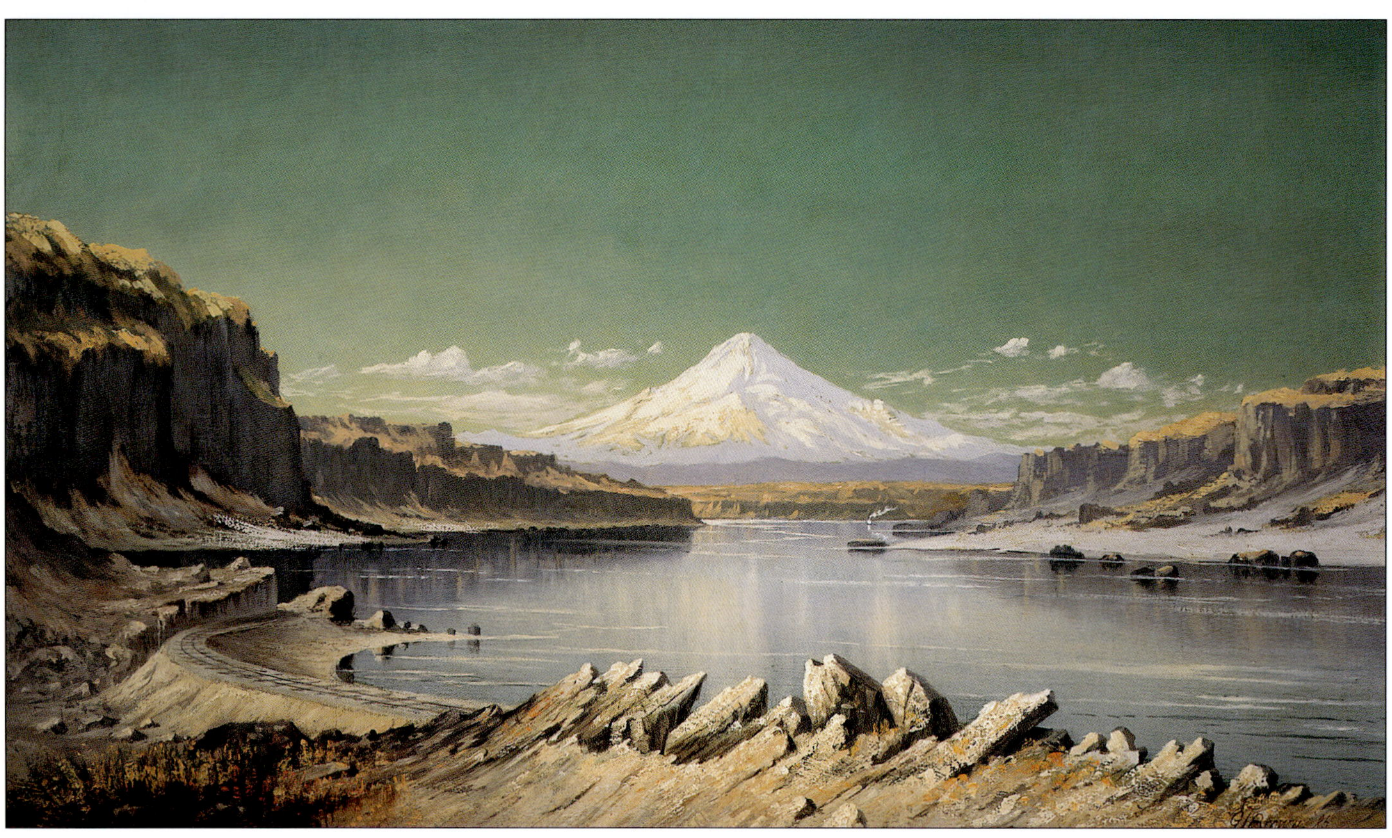

GRAFTON TYLER
BROWN

3.

*Mt. Hood from John Day's
Station,* 1884–1885

Oil on canvas

15.5" x 25.5"

Born of free parentage in Pennsylvania, Grafton Tyler Brown followed the lure of the West to California in the mid-1850s, participating in the expansion that would change the face of the nation. He was able to find work as a lithographer in San Francisco and eventually formed his own business in 1866. Brown is considered the first African American professional artist in California. His early work consisted of illustrating and documenting the emerging settlements, gold-rush towns, and ranches that were springing up in the territories surrounding San Francisco. His work, and that of others in his field who created appealing images of the West, served as part of the commercialization of the developing nation. Although his business as a commercial draftsman was successful, Brown sold it in 1879 and in 1882 left the Bay Area for Canada, where many African Americans found a more racially tolerant environment. Brown turned to paint as his primary medium and began to focus on the beauty of the Canadian landscape. With no formal training, his experience as a draftsman was the foundation he needed to establish himself as an artist.

By 1885 Grafton Tyler Brown had moved on to the Pacific Northwest, where he was inspired by the mountainous landscapes. *Mt. Hood from John Day's Station* of 1884–1885 is a dramatic view of Washington state's Mount Hood. Brown's soft palette imbues this sun-drenched vista with awe-inspiring majesty, a quality that characterized his grand landscapes. Brown frequently included railroad tracks and ferry boats in his landscapes, which serve as subtle but poignant reminders of the encroachment of civilization.   A. L. C.

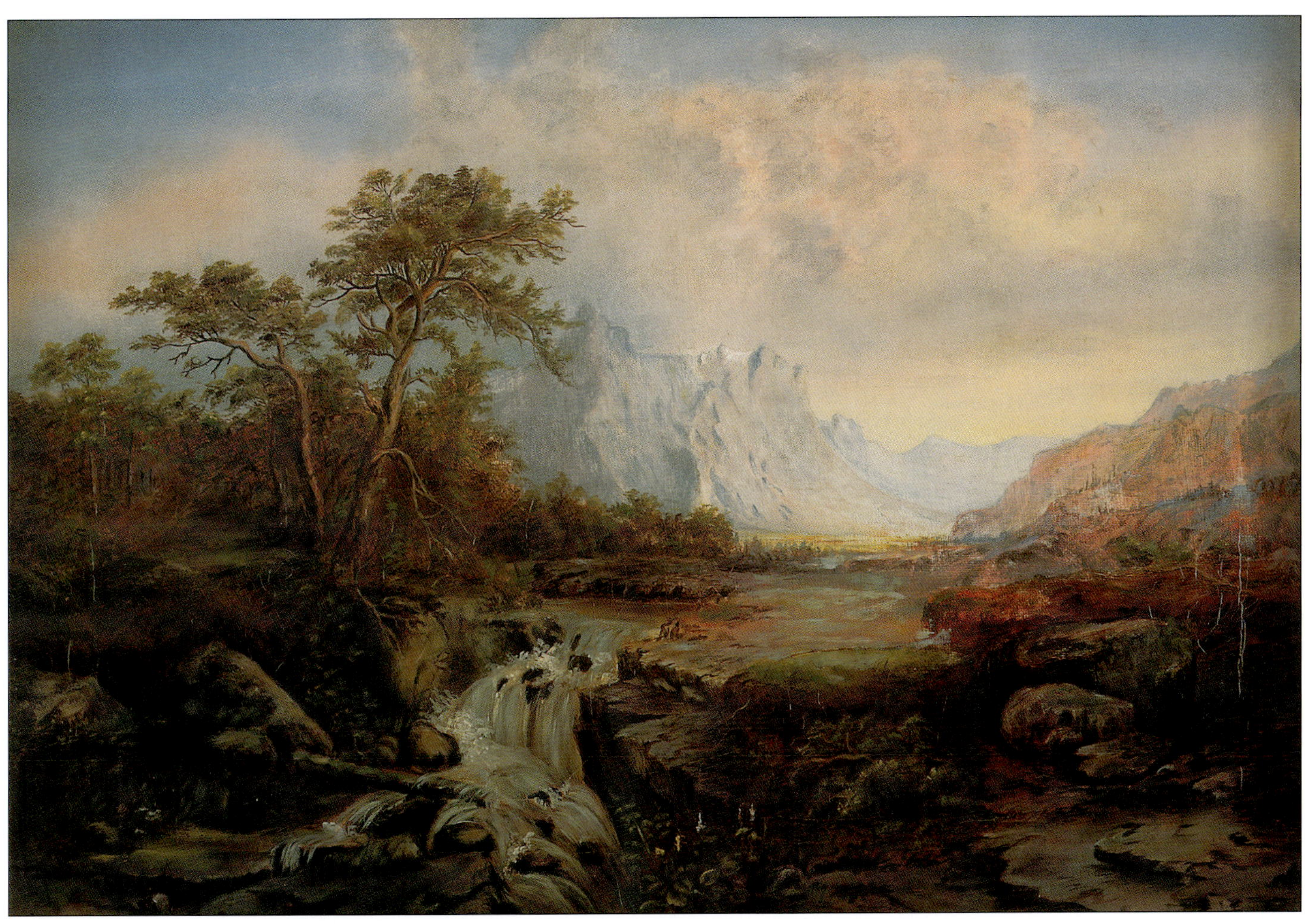

Robert Scott
Duncanson

4.

Scottish Landscape, c. 1870

Oil on canvas

15" x 21"

Scottish Landscape has been attributed to nineteenth-century African American painter Robert S. Duncanson. Duncanson worked in and around the Cincinnati, Ohio, area, a thriving arts center on the frontier of an expanding United States. Heavily influenced by the Hudson River School aesthetic of landscape painting, Duncanson also sought inspiration from European landscape and literary traditions. His absorption of European and mainstream American aesthetic standards undoubtedly assured his commercial success and popularity; however, he was not isolated from the racial issues that were paramount in America during the middle of the nineteenth century. Duncanson benefited from abolitionist patronage and actively supported the antislavery movement.

He remained steadfast in his pursuit of achievement in landscape painting in an international arena and traveled to Europe, England, Scotland, and Canada, where he gained experience and inspiration. Scotland was a particularly rich source of inspiration for Duncanson who, on his return from abroad in the mid-1860s, began a series of Scottish landscapes in keeping with the style and structure of the Driskell Collection's *Scottish Landscape*. From the immediacy of the rocks in the foreground to the majesty of the mountains and clouds, Duncanson creates a vantage point in which nature's elements of sun, sky, water, land, and foliage converge in a rugged landscape.   A. L. C.

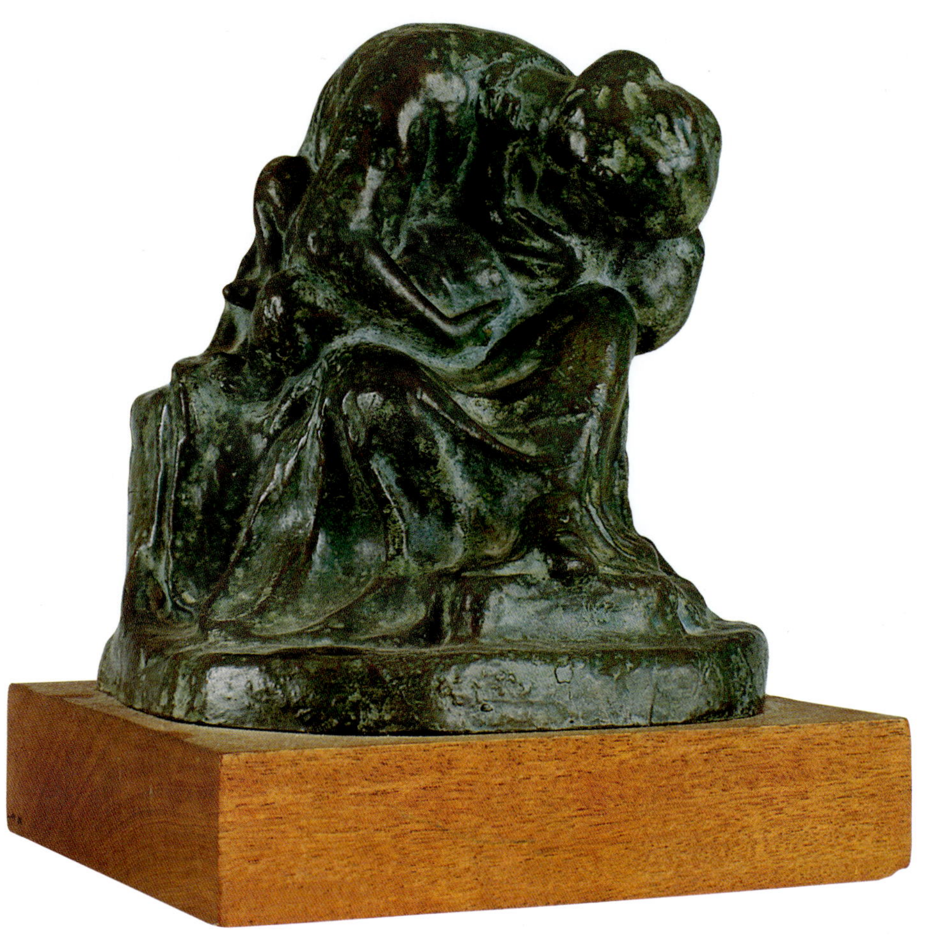

Meta Warrick Fuller was one of a handful of academically trained African American artists who studied both in America and Europe around the turn of the century. Fuller's work featuring black themes is generally considered a prelude to the Harlem Renaissance in its celebration of the black physique and African and African American cultures. Philadelphia-born Fuller studied at the Pennsylvania Academy of Fine Arts in Philadelphia as well as in Paris at L'École des Beaux Arts and Académie Colarossi, where the presence of a black American female was a rarity. While in Paris, Fuller met sculptor Auguste Rodin, whose influence was principal in the development of her work. Scholars have called Fuller's work macabre, expressive, and emotionally intense. Fuller, active in her church during the 1930s and 1940s, frequently explored religious themes in sculpture. The traditional Christian theme of the Pietà embodies the drama of human despair and is deftly communicated by Fuller in her small bronze *Pietà* of the 1930s.
A. L. C.

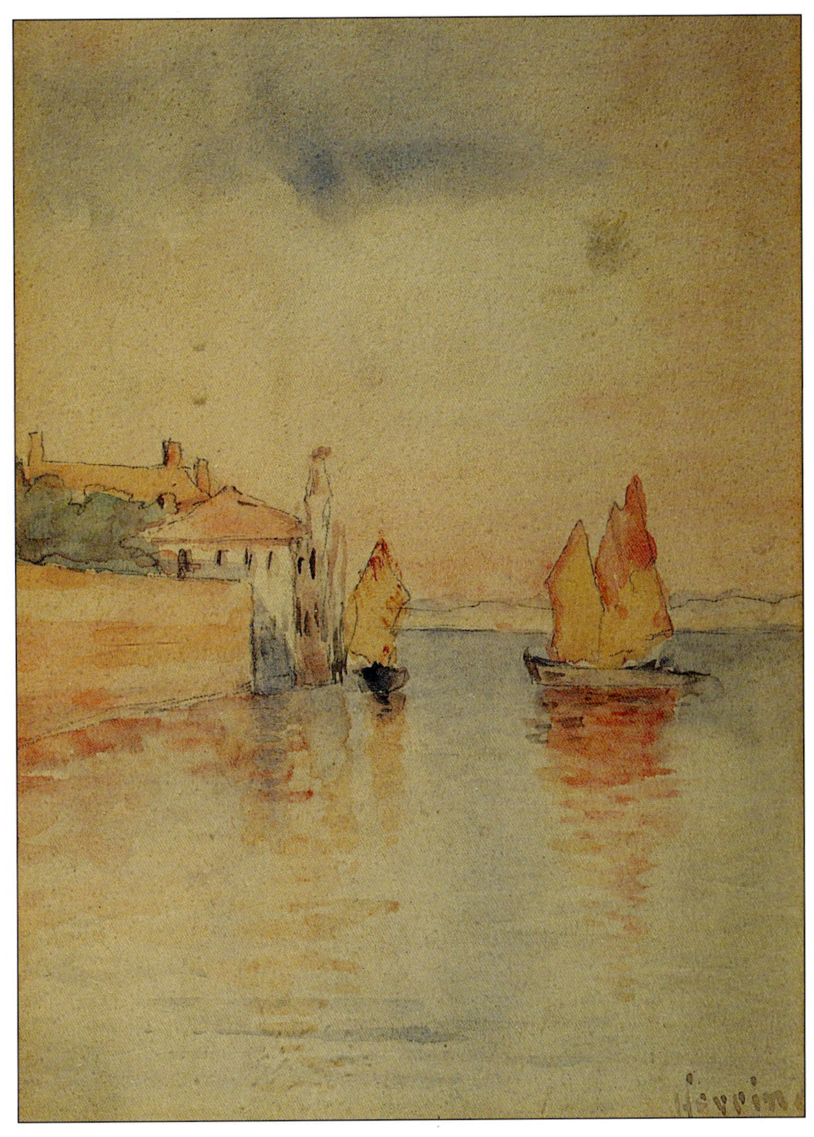

James V. Herring

6.

Newport Scene, n.d.

Watercolor on paper

7" x 5"

James V. Herring is primarily known as the founder of the Howard University Art Department. As an artist, Herring followed academic trends that were prevalent in early twentieth-century American art. *Newport Scene* presents a traditional seaside vista, using popular Impressionist treatment of light and reflection. Although the Impressionist movement began as a radical departure from academic painting, by the early twentieth century it had become established as a part of the Western tradition. Herring and many other African American artists used this vocabulary to express their artistic vision and establish themselves as viable participants in a long-standing and widely accepted artistic tradition.   A. L. C.

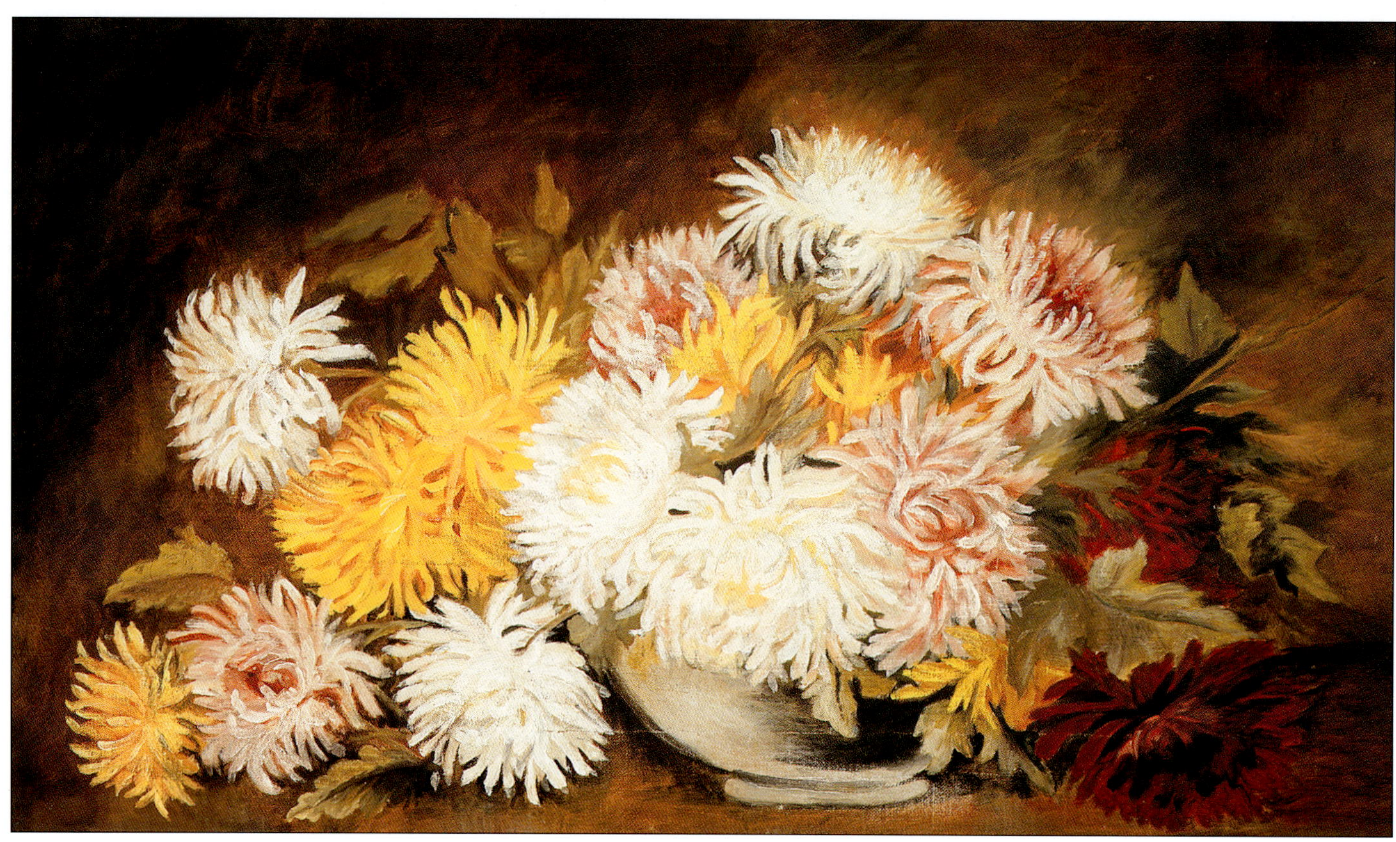

7.

Untitled (Still Life: Mums
in a Bowl), n.d.

Oil on canvas

11.75" x 19.5"

The Driskell Collection's *Untitled* (Still Life: Mums in a Bowl) has been attributed to Hartford, Connecticut, still-life artist Charles Ethan Porter. Like other black artists of his time, Porter followed the European aesthetic tradition as it was the standard for commercial success. Thus he became one of an elite group of African Americans in the late nineteenth century who were able to make their living as professional artists. The Driskell Collection still life features chrysanthemums, a type of flower Porter often revisited. Although still life was considered a lesser genre in the sense of the European hierarchy of painting, it was an important aesthetic aspect of the Victorian domestic interior and would have been found in households across racial lines in America.   A. L. C.

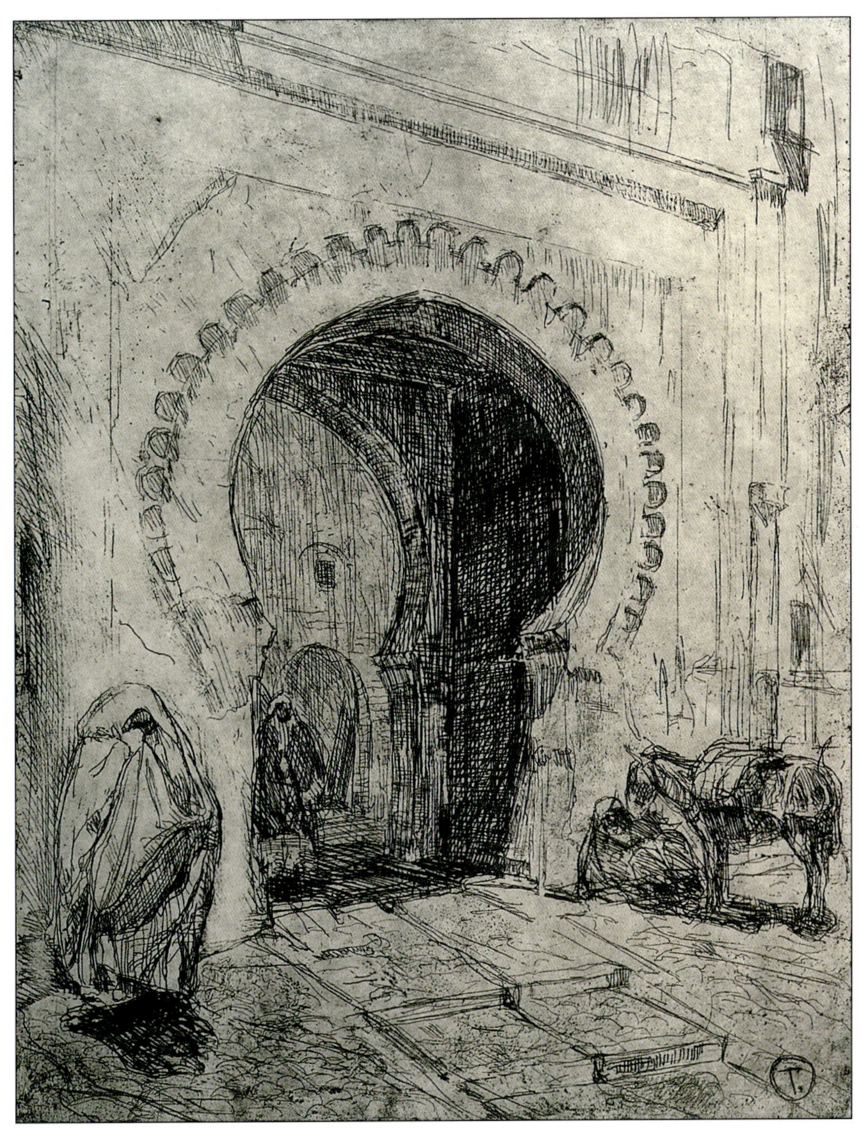

HENRY O. TANNER

8.

Gate at Tangier, 1910

Etching on paper

9.5" x 7"

Henry O. Tanner, America's premier expatriate African American artist at the turn of the century, made his first trip to North Africa in 1908. His travels inspired what are considered his Orientalist works as well as some of his most eloquent biblical scenes. *Gate at Tangier* is one of Tanner's many iterations of the shadowy archways connecting the streets and passages of Tangier, through which heavily draped figures pursue their daily activities. Tanner's sensitive treatment of North African subject matter is a marked departure from the exoticized view of the East that was the foundation of European Orientalist tradition.   A. L. C.

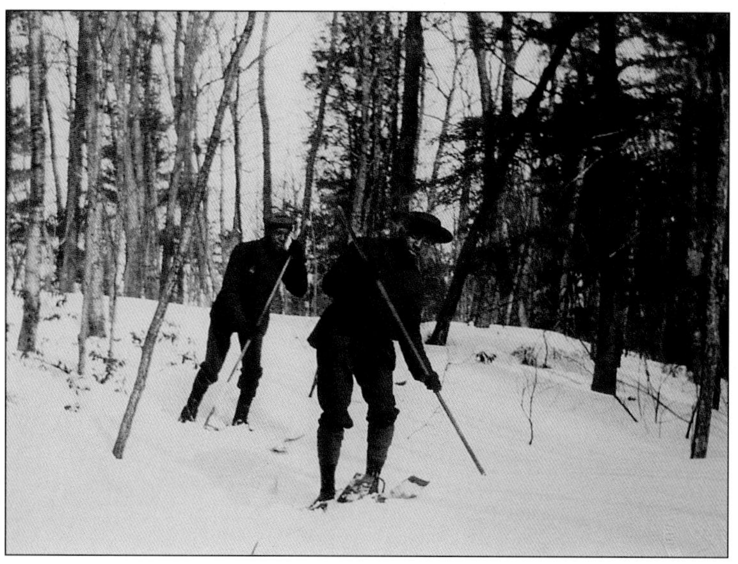

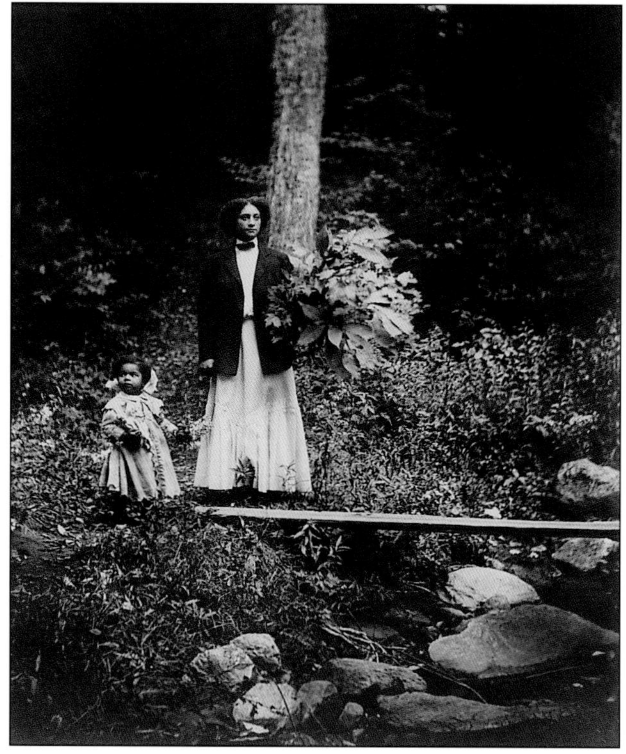

James VanDerZee

9.

VanDerZee Boys, c. 1900

Black-and-white photograph

7" x 9.5"

10.

*Portrait of First Wife and
Daughter (In the Woods),* n.d.

(also known as *Kate
and Rachel*)

Black-and-white photograph

10" x 8"

James VanDerZee's early years were spent with his family in Lenox, Massachusetts. The small community of African Americans living in Lenox primarily made their livings providing service to the wealthy New Englanders who spent summers in the hotels and estates of the mountain resort. It was while working as a waiter at the luxurious Hotel Aspinwall that VanDerZee purchased his first camera from a mail-order company. The 1900 photo *VanDerZee Boys* is among his earliest works. It features two of the VanDerZee brothers skiing in a snowy landscape. This photo provides a rare image of African Americans participating in what was considered an elite pastime and challenged stereotypical notions of blacks as they were represented in popular culture.

VanDerZee married Kate L. Brown of Virginia in 1907. In 1908, after the birth of their daughter Rachel, they moved to Harlem. At that time Harlem was just opening up to African Americans and held much promise for those looking to participate in the urban American economy. VanDerZee worked waiting tables and operating an elevator during these early years in Harlem. His only photographs from this period are outdoor studies of his wife and daughter and other family members. Kate's sober countenance and stiff stance, typical of Victorian era photography, are softened by the lush woods surrounding them. This is a sensitive portrayal of VanDerZee's young family that would unfortunately dissolve prematurely. Kate left VanDerZee in 1916 because of the uncertainty of the photography business, and, sadly, his daughter Rachel experienced an untimely death in 1927.   A. L. C.

II. Emergence: The New Negro Movement and Definitions of Race

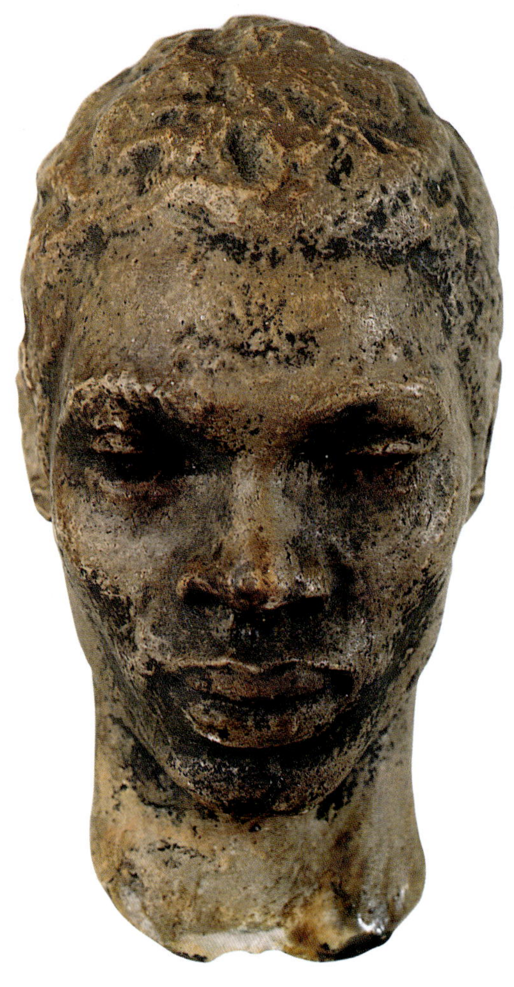

RICHMOND BARTHÉ

11.

Untitled (Head of a Man),
c. 1935

Terra cotta

4" x 1" x 1"

By the late 1930s, sculptor Richmond Barthé had become the most widely exhibited African American artist in the United States. Although he chose not to limit himself to the depiction of a particular race or theme, his dignified portrayals of African American men and women were a source of pride within the African American arts community.

Barthé created his first sculptures in 1928, during his senior year at the Art Institute of Chicago. Although he enrolled in the program with the intention of becoming a painter, his advisor, German artist Charles Shroeder, suggested that Barthé try his hand at modeling as an exercise to increase his skill at painting in three dimensions. Barthé followed his professor's advice and created his first two sculpture busts, which he modeled from the images of two of his friends. These works were so well received that the organizers of Chicago's Negro Art Week commissioned Barthé to create two busts, the head of artist Henry O. Tanner and Haitian general Toussaint L'Ouverture. From 1929 to the end of his career, Barthé continued to model positive and diverse images of Africans and African Americans such as *Masai,* 1933; *Boxer,* 1942; *Black Madonna*, 1961; and *Paul Robeson as Othello*, 1975.

Barthé's miniature sculptural head of an unidentified African American man visually attests to his facility for sensitively modeling African American features and expressions. Its unusually diminutive size also demonstrates his ability to work competently in a variety of scales and materials.   T. F.

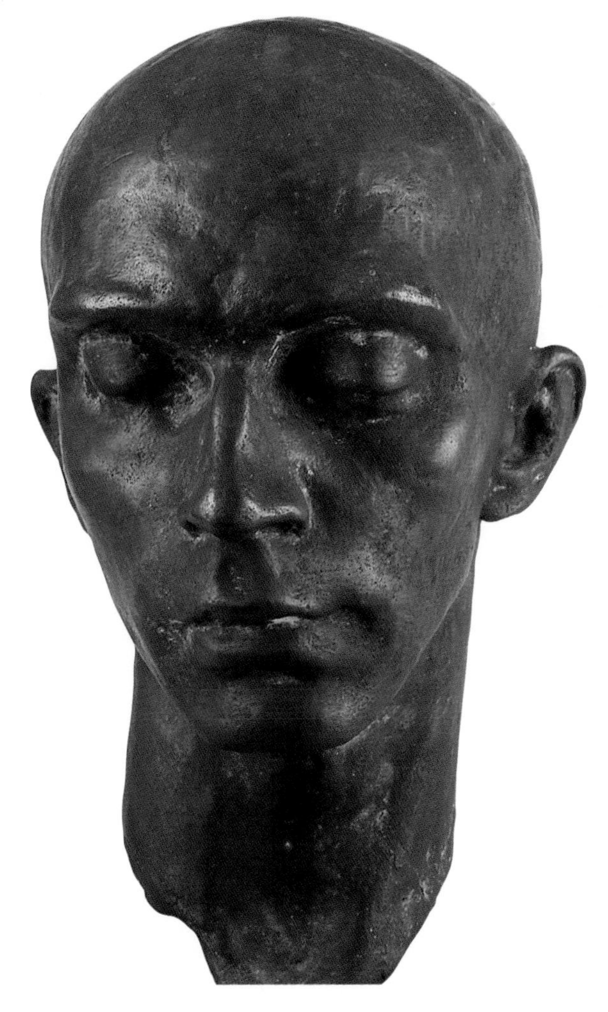

Even though Barthé is best remembered for his sensitive renderings of African and African American figures and portrait busts, he did not limit himself to that genre. In addition to his work within an African/African American thematic structure, Barthé also displayed a particular interest in dance and theater.

According to Bearden's and Henderson's 1993 *A History of African-American Artists,* during the 1930s, Barthé's fascination with the movements and expressions of dance inspired him to join a modern dance group under May Radin at Martha Graham's studio. Barthé utilized his experiences as a dance student to increase his knowledge of the body's musculature. According to Driskell, Barthé's portrait bust of Russian dancer Harold Kruetzberg reflects his interest in dance as well as his ability to communicate the innermost essence of his subject's humanity, irrespective of race.   T. F.

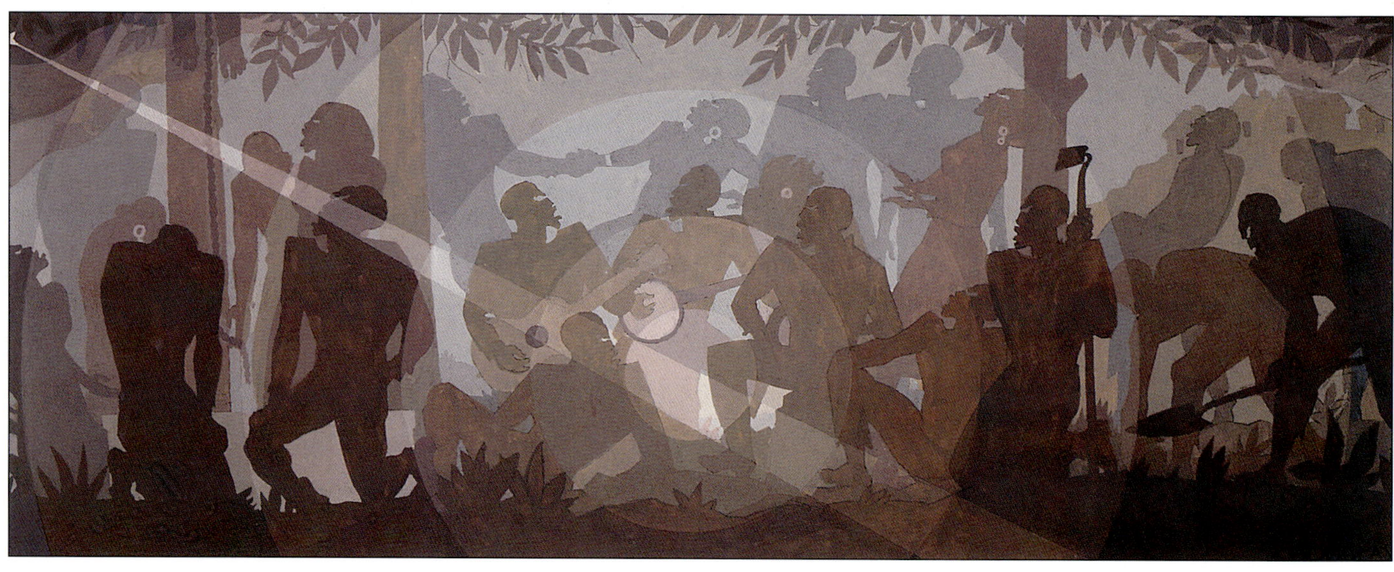

13.

Aspects of Negro Life: An Idyll of the Deep South (study), late 1930s

Tempera on paper

9.75" x 42"

Toward the end of the Harlem Renaissance, Aaron Douglas began to incorporate distinct political and social messages into his stylistic vocabulary. A primary example of this new political symbolism can be observed in the tempera on paper version of *An Idyll of the Deep South*. The Driskell Collection image is a smaller version of the third panel of Douglas's mural series *Aspects of Negro Life,* commissioned in 1934 by the WPA for the Harlem Branch of the New York City Public Library.

In *An Idyll of the Deep South,* Douglas subverts the myth of the "happy southern plantation Negro" by flanking the central theme of the painting—cheerful and contented African Americans singing, dancing, and playing music—with the images of black southern reality, the aftermath of a brutal lynching and black workers toiling in the fields. This reality of racism and economic hardship is underscored through Douglas's incorporation of a star and its emanating ray of light in the left-hand corner of the composition. Although this star has generally been perceived as a representation of the North Star, in April of 1971, during a conversation with David Driskell, Douglas revealed that in fact the star was his version of the red star of Communism. Douglas added that he had included this star in *An Idyll of the Deep South* to illustrate the hope held by some black Harlem intellectuals that true equality might be attained through the alternative policies of communism and socialism.   T. F.

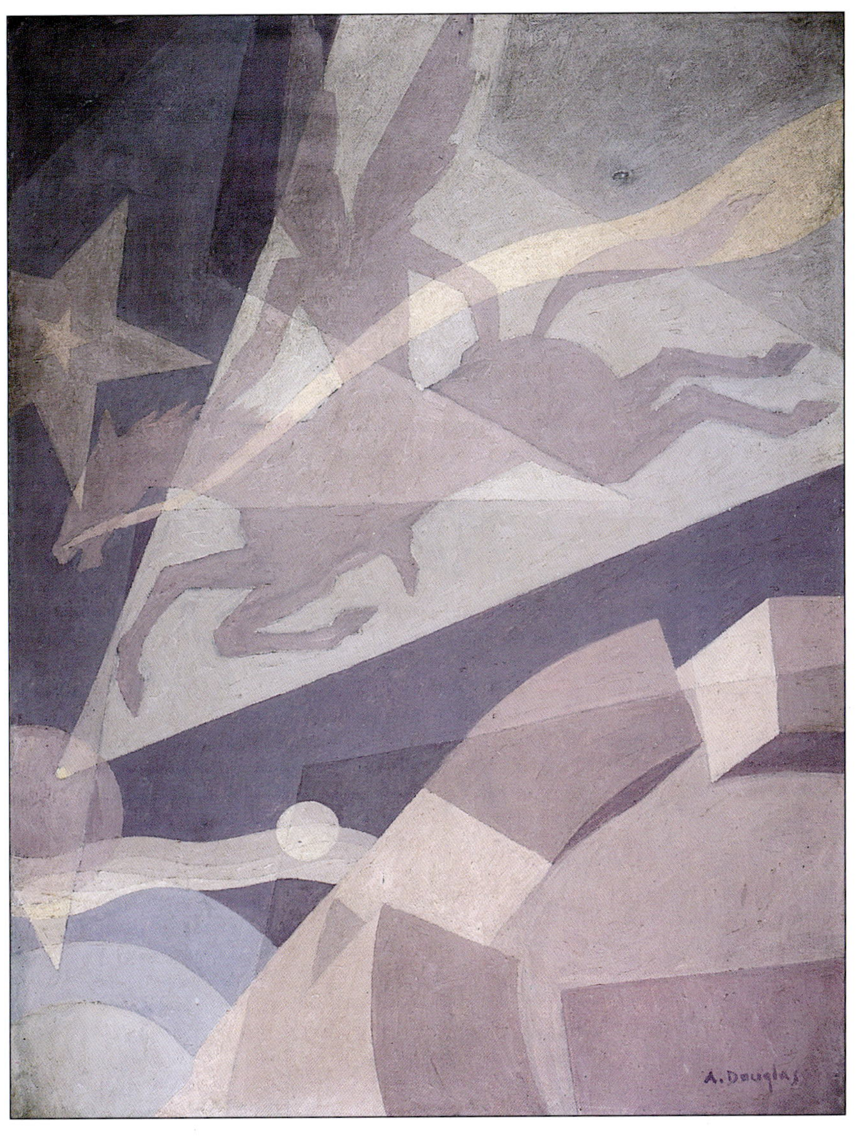

AARON DOUGLAS

14.

Go Down Death, 1934

Oil on Masonite

48" x 36"

In 1934, Aaron Douglas returned to his "God's Trombones" series, originally created as illustrations to accompany James Weldon Johnson's 1927 book of Negro spirituals in verse, *God's Trombones.* Douglas's illustration *Go Down Death* accompanied Johnson's funeral sermon of the same name. The sermon describes God's decision to have the Angel of Death ride down on his winged horse and carry Sister Caroline from a life of pain into the arms of Jesus. Douglas's interpretation shows Death as he rides down from heaven on a steed whose wings are borrowed from the archangel Gabriel. His 1934 re-working of that composition adds a radiating star in the upper left-hand corner of the work. This element illustrates another aspect of Johnson's sermon, in which the arrival of Old Death is likened to a falling star. It may also refer, as in other works, to Douglas's new-found interest in Communist theory. Using symbolic encoding in much the same manner as did the spirituals, Douglas gives descending Death and the star both religious and political implications. Death is portrayed as a religious journey of the spirit and as a release from the world of slavery. The radiating star symbolizes both the North Star that led fugitive slaves to freedom and the embodiment of political principles that would lead twentieth-century African Americans to freedom as well.   T. F.

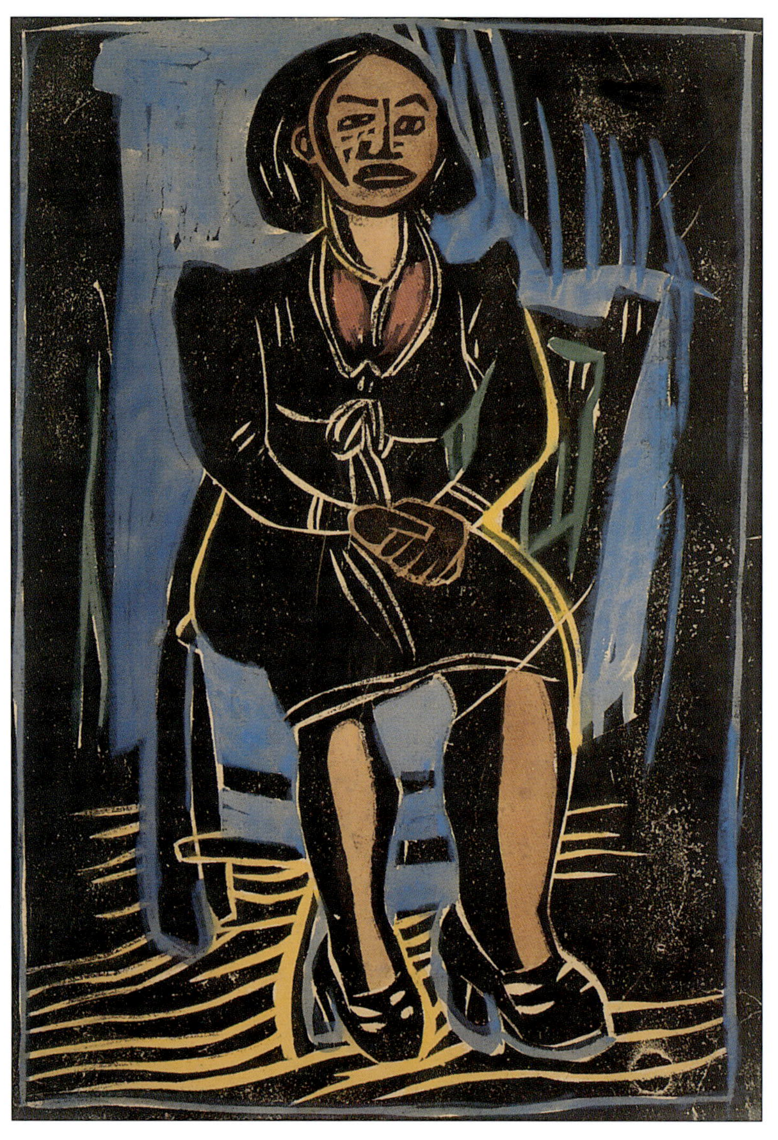

William H.
Johnson

15.

Seated Woman, c. 1939

Hand-colored linocut
on paper

18" x 12"

Constantly looking for new and challenging opportunities, William H. Johnson left his
native North Carolina to study fine art in New York City and later throughout Europe. Fascinated by German Expressionism and the works of Chaim Soutine, Johnson traveled to Europe
to study Modernism. Upon his return to America, he relinquished his experiments in Expressionism to pursue a "primitive" style, which he felt was a more suitable vehicle for the expression of African American experiences.

Seated Woman is an early work that combines Expressionism with the beginnings of his
burgeoning new simplified style. Thick incised lines define an anonymous portrait of a seated
African American female figure. The somber expression and color tones are Expressionist rem-
nants that Johnson would soon leave behind for a caricatured treatment of the figure and a
vibrant palette. This is a departure from his earlier work not only in style but in its uniqueness
of subject matter: a solitary modern urban woman, wearing a contemporary dress and matching
high-heeled shoes.   K.A.K.

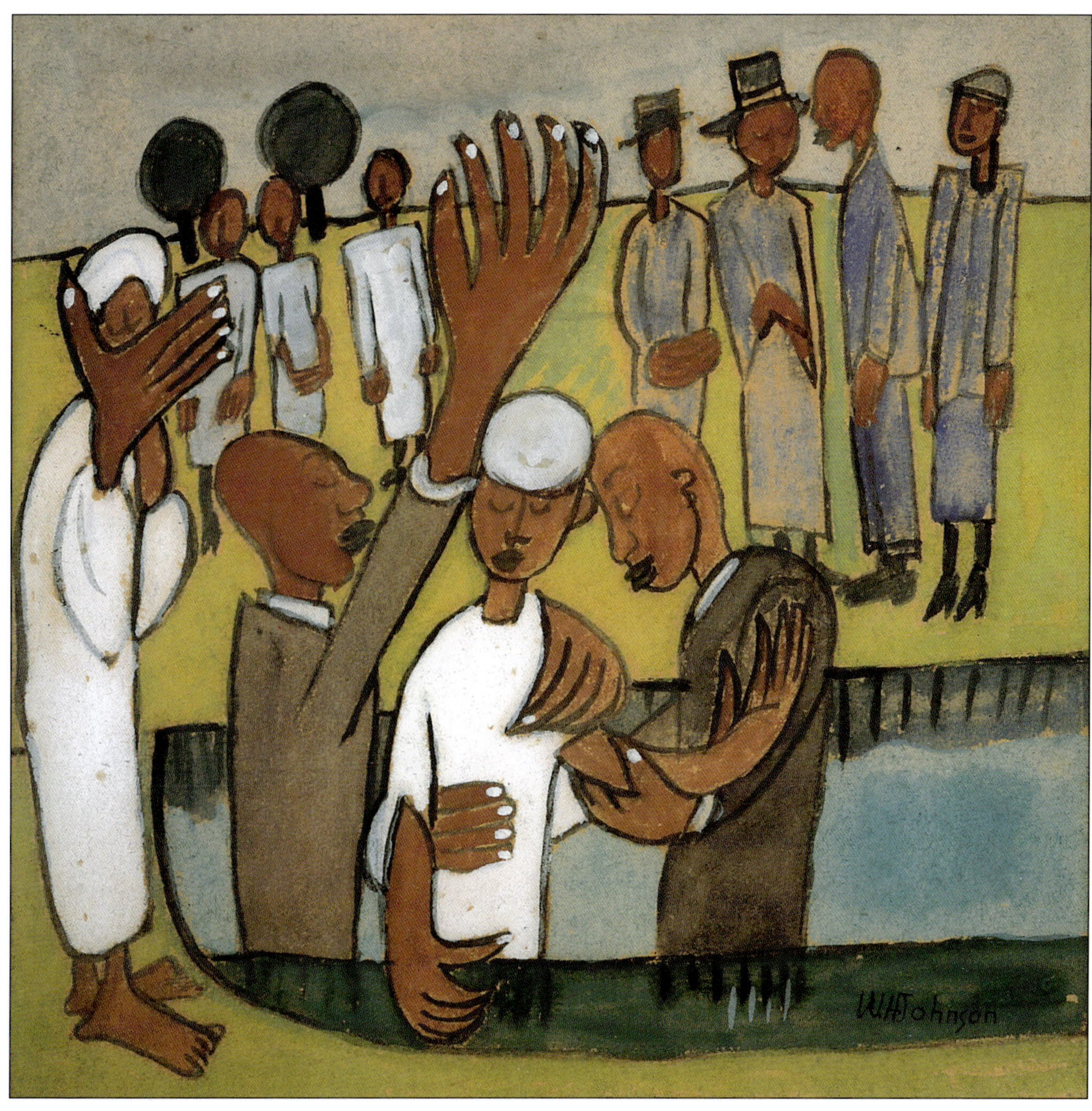

WILLIAM H.
JOHNSON

16.

I Baptize Thee (study), n.d.

Watercolor on paper

8" x 8"

Johnson used a "primitivist" style to encapsulate African American experiences of religious, genre, and military scenes. The term was not meant pejoratively. To Johnson it symbolized a culture and style that were closer to nature and art. A vibrantly contrasting palette, exaggerated figures, simplified landscape, and the use of heavy black outlining reveal his exposure to the Japanese woodblock prints that so influenced European Modernism. In *I Baptize Thee* (study), the setting for the baptism of an African American youth is a sparse outdoor landscape. The flatness of the figures and the landscape create a sensitive, scaled-down depiction of religious involvement in the everyday life of African Americans. While many artists of the time period were focusing on more urban or Africanized subject matter, Johnson looked to his native South Carolina for inspiration for his examination of the intimate gatherings of rural African Americans. K. A. K.

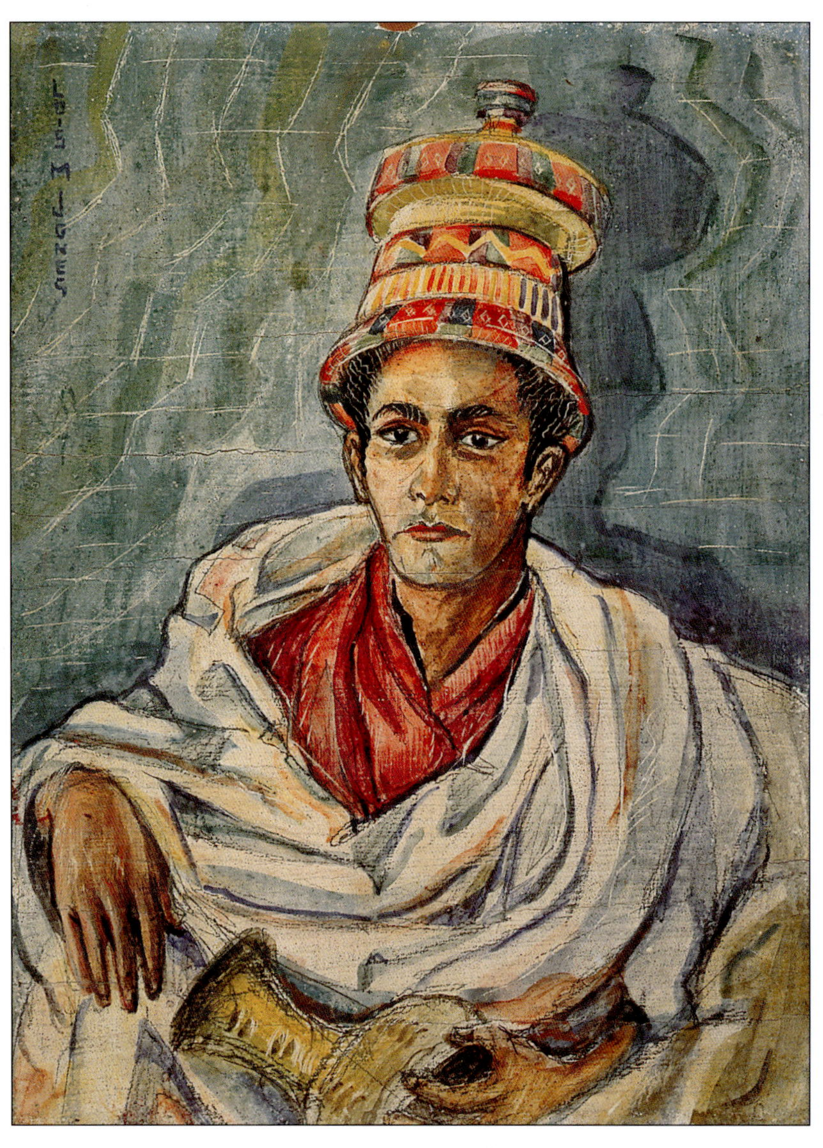

Loïs Mailou Jones

17.

Ethiopian Boy, 1948

Tempera on paper

7.75" x 5.75"

Loïs Mailou Jones's interest in visually depicting African subjects and aesthetics in her work began in 1932 with the creation of the painting *The Ascent of Ethiopia.* Over the next few years, Jones continued to create images reflecting African themes and material culture in works such as *Africa,* 1935; *African Bathers,* 1937; *Les Fétiches,* 1938; and her illustrations for Carter G. Woodson's publication, *African Heroes and Heroines,* 1939.

Jones's interest in the illustration of African culture was reinforced during the late 1930s by Howard University professor and philosopher Alain Locke who, according to art historian Tritobia Benjamin, strongly encouraged Jones to take her heritage more seriously. Jones warmly received Locke's advice and, during the 1940s, began to increase her artistic focus on the portrayal of Americans of African descent. *Ethiopian Boy,* 1948, exemplifies the romanticized manner in which she painted her subjects. Although the identity of the sitter is unknown and may in fact be a portrait of a model rather than an Ethiopian citizen, Jones's dignified portrayal of the "African" youth reflects a positive and uplifting image of African people that was rare during the era of this work's creation.   T. F.

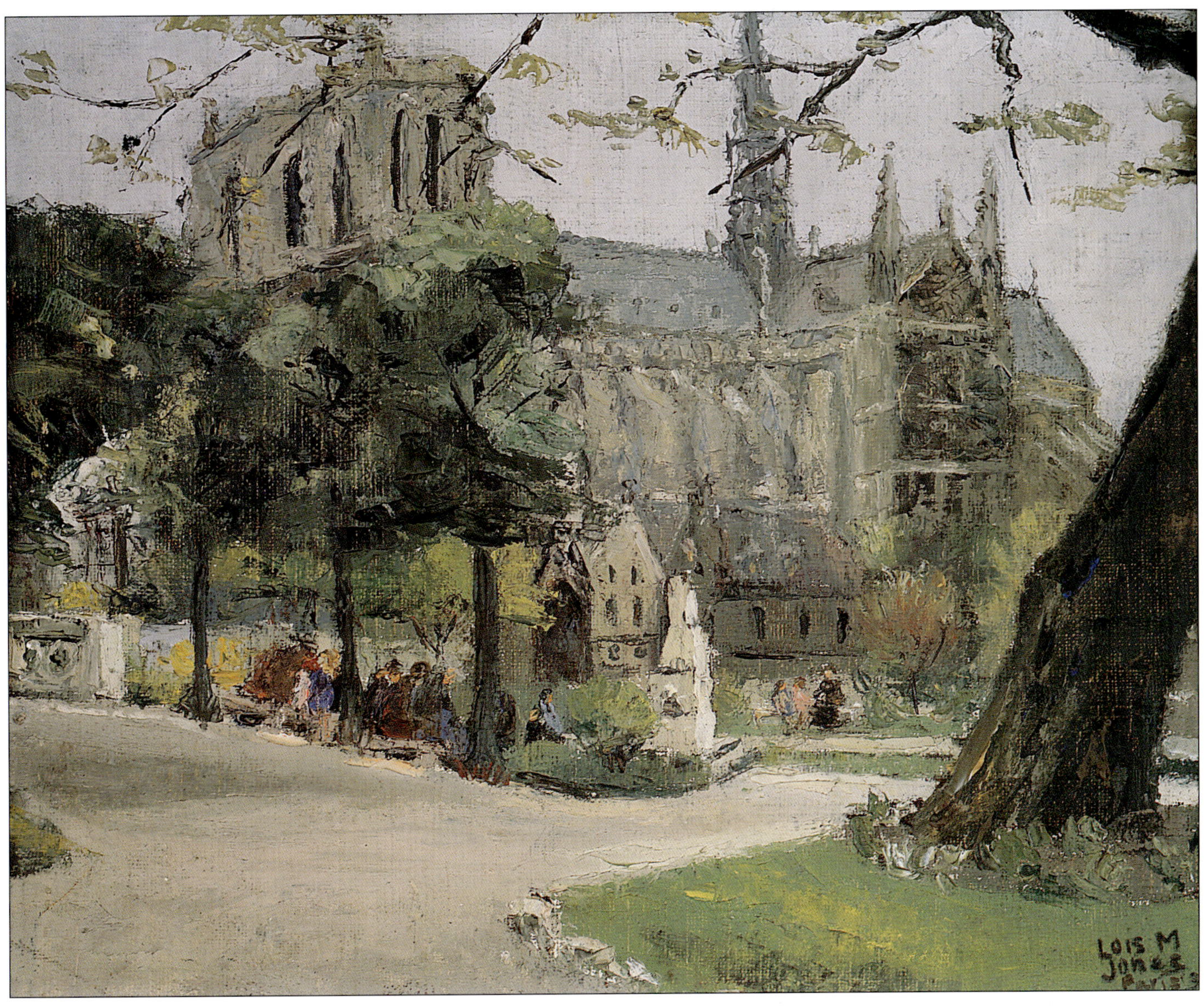

LOÏS MAILOU JONES

18.

Notre-Dame de Paris, 1936

Oil on canvas

14.25" x 17.25"

During the 1937–1938 academic year, after receiving a General Education Board fellowship to study at the Académie Julian, Loïs Mailou Jones traveled to Paris with the hopes of following in the footsteps of respected artists such as Picasso, Monet, and Tanner. Impressed by Paris's racially progressive atmosphere, Jones painted at a prolific pace, capturing France's gardens, historic churches, quaint urban scenes, and landscapes. Working primarily as a *plein air* painter, Jones's style rapidly evolved from design-based illustration into the impressionistic palette exemplified in her *Notre-Dame de Paris.*

In 1952 Jones published a reproduction of *Notre-Dame de Paris* in an ambitious artist's book entitled *Loïs Mailou Jones: Peintures 1937–1951.* After its publication, Jones incorporated the book into her classroom lectures at Howard University as a required text for her course. Driskell, who in 1952 was among Jones's many aspiring art students, fondly recalls this text as his first African American art book purchase. Although Jones was not the only art professor at Howard to impress upon students the importance of art acquisition, her dedication to the creation and promotion of African American art and aesthetics undoubtedly had a lasting influence upon the young David Driskell. Thus, it seems only fitting that as Driskell matured as a patron of the arts, he would acquire Jones's original painting of *Notre-Dame de Paris* for his own collection. T. F.

Jacob Lawrence was only twenty-one years old when he completed the monumental forty-one panel *Toussaint L'Ouverture* series in 1938. This series, based upon Toussaint L'Ouverture's epic struggle to emancipate Haiti from the tyranny of the Spanish and the French in the late eighteenth and early nineteenth centuries, set the standard for Lawrence's lifelong dedication to the visual description of black life and history within a narrative context.

Inspired by Harlem's unique social environment, which promoted an awareness of black history generally omitted from mainstream textbooks, Lawrence began to pursue what would become a lifelong inquiry into, and a visual revelation of, the historic accomplishments of people of African descent. After significant research, Lawrence settled on what would be his first monumental series documenting black history: the establishment of the first black Western republic through the heroic efforts of military leader Toussaint L'Ouverture.

Lawrence painted forty-one small tempera-on-white-paper works that chronologically documented the history of the Haitian revolution from Columbus's discovery of the island on December 6, 1492, through Toussaint's victory over the French with the signing of the Declaration of Independence on January 1, 1804. Instead of traditional titles, Lawrence utilized descriptive quotations to function as a verbal description and to accentuate the narrative theme of the series. For instance, *General Toussaint L'Ouverture,* number twenty in the series, is labeled "statesman and military genius, esteemed by the Spaniards, feared by the English, dreaded by the French, hated by the planters, and revered by the blacks."

In 1938 the *Toussaint L'Ouverture* series premiered during Lawrence's first solo exhibition outside of Harlem at the De Porres Interracial Council headquarters. Since its premier, the series has been exhibited at the Baltimore Museum and at the 1940 Chicago Negro Exposition, and was reproduced in the March 1939 issue of *Survey Graphic.* The series is currently located in the Amistad Research Center's Aaron Douglas Collection, New Orleans.

Lawrence's original intention in creating the *Toussaint L'Ouverture* series was to provide African Americans with a sense of pride, accomplishment, and hope during an era when many blacks were experiencing extreme political, economic, and racial difficulties. In 1986, the Spradling Ames Corporation and the Amistad Research Center, in conjunction with Lawrence and silk-screen artist Lou Stovall, decided to publish the series in a silk-screen edition. *General Toussaint L'Ouverture* was the first painting to be issued within a silk-screen edition and has been described by Driskell as "perhaps Jacob Lawrence's most heroic painting and in the silk-screen edition maybe his most decorative."   T. F.

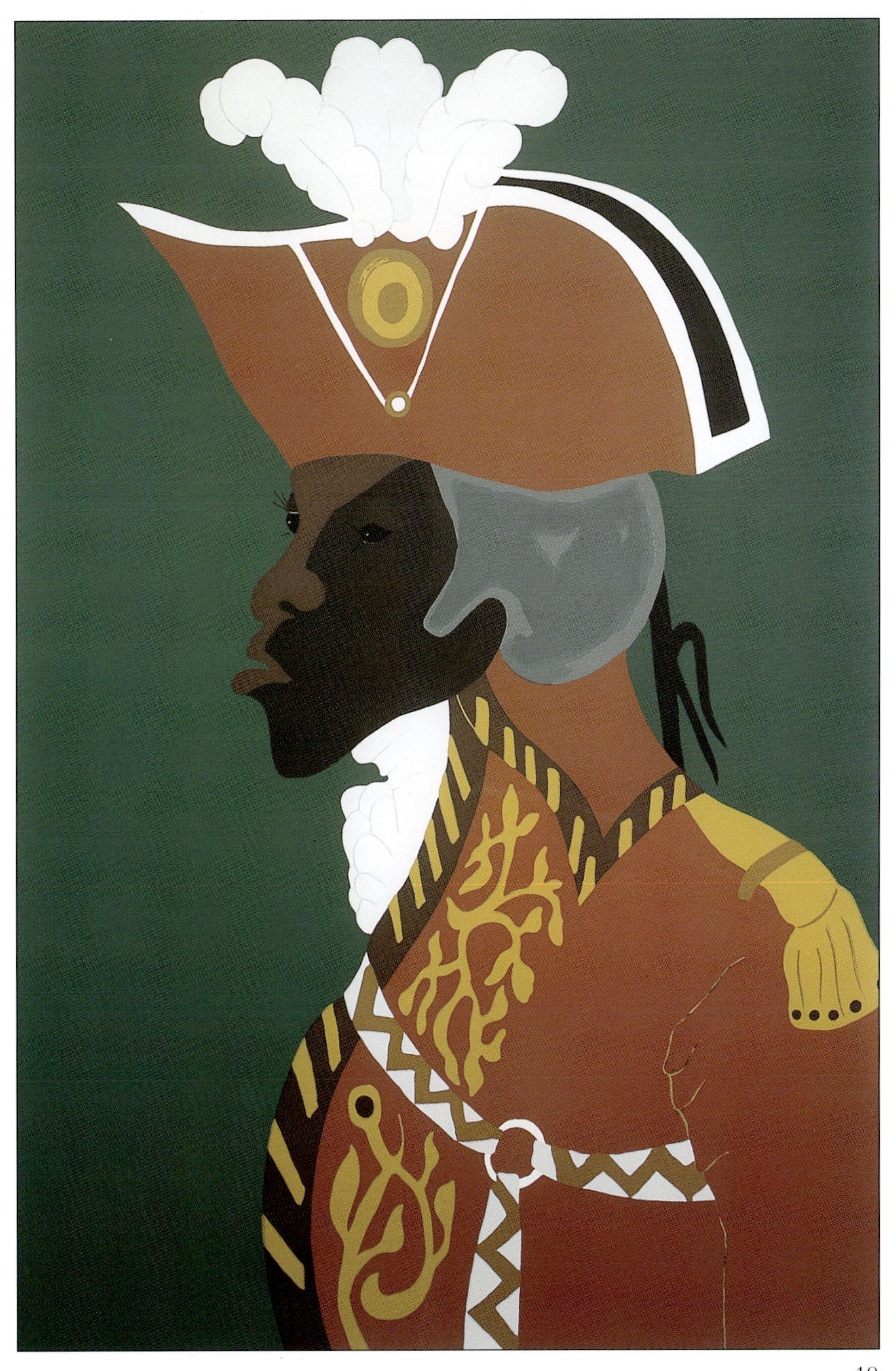

19.

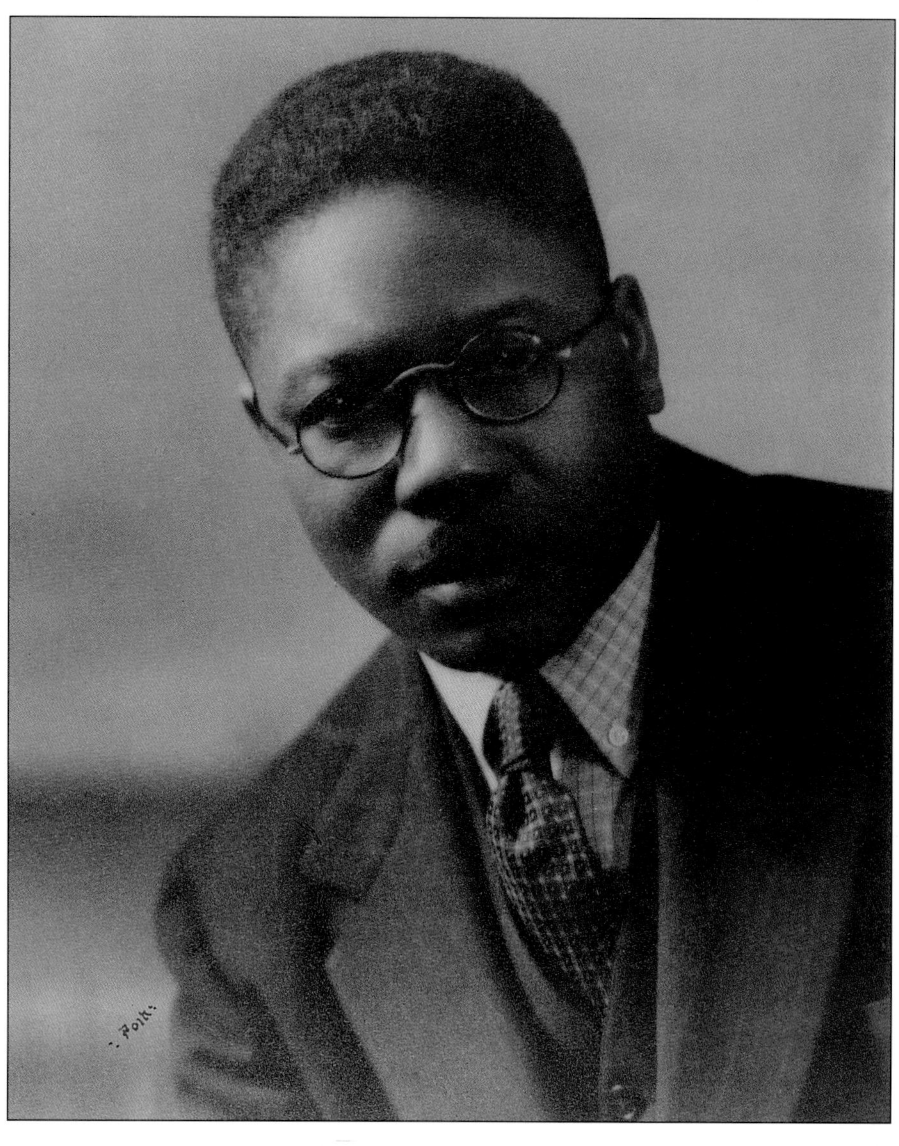

P. H. POLK

20.

Portrait of Aaron Douglas,
c. 1933

Black-and-white photograph

10" x 8"

Portrait photographer P. H. Polk firmly believed in the importance of allowing the personalities of his sitters to shine through in his work. Polk began his career as a student at Tuskegee Institute, Alabama, where he studied with black photographer C. M. Battey. Because his race barred his admittance to white photography schools, in 1922—two years after completing his study at Tuskegee—he continued his artistic education through a correspondence course.

Polk did not allow America's racial barriers to deter him from his desire to become a first-rate photographer. He recalled one of the lessons he gained from the course, which he continued to use throughout his career, stating that, "if you look at my pictures, you'll see most of them are from the shadow side. My correspondence course said you can get better details from the shadow side. It helps you leave people near as you can to who they are."

Polk's intimate *Portrait of Aaron Douglas* exemplifies his use of the shadow side technique. During the thirties, when the photograph was taken, Douglas was considered by such notables as Alain Locke and W. E. B. Du Bois to be the leading black artist in the United States. Although Polk, Tuskegee's official photographer, was often called upon to photograph important personalities, his images generally de-emphasized the celebrity status of his sitters in favor of capturing what he described in 1979 as "the picture that I felt within myself." Thus, Polk's *Portrait of Aaron Douglas* does not focus on Douglas's notoriety as the leading Harlem Renaissance artist; instead it seems to celebrate the quiet demeanor, dignified carriage, soft-spoken intelligence of the artist as a man.   T. F.

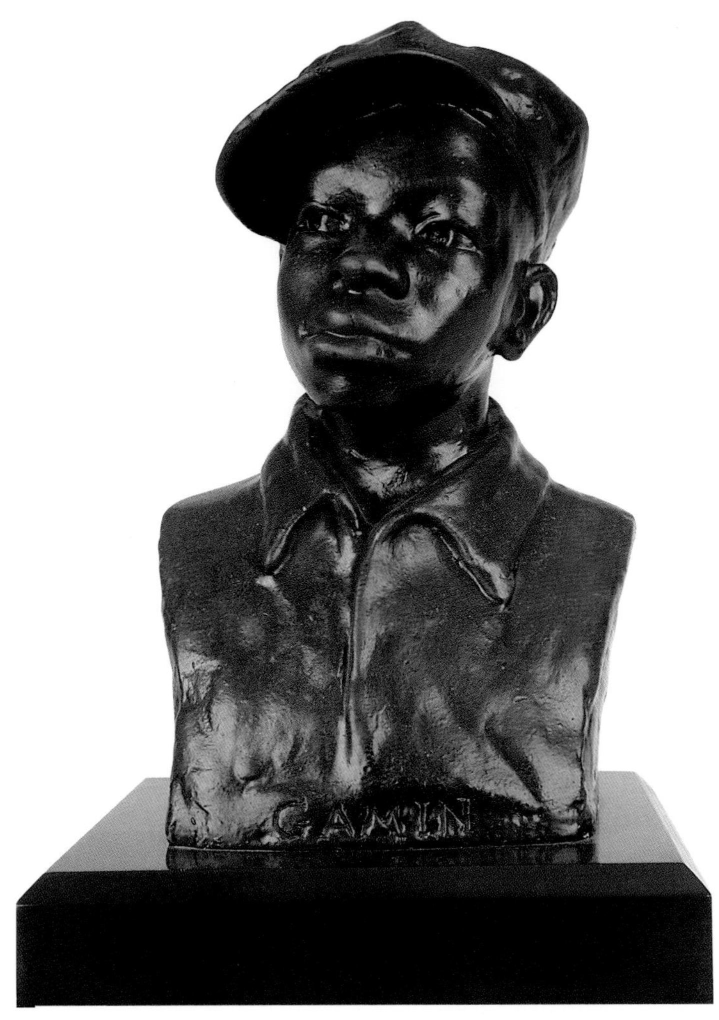

AUGUSTA SAVAGE

21.

Gamin, 1929

Bronze

9" x 5.5" x 3.5"

Sculpted in plaster over a weekend, Augusta Savage's bust of a young, attractive, street–smart young man, *Gamin,* is widely considered her best-known and most successful sculpture. Although Juanita Holland has discovered that the identity of *Gamin* is actually that of Savage's young nephew, Ellis Ford, the image of the savvy youth was immediately related by her New York audience to the images of thousands of other similar young men who roamed the streets of Harlem.

In fact, *Gamin* was so well received in New York that both the Urban League's Eugene Kinckle Jones and real estate operator John E. Nail agreed to assist in raising funds for Savage to study abroad. After *Gamin's* debut, Savage received two successive fellowships from the Rosenwald Fund and money for travel expenses, raised by members of the African American community in Harlem and Greenwich Village and by teachers at Florida A&M University. In 1929 Savage used these funds to travel to Paris and enroll in the Académie de la Grande Chaumière, where she studied with portraitists Felix Benneteau-Desgrois and Charles Despiau.

Driskell's *Gamin* is a later bronze casting of the original plaster sculpture.   T. F.

22.

Roberts and Johnson, 1932

(also known as
Looking Backward)

Black-and-white photograph
10" x 8"

23.

Barefoot Prophet, 1929

Black-and-white photograph
10" x 8"

24.

Undeclared War, 1929

(also known as
Just Before the Battle)

Black-and-white photograph
10" x 8"

25.

Couple in Raccoon Coats, 1932

Black-and-white photograph
8" x 10"

During James VanDerZee's twenty-year tenure as Harlem's premier photographer, he witnessed many important social and political events that had great impact on the community, one of which was the First World War. The advent of World War I saw African Americans called to service in record numbers. VanDerZee's portraits of war heroes and soldiers serve to document the Harlemites' participation in this global crisis. *Roberts and Johnson* is the second double portrait VanDerZee shot of Needham Roberts and Henry Johnson, two decorated war heroes. VanDerZee first photographed them in 1920, after their triumphant return to Harlem from Europe as part of the 369th Infantry Regiment, also known as the Harlem Hellfighters. Depicted wearing their medals in a signature VanDerZee interior, they are the embodiment of pride and patriotism. VanDerZee's treatment of blacks who participated in World War I pays tribute to a group of patriots whose service went unrecognized for decades. This photo is an example of how VanDerZee used photomontage to add a sentimental or dramatic dimension to the image, a technique he frequently employed. Although the photograph was dated 1916, this image clearly postdates the 1920 photo of the young soldiers just back from the war and, according to Deborah Willis-Braithwaite, was probably made in 1932, when VanDerZee photographed Needham Roberts alone.

Among the many aspects of Harlem life that VanDerZee captured on film, he is perhaps most noted for his studio portraits. Individuals from all walks of life came to VanDerZee's studio to be photographed by the most popular image-maker in Harlem. VanDerZee's use of props, garments, and elaborate backdrops enabled him to construct an atmosphere around the sitter that could enhance the image of the individual or create an entirely new identity. *Barefoot Prophet* of 1929 is a photograph of Elder Clayhorn Martin, also known as Prophet Martin and the Barefoot Prophet, an eccentric street preacher. VanDerZee constructs a serious image of this well-known Harlem character by depicting him contemplating the Bible and surrounded by the traditional religious symbols of the crucifix and the Virgin Mary. However, his unconventional style is revealed by the inclusion of a tambourine under his chair and his notorious bare feet.

Wives waiting up for their husbands was the theme of the calendar for which VanDerZee's 1929 photograph *Undeclared War* was planned. Here VanDerZee has constructed a photographic vignette of a woman waiting by the door for her tardy husband. She is armed for the battle with a rolling pin, milk bottles, and other domestic objects. VanDerZee injects humor into this light-hearted depiction of the "undeclared war" of the sexes.

When James VanDerZee's photos were rediscovered in 1969, the history, excitement, and glamour of the Harlem of the 1920s dazzled the American public. VanDerZee's images of Harlemites gave faces to the "New Negroes" of the growing black urban middle class. *Couple in Raccoon Coats* has become the quintessential image of Jazz Age Harlem. The fur-shrouded black couple in front of a shiny Cadillac are the embodiments of style, prosperity, and class. The faces and places that populate VanDerZee's body of work constitute a virtual lexicon of New Negro identity as it developed during the Harlem Renaissance.   A. L. C.

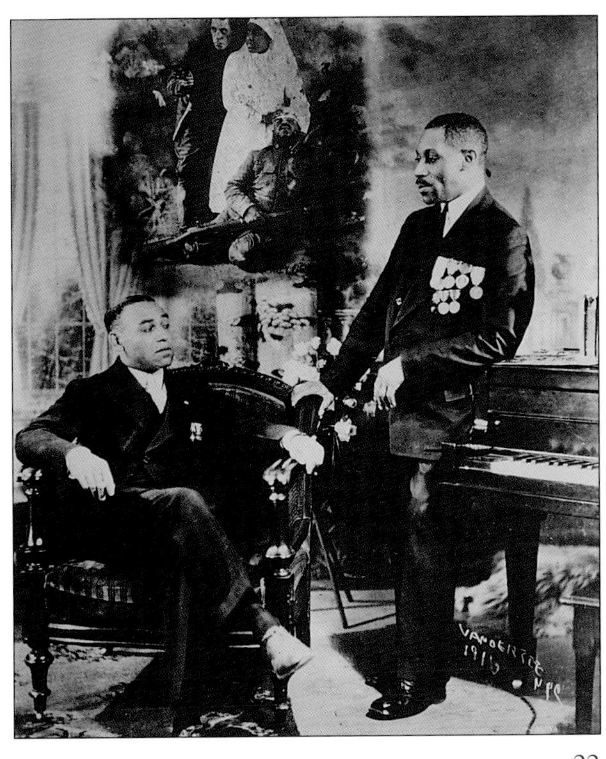

22.

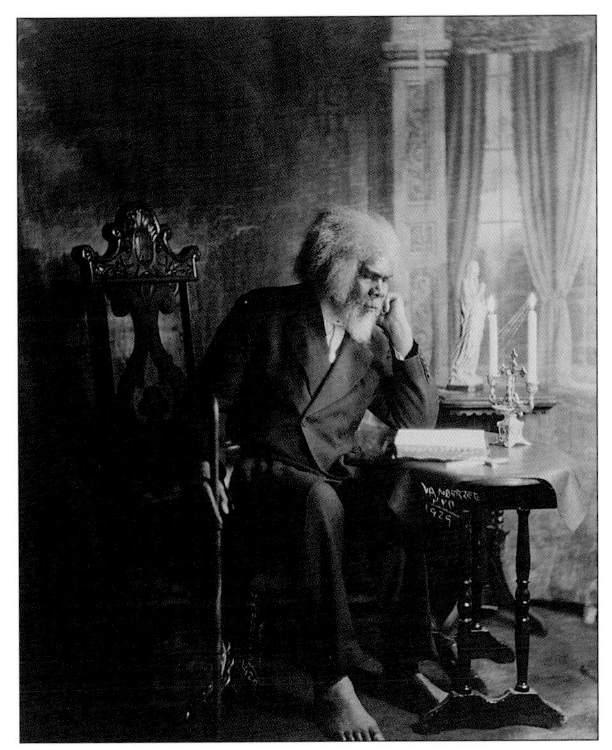

23.

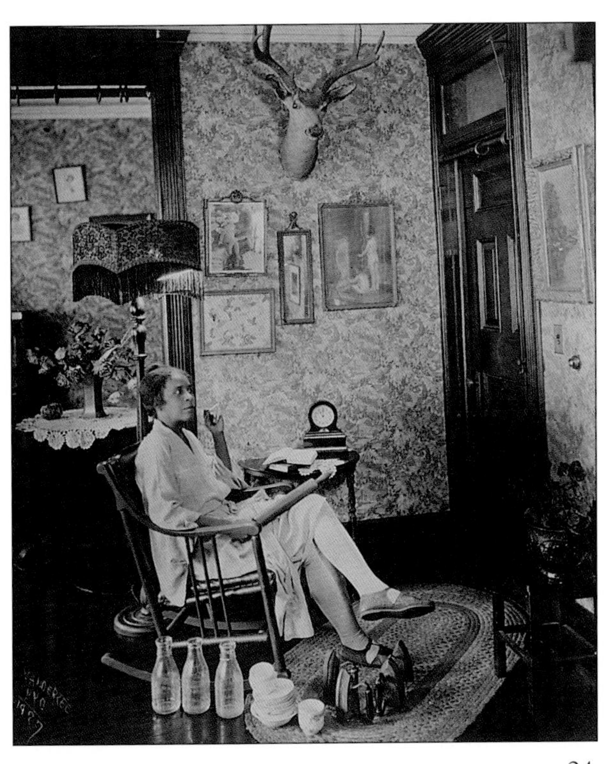

24.

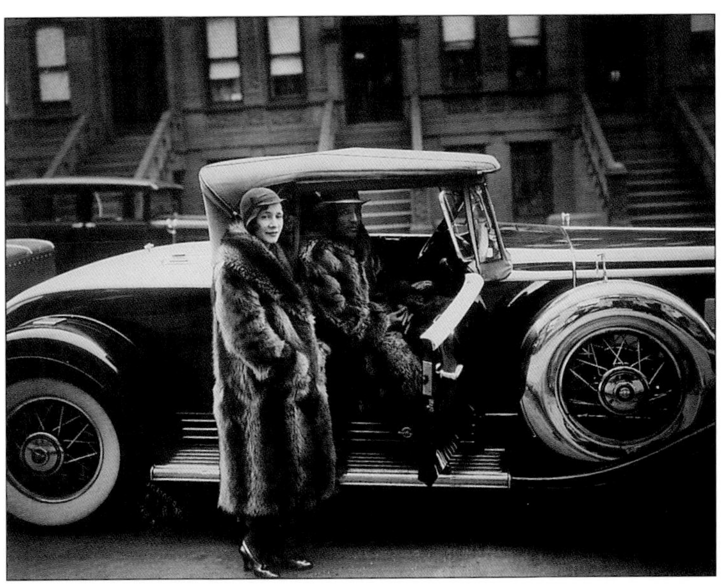

25.

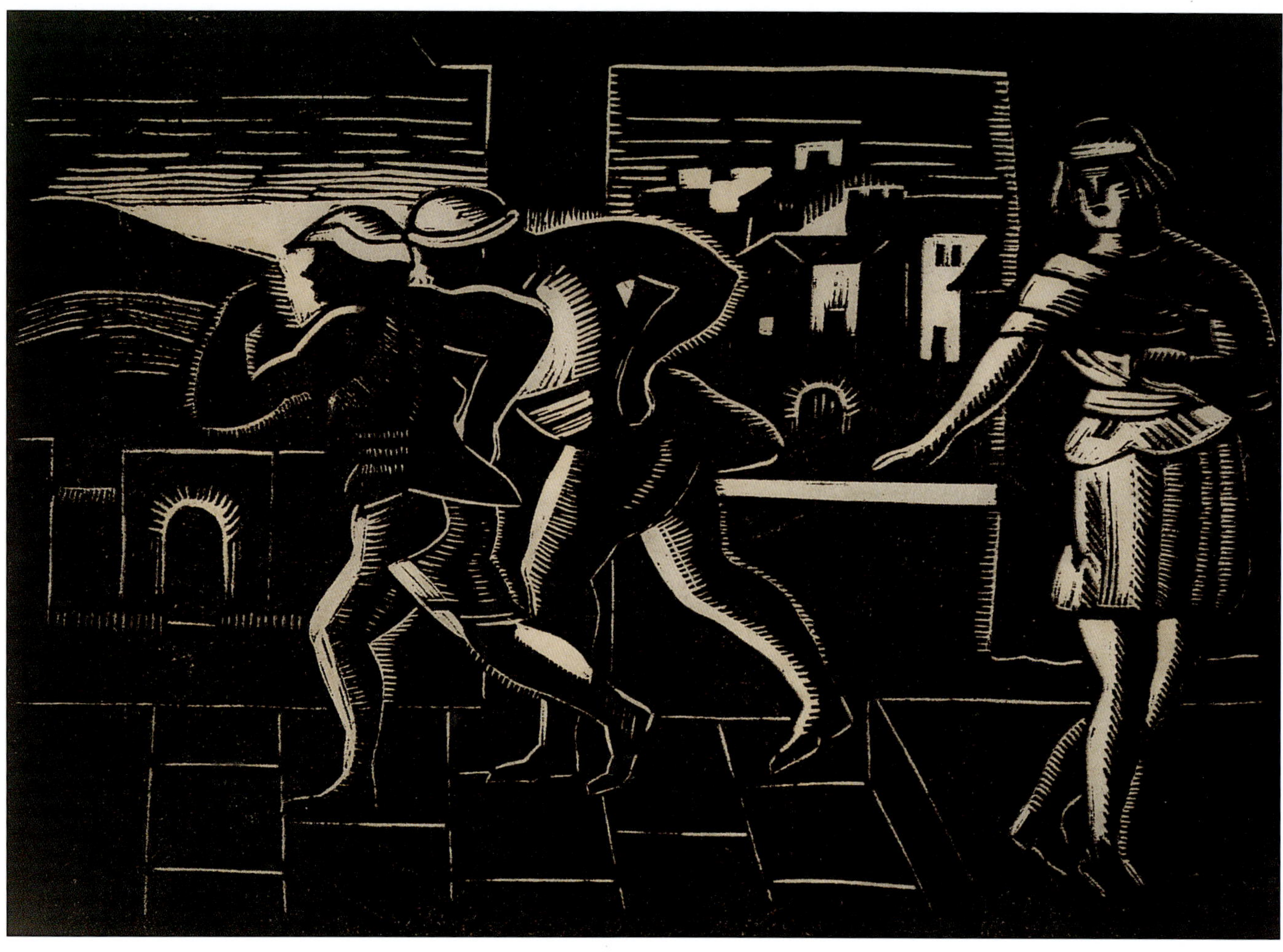

Touted as the "dean of the Negro printmakers" by James A. Porter in 1943, James Lesesne Wells was among the young artists of the period whose work addressed the black experience in America and helped to shape the developing African American aesthetic tradition. Son of a Baptist minister, Wells became known for his treatment of Biblical themes. *Escape of the Spies from Canaan* represents the Old Testament story from the Book of Numbers that recounts the plight of the Israelites as they approach Canaan, the land promised them by God. Wells's rendition illustrates the drama of the moment when the spies, sent by God to search out Canaan, flee the walled city that they find inhabited by man-eating giants. The racial designations, with the fleeing spies as black and the giant as white, evoke the striking parallel between this biblical story and the migration of southern blacks to the urban North in the early twentieth century. Regarding the potential opportunity that the north represented for southern blacks, it was often referred to as the Promised Land. The appropriation of biblical imagery to characterize the plight of African Americans has had a long tradition in African American culture.

Sisters is typical of James Wells's early linoleum-cut illustrations, many of which he created for African American journals such as *The Crisis* and *Opportunity,* which were the main arteries of the New Negro intellectual movement. Wells's 1929 *Sisters* is among the many works of that era that he indicated were inspired by African and Egyptian art. *Sisters* depicts the heads of two virtually identical "modern" black women in contrasting fashionable hats against the backdrop of a rhythmic circular motif. This combination of black subject matter and exoticized Art Deco style reflects the essence of "New Negro" as a participant in modern culture on his/her own terms and captures the flavor of that moment in history known as the Harlem Renaissance. A. L. C.

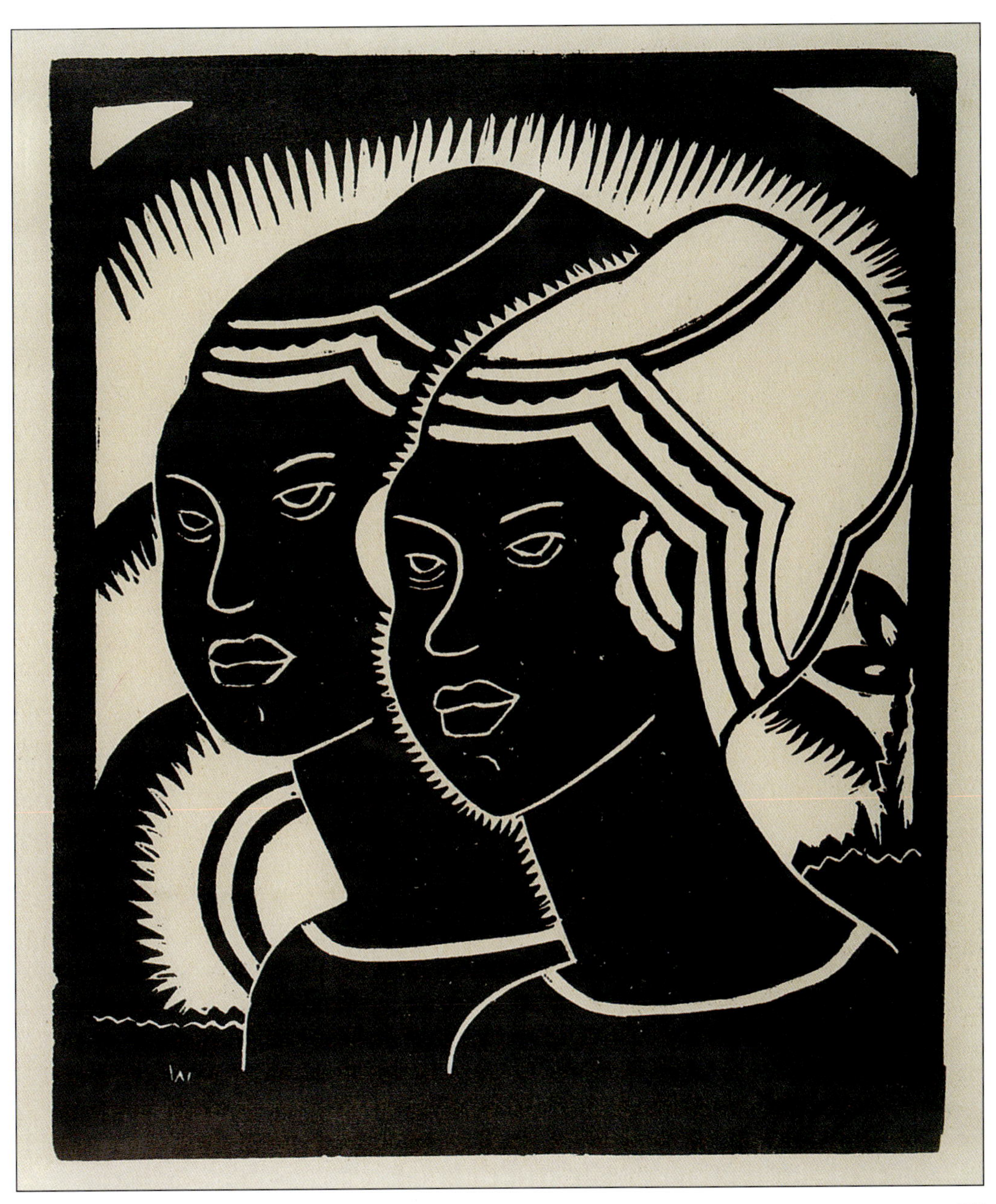

27.

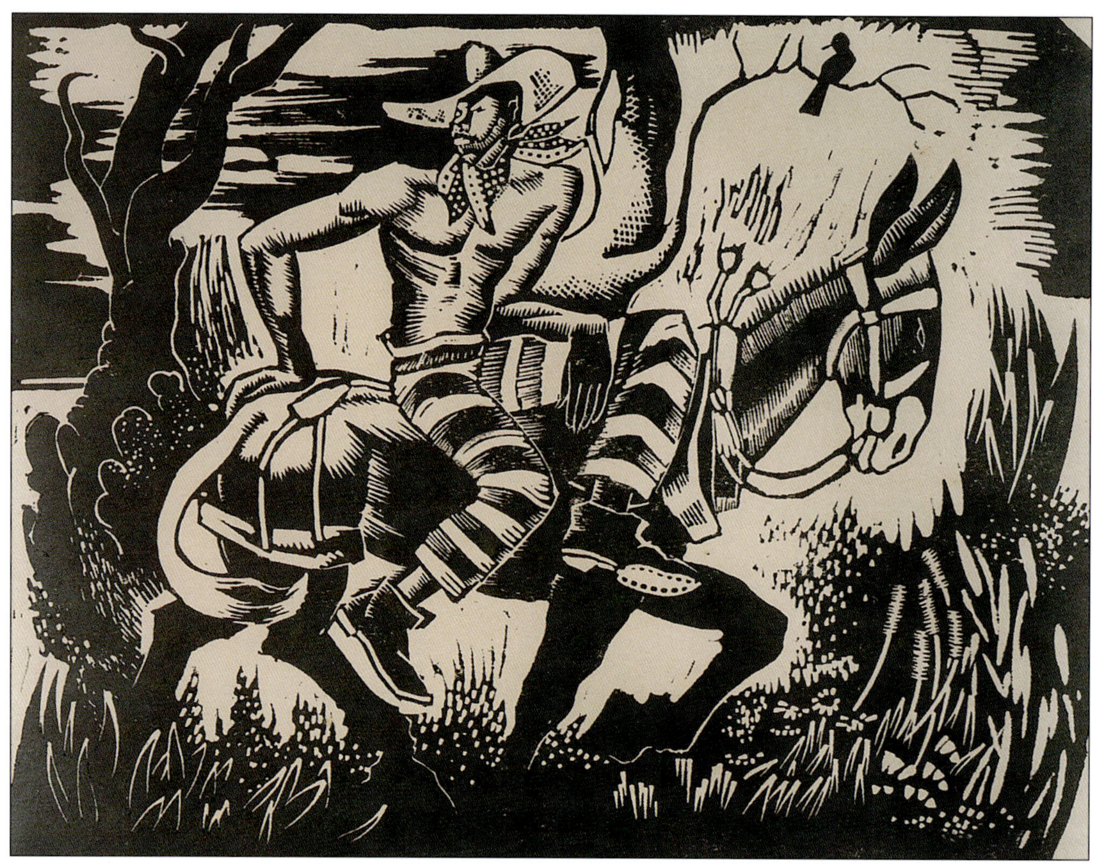

Upon his return to the United States in 1931, after four years of study in France, Hale Woodruff joined the staff of Atlanta University. As the first extensively trained African American artist to teach at a black southern university, Woodruff encountered a myriad of obstacles such as inadequate studio space (he taught in two basement rooms of Spelman College) and a meager selection of art resources. Additionally, Woodruff felt ambivalent about the relevance of teaching Cubist technique and modernist theory—which he had studied intensely in Paris—to his eager yet artistically inexperienced students.

These unique circumstances, combined with the devastating impact of the Great Depression and the shift in American art from traditionalism to regionalism, lead Woodruff to drastically alter his former Cézanne-like palette into his own version of American regionalism. In an effort to translate this latest trend in American art into a format that he perceived as relevant to his pupils, Woodruff organized his students into a "Painter's Guild." In a 1942 interview for *Time,* Woodruff explained that he created the guild so that his students could gain a sense of identity and purpose through the expression of the "South as a field, as a territory: its peculiar rundown landscapes, its social and economic problems, and Negro People…"

In addition to teaching, Woodruff also encouraged his students by example. According to artist Romare Bearden and historical journalist Harry Henderson, Woodruff utilized one of his two allotted rooms at Spelman College as both an office and a studio, and "urged his students to come at any hour, letting them see that he was constantly working…" During his tenure at Atlanta University, Woodruff created an assortment of superbly designed woodcut prints, such as his 1939 work entitled *Trusty on a Mule.* The work is Woodruff's characterization of the trustworthy and dependable convict, popularly referred to as "trusty," who is often granted special privileges during his incarceration.   T. F.

III. THE BLACK ACADEMY:
TEACHERS, MENTORS, AND
INSTITUTIONAL PATRONAGE

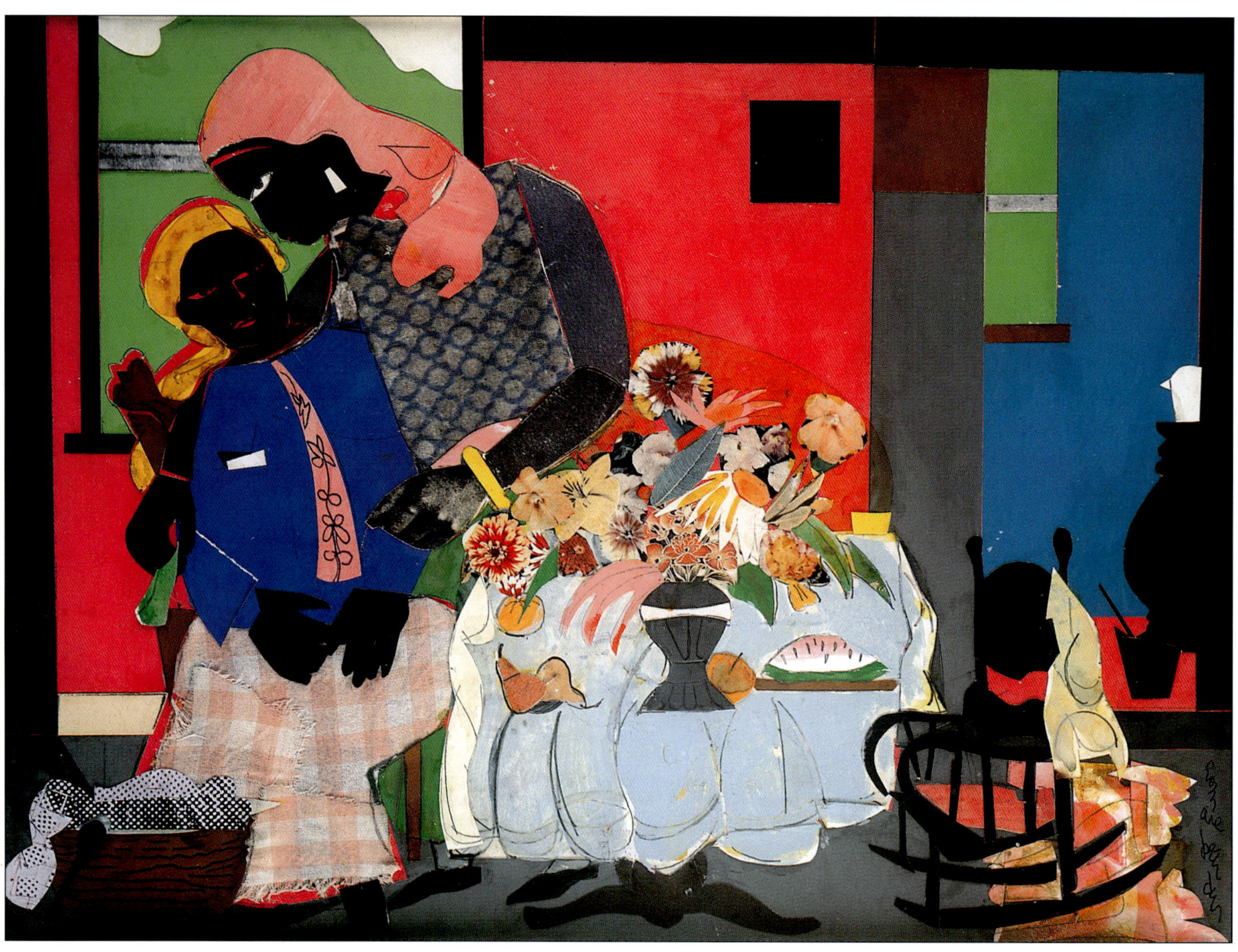

ROMARE BEARDEN

29.

Morning, 1975

Collage on paper

13.5" x 17.5"

© Romare Bearden Foundation
Licensed by VAGA, New York, NY

Romare Bearden is considered America's premier collagist, and, in terms of mainstream recognition, the most noted African American artist of the twentieth century. Bearden's long and distinguished career, beginning in the early 1940s, led him from social realism through semi-abstraction to non-representation. When he turned to collage as his primary medium in 1963, he found a language that was innovative and that eloquently served his desire to represent black American culture. *Morning* demonstrates Bearden's interest in black genre and is a testament not only to his own memory of family but to the collective memory of African American family life. The rocking chair and potbellied stove lend an air of "Americana" and squarely locate the black family within the realm of traditional domesticity.   A. L. C.

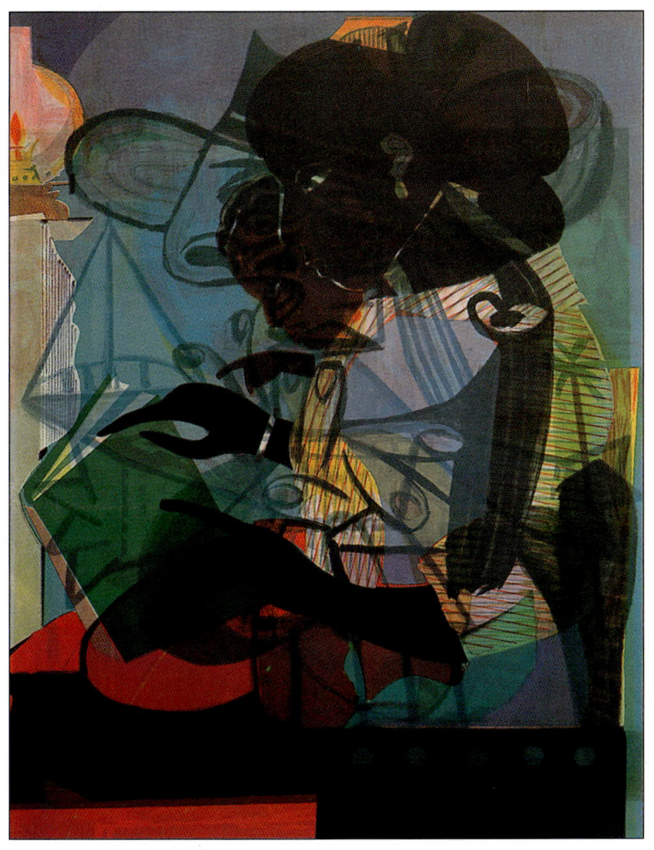

30.

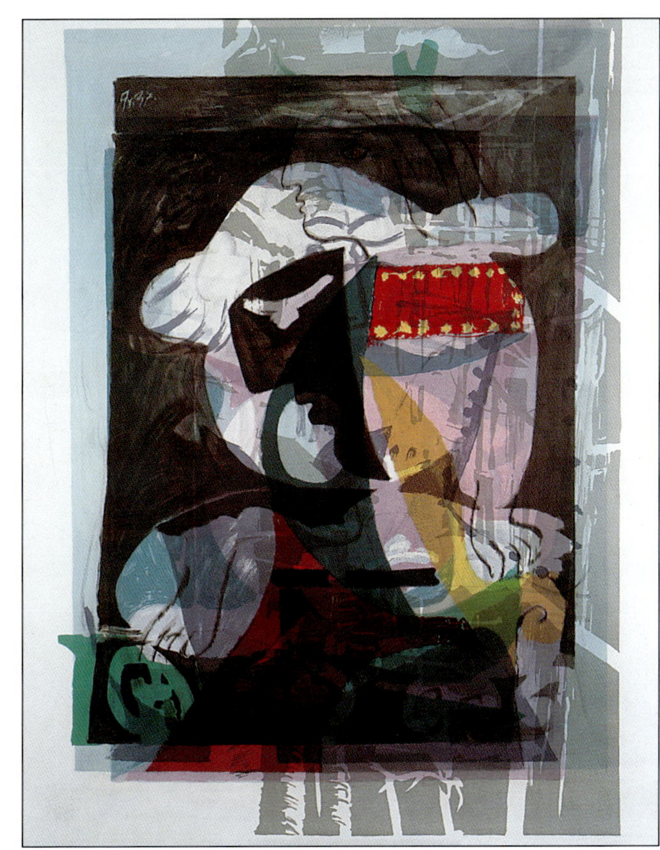

31.

ROMARE BEARDEN

30.

Woman and Child Reading, 1977

Lithograph

25.5" x 18.5"

© Romare Bearden Foundation
Licensed by VAGA, New York, NY

31.

Untitled (Verso), 1977

Lithograph

25.5" x 18"

© Romare Bearden Foundation
Licensed by VAGA, New York, NY

The notion of a black academic tradition in the arts must encompass not only the institutional structures but include the informal alliances and community groups that lent much-needed support to artists who were shut out of the traditional academic world. Romare Bearden played a large role in the nontraditional education of black artists. As early as the 1930s, Bearden was involved in "306 Group," an informal association of black artists in Harlem. It was through this organization that Bearden had his first one-man show. He went on to form alliances with mainstream contemporary galleries in New York but maintained his involvement with black artists. In 1963 Bearden was instrumental in forming the Spiral group, composed of black artists who sought to make a contribution to the civil rights movement. He also served for many years as the art director of the Harlem Cultural Council. Bearden's support of the black artist was manifest in the form of scholarship as well. An advocate of the importance of the history of art, Bearden wrote several books on African American art, including *A History of African-American Artists,* published posthumously in 1993.

Given to David Driskell by the artist in 1983, the lithographs *Woman and Child Reading* and *Untitled* are unusual in that they are printed on both sides of the same paper. The multi-layering of colors and shapes results in the collage-like treatment of form that is his signature style.   A. L. C.

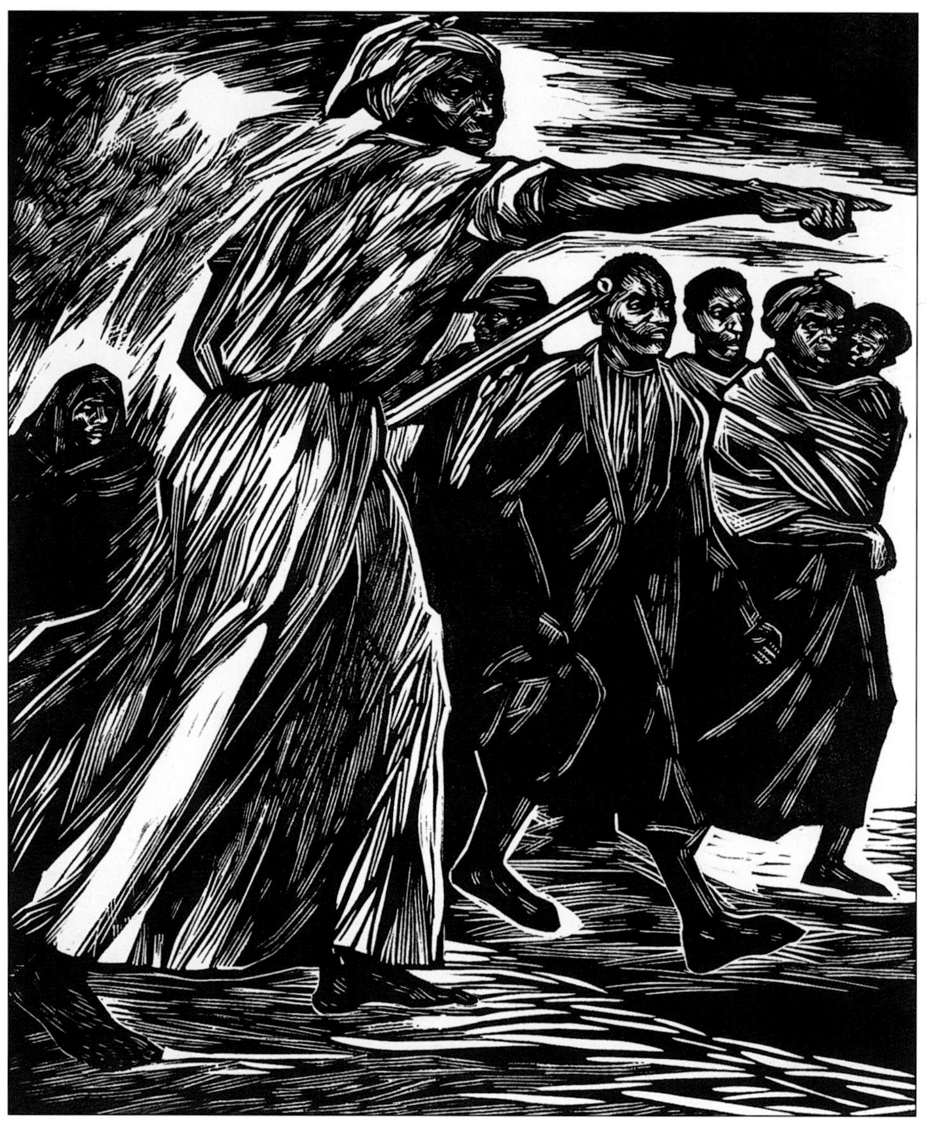

As an artist/educator, Elizabeth Catlett was a highly influential teacher who was herself a beneficiary of the black academy. As a student at Howard University in the early 1930s, Catlett was influenced by Loïs Mailou Jones, James V. Herring, and James A. Porter, three of the founders of the black academic tradition in the arts. Catlett went on to hold teaching positions at Dillard University, in New Orleans; Hampton Institute, in Virginia; and the George Washington Carver School, in Harlem. As a member of the Taller de Gráfica Popular in Mexico City, Catlett worked collectively with other artists in developing the art of the socially relevant print. By 1956, having established herself as an artist and educator, Elizabeth Catlett became the first female professor to head the sculpture department at the National Autonomous University of Mexico.

Elizabeth Catlett portrayed Harriet Tubman in print three times between 1946 and 1975. A monumental character in the history of black women in America, Tubman played a central role in the fight against slavery and is an icon of strength and leadership. Catlett's 1975 print *Harriet* portrays a dynamic Tubman in the act of directing a group of fleeing slaves toward freedom and demonstrates Catlett's commitment to the struggles of black women.   A. L. C.

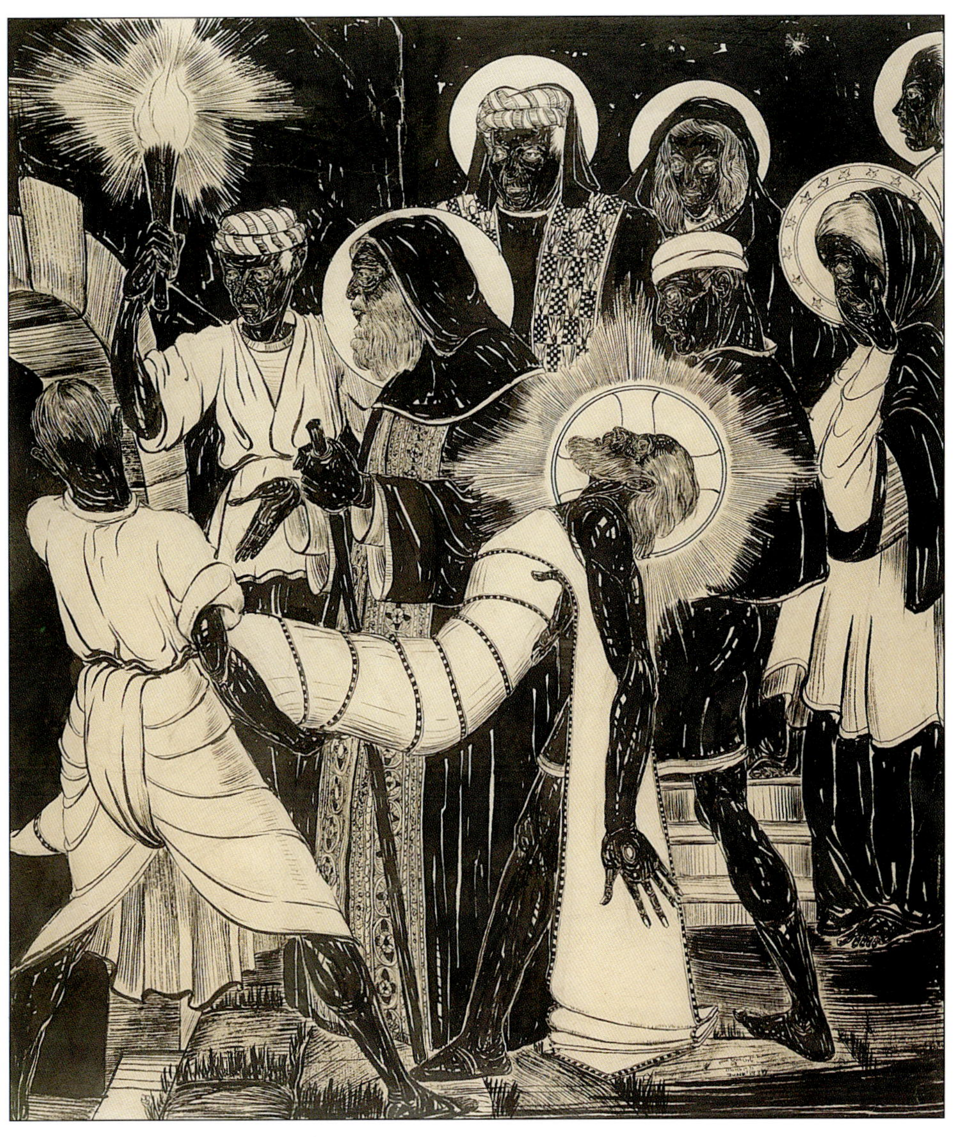

ALLAN ROHAN
CRITE

33.

*Last Station: Suggestion for
the Station of the Cross,* 1935

Ink on paper

18" x 15"

"For a long time, I felt as far as the Church was concerned, that there was too much the impression of a mostly European institution, practically to the exclusion of anything else," wrote Boston artist Allan Crite in his *An Autobiographical Sketch.* His *Last Station* is a typical example of the type of liturgical art he produced in the 1930s. During this time period, he was acutely sensitive to stereotypes of African Americans, and like many middle-class African Americans, felt unsure about the merits of jazz and "church revivalist" imagery. As a result, Crite adopted a "high" Episcopalian or Catholic visual vocabulary from the liturgical movement of which he was a part. In *Last Station,* by combining formal church "vocabulary," such as Christ's tripartite halo (which refers to the Trinity) with solemn black figures, Crite conveys the dignity and deep spirituality that he insisted African Americans possessed.

Crite has always used his art to teach, whether for religious or historical reasons. Unlike its Harlem counterpart, 1930s Boston possessed a small African American community with few black artists. Years later, Crite contributed to Boston's African American art scene by creating the Artists' Collective, a forum for emerging African American artists. Well known in the Boston community, he has lectured frequently and served as a mentor to many new artists, prompting him to joke that "I'm looked upon as the 'patriarch' of artists in this area, which means almost that if I say anything, it sounds like an ex cathedra statement…." His community involvement has extended to schools as well; in 1968, he initiated a project for schoolchildren on the cultural heritage of the United States.   J. S.

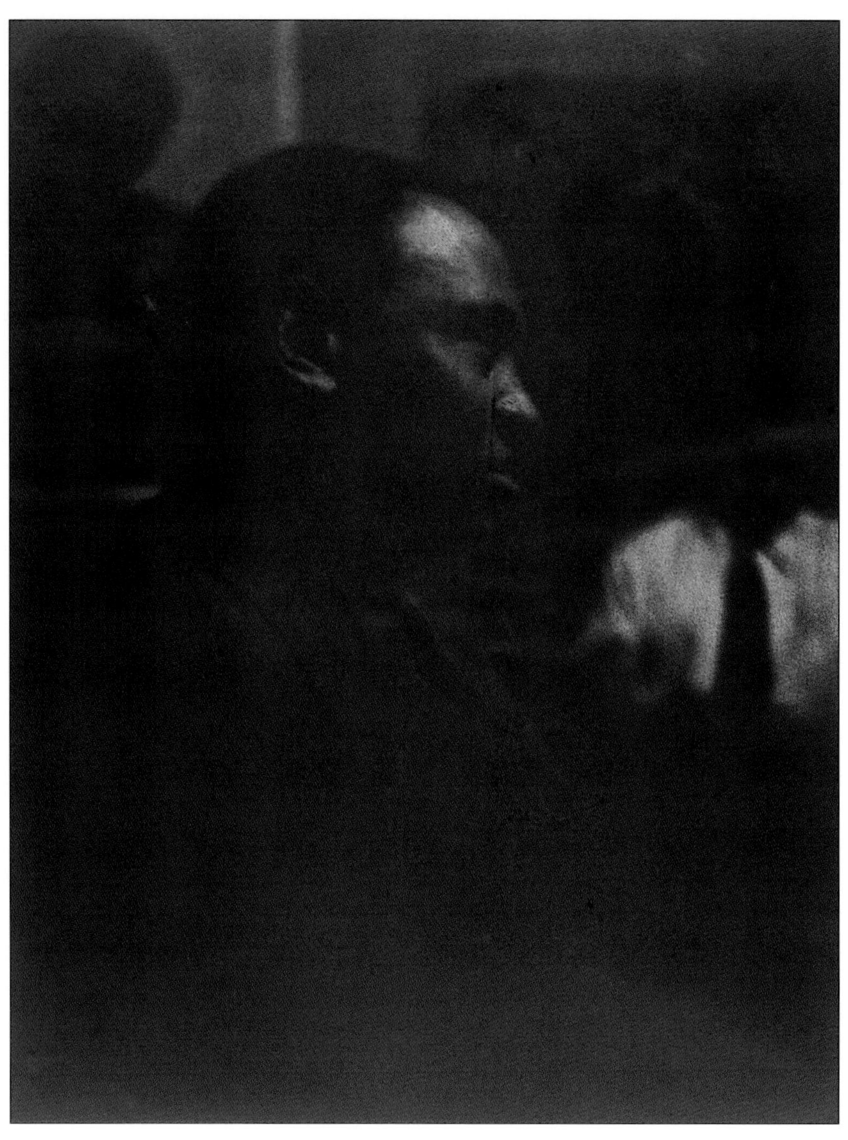

ROY DECARAVA

34.

Portrait of Paul Robeson, 1950

Black-and-white photograph

11" x 8"

Employing the dramatic properties of shadow and dark tonalities, elements that constitute his signature style, Roy DeCarava creates a moody portrayal of one of the most luminous figures of the Harlem Renaissance, Paul Robeson. DeCarava's melancholy Robeson in an austere interior is a far different characterization from that of the robust, almost mythical figure who was America's leading black actor of the 1920s and 1930s. This 1950 photograph of Robeson typifies DeCarava's expressionistic view of postwar Harlem. From Harlem notables to the man on the street, DeCarava's lens does more than document; it orchestrates an interplay of tone and form that results in an aestheticized journey through one of the most compelling strands of African American culture.   A. L. C.

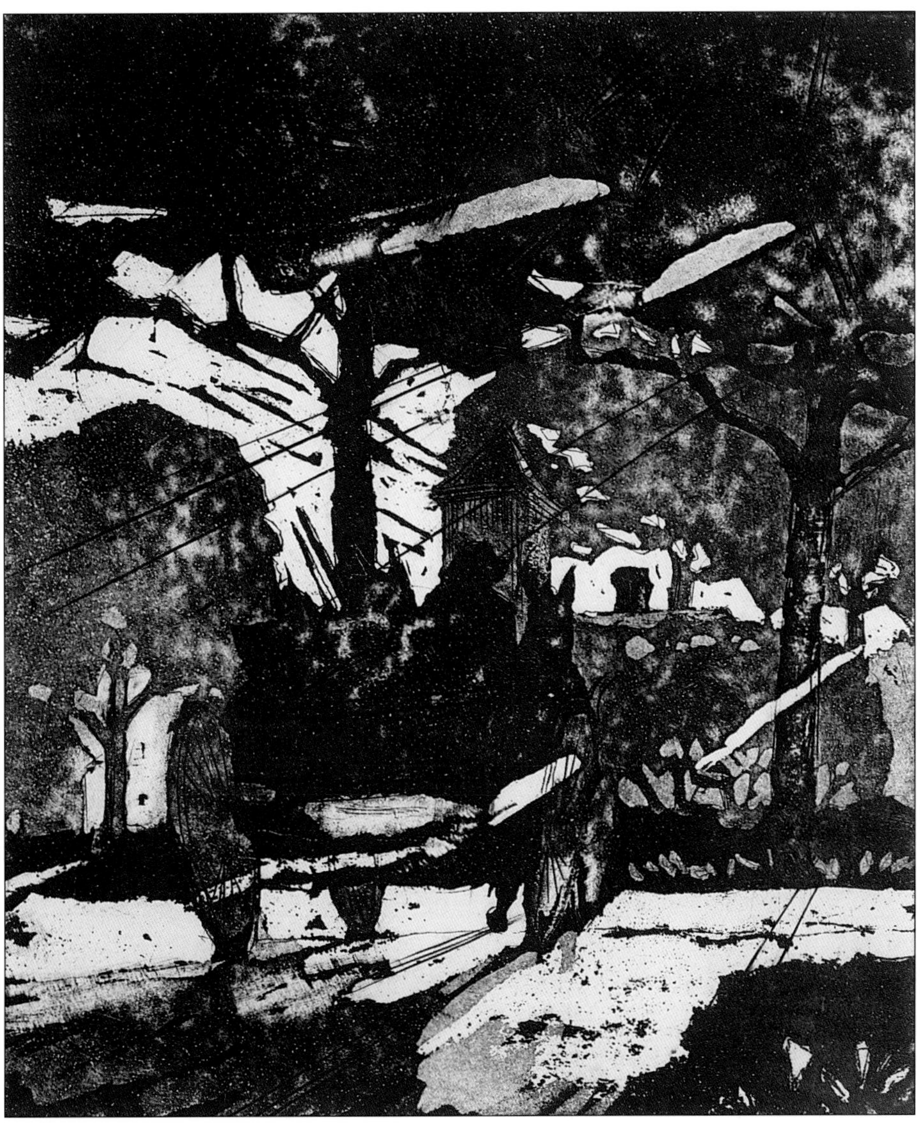

Like his 1956 watercolor *City Scape,* Aaron Douglas's etching *The Junk Man* differs in terms of both style and medium from the monochromatic, Art Deco- and Egyptian-inspired compositions that gained him international recognition during the period of the Harlem Renaissance. Although stylistically different from the compositions such as *Aspects of Negro Life,* 1934, many of the elements relating to the working-class ideology found in the majority of his Harlem Renaissance works are present in *The Junk Man* as well.

Douglas's Harlem Renaissance compositions focused on the lives and concerns of everyday African American men and women in America. He believed that depictions of the working class formed the essence of what he described as the "Negro thing"—an idea upon which the Harlem Renaissance was developed. With regard to his opinion on his depiction of the black working class, Douglas recalled, "Yes, we have higher, we have lower and so on, but here [the black working class] is the base of the thing. We all understood that. We all were only one jump ahead of this person that I was trying to set forth here."

The Junk Man is the dignified and sensitive portrayal of a serene and solitary moment in the life of a junk dealer. Like Douglas's stylized, geometric silhouettes, *The Junk Man* is an anonymous figure whose horse-drawn cart and worn hat serve as reminders of the humble surroundings that most African Americans were still living in or were in the process of emerging from.
T. F.

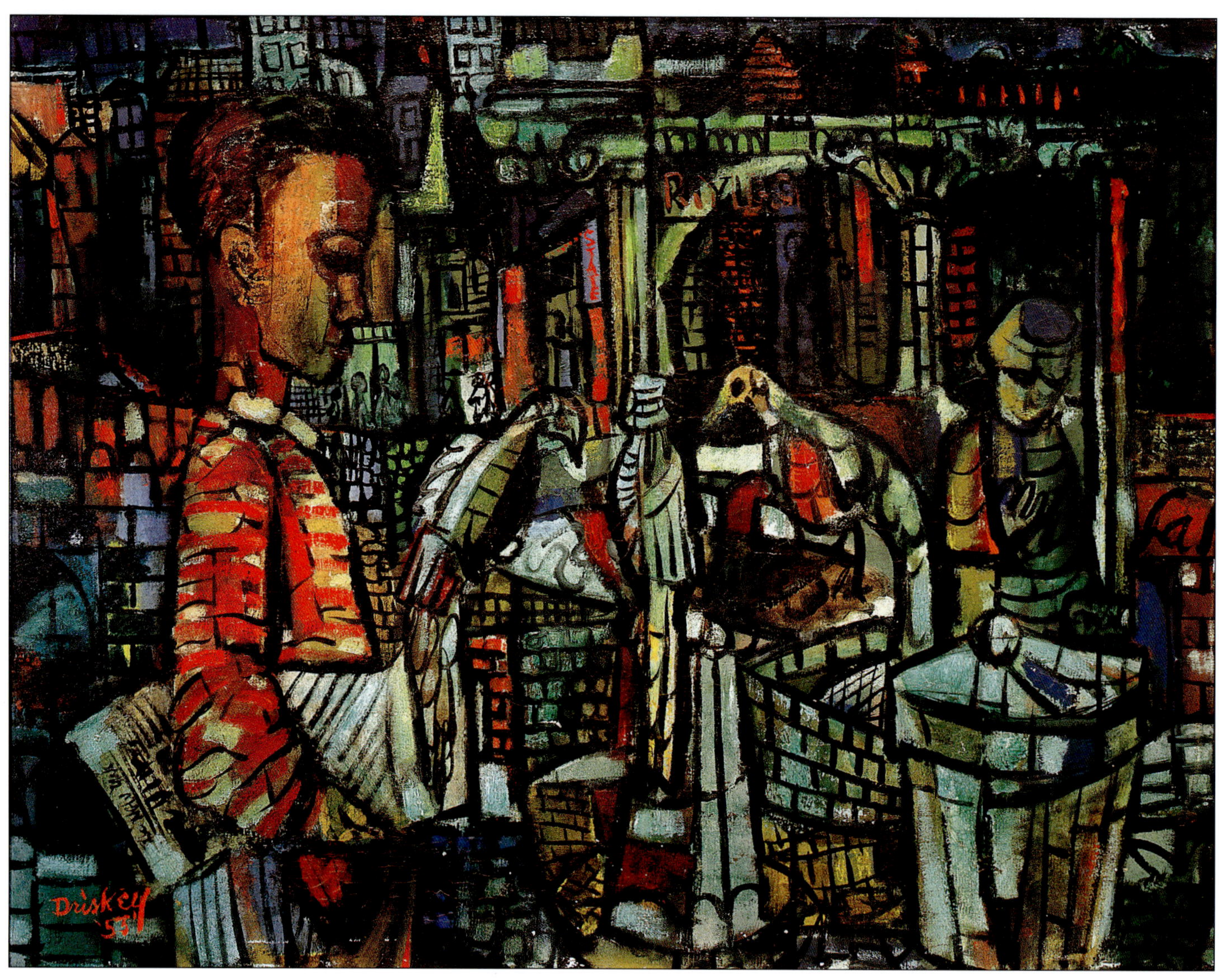

DAVID C. DRISKELL

36.

Boy with Birds, 1953

Oil on canvas

23.5" x 29.5"

As an artist/scholar and educator, David C. Driskell has mentored and served as a role model for young artists and art historians for more than forty years. As Driskell's students are fortunate to benefit from the compassionate leadership of a renowned artist and scholar, Driskell himself benefited from the support of mentors James A. Porter and James V. Herring, as well as Loïs Jones and Morris Louis at Howard University, and with much success carries on their legacy today.

After spending the summer of 1953 at Skowhegan studying under Social Realist artist Jack Levine, Driskell became interested in commenting on African American life and urban culture. When he returned to Howard University, he embarked on a series of social realist paintings entitled *City Quartet.* One of the four works from the series, *Boy with Birds* is a nocturnal urban scene in which the use of light and color reveal a sense of beauty in the otherwise tragic street life of children. The use of outlining and jewel tones found in *Boy with Birds* is the beginning of a design interest in stained glass that has recently culminated in sixty-five stained-glass windows designed by Driskell for the DeForest Chapel at Talladega College, Talladega, Alabama.   A. L. C.

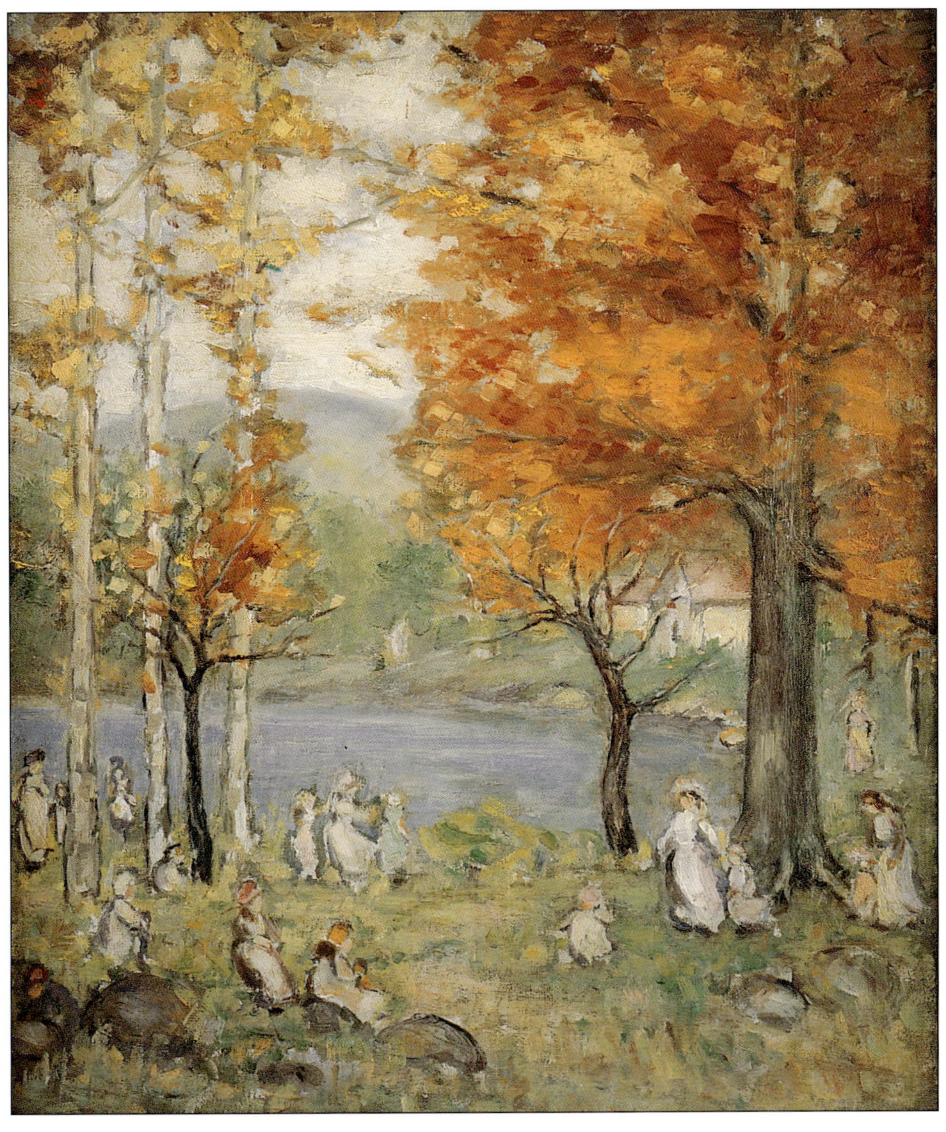

JAMES V. HERRING

37.

Campus Landscape, 1922

Oil on canvas

9.5" x 7.5"

Artist and educator James V. Herring was an extremely important figure in the development of both the academic and commercial aspects of African American art in the first part of the twentieth century. Herring founded the Howard University Art Department in 1922 and served as mentor to artists/art historians James A. Porter and David C. Driskell. In 1930, Herring organized the art gallery at Howard, the first in the United States to be directed and controlled by blacks. Along with Alonzo J. Aden, Herring opened the Barnett-Aden Gallery in 1943, one of the few institutions dedicated to the collection, preservation, and exhibition of African American art. The Barnett-Aden Collection went on to become one of the richest collections of African American art in the U. S.

    As an artist, Herring was trained in the academic tradition. *Campus Landscape* of 1922 is a view of students near the reservoir at the Howard University campus. Herring's hazy figures congregating in a vibrant fall landscape recall the French Impressionists of the latter part of the nineteenth century.   A. L. C.

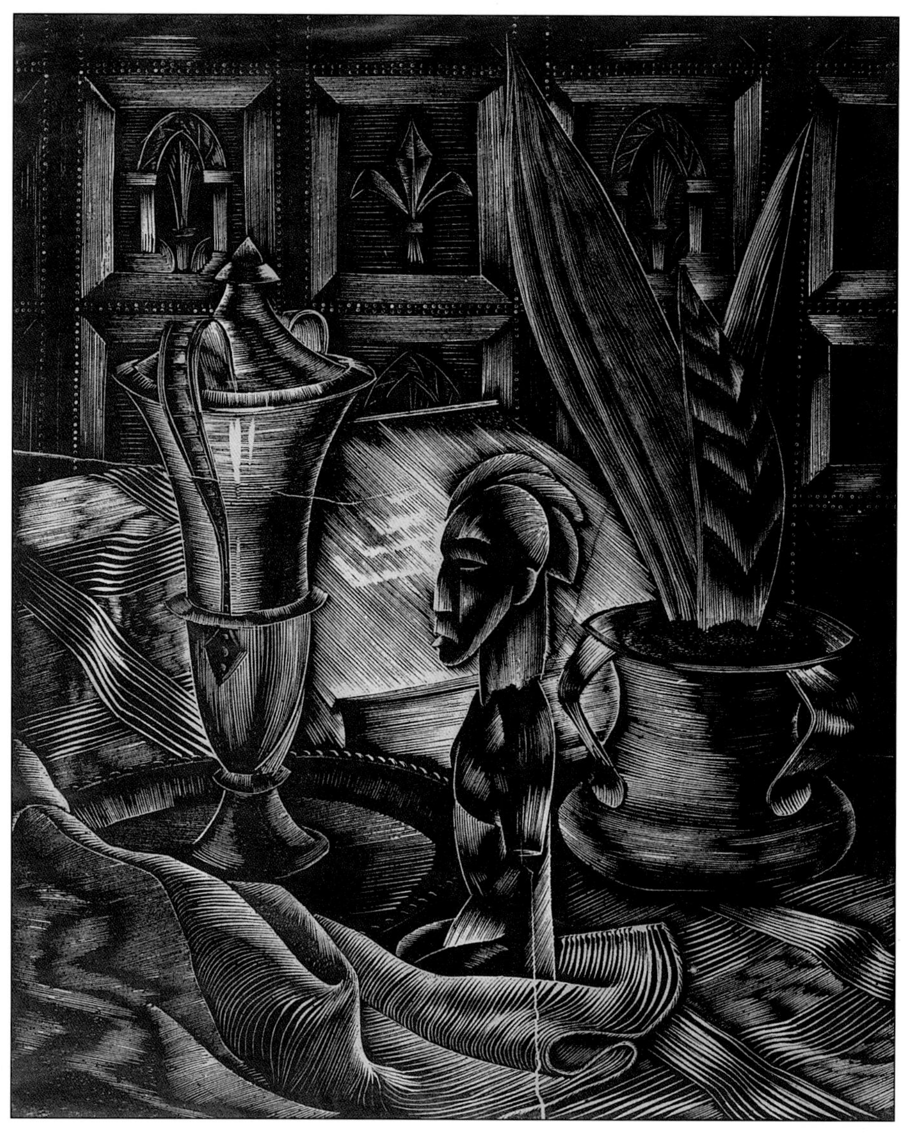

Wilmer Jennings was one of many African American artists who benefited from the printmaking programs offered by the WPA between 1935 and 1943. Through WPA programs established in urban community arts centers, black artists gained valuable technical and artistic experience as both teachers and students. Although there were relatively few black printmakers during this period, the WPA program in particular was responsible for bringing into the world of printmaking many more African Americans than had been involved heretofore, many of whom went on to become the most important African American artists of the twentieth century.

Wilmer Jennings, who worked for the WPA in both Atlanta and Providence in the mid-1930s, was most famous for his black-and-white wood engravings. *Still Life* uses the traditional format of objects assembled on a table top as a vehicle for exploration of form and ideas. The elongated, cylindrical forms of the urn, the African statue, and the plant contrast with the square modularity of the tablecloth, book, and background motif. Jennings's incorporation of African sculpture into a still life composition with non-African objects recalls the use of this device by Harlem Renaissance artists who used African motifs to assert a sense of pride in an African heritage while maintaining an identity as Americans.   A. L. C.

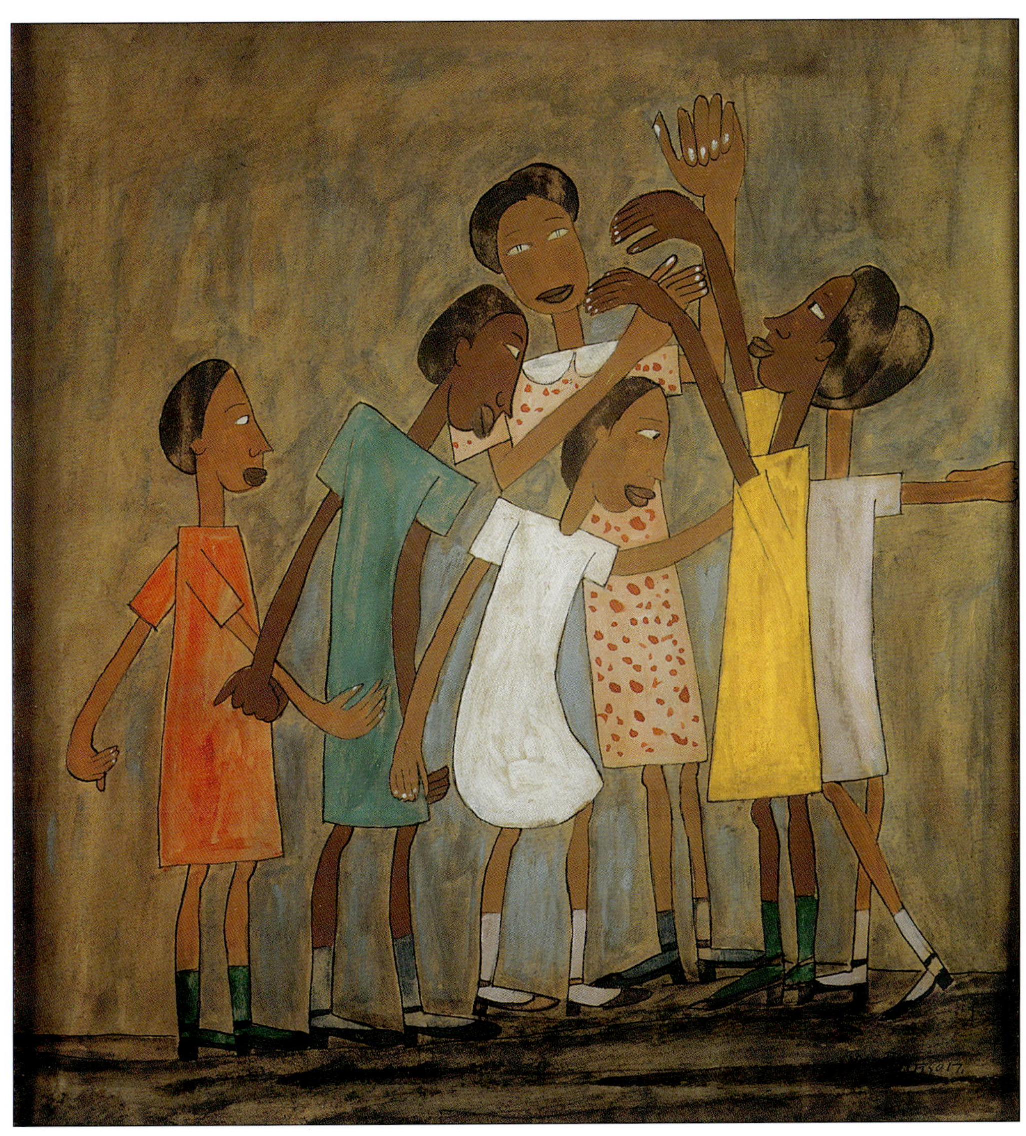

WILLIAM H.
JOHNSON

39.

*Children Playing
London Bridge,* c. 1942

Watercolor on paper

12" x 10.5"

With the threat of war looming over Europe in the late 1930s, black American expatriate William H. Johnson, a prolific artist whose style had been greatly influenced by European Expressionism, returned to the United States. Upon his return to America in 1938, Johnson entered into a new stylistic phase typified by bright colors and simplified, heavily outlined forms, an approach that would be the hallmark of his work until he stopped painting in 1946. In addition to stylistic developments, Johnson's focus shifted to characterizations of black life, both rural and urban, and to the depiction of religious themes using black figures.

Johnson's self-ascribed "primitivism" was explored through his depictions of African American everyday life and rooted in his childhood memories of South Carolina. *Children Playing London Bridge* is a cartoon-like depiction of children at imaginative play. It is a heavy composition of thin, blocky figures playing amongst each other through the rhythmic interweaving of each figure's arms.   K. A. K.

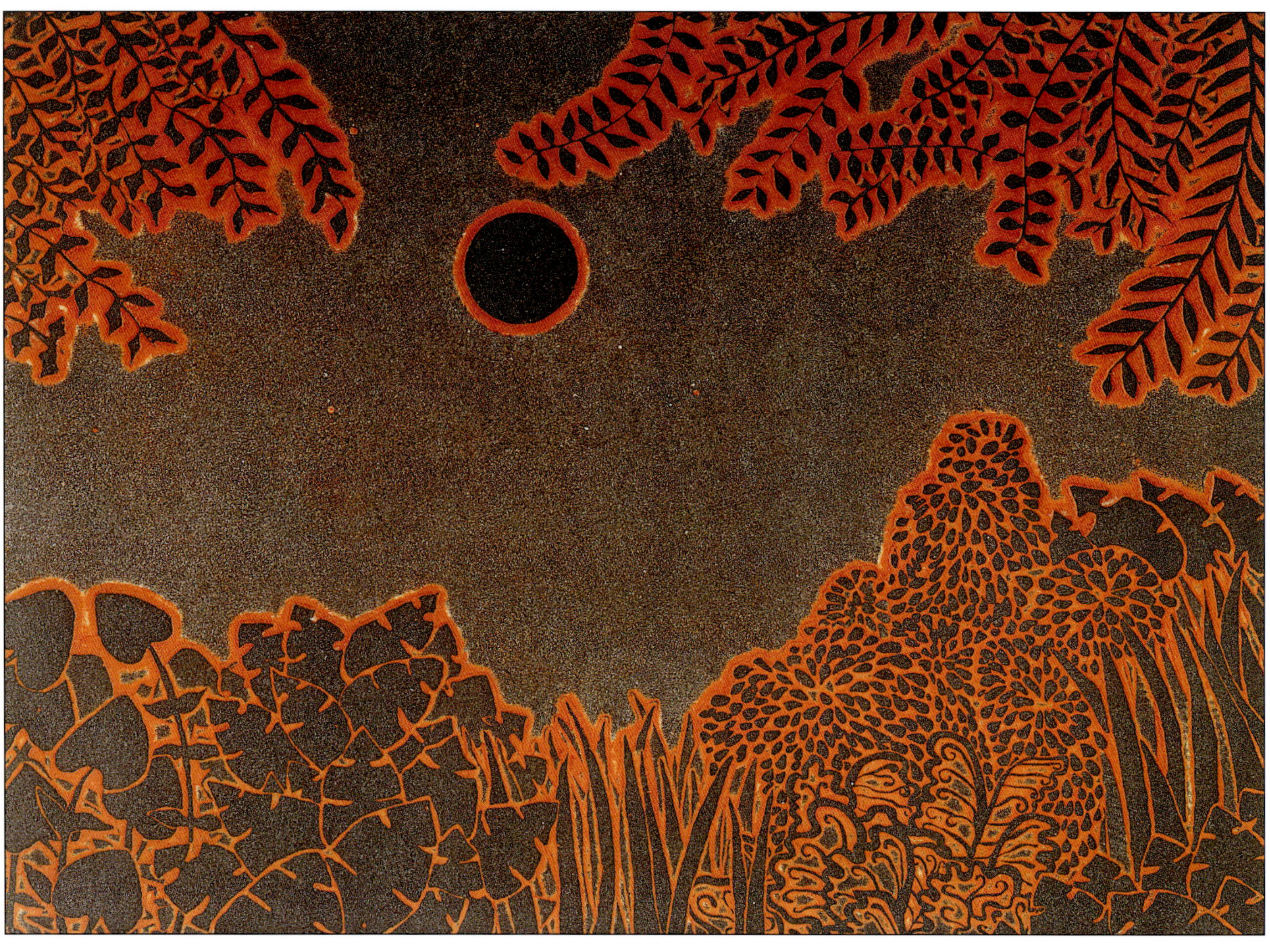

STEPHANIE POGUE

40.

Aaron's Meadow, 1977

Color viscosity etching
on paper

15" x 21"

Like that of David Driskell, Stephanie Pogue's career as an art professor and art collector has had a lasting impact upon her growth and development as an artist. Her 1977 etching *Aaron's Meadow,* for example, was created as an homage to the renowned Harlem Renaissance artist Aaron Douglas. An avid collector of Douglas's work, Pogue created *Aaron's Meadow* as a testament to the quiet, genteel, highly intellectual man who had dedicated his life to the production and promotion of dignified, positive images of African American life and history.

Pogue's inclusion of Douglas's distinctive vegetation, which appeared in such works as his 1934 mural *Aspects of Negro Life* and the 1935 mural *Evolution of the Negro Dance,* pays homage to Douglas's aesthetic sensibilities. Pogue explained that she combined the concept of a peaceful meadow with images from Douglas's own stylistic vocabulary to infuse the work with an aura of quiet contemplation, creating a feeling of intimacy between the audience and her testament to Douglas.   T. F.

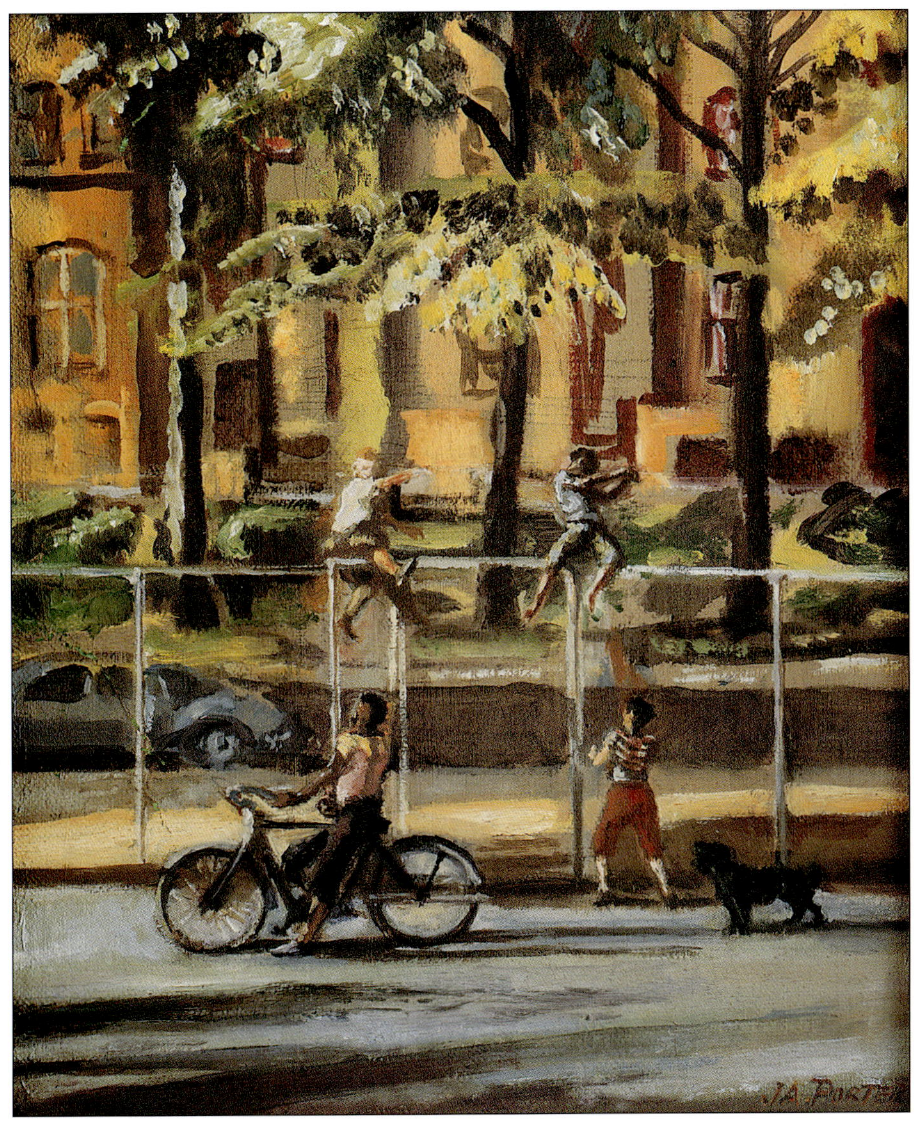

James A. Porter

41.

Playground, n.d.

Oil on canvas

10" x 8"

David Driskell cites James A. Porter not only as his mentor and professor but also as the man who inspired him to see art, and particularly the practice of painting, as a necessary accompaniment to the study of art history. Porter himself was both an art historian and a painter. Although he is best remembered for his sensitive portraits of his family and friends, he also painted still lifes, landscapes, and genre scenes from both his immediate surroundings and his extensive travels throughout Africa, Cuba, Mexico, and the United States.

As a student, Driskell had always been impressed with the content and quality of Porter's work. Driskell was especially attracted to the small scale and quaint depiction of children at play in Porter's *Playground,* a composition he personally requested of the artist. Porter agreed to give Driskell *Playground* in exchange for a comparable work from his young mentee. Although Porter died before being able to personally deliver the painting, his wife, librarian and scholar Dorothy Porter-Wesley, later completed the transaction in her husband's memory.   T. F.

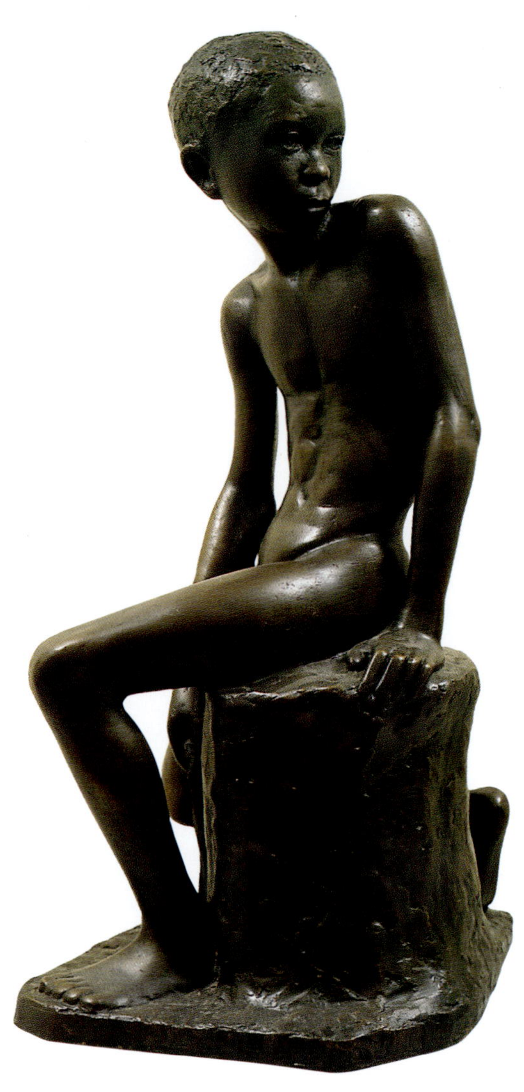

Augusta Savage was a leading proponent for the rights of African American artists and a champion for positive visual representations of African American life and history. Because Eurocentric culture and artistic training were the norm for blacks in the United States, she did not agree with the philosophy (promoted by Howard philosopher Alain Locke) that African American artists should mine only African art for inspiration. Although Savage was primarily interested in the dignified portrayal of African American life, her style, exemplified in her sculpture *Boy on a Stump,* was distinctly European.

Throughout her career as artist, teacher, and activist Augusta Savage fought valiantly to destroy the political, social, and educational barriers that so often prevented African American artists from realizing their full potential in the United States. Savage fought this battle against racial injustice within her own career as she struggled to acquire the financial support necessary for her to continue her artistic education. She also challenged these barriers through her involvement as a teacher/director for the Savage Studio of Arts and Crafts, located in a basement apartment on West 143rd Street in Harlem, New York.

Savage's Studio, which later evolved into the WPA-funded Harlem Community Art Center, was the largest art center in the nation. As director of the Harlem Community Art Center, Savage soon began to contest the racially biased hiring practices of WPA administrators. Savage's unyielding dedication to the fight for black empowerment within the WPA resulted in the organization of the Harlem Artists Guild in which she served in various leadership capacities. T. F.

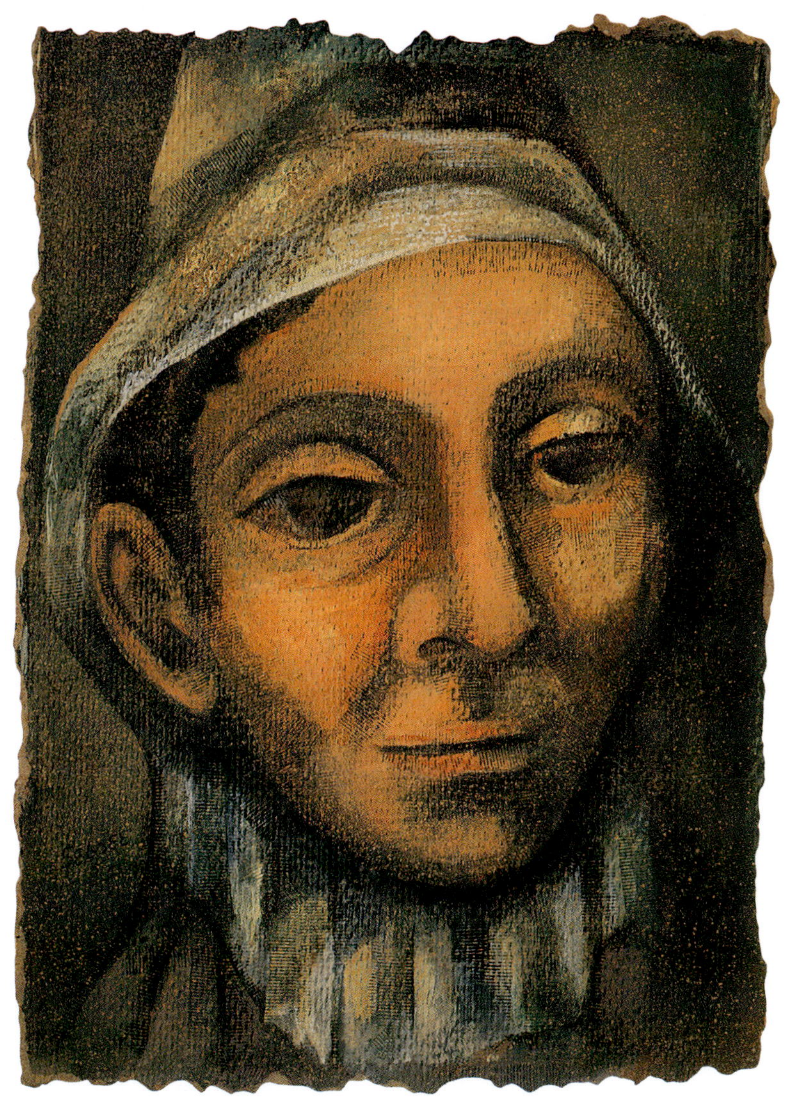

Charles Sebree was one of many noted artists to emerge out of Chicago's black arts scene of the 1930s and 1940s. The network of support created through alliances with other artists and affiliations with such institutions as the South Side Community Arts Center and the Art Institute constituted a system through which black artists could forge a career for themselves in a landscape that remained largely hostile to their ambitions. After attending the Art Institute of Chicago, Sebree remained there and interacted with a group of artists centered in Chicago's South Side. The vitality of Chicago's black arts movement came to rival that of Harlem, and Sebree benefited from the involvement with colleagues such as Margaret Burroughs and Eldzier Cortor. Sebree also maintained a strong interest in the theater and often produced images of saltimbanques and harlequins. The Driskell Collection's untitled pastel features a harlequinesque head whose pale skin tone and large dark eyes are typical of Sebree's expressionist approach to the human visage.   A. L. C.

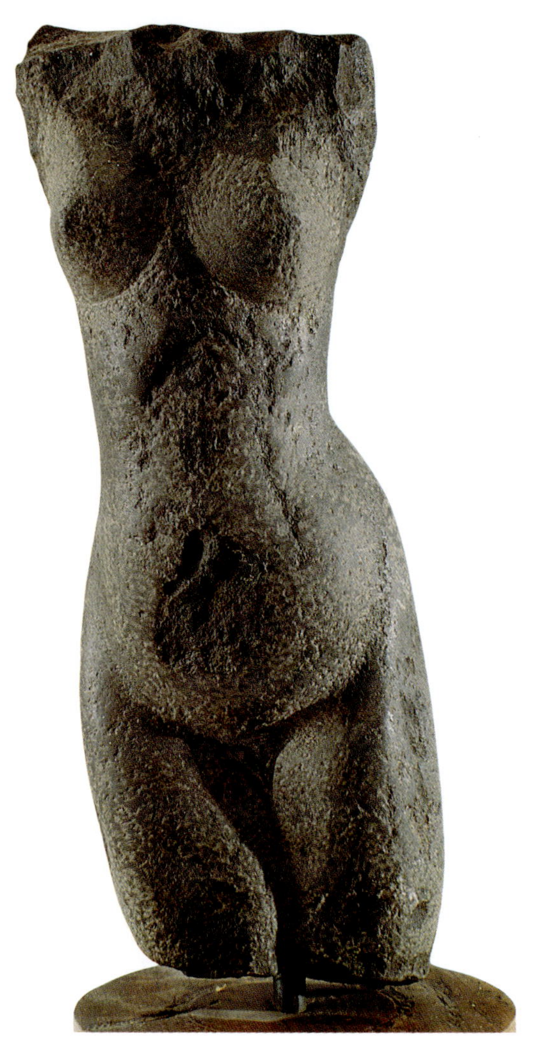

BILL TAYLOR

44.

Torso, c. 1965

Stone

15" x 5.5" x 3"

Torso's small size creates intimacy, inviting the viewer to approach and admire this female nude's forms and smooth silhouette. Taylor studied under both Alma Thomas and Alexander Giampietro, an Italian sculptor. Perhaps because of Giampietro's influence, as well as Taylor's interest in many different artistic traditions, a preoccupation with subjects that were associated with classical and Italian Renaissance art history is evident in many of his works. From the 1960s through the 1990s, Taylor worked often with female, mother and child, and Christian religious imagery. Additionally, the weathered, limbless appearance of *Torso* suggests the passage of time and the condition in which many Renaissance and classical works are found. Although it is not apparent in *Torso,* Taylor's works frequently incorporate African American features, adding another dimension from his own heritage to the many artistic traditions he explores in his sculptures. J. S.

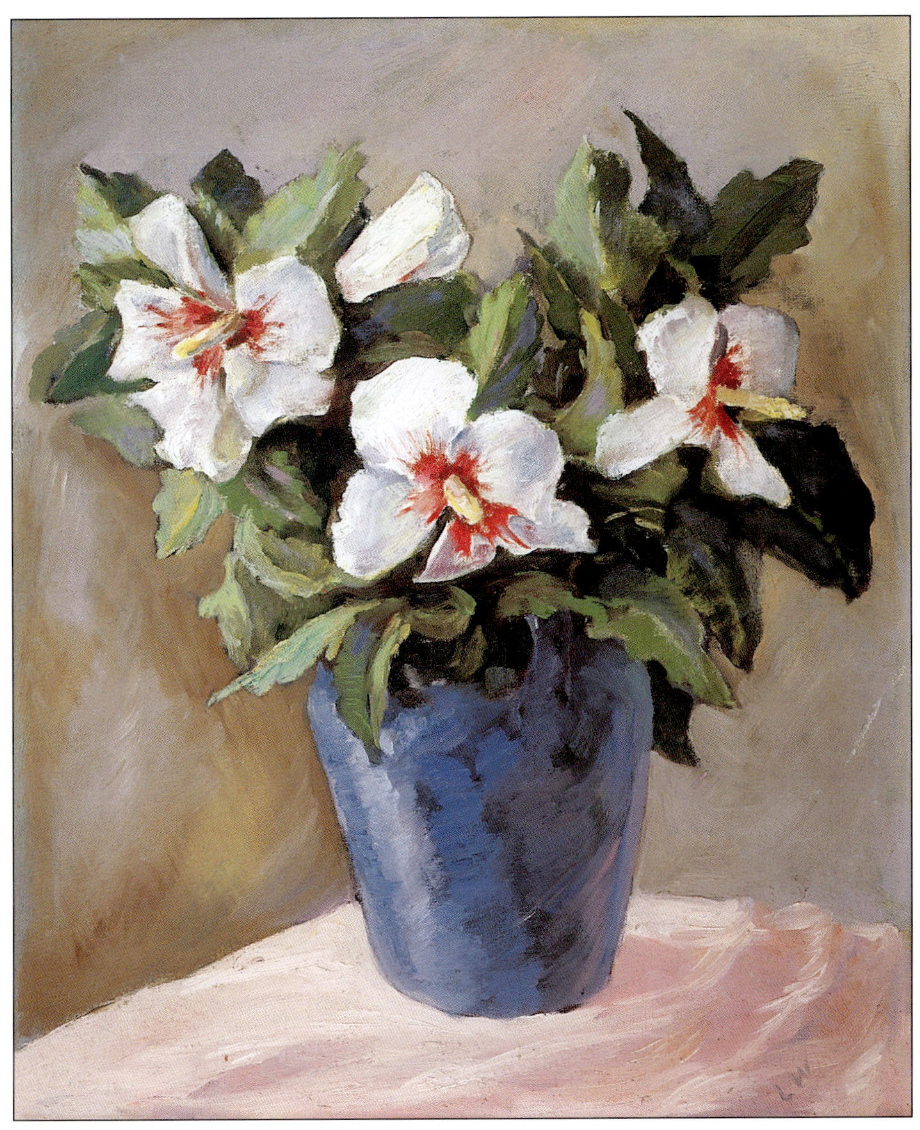

Laura Wheeler Waring

45.

Rose of Sharon, n.d.

Oil on canvas

19.25" x 15.25"

Laura Wheeler Waring is known both for her lifelong dedication as art instructor and department head at Cheyney Training School for Teachers in Pennsylvania and for her artistic accomplishments as a portrait painter and illustrator. During her distinguished career Waring created a number of landscapes and still lifes, such as *Rose of Sharon*. Painted in the impressionistic style characteristic of the majority of her works, *Rose of Sharon* is an interesting example of her mastery of academic realism.

The title *Rose of Sharon* is a biblical phrase quoted from a collection of love poems between a lover and his beloved in the *Song of Songs*. Although according to religious historian Dr. William Smith, the "Rose of Sharon" is generally believed to be the Sweet-Scented Narcissus, a flower native to Palestine, in Waring's painting the flowers are hibiscus.

Waring's choice to use biblical verse and subjects for her works was undoubtedly influenced by her middle-class, socially conscious upbringing and the strong religious presence of her father, Reverend Robert F. Wheeler, and her maternal grandfather, Reverend Amos Noe Freeman.   T. F.

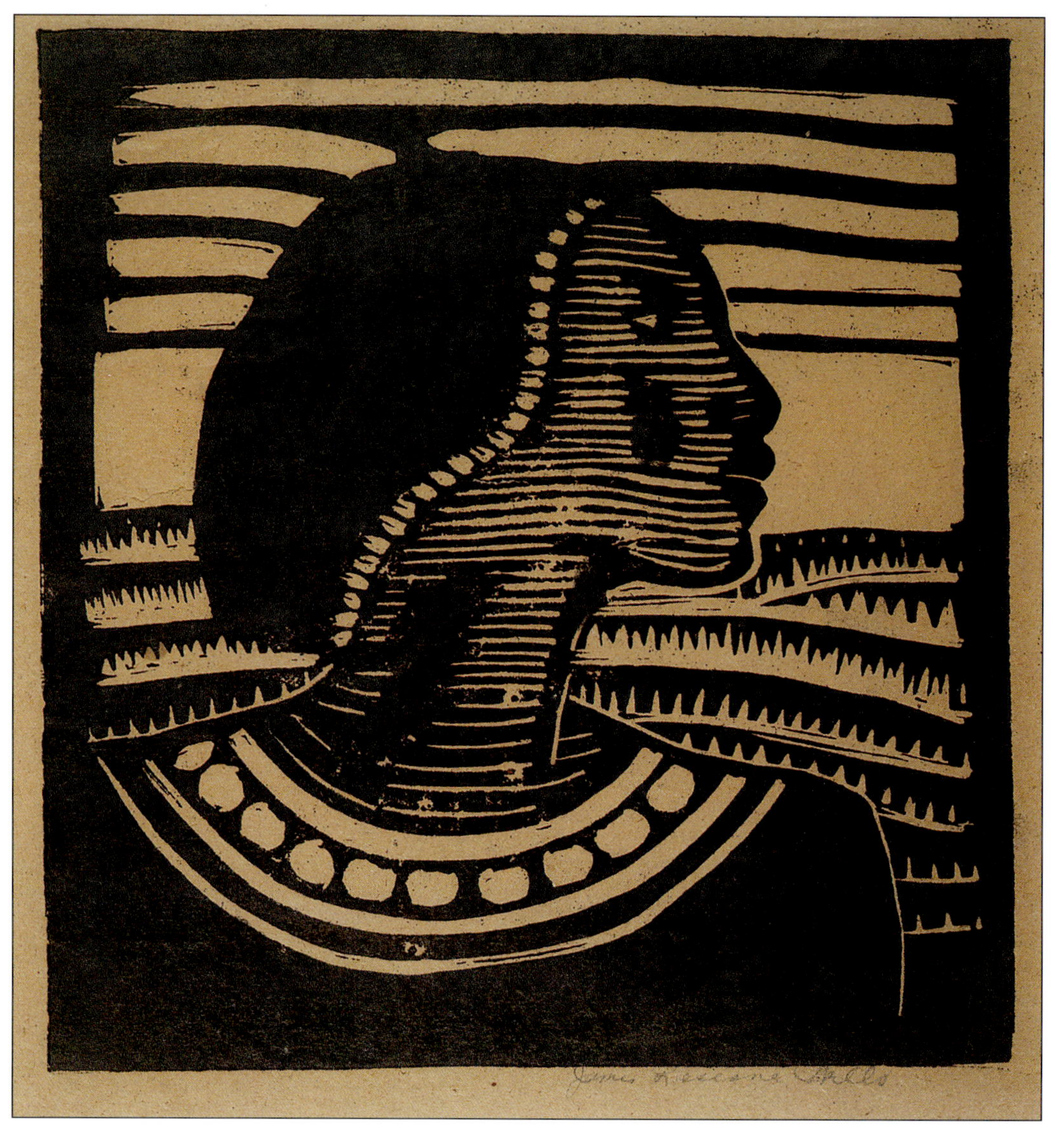

JAMES LESESNE
WELLS

46.

Primitive Girl, 1929

Linocut on paper

7.5" x 7"

In James Wells's forty years as an educator, he had a tremendous impact on African American art as it developed in this century. He began as an instructor in 1929 at Howard University, where his skill as a master craftsman, artist, and teacher benefited a long line of African American artists until his retirement in 1969. During the summer of 1933, his influence spread as he was appointed director of the Harlem Art Workshop and Studio, where he taught children and adults. David Driskell was among the many noted artists inspired by Wells's nurturing instruction. At the time of Well's's death in 1993, Driskell wrote of him: "These artistic colleagues with myself, are the lively voices that sing joyfully—the lyrical memories of one man's kindly devotion to helping us understand beauty, truth and the unity of form in what often seemed like a world without order."

Primitive Girl emerges out of the New Negro Movement, an era when black artists began to investigate their relationship to the ancestral arts and incorporate them into a discourse on contemporary black identity. This work constitutes Wells's celebration of the essence of African ancestral arts vibrantly articulated by his signature vocabulary of pattern, rhythm, and contrast. A. L. C.

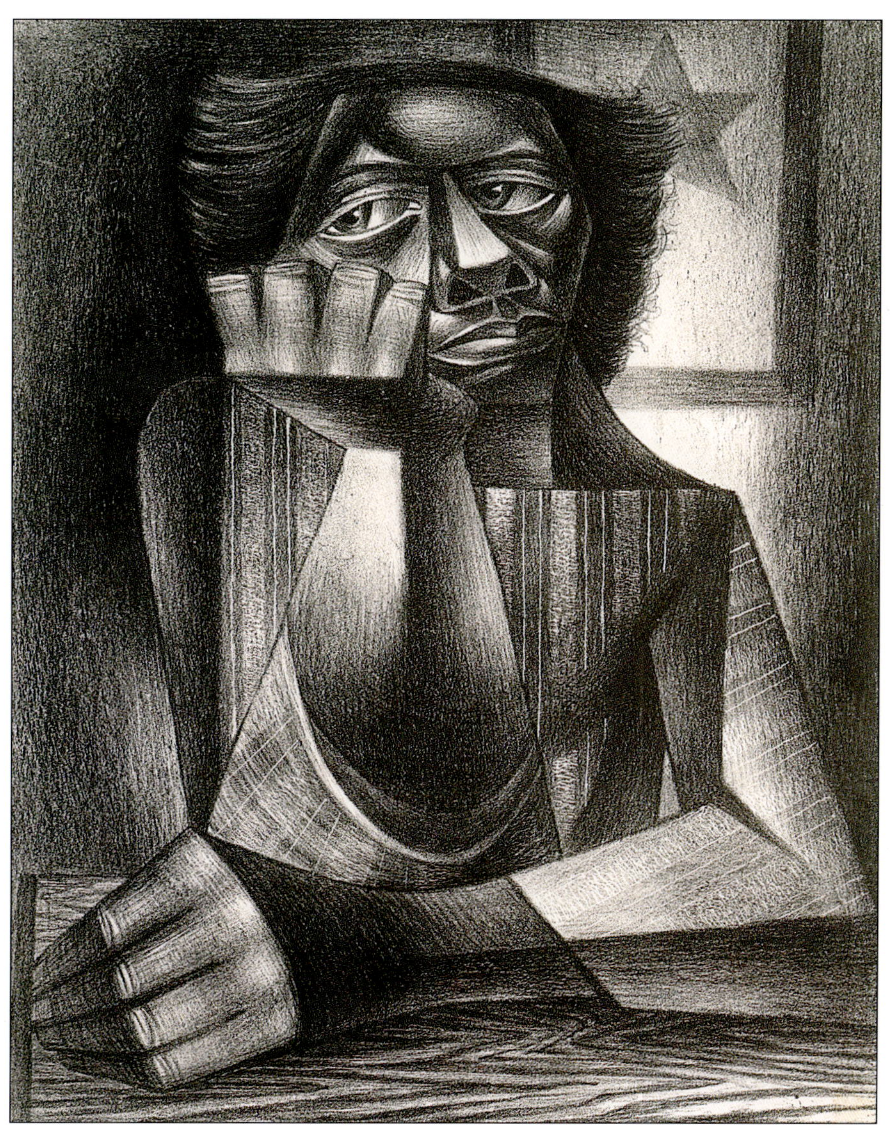

The highly stylized figure of a woman anxiously awaiting the return of her loved one from military service during World War II is a gripping portrait of the pain and suffering experienced by the friends, relatives, and lovers of the men who fought for their country. According to Bearden's and Henderson's 1993 *A History of African-American Artists,* the partially concealed star in the background of White's anonymous portrait serves as a "reminder that there were African-American Gold Star mothers and wives in World War II."

The interesting combination of stylized symbolic imagery, anonymous figures, and black and white tones within *Awaiting His Return* represents an important shift in White's work. During the late 1930s and early 1940s White was primarily considered a historical painter who specialized in murals. However, in 1942, upon the advice of leading Art Student League instructor Harry Sternberg, White began to shift his style from monumental historical themes strongly influenced by the Mexican muralist movement to more individualized and humanistic portraits of everyday people in contemporary situations. Sternberg not only influenced White to pay more attention to the human figure but also stimulated his interest in the art of precision draftsmanship. White believed that his shift from painting to drawing evolved naturally in his career. He attributed his love of black and white to his interest in the work of German artist Käthe Kollwitz, the relative ease of lithographic reproduction, and the fact that he loved to draw. T. F.

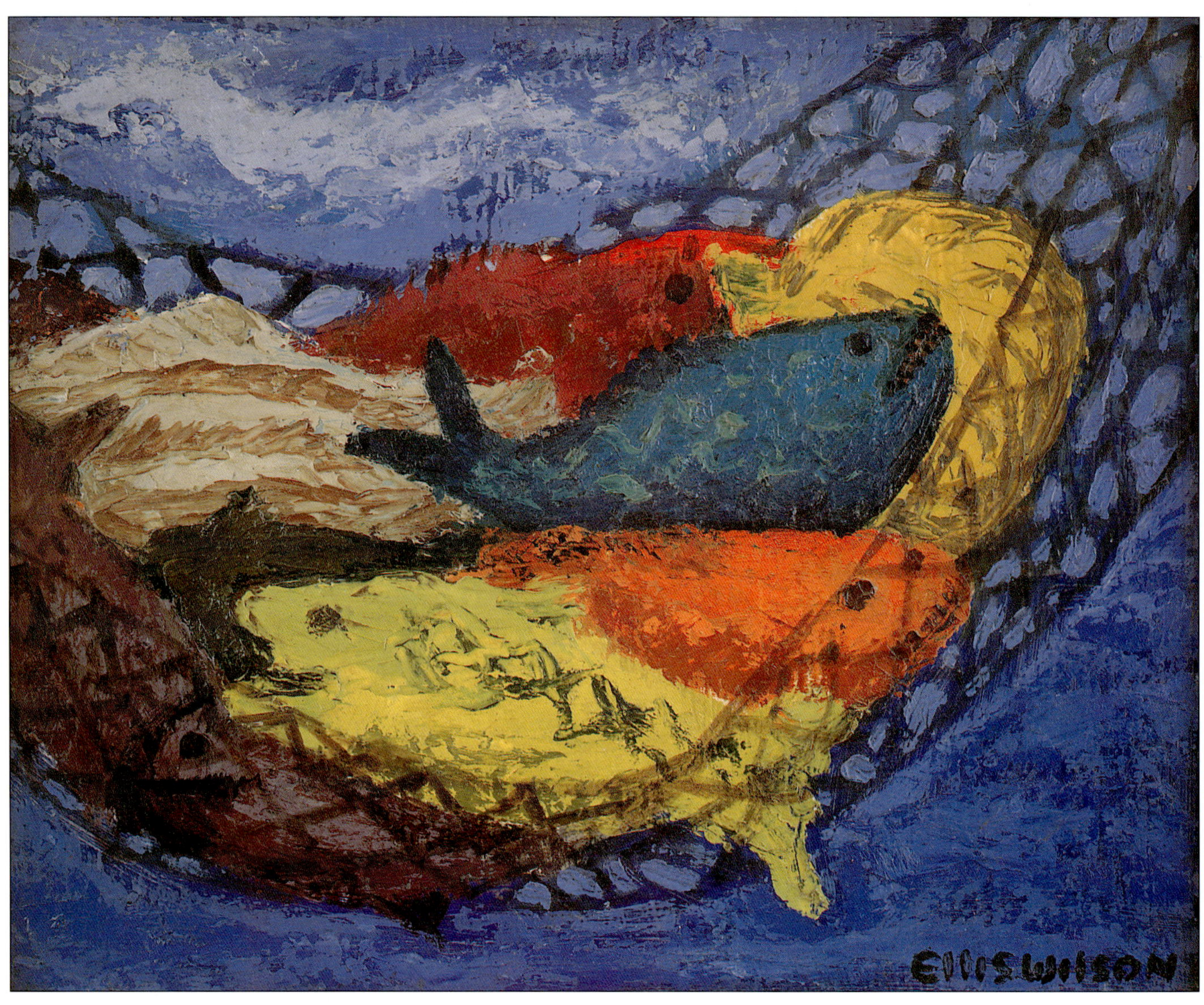

ELLIS WILSON

48.

Untitled (Fish in Net), n.d.

Oil on Masonite

9" x 12"

Ellis Wilson, like many southern black artists of his time, went north to Chicago in the early 1920s to study and participate in the black arts movement that was emerging in urban centers. In 1928 he moved to New York, where he participated in WPA art programs and exhibited through the Harmon Foundation. In spite of the distance between Willis and his roots in rural Kentucky, black southern genre was his theme of choice. He followed his interest in the everyday lives of diasporan peoples from the open air markets of Charleston, South Carolina, to the marketplaces and seashores of Haiti. The Driskell Collection's *Untitled* demonstrates Wilson's love of seaside culture. The colorful fish emerging from the water in a fishing net call to mind the bounty of the ocean that was an integral part of the lives of coastal black cultures in the Americas and the Caribbean.   A. L. C.

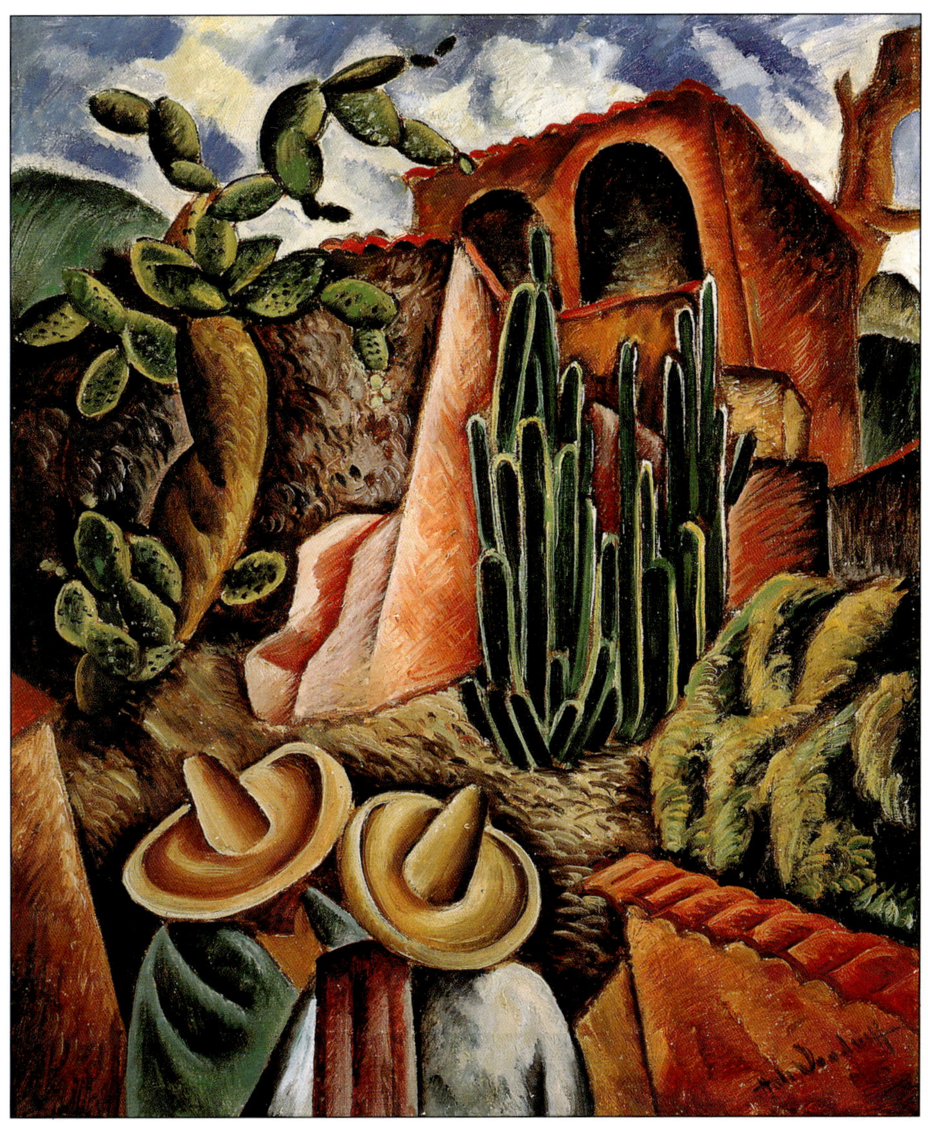

HALE WOODRUFF

49.

Two Figures in a Mexican Landscape, c. 1934

Oil on canvas

22" x 18"

In July of 1934, Hale Woodruff received a grant to travel to Mexico and study the work of the great Mexican muralists. Upon his arrival, Woodruff apprenticed himself to Diego Rivera and assisted him with the preparation of colors, the transferal of his figurative cartoons to the wall, and other necessities while Rivera painted his famous Hotel Reforma mural in Mexico City. Woodruff, like many other African American artists, admired the social and historical significance of Mexican murals and hoped that his experience would assist him not only in learning how to create murals but also in enhancing his work as an artist.

Although Woodruff traveled to Mexico to enhance his technique, it remains unclear whether Woodruff painted *Two Figures in a Mexican Landscape* while he was in Mexico; however, the work's reference to Mexico's unique landscape and architecture is clear.   T. F.

IV. Radical Politics,

Protest, and Art

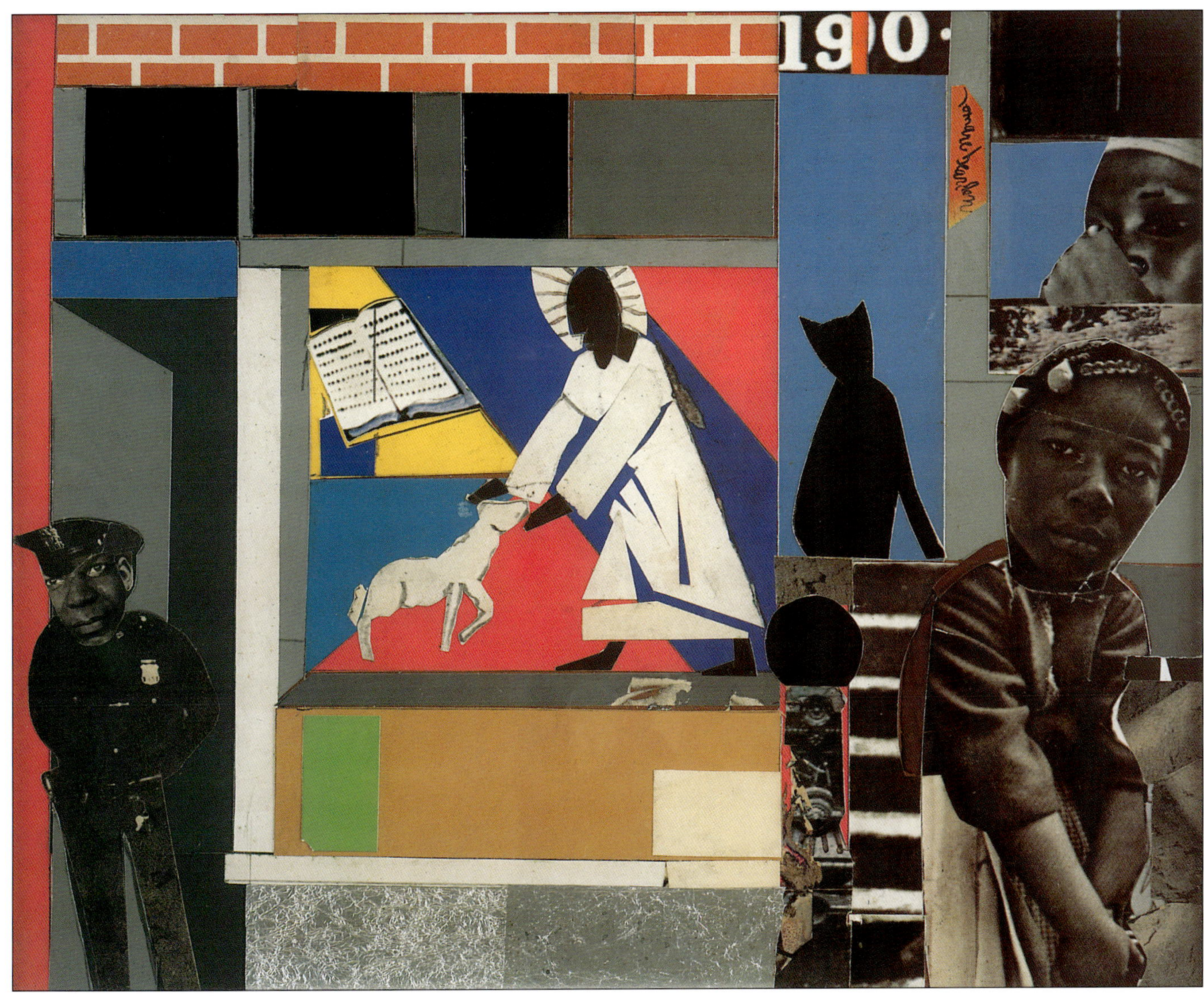

ROMARE BEARDEN

50.

Urban Street Scene,
early 1970s

Collage on paper

11.75" x 9.75"

Romare Bearden made the conscious decision to move from abstraction to the figurative in an effort to more clearly articulate the black experience. With collage as his principal medium, he called on his memories of the rural South and his urban experiences to inform his epic pictorial on black life in America. His synthesis of the sights and sounds of black America has been called the "blues aesthetic," aptly comparing his images to the rhythm, pathos, and poetry of the blues. *Urban Street Scene* addresses the various forces that compete for control of the urban streets. The young black male, the policeman, and the black Jesus on the storefront church could have been found in any American city in the early 1970s, when issues of law enforcement were paramount in the black community.   A. L. C.

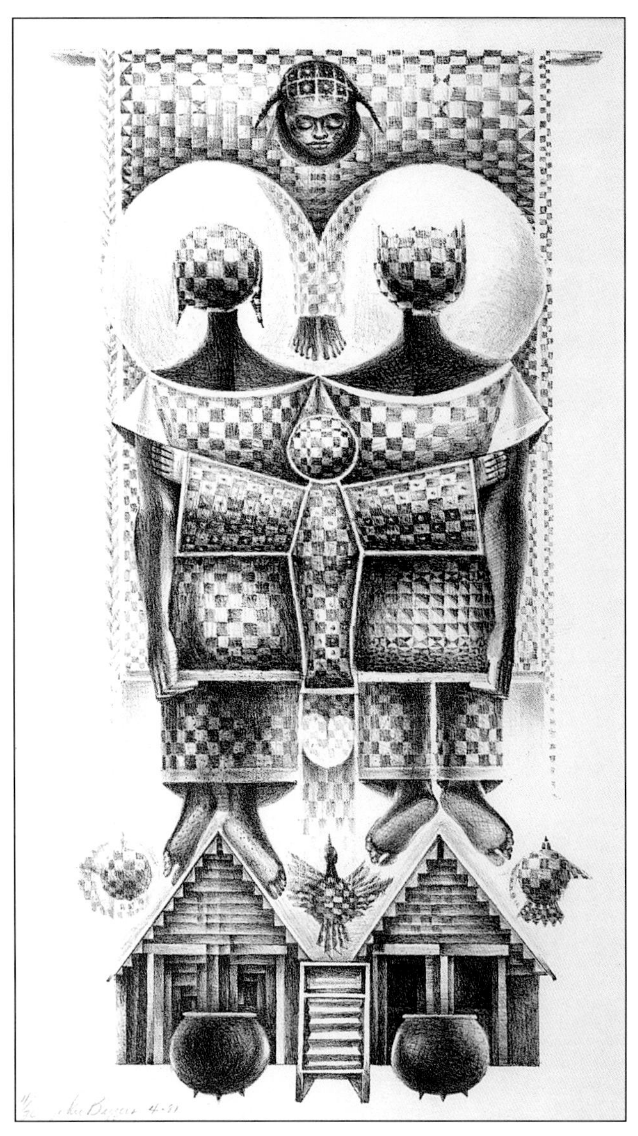

JOHN BIGGERS

51.

Quilting Party, 1981

From the *Shotgun Series*

Lithograph

22.25" x 15"

John Biggers's interest in African cultural systems, along with his own experiences in the American South, inform his highly personal aesthetic and contribute to his rich symbolic language. Biggers's images impart layered meanings both as immediately recognizable symbols of everyday life and as spiritual connections to an African heritage. In *Quilting Party* from the *Shotgun Series,* Biggers's complex symbology unfolds within the highly patternistic, quilt-like approach to form. Black women symbolize the eternal ancestor and the nurturing womb, and maintain a mystical presence throughout Biggers's body of work. Quilts, pots, kettles, and washboards evoke memories of domestic and spiritual arts performed by African and southern black women. Shotgun houses are icons of southern black architecture, with roots in Africa, via the Caribbean. The two female figures in the 1981 lithograph are echoed in Biggers's major mural *Quilting Party* from 1980–1981 at the Music Hall in Houston, Texas.   A. L. C.

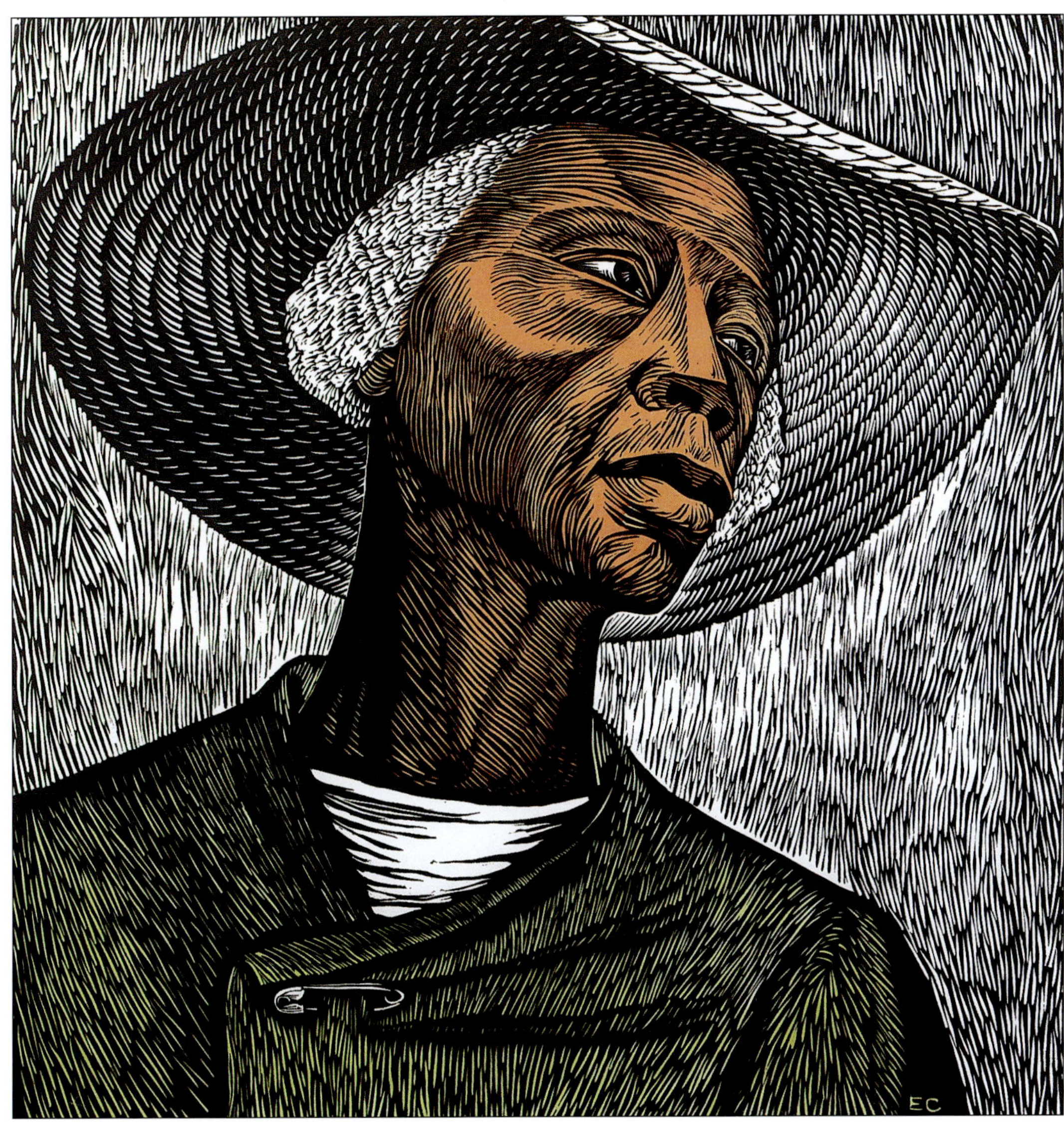

Elizabeth Catlett's intimate portrayal of an elderly black female sharecropper is perhaps the most recognizable example of her commitment to the working woman, a theme that is reiterated throughout her print work. *Sharecropper* embodies the struggles and the dignities of black womanhood and additionally demonstrates her interest in combining politics and art, an ethic that was furthered by her work at the Taller de Gráfica Popular in Mexico, where many of her prints were produced. Throughout her career as an artist, Catlett has given expression to the plight of the working-class woman of color both in Mexico and the United States and has used her art as a political tool to articulate the struggles of oppressed peoples.

Considered by many to be one of the first black feminist artists, Elizabeth Catlett's body of work is a testament to her commitment to the black woman. Although she expatriated to Mexico in 1946, Catlett's work embodies the spirit of protest that fueled the black political movements of the 1970s in America. *The Black Woman Speaks* is a stylized head of a black female fashioned out of cedar, with a smooth finish that enhances the wood's natural grain. The large painted eyes and open mouth attest to an alert, active woman whose voice will not be contained.   A. L. C.

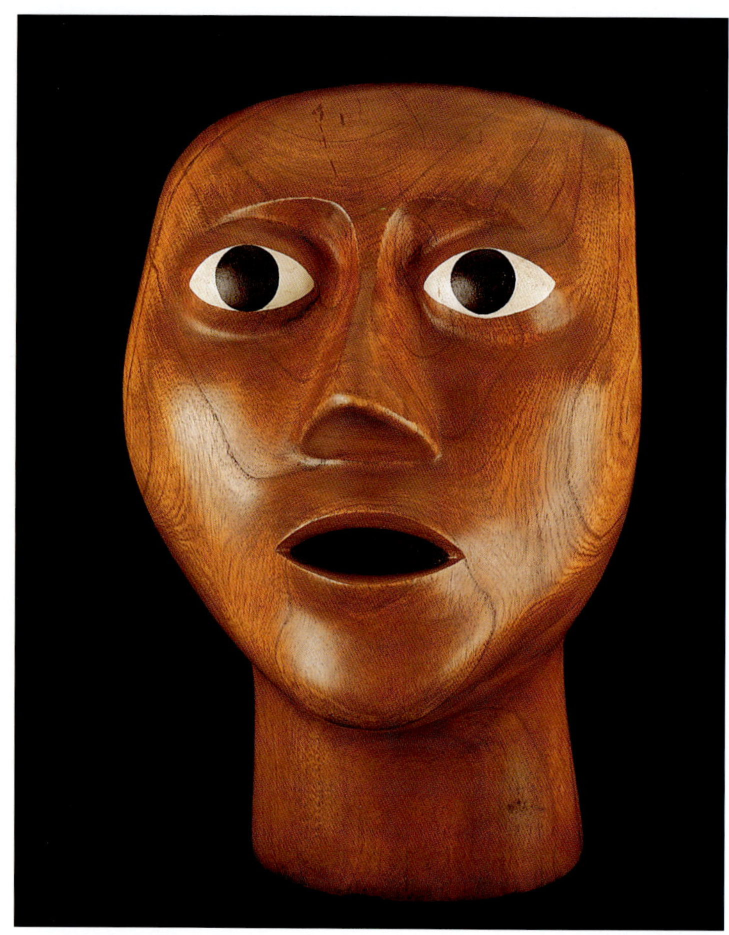

53a.

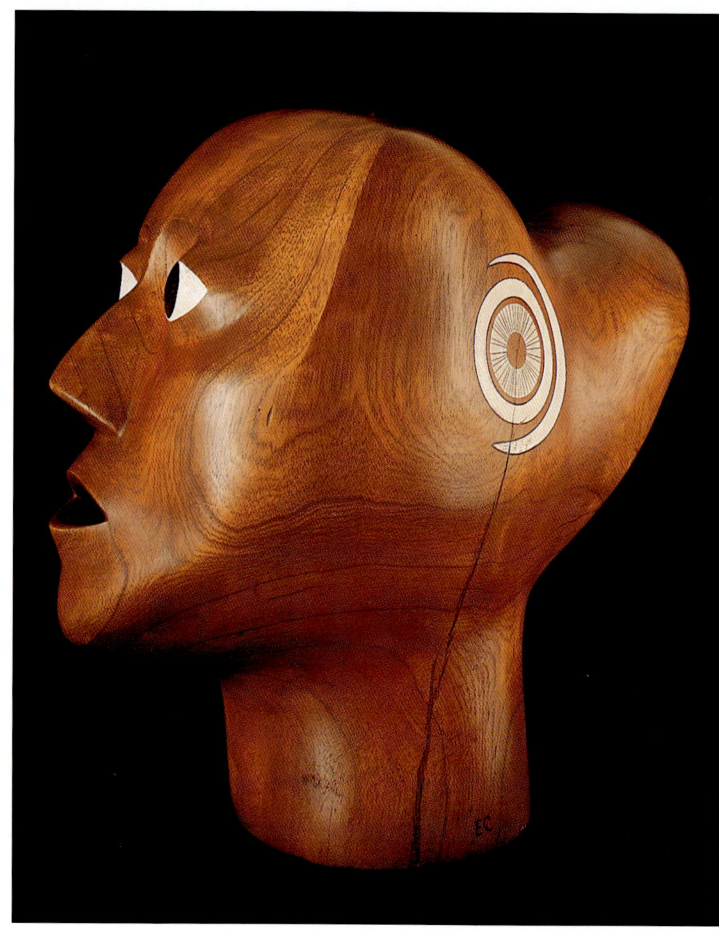

53b.

120

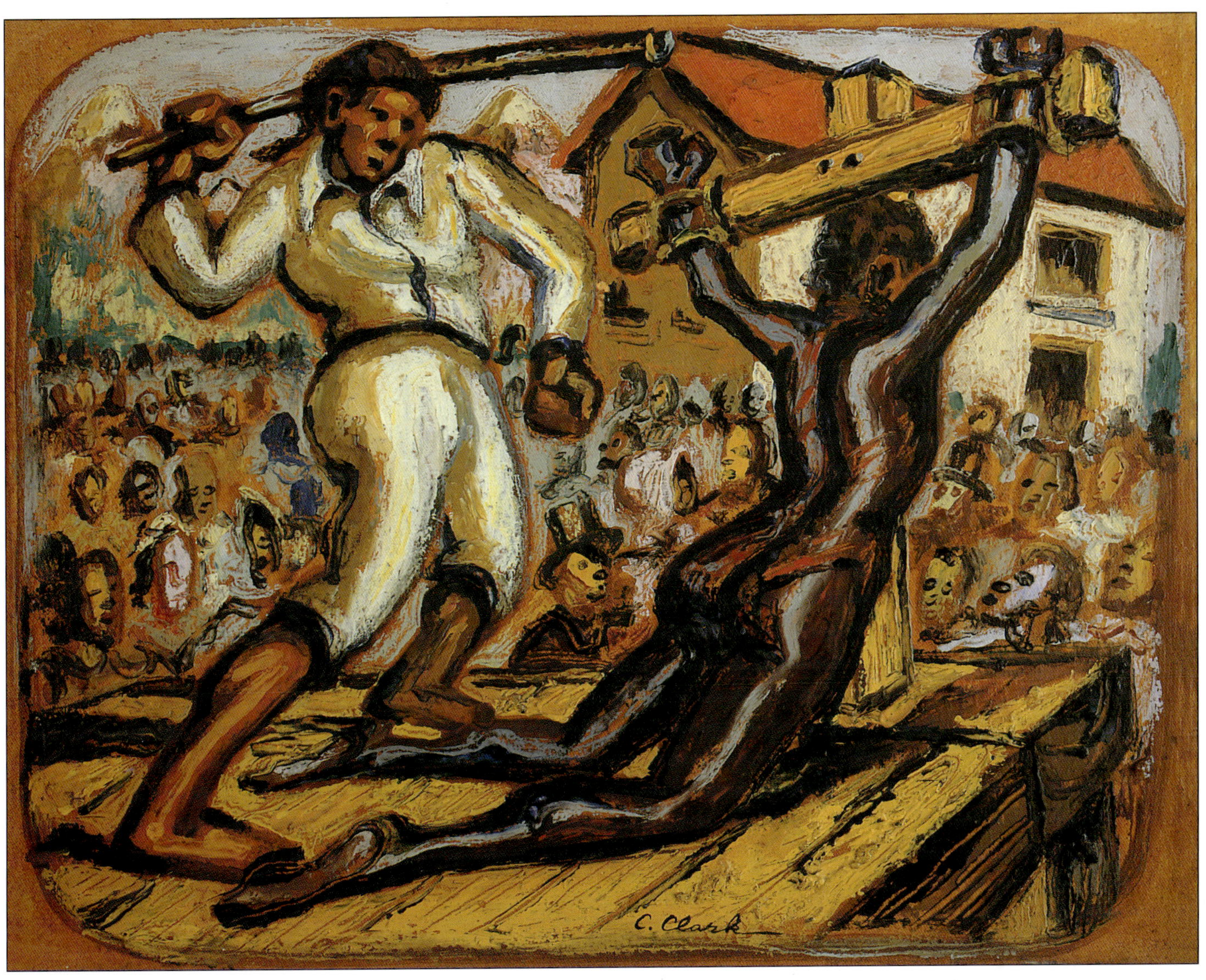

CLAUDE CLARK

54.

Slave Lynching, 1946

Oil on canvas

13.25" x 16.5"

One of America's most respected black artists, Claude Clark was an influential educator as well. As an art instructor, Clark was instrumental in establishing the Art Department at Alabama's Talladega College. He taught there from 1948 until 1955, when he was succeeded by the young David Driskell. Clark's influence spread as he moved to Oakland, California, where, after obtaining his master's degree from the University of California at Berkeley, he taught art at a juvenile justice facility until 1967. In 1969 he joined the staff of Oakland's Merritt College, where he responded to the call by the Black Panther party to develop a curriculum that was relevant to black culture by writing *A Black Art Perspective: A Black Teacher's Guide to a Black Visual Arts Curriculum*.

From black genre to political commentary, Claude Clark's own work focused on the varied experiences of black people in the Americas. Clark's 1946 *Slave Lynching* is a dramatic illustration of the inhumanity of slavery. The public lynching, or flogging, of a black slave by a white male demonstrated the type of violence that was the legacy of this system of exploitation and cruelty. Clark's use of the palette knife to apply his pigment results in a highly textured, expressionistic style that enhances the movement as well as the emotion of this horrific scene.   A. L. C.

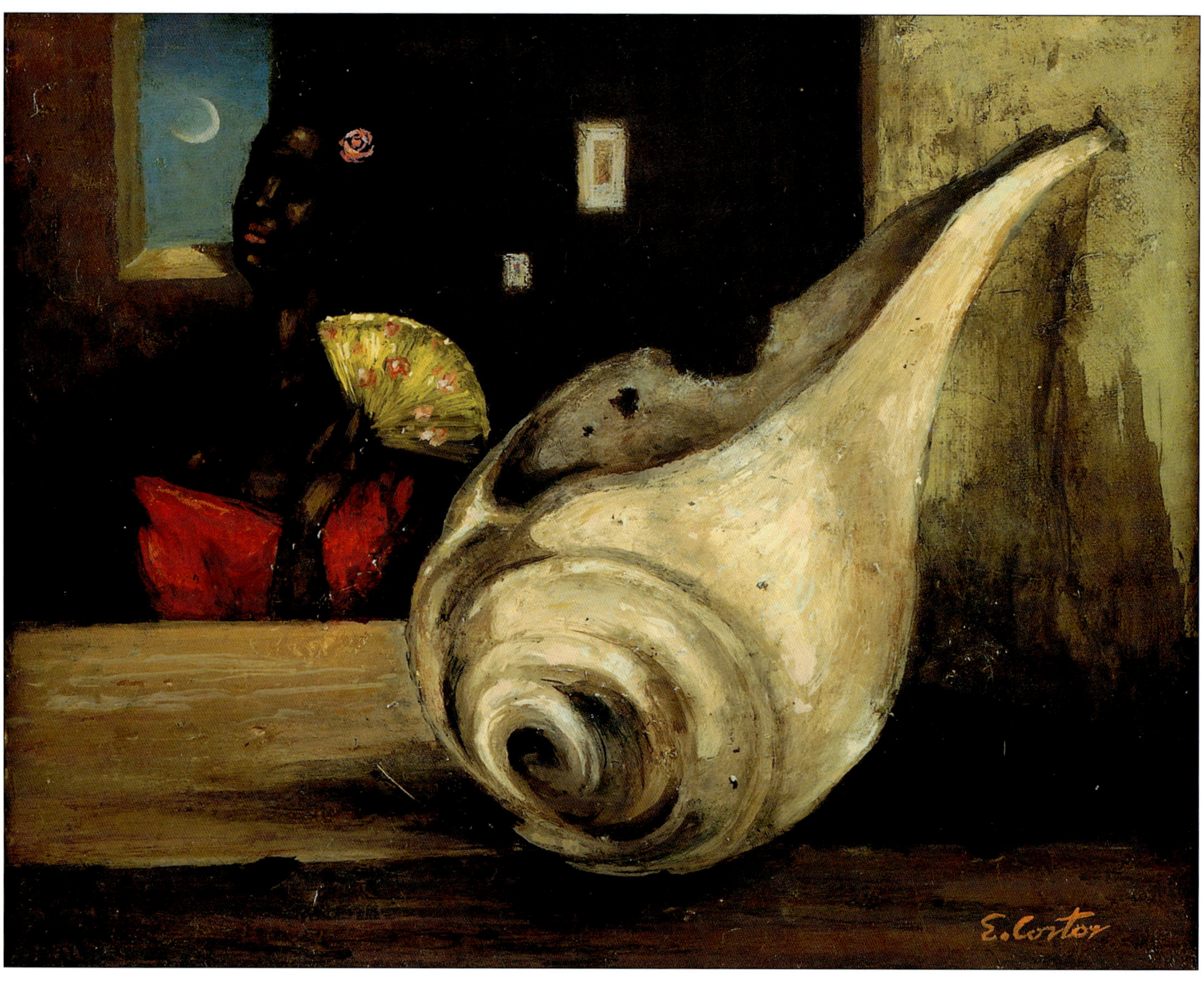

ELDZIER CORTOR

55.

Cuban Souvenir, n.d.

Oil on canvas

8" x 10"

The moody interior of Eldzier Cortor's *Cuban Souvenir* typifies the artist's poetic approach to the black female, a subject that has remained paramount in his work throughout his career. After studying diasporan peoples in the Sea Islands, South Carolina, Haiti, Jamaica, and Cuba, Cortor developed an interest in African customs practiced in New World locations, particularly in relation to black female culture. In *Cuban Souvenir* Cortor presents an exoticized black woman whose red dress, red lips, rose hair ornament, and fan evoke the stereotypical notion of Latin female sexuality. His use of the sea shell still life in the foreground recalls the close ties of both African and island cultures to the ocean. Set in the tropics or an urban tenement, Cortor's black women remain sensuous, introspective, and self-contained.   A. L. C.

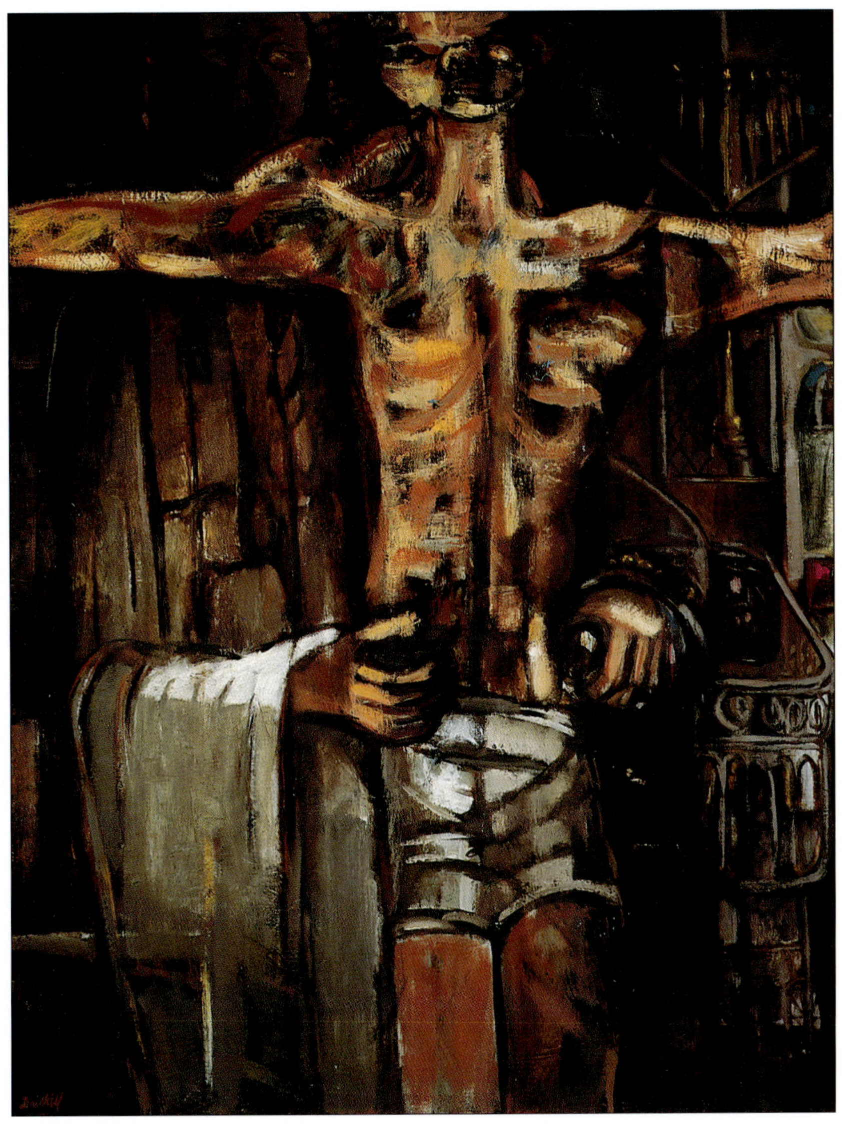

David C. Driskell

56.

Behold Thy Son, 1956

Oil on canvas

40 x 30

As the Civil Rights movement gained momentum in America, David Driskell and many of his colleagues began to use their art to address serious concerns about racial injustice. Driskell became interested in the art of social commentary while studying with Jack Levine at Skowhegan School of Painting and Sculpture in Maine during the summer of 1953. The 1955 murder in Mississippi of Emmett Till, the black youth who was lynched after having been accused of whistling at a white woman, outraged Driskell and inspired *Behold Thy Son*, one of his earliest attempts to address racial prejudice in his work.

Driskell's poignant image portrays Till's mother presenting her son in death to the church. The outstretched arms and bruised body of the young man recall the crucifixion of Christ and signify the sacrifice of many young lives for freedom. The extreme foregrounding of the figures demonstrates the artist's interest in the mono-dimensional spirituality of Byzantine art while his expressionistic style and coloration add warmth and emotion to the drama being represented. A. L. C.

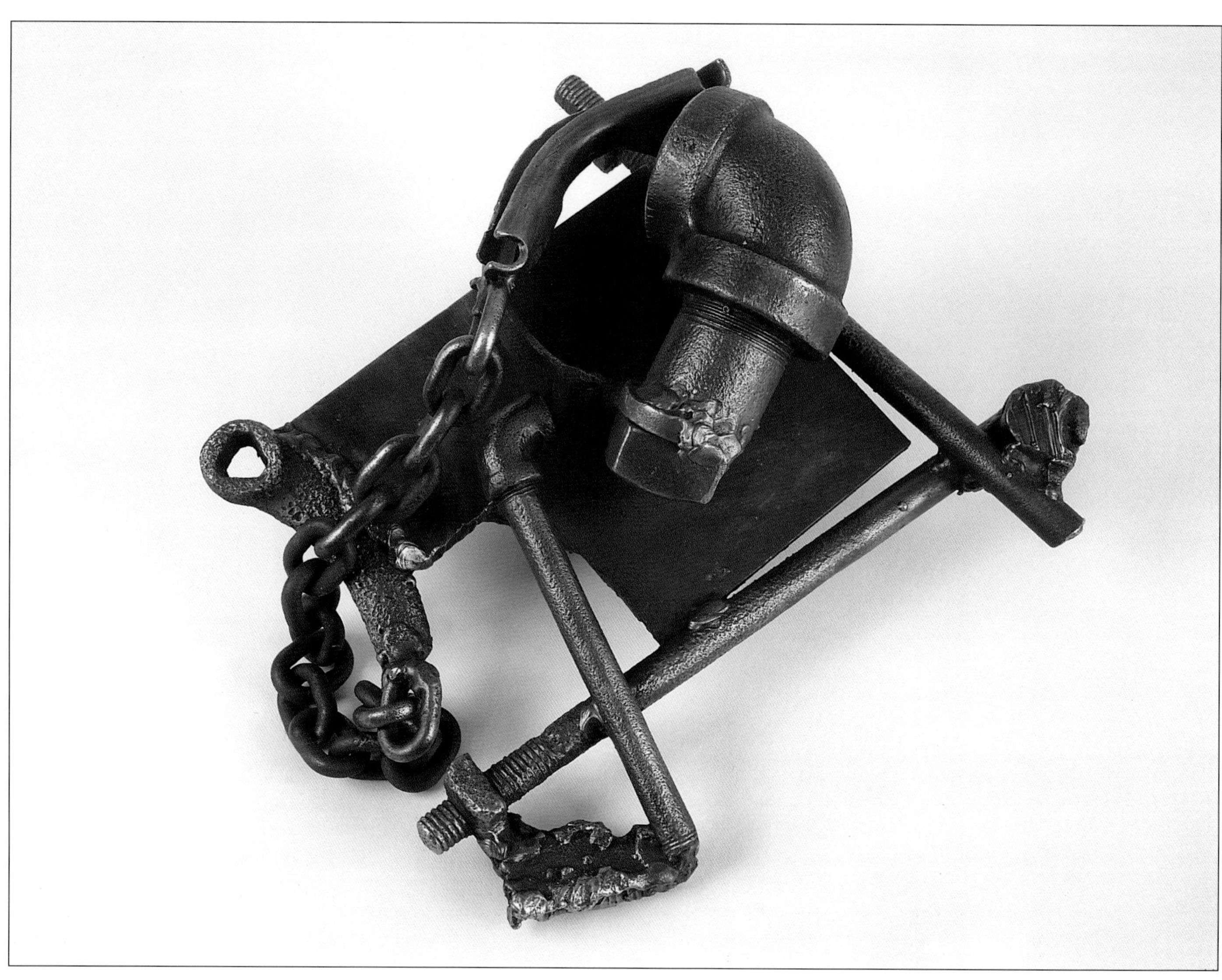

MELVIN EDWARDS

57.

Sippi Eye, c. 1988

From the *Lynch Fragment Series*

Steel and cast iron

13" x 13"

Melvin Edwards's works in steel often address political issues of historic and/or contemporary concern to the African American community. Edwards describes the *Lynch Fragment Series* as a "private conversation," which, unlike his public works, is meant to create a "one-on-one" experience between object and viewer. This series, begun in 1963, speaks to the threat of lynching as a powerful controlling tool of a racist society. Like other works in the series, Edwards uses welded steel forms that evoke the shapes of farm implements, weapons, and shackles of bondage to powerfully remind us of the violence and horrors of lynching, which survived as common practice in the country until almost the middle of this century. "I decided that the forms should hang on the wall," Edwards explained, "because hanging was symbolic." Each piece is individually named, and each seeks to invoke both historical memory of this vigilante practice and the malignancy and power of lynching as a constant threat for so long in black Americans' experience.   A. L. C.

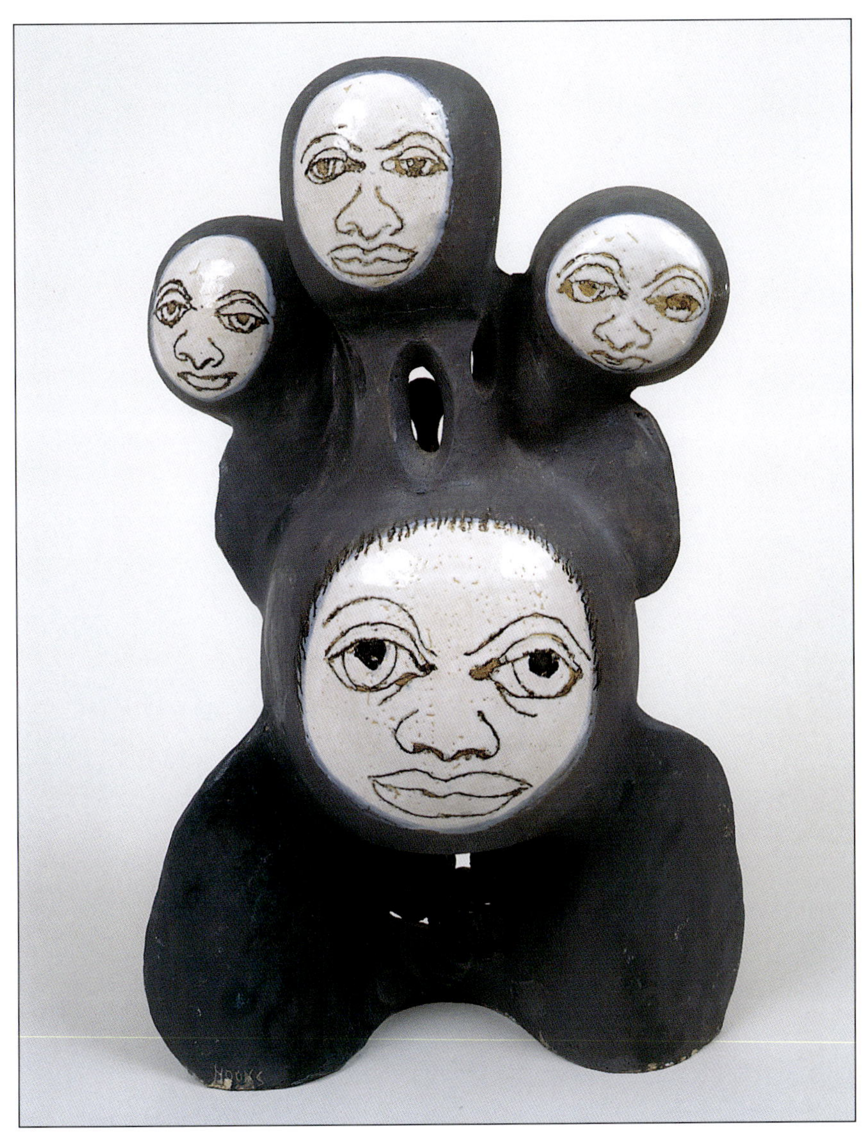

EARL HOOKS

58.

Maternal Family, 1974

Ceramic

16" x 10" x 6"

Earl Hooks began his career during the early 1950s as a crafts and ceramics instructor at a Washington, D. C., adult recreation program. He continued to teach for a number of years, first at Shaw University in Raleigh, North Carolina (1953–1954) and then at Indiana University North Campus (1954–1961). Between 1961 and the year of his retirement, 1967, Hooks served as both a professor and chair of the department of art at Fisk University, Nashville, Tennessee.

During his sixteen years as an art instructor, Hooks taught his students, both through lectures and by example, the value of taking risks and a deep appreciation of the natural world and humanity's proper situation within that structure. Created four years after his retirement from Fisk, Earl Hook's *Maternal Family* is a unique expression of the complex interrelationships between life, nature, and humanity. The central focus of *Maternal Family* is the connection of the individual—through either familial or personal relationships—to the larger structure of humanity and nature.   T. F.

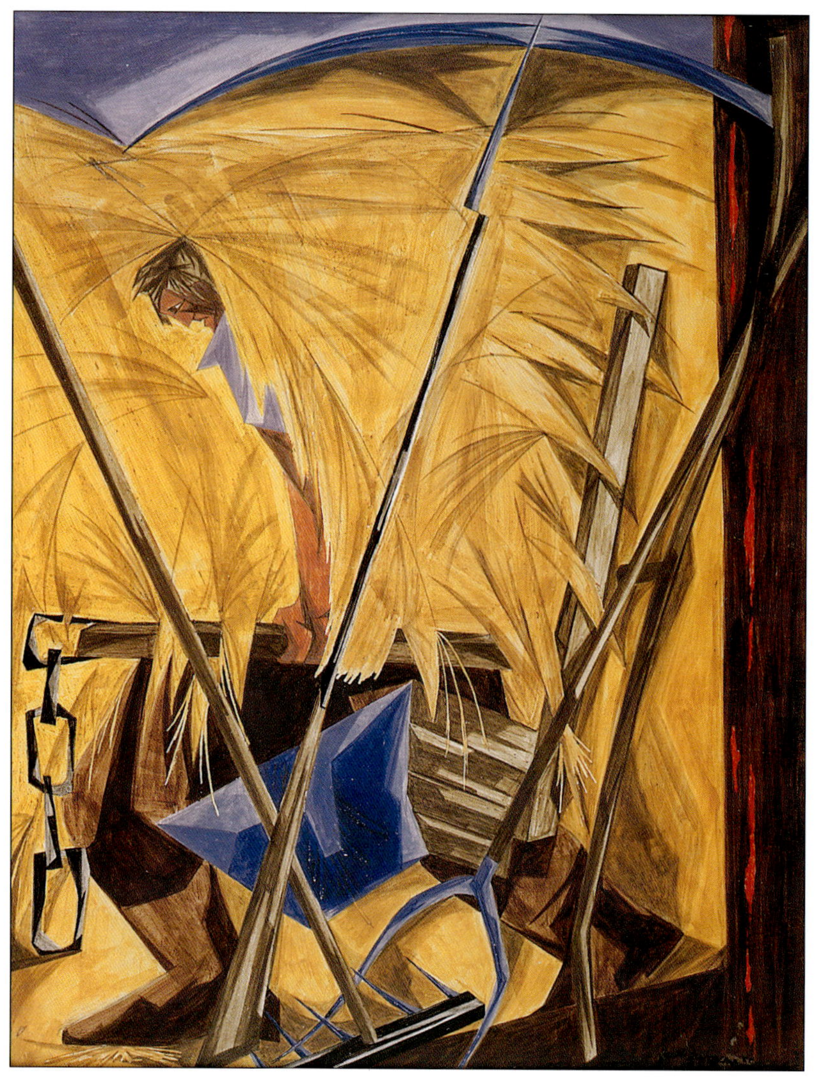

JACOB LAWRENCE

59.

*We Declare Ourselves
Independents,* 1955

From the *Struggle Series*

Egg tempera on cardboard

16" x 12"

In 1955, while in residency at the Yaddo Foundation in Saratoga Springs, New York, Jacob Lawrence began the series entitled *Struggle: From the History of the American People* as a testament to man's general struggle for freedom as the United States gained independence and self-sufficiency as a nation.

We Declare Ourselves Independent, the sixth painting of the thirty-panel *Struggle Series,* illustrates a man pulling an enormous load of what appears to be hay or wheat. Using the technique of abbreviated composition, Lawrence eliminated the standard foreground, middle, and background in this work in favor of the extreme close-up. This absence of compositional depth enhances Lawrence's use of light and dark, color, and form. In this case, the farmer and his crop become intertwined, together forming one massive entity severed only by the strong diagonal lines of the farmer's scythe, rake, and pitch fork.

In a similar fashion to his earlier series, Lawrence included historical quotations within *Struggle* to emphasize its narrative structure. For instance, the quotation for the panel *We Declare Ourselves Independent,* taken from the Declaration of Independence, July 4, 1776, states, "…we mutually pledge to each other our Lives, our Fortunes, and our sacred Honour." This statement combined with Lawrence's use of a magnified perspective underscores the importance of the common man and his efforts both individually and as a group in the struggle for a better life. Lawrence would later reassert his beliefs in the importance of struggle during a lecture in 1982: "Man's struggle is a very beautiful thing…the struggle that we go through as human beings enables us to develop, to take on further dimension."   T. F.

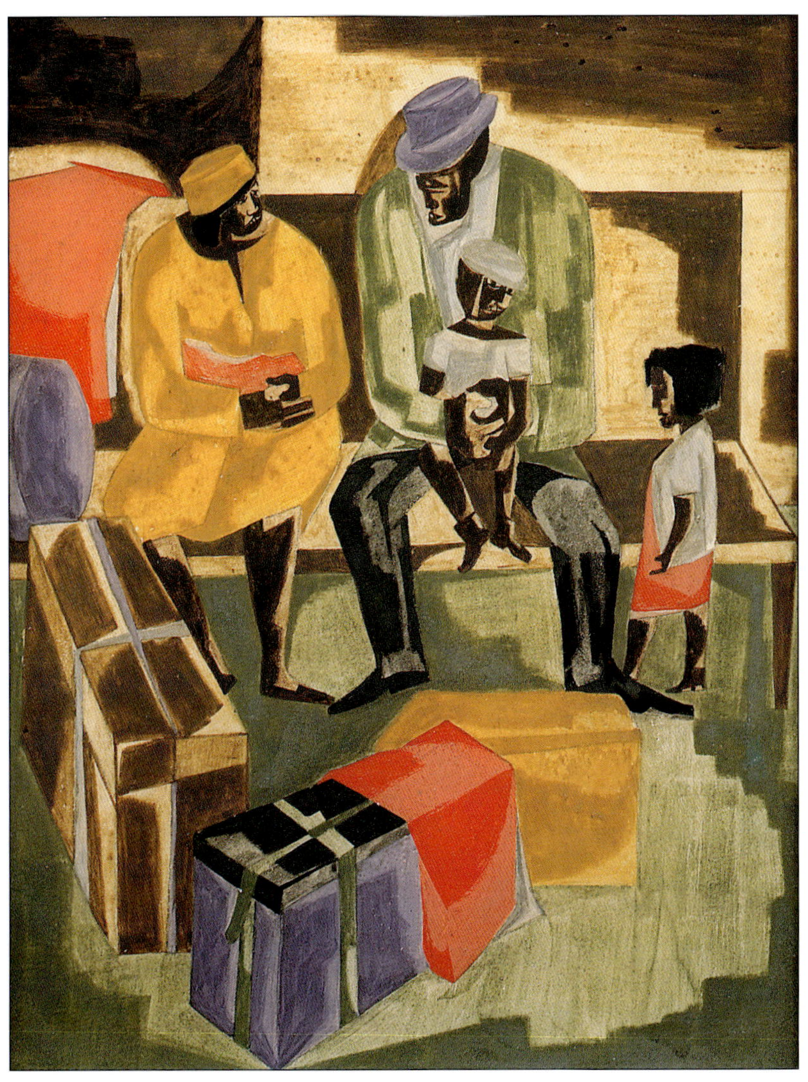

JACOB LAWRENCE

60.

The Travelers, 1961

Egg tempera on Masonite

11.5" x 8.5"

Between the years 1961 and 1969, Jacob Lawrence created a series of paintings based upon many of the jarring political and social events that occurred between 1954 and 1964. Among the works he created during this period were *The Ordeal of Alice* (1963), which illustrates the horrors of racial protest and violence many black children endured during the process of forced integration, and *Invisible Man Among the Scholars* (1963), which questions the chances of success for a black man within a white educational establishment.

In *The Travelers* (1961), Lawrence utilizes elements of color and form to create the image of a tightly knit family unit with their material belongings waiting patiently before they embark upon their journey. Undoubtedly, this family would have had to deal with many of the problems of segregation in public transportation that were receiving national attention, including the 1955 massive protest of the Montgomery Bus Boycott and the brave determination displayed by the CORE-sponsored Freedom Riders in 1961. Although *The Travelers* is not as visually didactic as the other two works mentioned above, its theme of a traveling African American family recalls many of the issues involving segregated public transportation that were on the minds of United States citizens in 1961.   T. F.

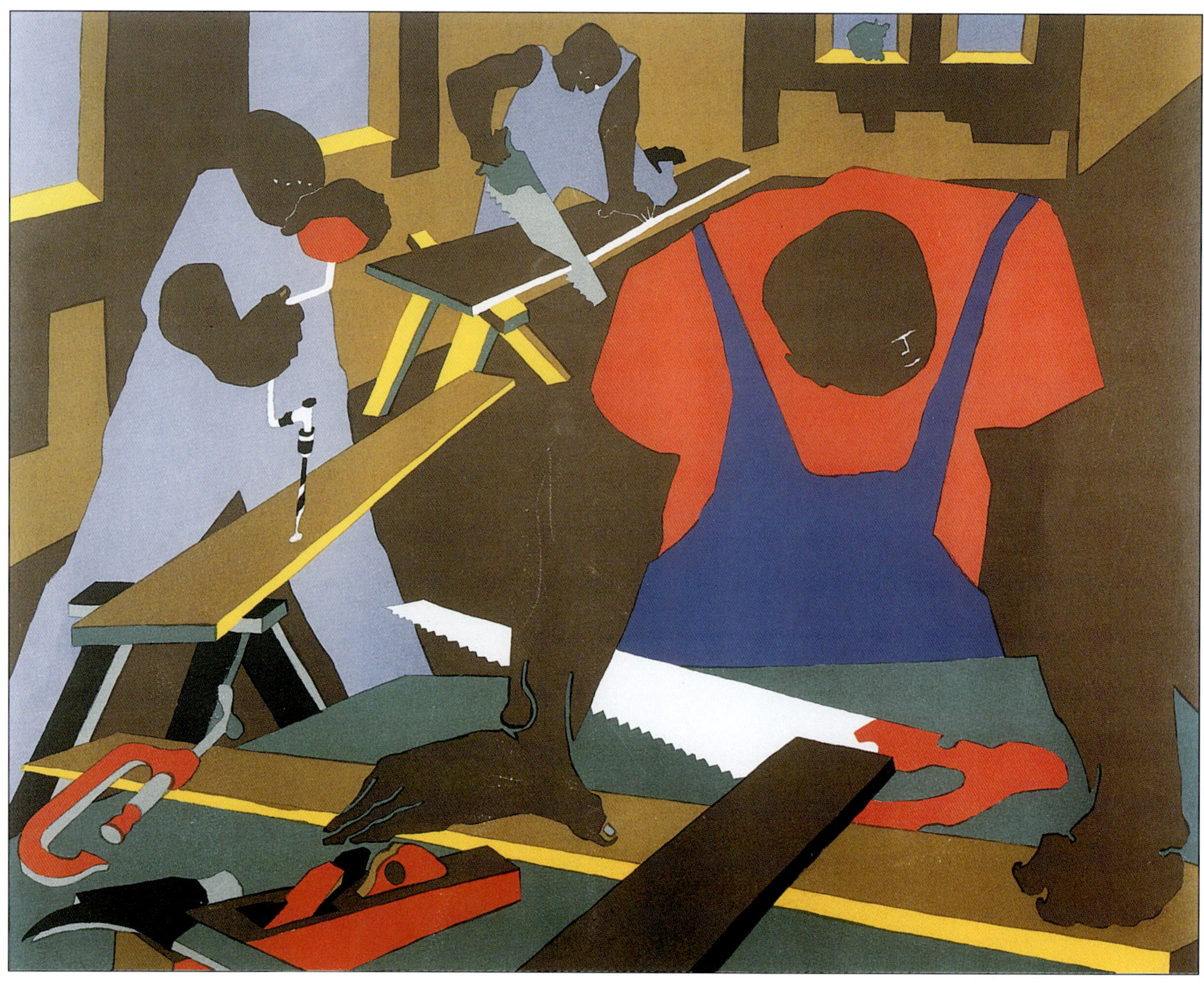

During the late 1960s and throughout the 1970s, Jacob Lawrence began to explore his interest in themes surrounding construction or building. Lawrence's 1977 silk-screen print, *Carpenters*, is based upon this theme, which incorporates elements from his own personal observations of the human condition. Lawrence was exposed to the process of building early on in his life while attending the Utopia Children's Center as a child in Harlem. In Ellen Harkens Wheat's biography of the artist, Lawrence recalls, "In Harlem there were some cabinetmakers named the Bates brothers, who were close to the arts. We all worked together at the center. . . They worked with tools that were aesthetically beautiful, like sculpture. . ."

As in Lawrence's description of his early childhood experiences, tools and the hands that wield them figure prominently in the composition *Carpenters*. Unlike his angry portrayals of racial injustice of the 1960s, the theme of Lawrence's *Builders* focuses on the more constructive process of creation.

This concept of constructive creation is not only thematically reflected in Lawrence's work but also manifests itself in the growing diversity of materials utilized to convey his theme. Whereas previously the majority of his work was created with water-base egg tempera on paper, during the 1970s Lawrence began to expand his repertoire to include prints, drawings, enamel murals, and graphic illustrations. Thus, the silk-screen print *Carpenters* embodies Lawrence's personal exploration: his tools combined with a theoretical consideration of tools and building as vehicles for man's most basic aspirations.   T. F.

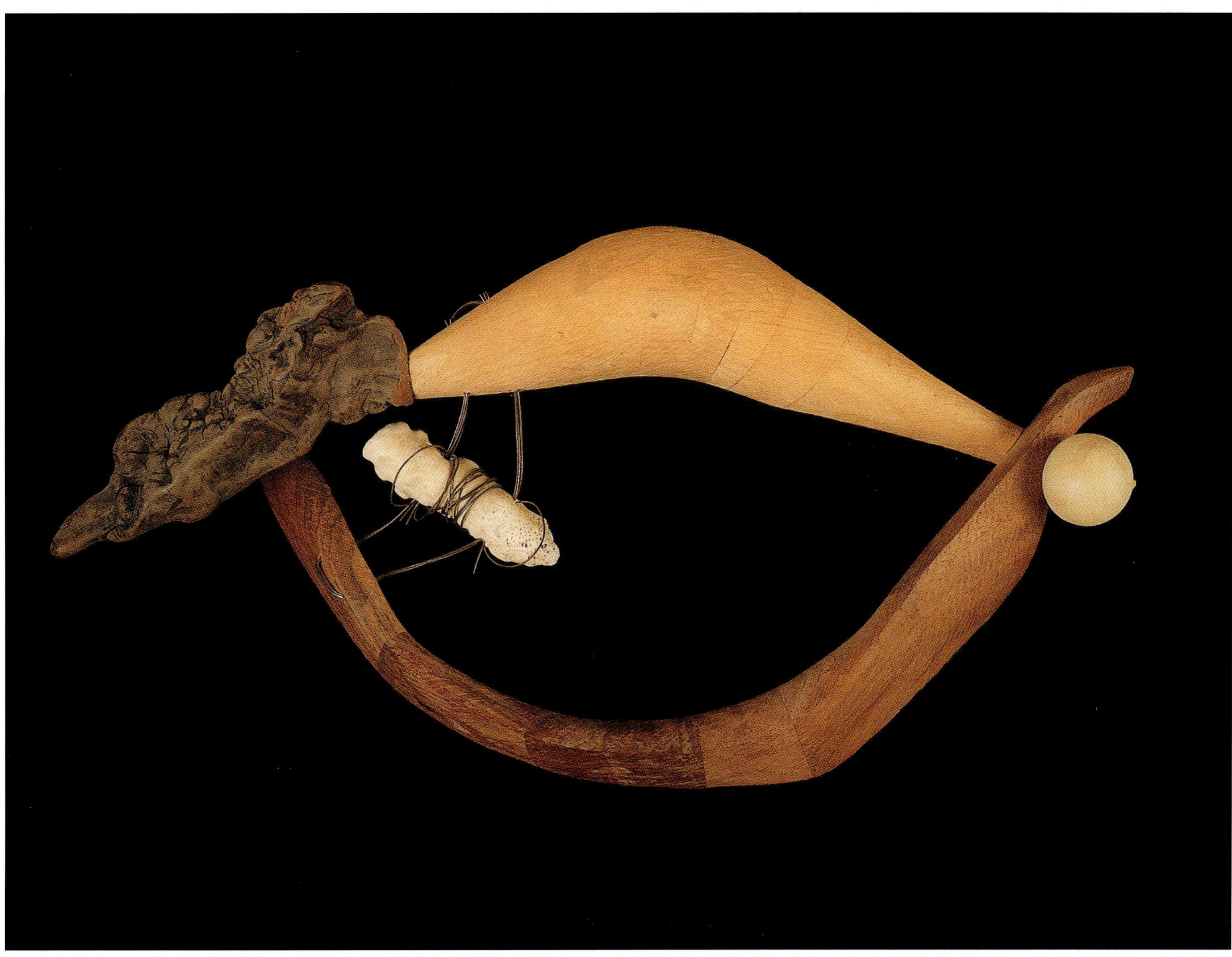

JEROME MEADOWS

62.

Bound Between, 1994

Mixed media

10" x 19.5"

A mixed media sculptor who has planned and executed more than seven major sculpture commissions over the past ten years, Jerome Meadows is a Washington, D. C., artist whose commissions can be seen in Alaska, Georgia, Virginia, New Mexico, and Maryland, among other states. Trained in the figure tradition, Meadows is fond of using a variety of media such as wood, stone, metal, and cast cement in one composition. The curve is used as a basic geometric element in many of the works of the late 1980s and early 1990s, and it often serves to unify two or more forms that are the dominant figure features of a given work. Meadows utilizes a variety of materials such as coral, wood, stone, steel, and wire in a harmonious relationship with compositional forms that are both abstract and organic.

In *Bound Between,* the artist places two curvilinear wooden forms in a parallel formation, thereby creating the action of smaller surges of energy from a bow about to be pulled upon. The result is a vibrant movement between two arches interacting on different planes.   A. L. C.

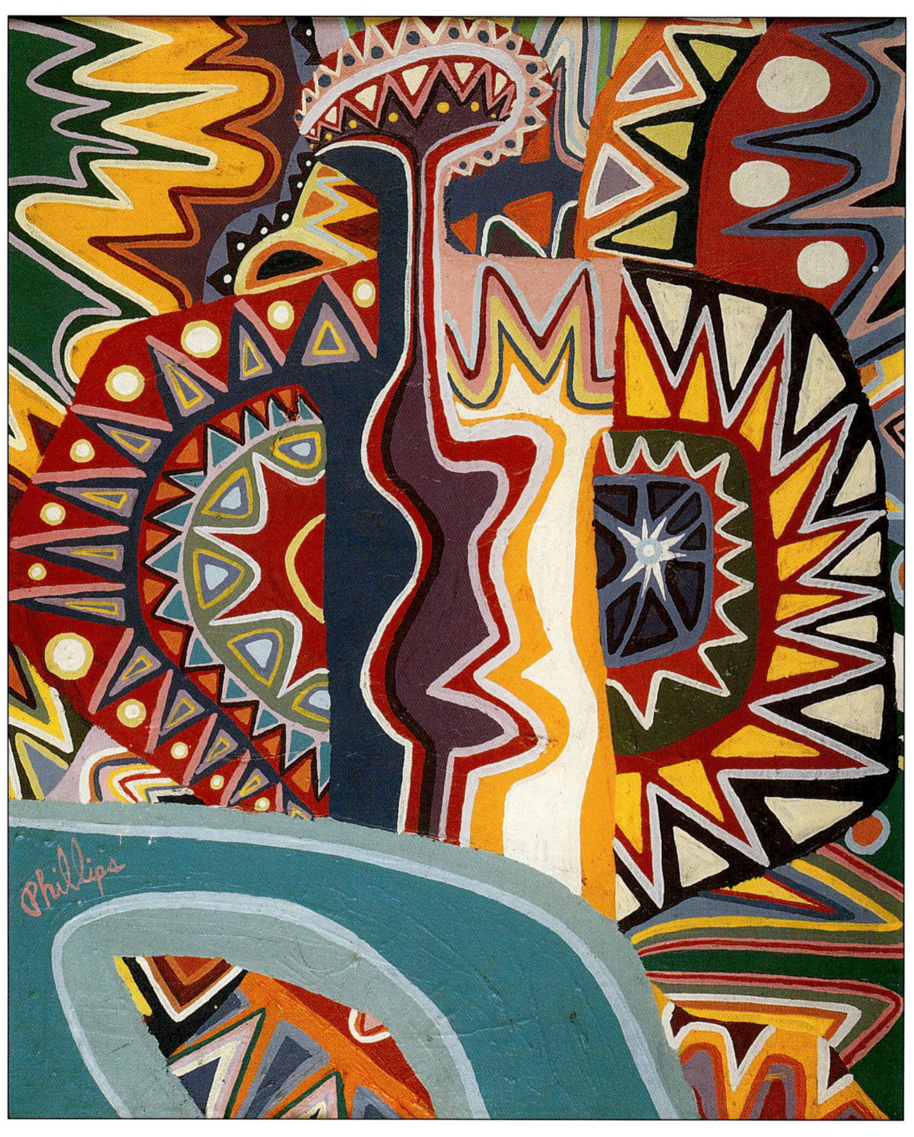

JAMES PHILLIPS

63.

The Dealer, 1966

From the *Junkie in the Twilight Zone Series*

Oil on canvas

20" x 16"

After graduating from the Philadelphia College of Art during the late 1960s, Weusi and Afri-Cobra painter and muralist James Phillips traveled to New York, where he became acquainted with several popular jazz musicians and artists. Phillips's experience with New York's musicians and artists inspired him to attempt to mimic the rhythms and moods of jazz music within his own work.

As evidenced in his 1966 painting *The Dealer,* Phillips began to incorporate jarring color combinations, sporadic zigzagging forms, and writhing compositions that alter the perception of reality. In similar fashion to the musical free jazz style of John Coltrane—an artist with whom Phillips was acquainted—*The Dealer* displays striking features of improvisation, layered rhythmic patterning, and violent bursts of colorful forms and accents.

In contrast, the title of Phillips's work, *The Dealer,* suggests a more sinister element to the world of music and art, that of the transforming, mind-altering effects of drug use and addiction.   T. F.

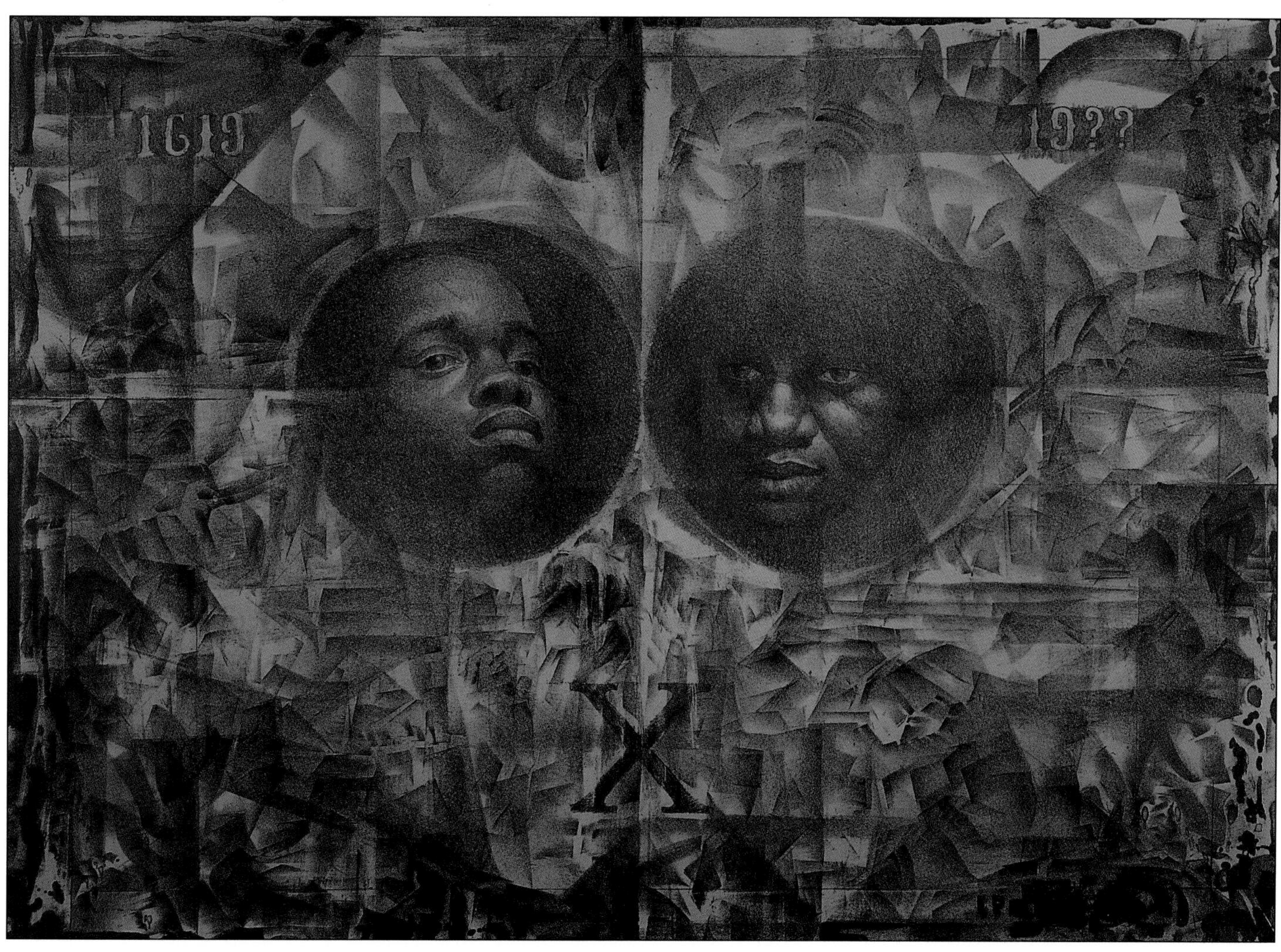

CHARLES WHITE

64.

Wanted Poster Series, 1970

Lithograph

21.5" x 29.25"

During the late 1960s, Charles White discovered a series of pre–Civil War posters advertising slave auctions and rewards for runaway slaves. These posters inspired White to create a series of paintings portraying contemporary African Americans against a background fabricated from the images of the old "wanted" posters. The original series was painted in oil on board in 1969. Later, in 1970, through the process of lithography, he reproduced the series on paper.

The lithograph in the Driskell Collection from the *Wanted Poster Series* depicts a mother and child set against the crinkled textured background of what appears to be an old slave-auction poster. On the top left-hand corner, White painted the year *1619*. In the center of the composition—underneath the two circular forms that frame the faces of a woman and child—he has prominently placed an *X*. And, in the far right-hand corner of the painting, he included the unfinished date *19??*. White's careful juxtaposing of dates, symbols, and images in this work may indicate his frustration regarding the cycle of oppression and degradation African Americans have historically endured from the first arrival of seventeen African slaves in Jamestown, Virginia, in 1619 to a date that has yet to be revealed.

The *X* in White's "wanted" poster composition appears to refer to the Nation of Islam's use of the letter as a symbolic replacement for the white slave name that black Americans chose or were forced to choose in lieu of their original African names. Such a reference is underscored by its placement under and between the child and woman, indicating the further separation of black American families—through slave auctions—from their cultural heritage.   T. F.

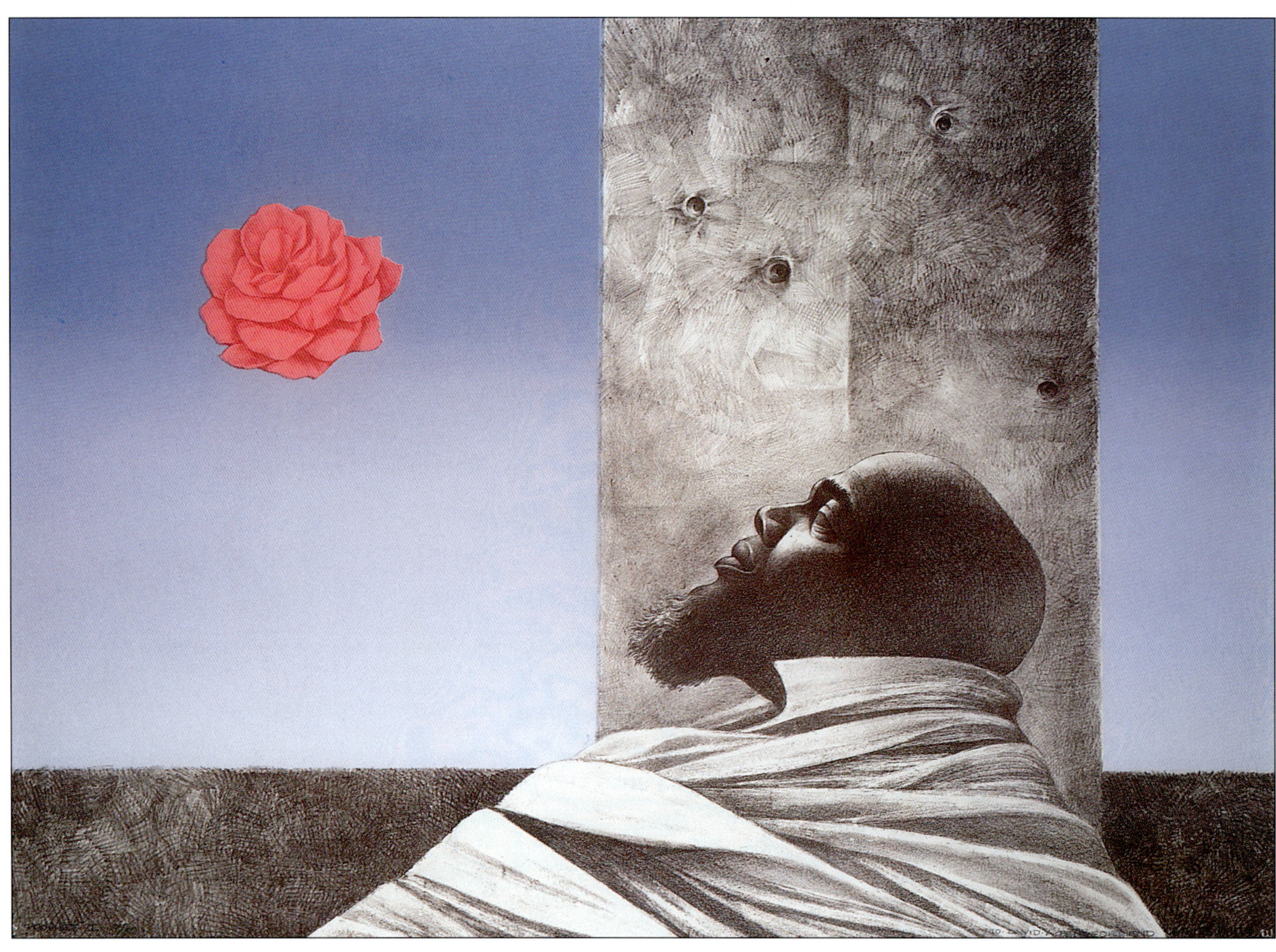

CHARLES WHITE

65.

The Prophet, 1975–1976

Lithograph

27" x 36.5"

During the mid- to late 1970s, Charles White began to move away from his characteristic black-and-white style of social realism toward a more surrealistic approach in his compositions. His new work was infused with intense color, often featured against an undefined background. This interesting combination of color, graphic realism, and sharply defined positive and negative space created a surrealistic effect reminiscent of the work of Hughie Lee-Smith.

The Prophet exemplifies this new approach in White's oeuvre, which features a portrait of a reclining man within a surreal landscape. The horizontal plane occupied by his torso and reinforced by the horizon is diametrically opposed by the vertical structure or column that frames his head. The sepia tones of the man, the horizon, and the column are nicely accented by the strong fuchsia color of the rose, which seems to float amidst the blue sky of the composition. T. F.

V. Diaspora Identities/Global Arts

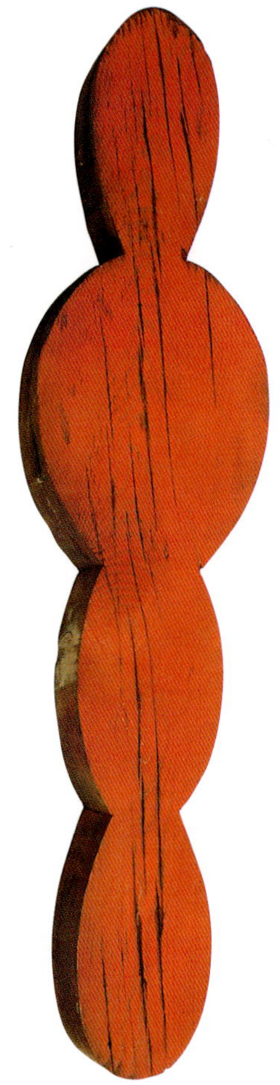

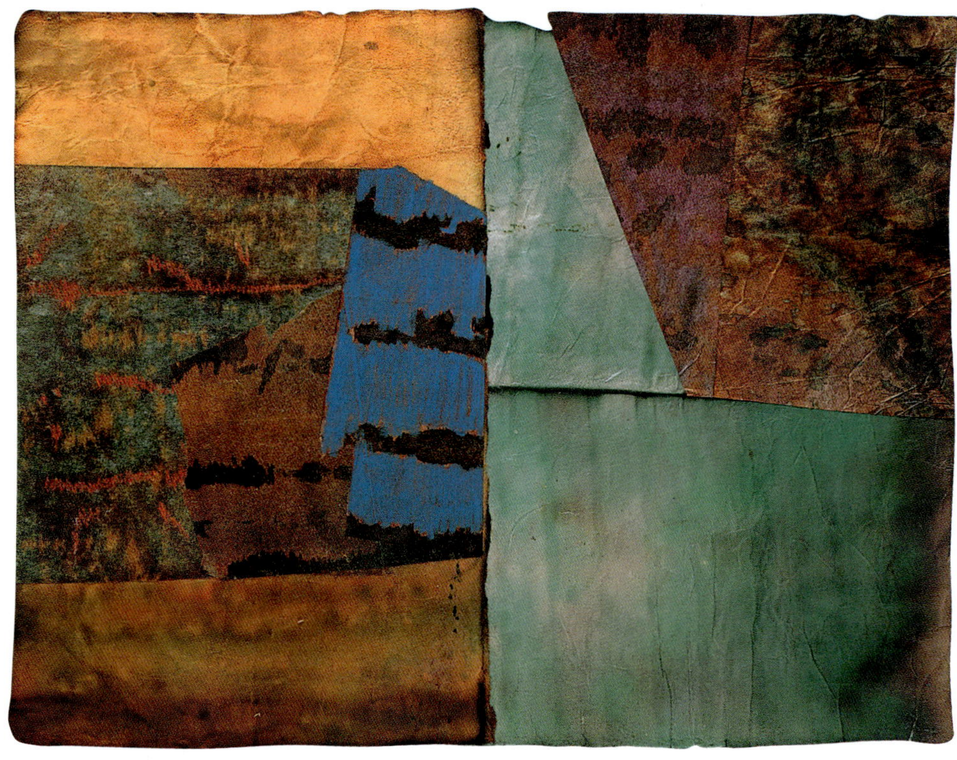

In 1990, Terry Adkins commented upon a group of his sculptures: "The language of this work is esoteric, symbolic, abstract…it embraces the legacy of all cultural traditions." *Budo* easily falls within the parameters of this statement. Like many of Adkins's titles, *Budo* suggests a non-Western influence. Adkins may be referring to the Japanese term "budo," which relates to martial-arts training; regardless of the precise intent, however, *Budo* still has an Asian connotation. The ambiguity of the term emphasizes the esoteric nature of the sculpture. In addition to Asian influences, some critics have suggested that Adkins's choice of a wood medium and his interest in African cultures may recall wood-carving traditions on the African continent. The symmetrical, swelling forms, however, transcend any of these possible references. Adkins's interest in music, his ability to play several instruments, and music's relationship to his works of art have been noted often; thus, *Budo*'s rhythmic forms may also be a visual link to musical rhythm.

Best known as a sculptor and performance artist, Terry Adkins also experiments with printmaking and multimedia. *Untitled #1* is a good example of his collages, which are layered with vibrant colors and abstract designs. The abstract shapes of which it is composed corresponds to the shapes found in his sculpture; they do not refer to one culture but rather reflect Adkins's interest in design and the many memories or objects that particular shapes or titles can evoke. J. S.

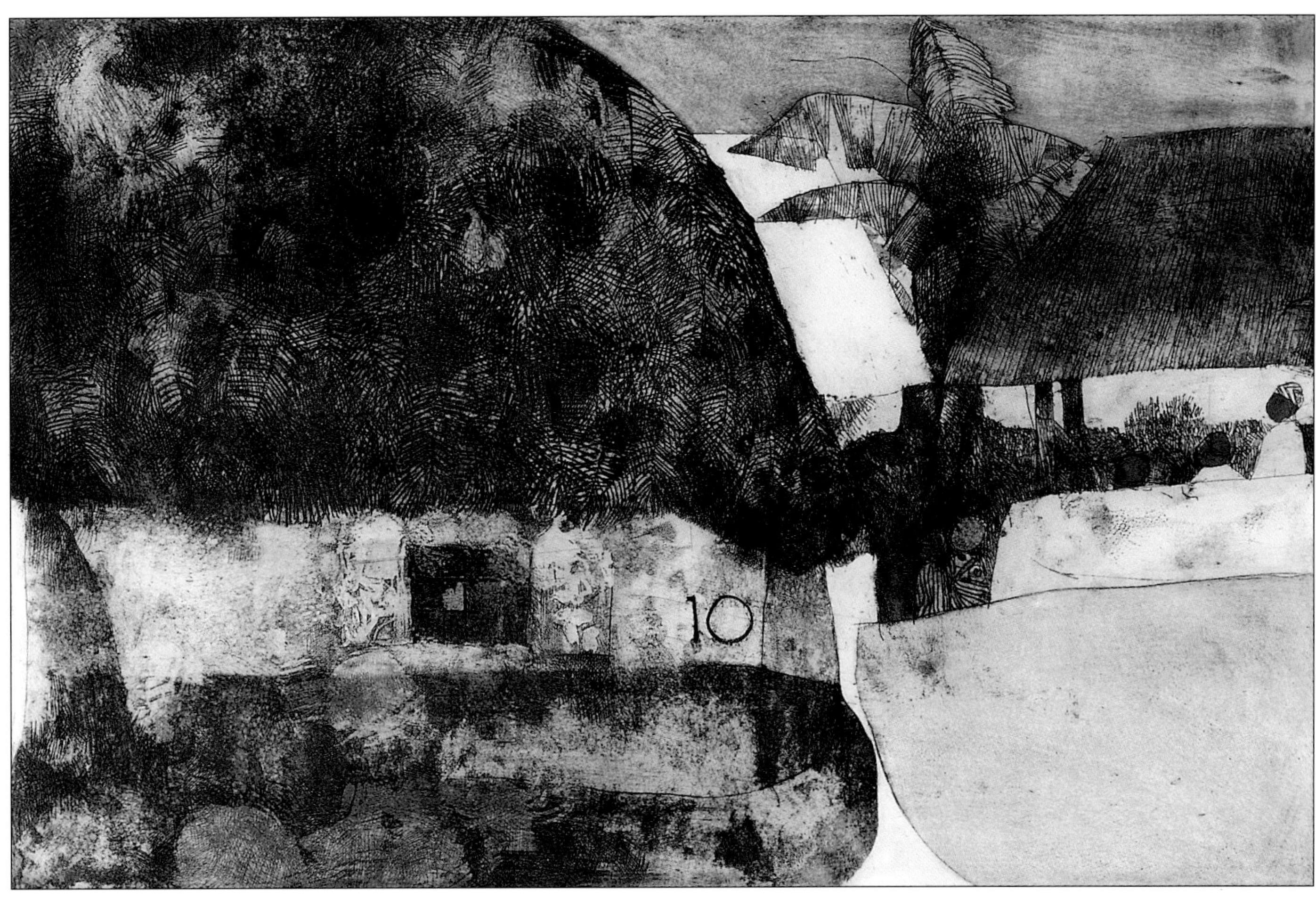

MARTIN PURYEAR

68.

Gbows Gård, 1967

Aquatint, engraving,
and etching

13" x 19.25"

Few artists working in America today have received the critical acclaim imparted to Martin Puryear. Puryear began his art career in 1959, under the direction of painter Nell Sonneman at The Catholic University of America in Washington, D.C. Between 1964 and 1966, working as a teacher in the Peace Corps in Sierra Leone, West Africa, Puryear independently studied West African arts and crafts. In 1967, while enrolled at the Swedish Royal Academy of Art in Stockholm, he began to study carpentry. It was in Sweden that Puryear shifted his artistic focus from painting to sculpture. The highly refined wood surfaces popularly associated with the majority of his oeuvre fully developed during his tenure at Yale University's Graduate School (1969–1971).

In both his sculpture and his graphic works, form is reduced to simple shapes that define the essence of a given subject. Puryear's studious investigation of indigenous architectural forms from around the world appears to have informed many of his sculptures and prints. *Gbows Gård* is among the early graphic works done by the artist. According to Puryear, *Gbows Gård* illustrates the view, from his personal studio, of a Swedish neighbor's house or compound.

Puryear is an artist whose consummate skill as a draftsman, printmaker, sculptor, and painter (particularly his painted sculptures) allows him the freedom to reduce forms to their essential structure without compromising the integrity of a given composition. This talent for seeing and representing the quintessential nature of form transverses Puryear's work regardless of his chosen medium.   T. F.

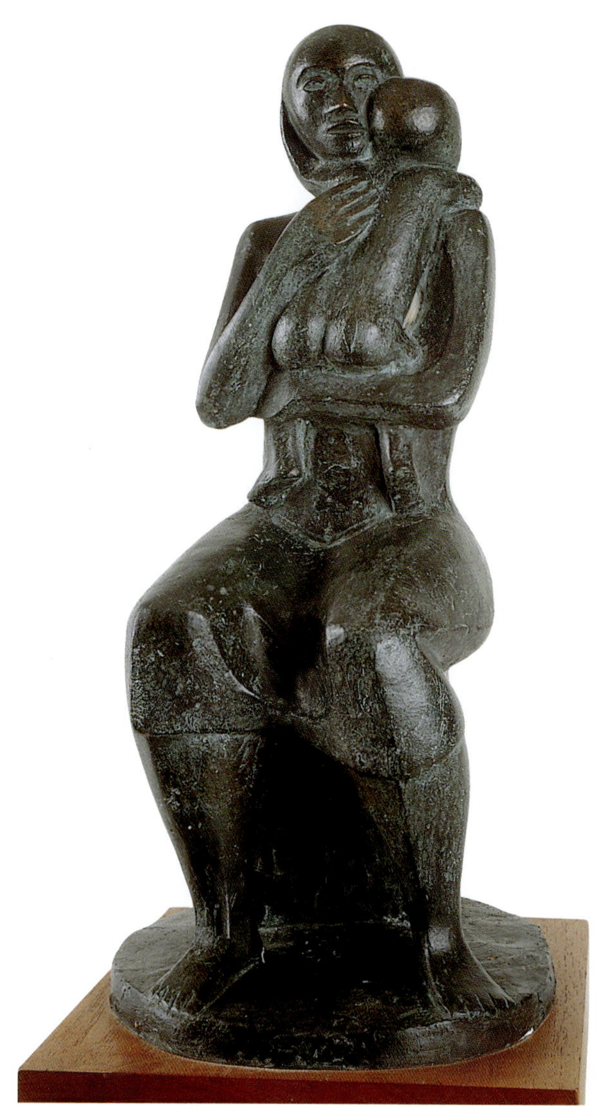

ELIZABETH
CATLETT

69.

Seated Mother and Child,
1982

Bronze

15.5" x 7" x 7"

As an artist, activist, feminist, and mother, Elizabeth Catlett has put form to the universality of motherhood for nearly sixty years. Catlett won the first prize in sculpture at the American Negro Exposition in Chicago in 1940 with a limestone *Mother and Child,* the same piece that had been her master's thesis from the University of Iowa. Throughout her career Catlett has repeatedly explored the role of woman as mother, both in print and sculpture. Although the image of mother and child recalls the Christian tradition of the Virgin Mother and the infant Jesus, the simplified forms and subtle gestures found in Catlett's *Seated Mother and Child* speak to the essential nature of motherhood, a fundamental aspect of the human condition that transcends religion, race, class, and nationality.   A. L. C.

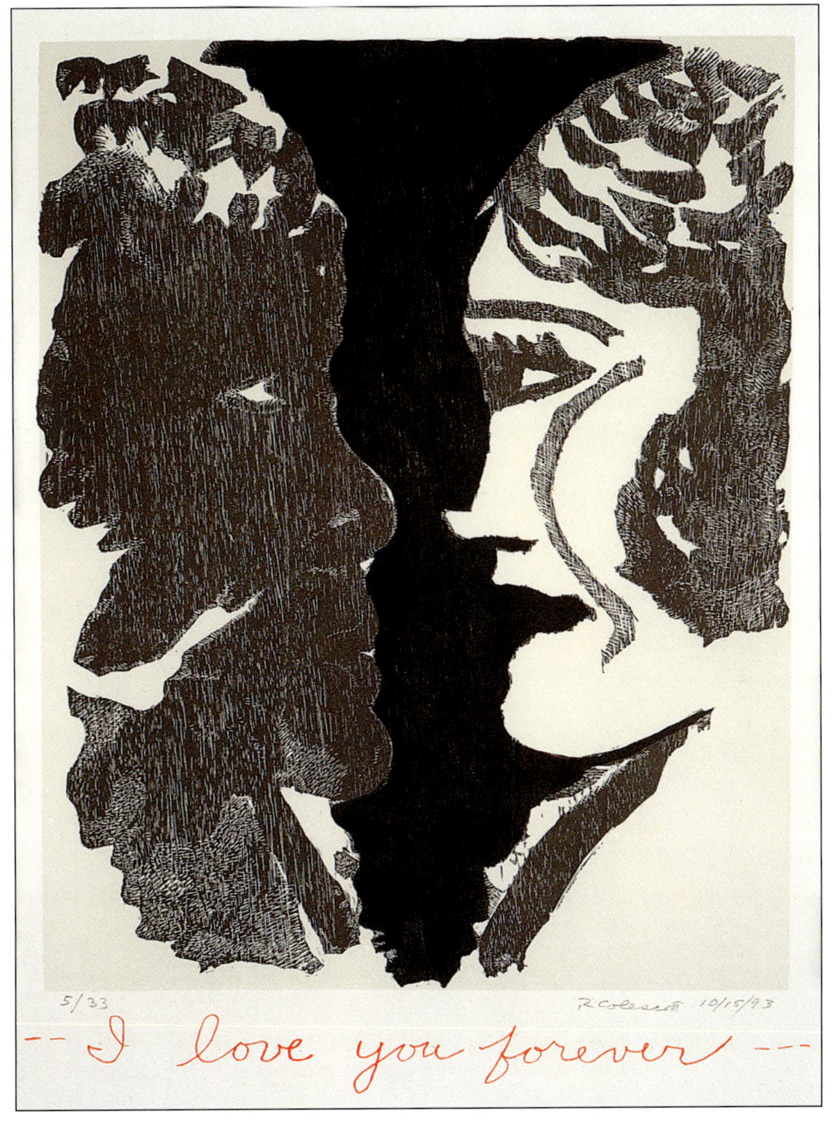

ROBERT
COLESCOTT

70.

I Love You Forever, 1993

Woodblock engraving

22" x 14"

In Robert Colescott's *I Love You Forever,* an African American man and a European American woman gaze into each other's eyes; the caption establishes a narrative, suggesting a relationship between the two. Is this a simple depiction of lovers? Considering the history of race relations and the unconscious assumptions viewers bring to a work of art, this couple's relationship becomes more ambiguous. Colescott plays on viewers' beliefs concerning interracial relations by reinforcing compositionally the hesitant nature of their relationship: The lovers face each other but do not touch. His lithograph forces viewers to confront stereotypes and assumptions about "the black man with the white woman." Even the word "forever," which sounds certain, could be interpreted as a desperate declaration, based upon the societal pressures that work to keep the couple apart. Colescott is well known for his art historical satires and subversions of stereotypes; in *I Love You Forever,* as in many of his other works, he explores the identities that people assign to others and assume themselves.   J. S.

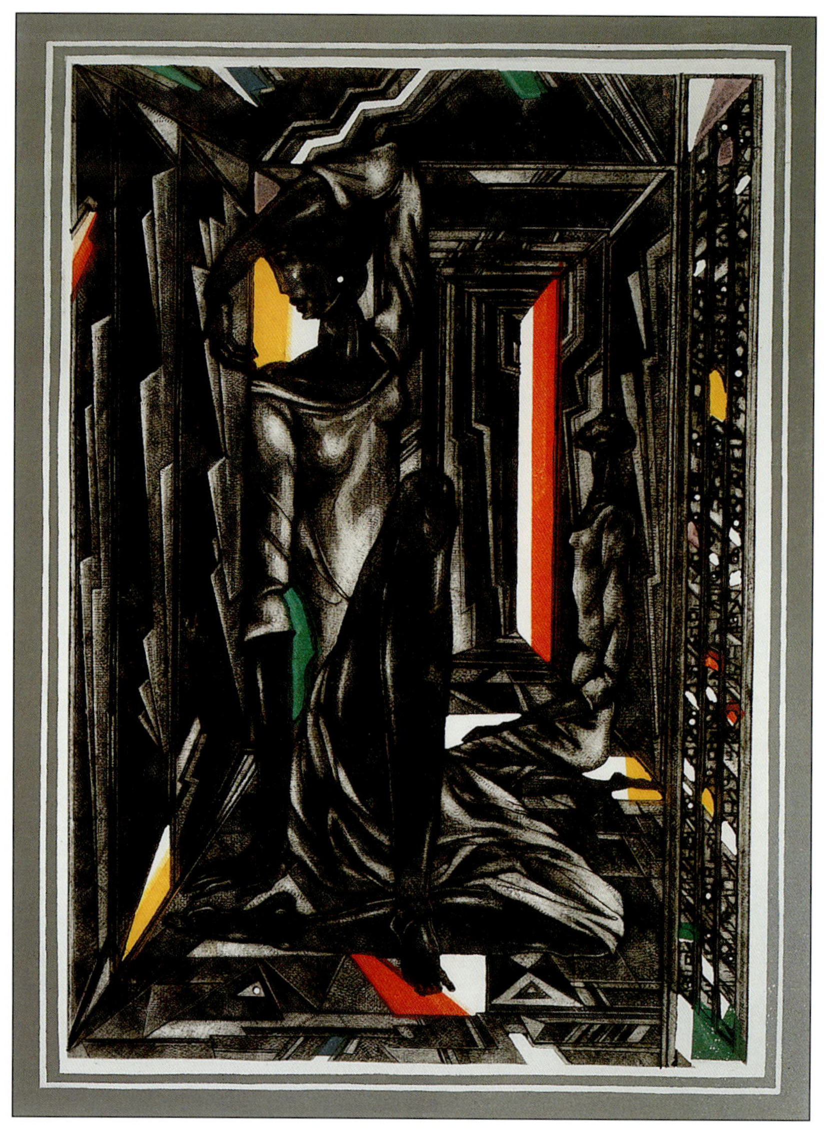

71.

Jewels / Theme V, c. 1980

Etching on paper

23" x 16.75"

One of the country's most respected African American artists, Cortor spent years studying diasporan peoples in the American South and the Caribbean, and, over the years, amalgamated various aspects of women of the African Diaspora into his prototypical black female. Eldzier Cortor was one of the first black male artists to explore the beauty and intensity of black womanhood. Sensuous and melancholy women of color inhabit Cortor's intimate spaces. Seated in a stylized interior, the elongated, gracefully introspective woman of *Jewel / Theme IV* represents Cortor's idealized black female.   A. L. C.

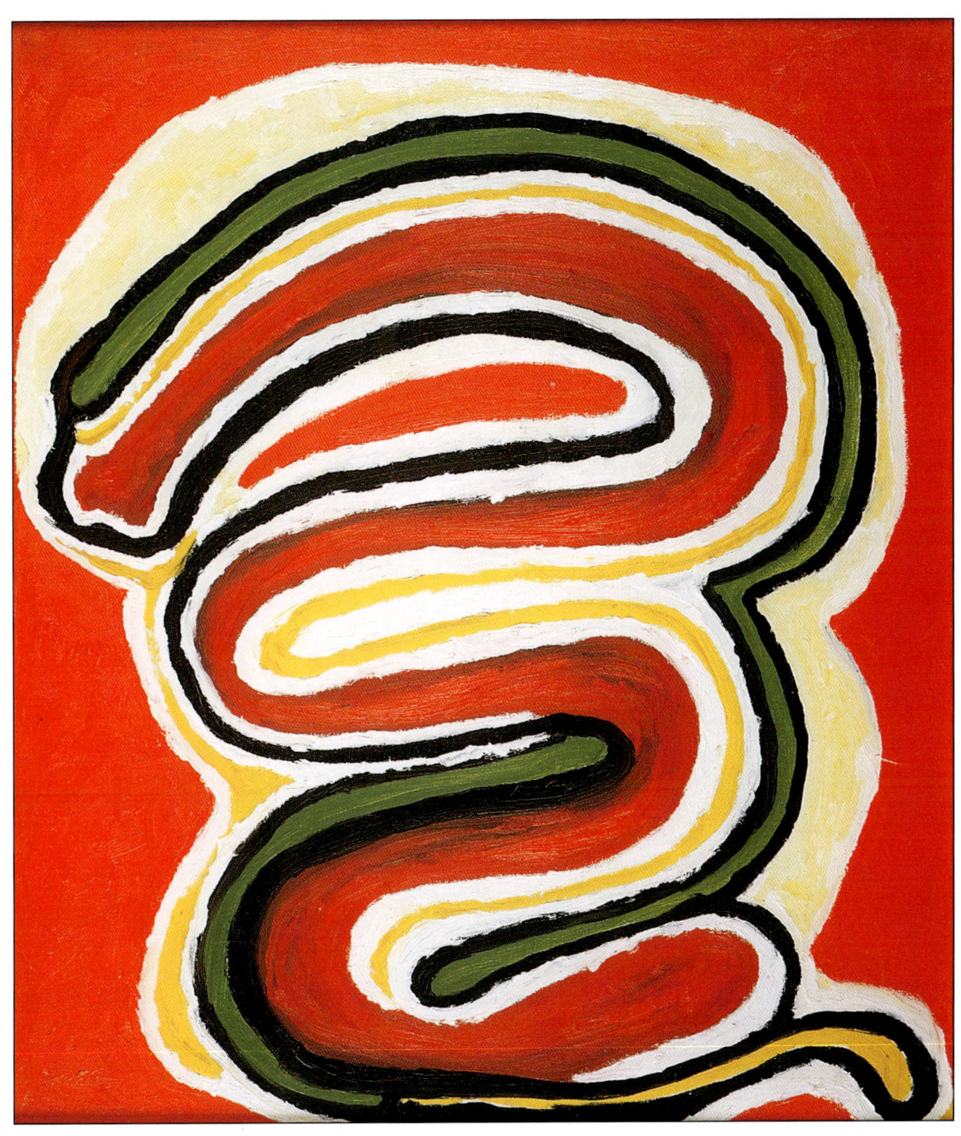

BEAUFORD
DELANEY

72.

Untitled, c. 1965

Oil on canvas

25.5" x 21.25"

Beauford Delaney's untitled 1965 abstraction demonstrates the bold use of color and expressive brush work that is the hallmark of his oeuvre. As a young artist Delaney lived in New York's Harlem and Greenwich Village. He supported himself by painting portraits of a spectrum of New York notables and established close relationships with Village artists and literati. Delaney's relationship with abstraction predated the notorious Abstract Expressionist movement, positioning him as a forerunner of one of the most important ideological and stylistic developments in twentieth-century American art. Although he chose not to identify himself with the movement, as the Abstract Expressionists began to gain notoriety in the late 1940s, Delaney's abstract work increasingly gained attention. Beauford Delaney expatriated to Paris in 1953, where he came to be considered the most important black American artist of his day and where he remained until his death in 1979. Delaney developed his commitment to abstraction during his years in Paris and continued to produce expressionist portraits of friends and patrons.   A. L. C.

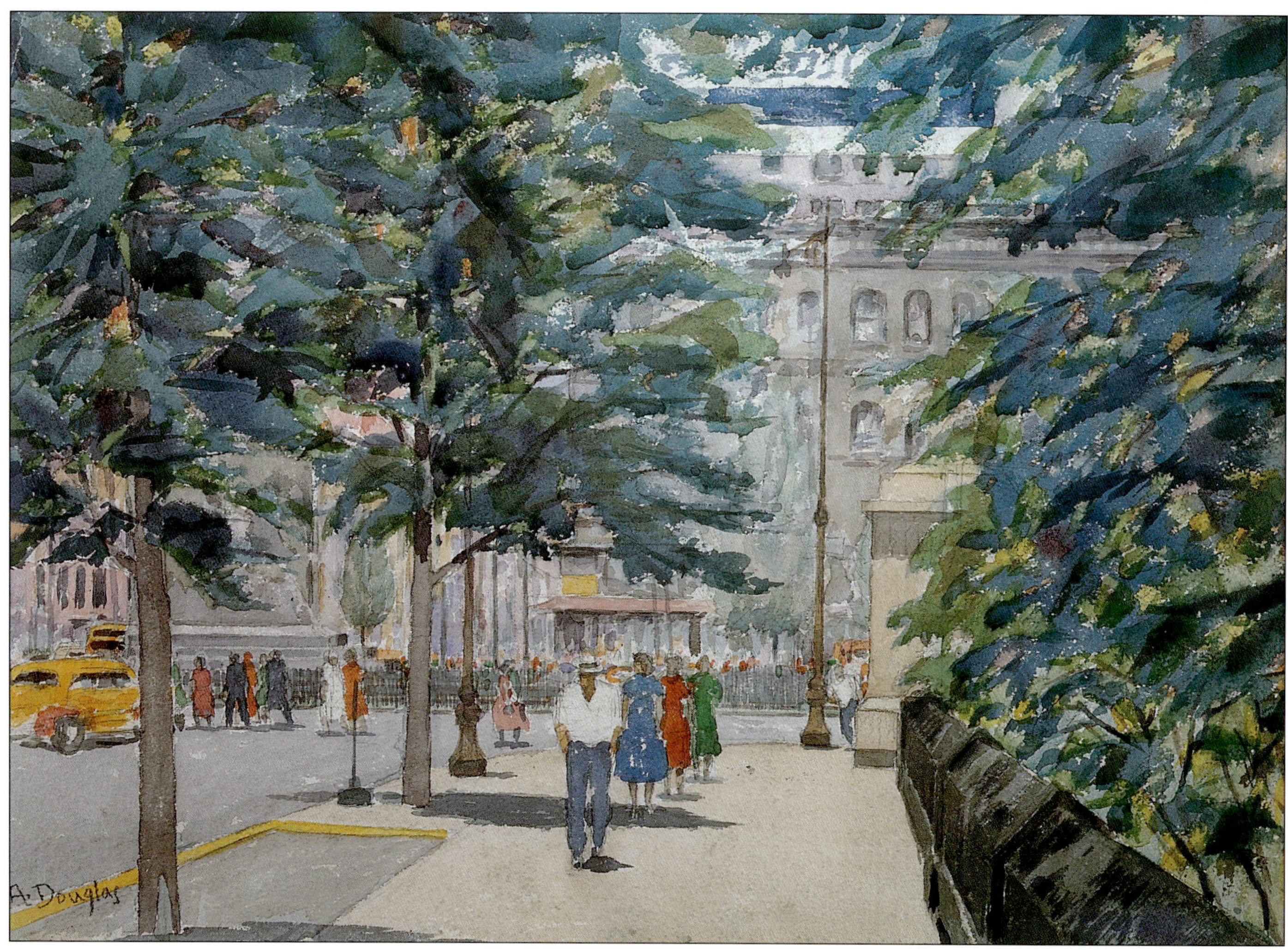

A a r o n   D o u g l a s

73.

City Scape, 1956

Watercolor on paper

14.5" x 19.5"

Although Aaron Douglas is best known for his monochromatic compositions, often inspired by Art Deco and Egyptian influences, he never abandoned the portraits and landscapes that were based on the European art traditions he learned early in his academic career. In one such work, *City Scape,* Douglas utilized a Post-Impressionist optical analysis of color while carefully delineating his freely drawn composition to capture the vitality of black urban life. This tranquil and romantic scene of black urban life likely reflects Douglas's lifelong and sentimental connections to the New York urban experience of his early career. Although by 1937 he had moved permanently to Nashville, Tennessee, he maintained his Harlem apartment at 409 Edgecombe Avenue until a few years prior to his death.   T. F.

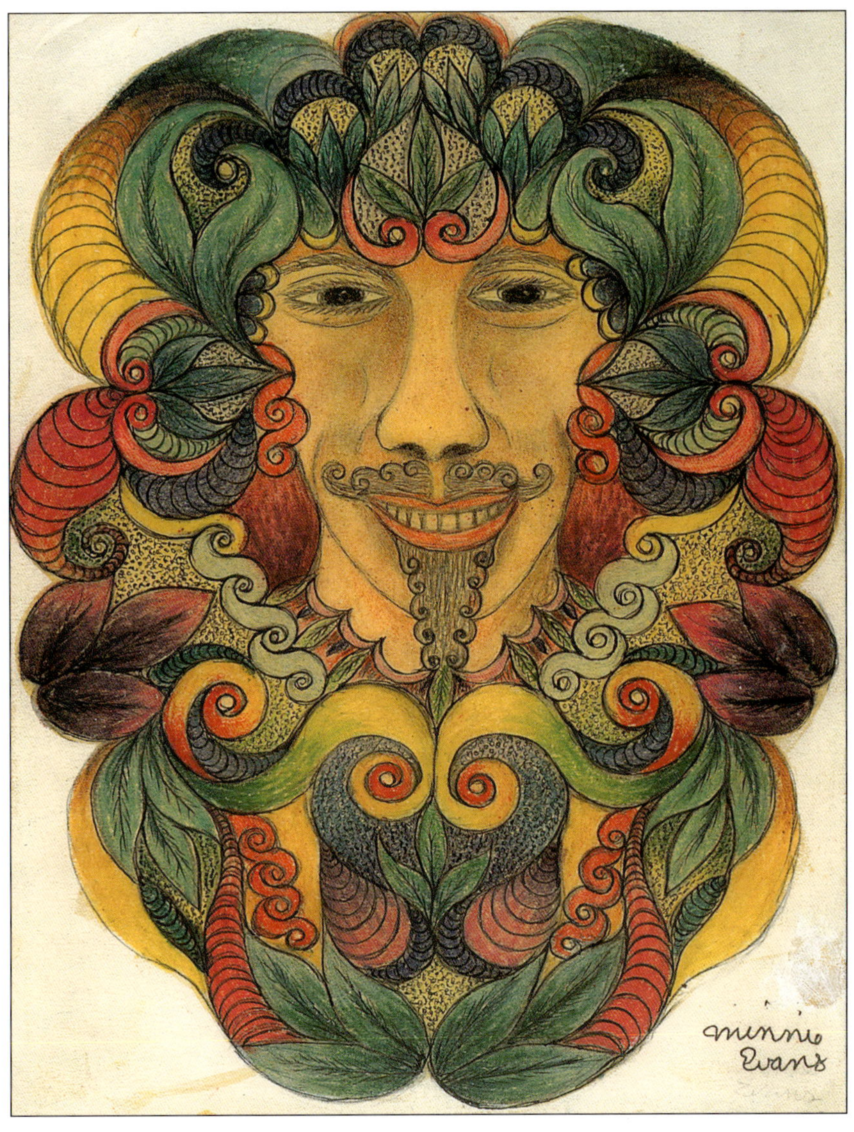

MINNIE EVANS

74.

Face of a Man, n.d.

Crayon and watercolor
on paper

12" x 9"

Regarded as one of America's most unique visionaries, Minnie Evans began fashioning her dreams into art in the early 1930s. Evans worked as a gatekeeper at a botanical garden in Wilmington, North Carolina, for more than twenty-five years. With no formal training, she began to create as a result of direct inspiration from God through her dreams. Her inscribed visions consist of magical fantasy-scapes inhabited with fantastic plant and animal life, floating eyes, and spiritual beings. *Face of a Man* is typical of her highly personal iconography and distinctive style. The mysterious head is intricately decorated with exotic flowers and foliage of her own design. Evans's beings are the human incarnation of her singular spirituality, articulated in a language that is at once highly personal and universal.   A. L. C.

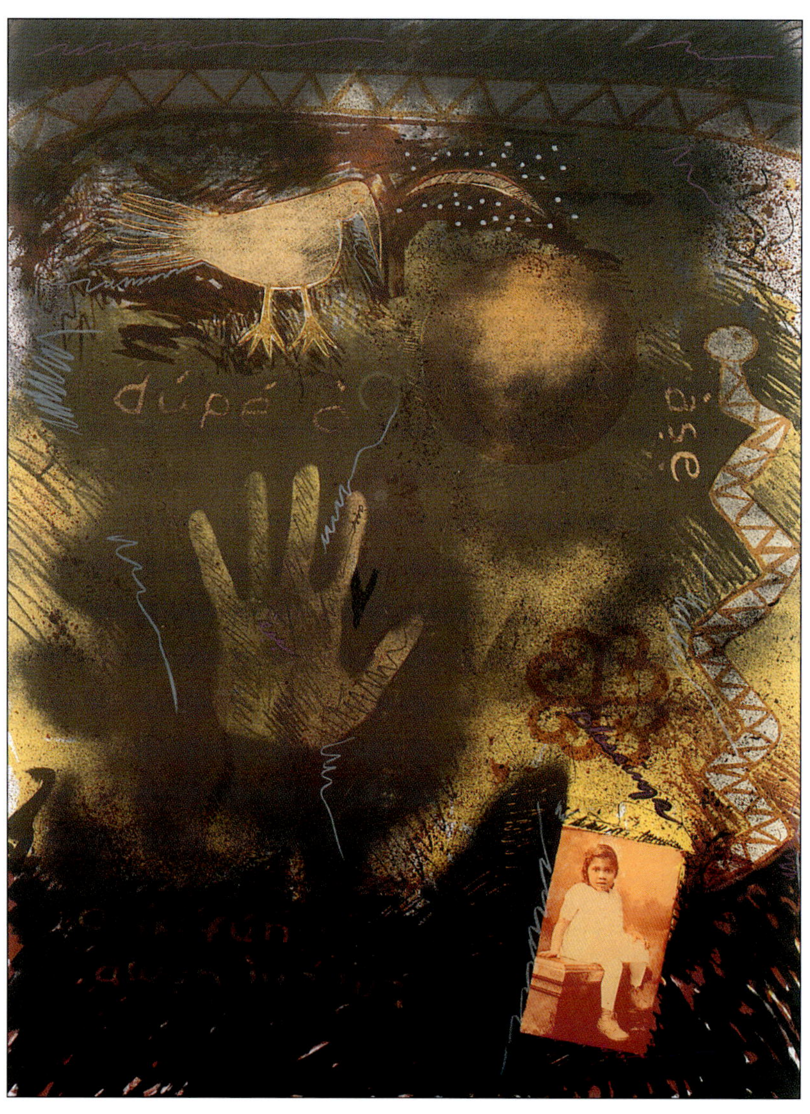

MICHAEL D. HARRIS

75.

Mothers and the Presence of Myth, 1997

Lithograph

30" x 21.25"

Art historian, artist, and AfriCobra member Michael D. Harris's conviction that art, at its best, is an "articulation of spiritual ideas or transformative intention" is reflected in his lithograph *Mothers and the Presence of Myth.* Harris combines elements of Yoruba religious aesthetics and symbols with the personal image of his mother to create a work that for him serves as an agent of personal and social transformation.

Mothers and the Presence of Myth was created at the Brandywine Workshop, Philadelphia, as part of a suite of works developed by the members of AfriCobra (African Commune of Bad Relevant Artists) between 1993 and 1995. Harris states that he designed this work, with its polychromatic areas of tonalities traditionally utilized by Yoruba women shrine painters, as a testament to the spiritual powers and positive attributes of black women. Harris's interest in female spirituality and transformation is further implied through his incorporation of such Yoruba religious symbols as the bird, which refers to the idea of motherhood; the snake, a symbol that African art historian Robert Farris Thompson believes represents the spiritual command *ashe* (defined by him as "God's own enabling light rendered accessible to men and women"); and the hand, a symbol that refers to the ability of an individual to create himself or herself with his or her own hand. Harris's inclusion of a photograph of his mother as a young girl serves as a symbolic bridge linking the past of African ancestors and his mother's individual history to the future, embodied in the life of her son and his children.   T. F.

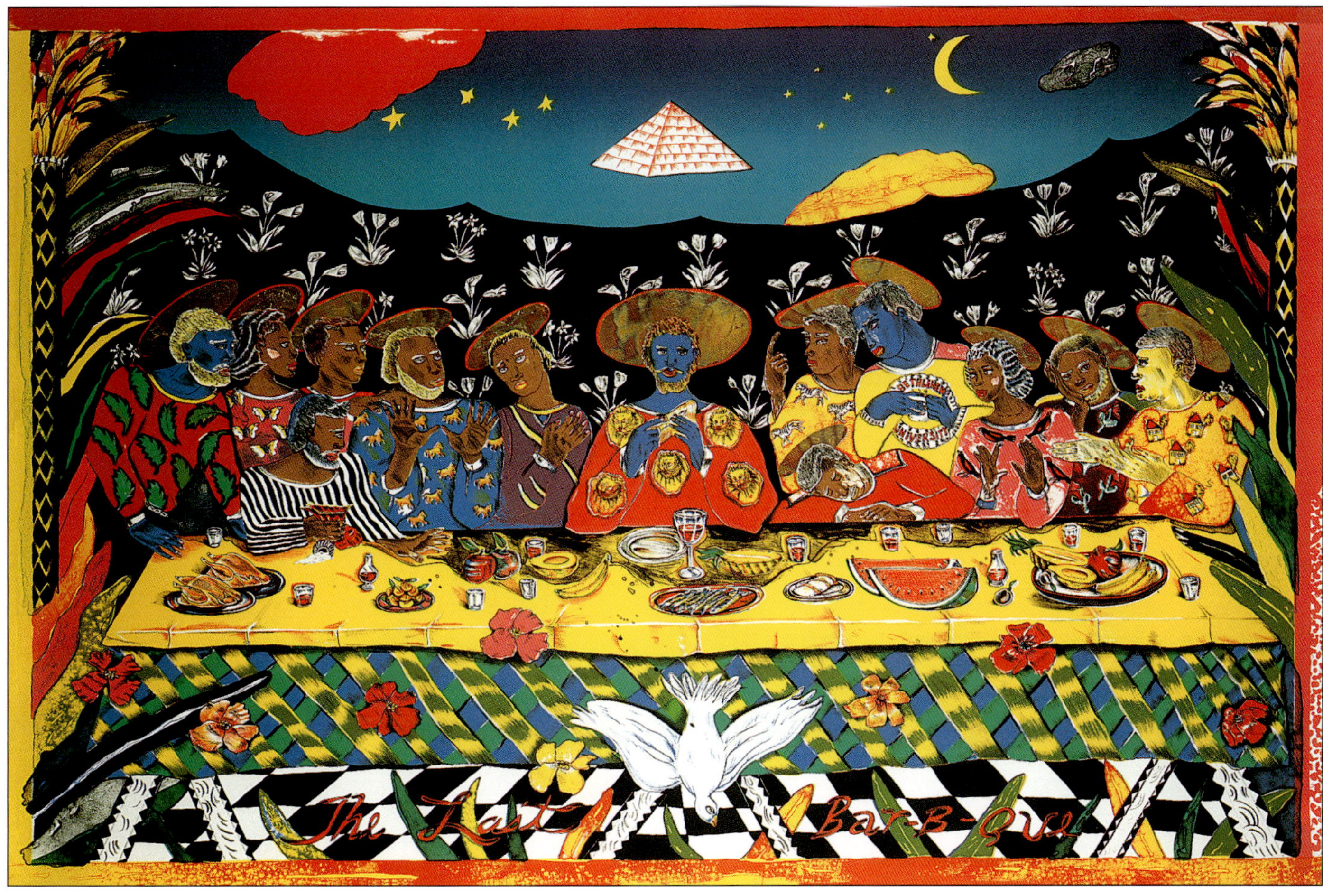

MARGO HUMPHREY

76.

The Last Bar-B-Que, 1989

Lithograph

26" x 38.5"

The Last Bar-B-Que is one of the most well-known lithographs of master printmaker Margo Humphrey. It required nearly three years of thought, during which Humphrey looked at other representations of the Last Supper by artists from Lorenzetti to Emil Nolde and considered what tone the potential work should possess. In the final version, *The Last Bar-B-Que* embraces many sources and traditions to create a scene that is meaningful, humorous, and visually beautiful. Like traditional representations of the Last Supper, Christ is shown seated at a table, surrounded by his disciples. Humor can be found in the title and in the watermelon and chicken that join the traditional bread and wine; however, the title also indicates a shift from a European American perspective to an African American one. The apostles and Christ are African American, while the presence of the pyramid and bright patterns of the clothing and the overall composition suggest African influences. Humphrey commented, "T*he Last Bar-B-Que* is a serious piece: a rewriting of history through the eyes of my ancestry, a portrayal of a savior who looks like my people."   J. S.

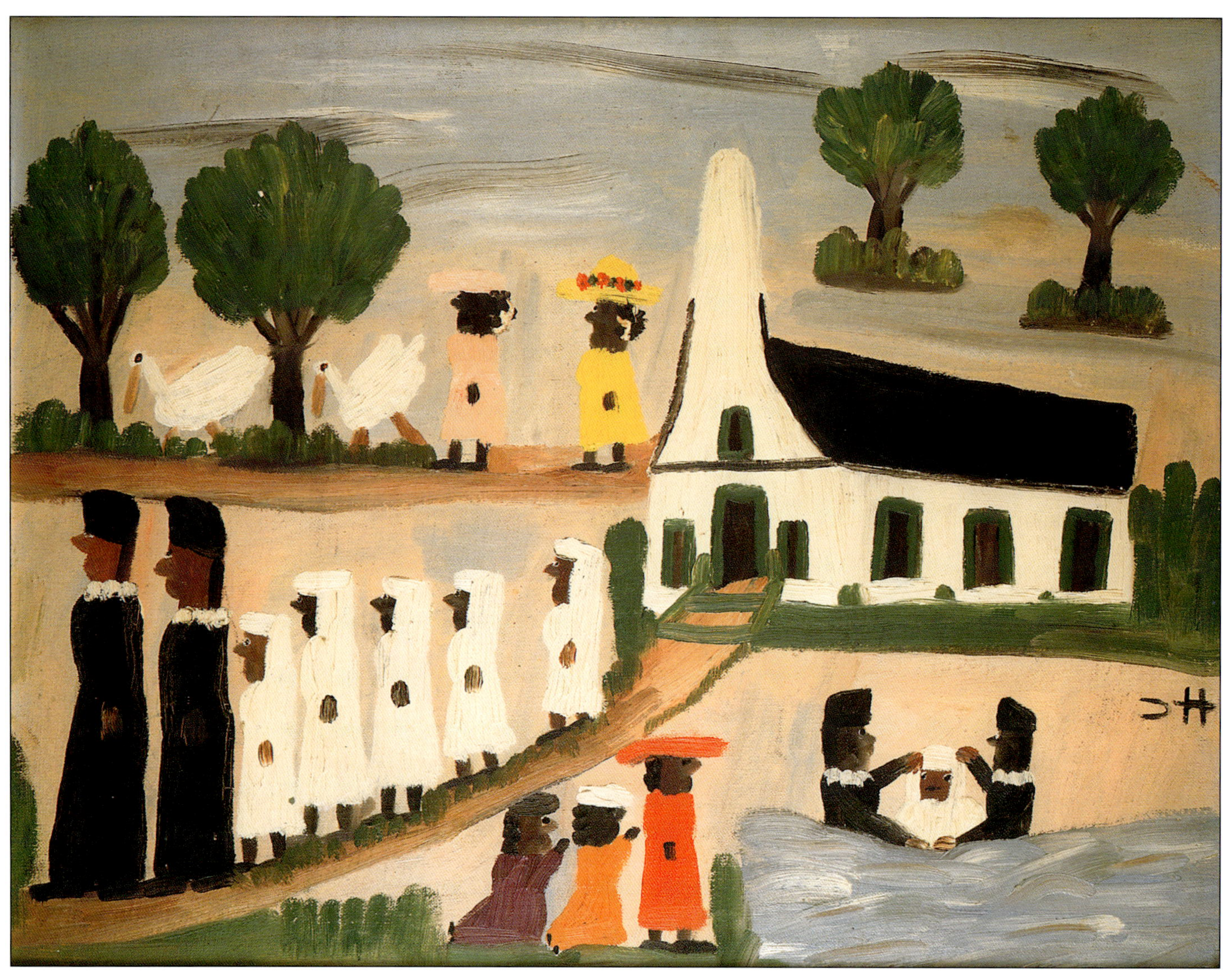

CLEMENTINE
HUNTER

77.

Baptism, c. 1964

Oil on canvas

15.5" x 19.5"

One of the most celebrated African American self-taught artists of the twentieth century, Clementine Hunter's entire body of work revolves around her more than 100 years of experience on a rural Louisiana plantation. Hunter's images are predominantly focused on those experiences shared by the community of African Americans who lived and worked on the historic Melrose Plantation, where she spent most of her life. *Baptism,* one of many similar works portraying the ceremony surrounding the baptism of a child, underscores the great importance of the black church in the rural south. Hunter's apolitical commentary combined with her frank, unself-conscious style provides us with a fascinating narrative of southern black culture from within the plantation system.   A. L. C.

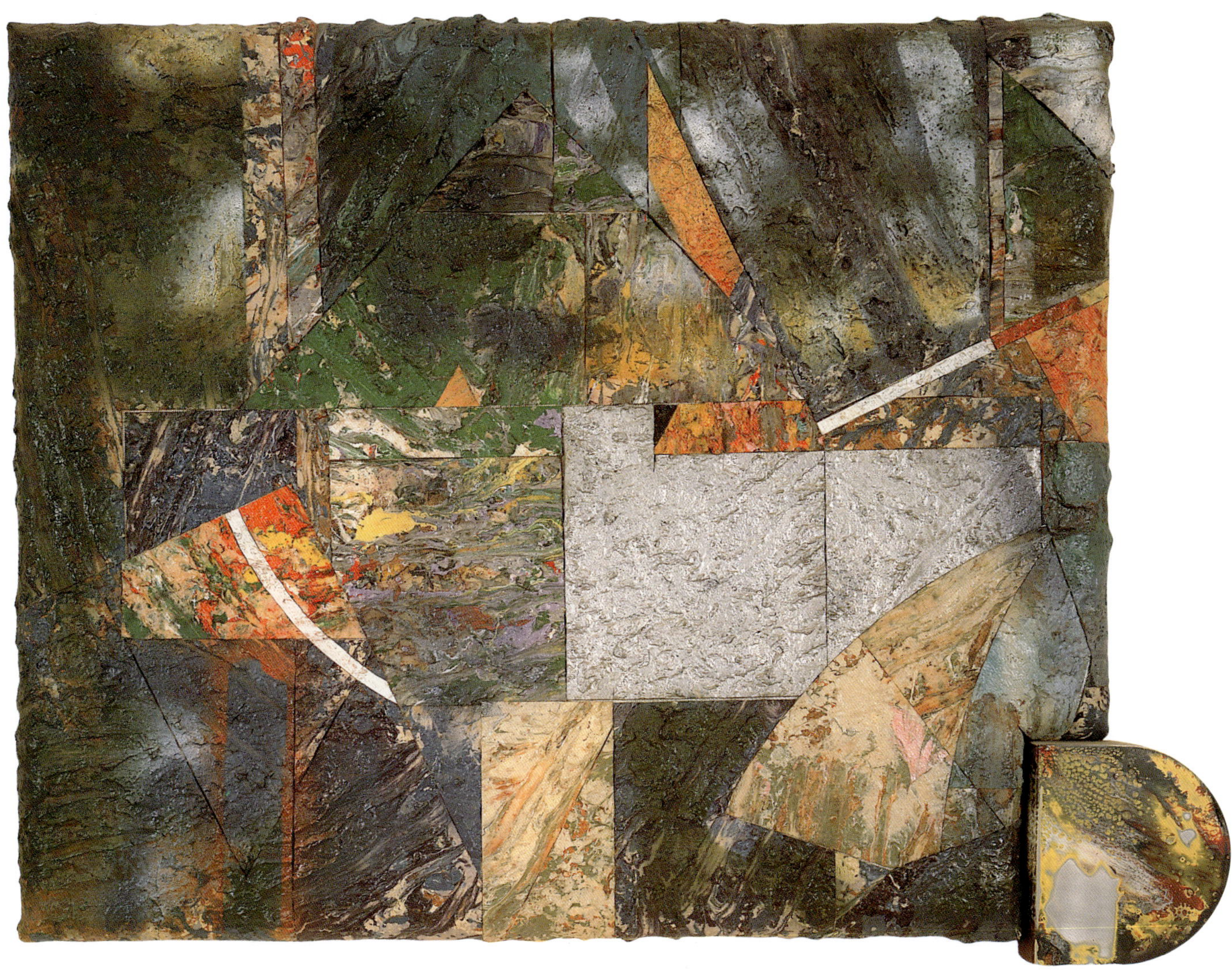

SAM GILLIAM

78.

From *The D Series,* 1982

Mixed media on canvas

32" x 42"

An abstract painter for more than thirty years, Sam Gilliam has worked through the Abstract Expressionism and Washington Color Field school movements to create his own unique style. Known as the "father of the draped canvas," Gilliam rose to fame in the 1960s by liberating the canvas from its frame, draping it from leather strings, and hanging it at the owner's discretion. This blurring of painting and sculpture is continued in *The D Series*. It also marks the end of narrative compositions for Gilliam, for this series is his first nonobjective, completely abstract work.

At the bottom right-hand corner of the canvas, a small, brightly painted metal D-shape is attached to the rectangular composition. This allows the composition to exist in three-dimensional space. The canvas itself is a rich collage of textures and patterns produced by paint and mixed media. While working to situate himself through multiple Western movements, Gilliam is systematically recalling his African and African American heritage. The rhythmic patchwork-like quality of the canvas is reminiscent of African American "crazy quilts" of the deep South and also of asymmetric West African textile prints.   K. A. K.

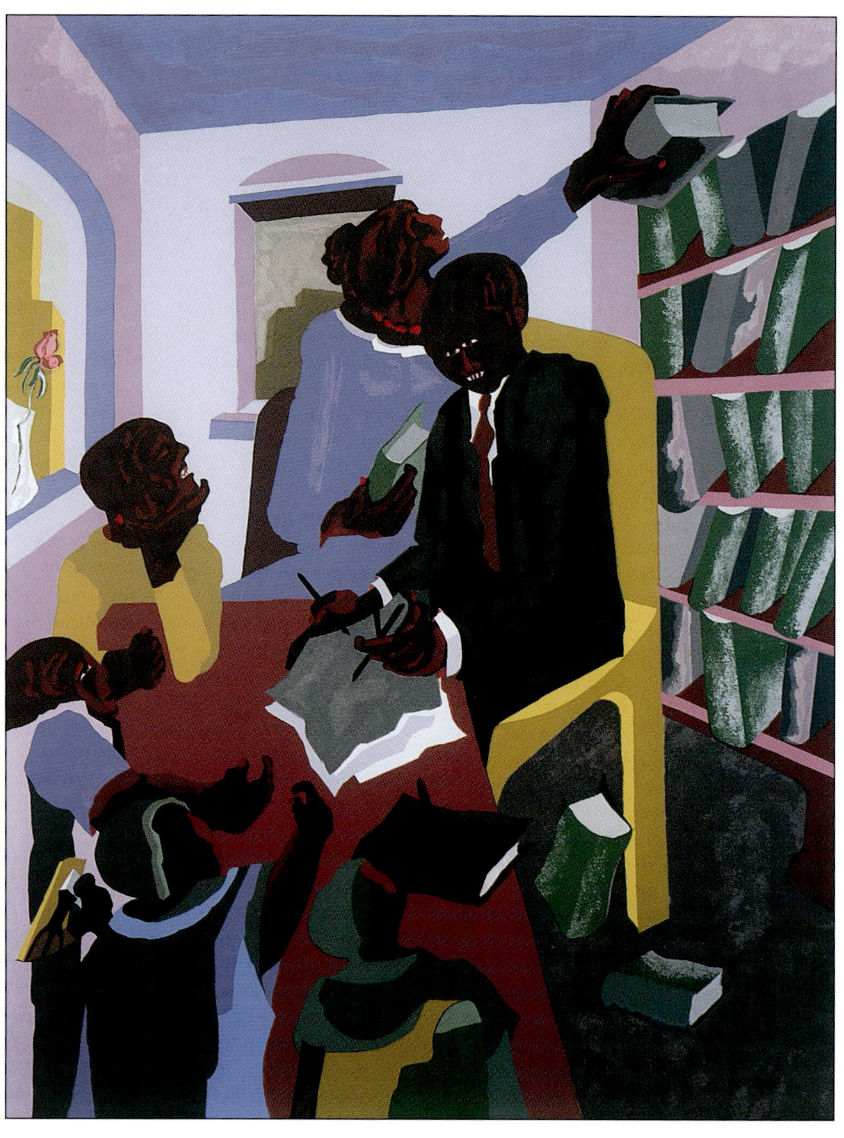

Jacob Lawrence's 1994 silk-screen print *Lawyer and Clients* depicts a family of young African Americans visiting a lawyer's office for legal advice and assistance. Although Lawrence chose not to inform his audience of the specific purpose of the visit, the tightly unified structure of the composition, which focuses on the tools of the lawyer's trade—the reference books on the shelf and in the possession of the woman in the background, the pens and paper in the counselor's hands, and his attentive and eager clientele—indicates that the importance of the meeting is clear to all who are involved within the scene.

Lawrence's decision to illustrate a black family seeking the advice of an African American lawyer is a significant statement relating to the crucial niche that black professionals occupy within the African American community.   T. F.

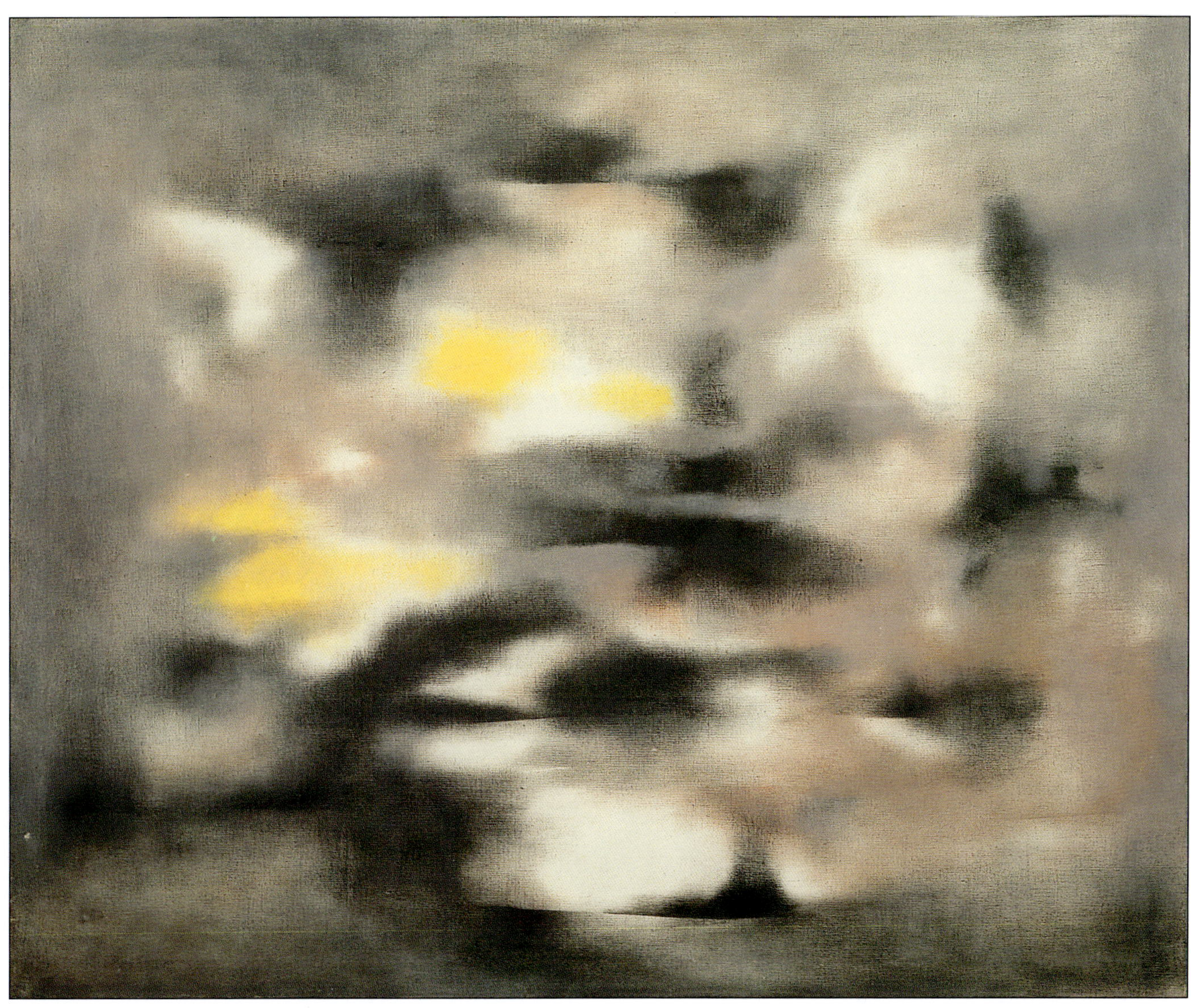

Norman Lewis was the first major African American Abstract Expressionist. Like many other Abstract Expressionists of the era, Lewis began his career during the 1930s as a Social Realist. He worked as a WPA artist under Augusta Savage and was well situated within the artistic milieu of Harlem, New York. After World War II, Lewis's interest shifted away from abstract figuration toward European modernism, popularized by artists such as Pablo Picasso, Georges Braque, Wassily Kandinsky, and Arshile Gorky. According to art historian Ann Gibson, "Lewis's wartime experiences…prompted him to question whether picturing 'the Negro' was the most effective means either of expressing his own identity or of furthering the interests of the Black community."

During the late 1940s and through the 1950s, Lewis believed that he had found in New York's Abstract Expressionist movement a style that could adequately express his own particular artistic identity. In a fashion similar to that of other New York Abstract Expressionists with whom Lewis closely associated at Artists Sessions at Studio 35 (organized by Willem de Kooning, Franz Kline, and other New York avant-garde artists to discuss art and theories of Abstract Expressionism), Lewis's work, as evidenced in the 1960 painting *Good Morning,* evolved into an aesthetic of pure abstraction.

Although the title and the yellow, blue, and hazy gray hues of *Good Morning* suggest a particular moment, such as an early morning sunrise, the absence of identifiable forms in Lewis's painting leaves its intent inconclusive.   T. F.

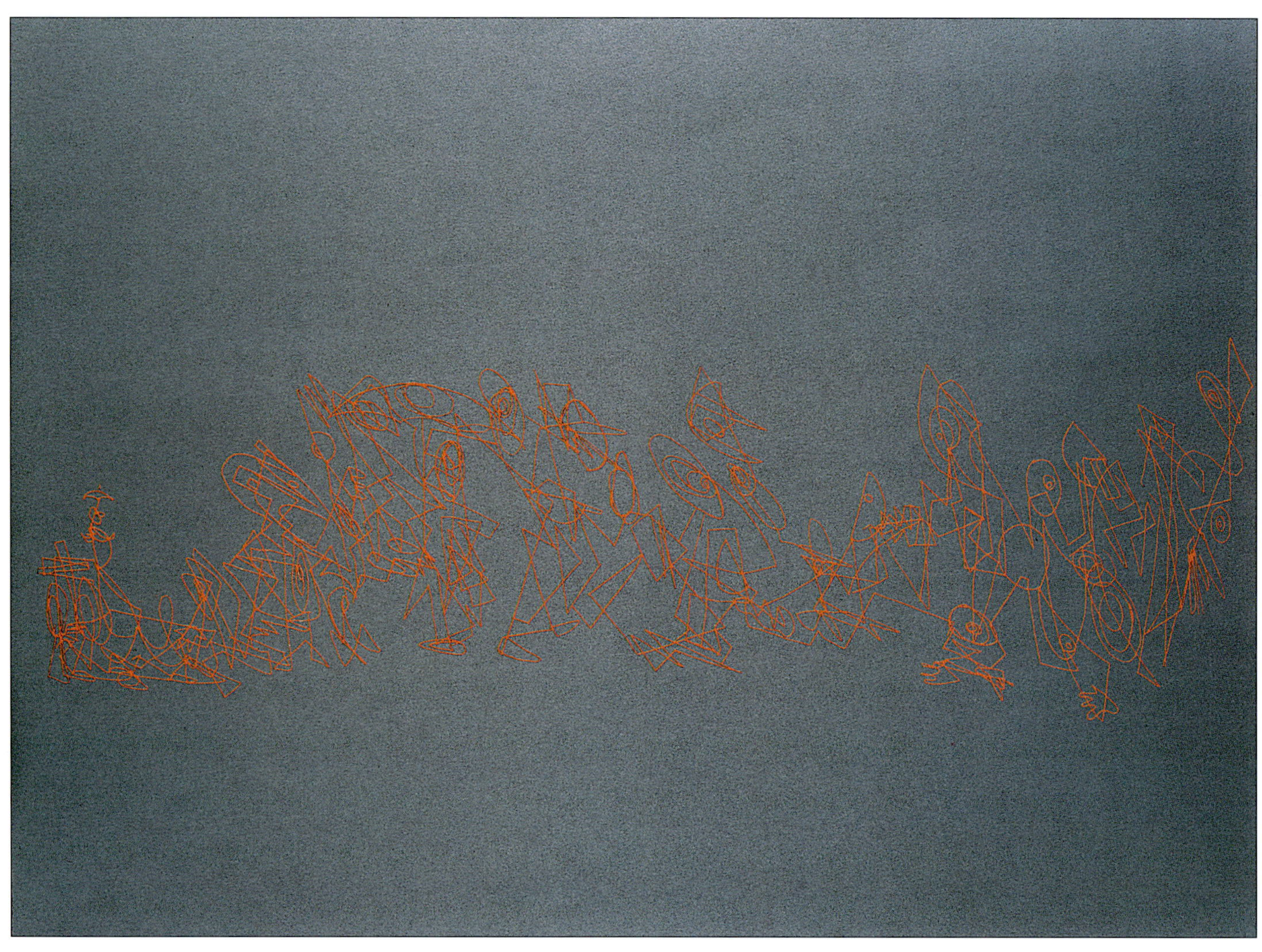

From the 1920s through the 1940s, many African American leaders, historians, and artists believed it was the social responsibility of black artists to create works that would heighten the awareness of cultural and political issues within the black community. However, in the 1940s, Lewis rejected the notion that art should be used as a tool for social protest and became an Abstract Expressionist. Because of his decision to abandon social realism in favor of nonobjective aesthetics, Lewis was heavily criticized by members of the African American arts community.

According to Bearden's and Henderson's 1993 *History of African-American Artists,* the criticism Lewis experienced during this period may have led him to feelings of extreme isolation in asserting his right to paint as he felt. From this isolation, they add, Lewis would often create works containing small clusters of trailing figures, symbolizing the absence of individuality and true independence in American culture.

Although undated, the abstracted figurative style in *The Red Umbrella* appears to relate the period of trailing figures in Lewis's work during the late 1950s and early 1960s. The line of figures actively wrestling with umbrellas might refer to Lewis's concepts of independence and interdependence.   T. F.

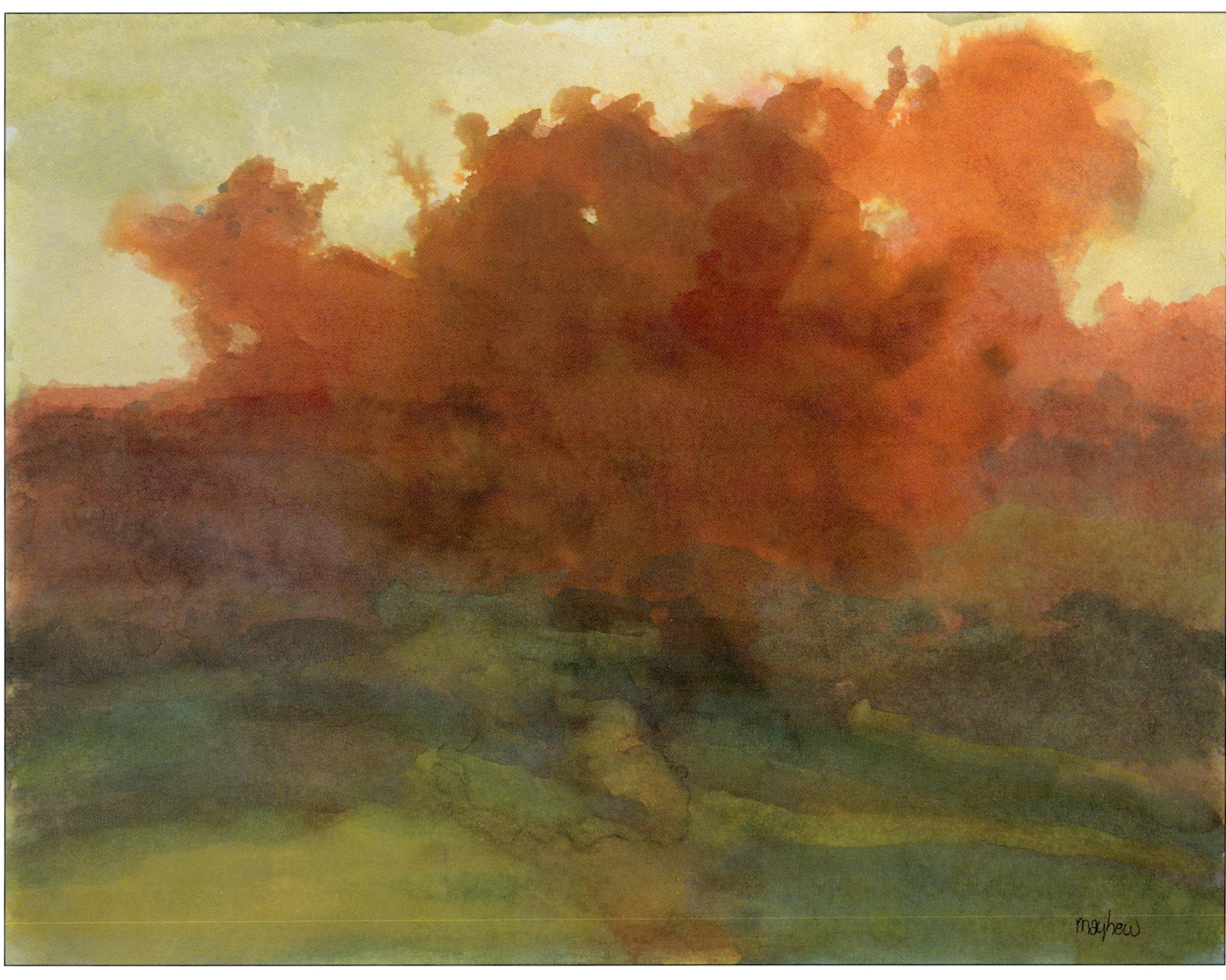

RICHARD MAYHEW

82.

Landscape, n.d.

Watercolor on paper

11" x 14"

Throughout his life, abstract expressionist painter and professor Richard Mayhew has been preoccupied with light and color and its effects on the natural environment. Mayhew's absorption with nature, which he attributes to his paternal grandmother's lessons in Native American traditions and attitudes regarding what he describes as "nature lore," is evident in his sensitively painted and richly colored landscapes of forests, fields, swamps, and outcroppings.

Perhaps the most outstanding feature in Mayhew's works is his exceptional mastery of color, illusion, and space. During the 1950s, Mayhew's interest in the effects of light led him to study the science of optics. By 1960, his attention shifted to an examination of color's effect on form. During the 1960s, Mayhew sought to apply color, space, and form within landscapes to express, in his words, "a universal space with the illusion of time." Although Mayhew's landscape paintings do not contain overt references to the African or African American experience, he believes that the timeless emotional quality of his works have an intimate connection to the warm and cool rhythms of jazz and the blues.

The solitary tree in Mayhew's *Landscape,* rooted in the cool green grass and softly framed by the warm sun and distant mountains, exemplifies his expertise in the use of color and space to psychologically identify abstract elements of the landscape with human emotions and ideas.
T. F.

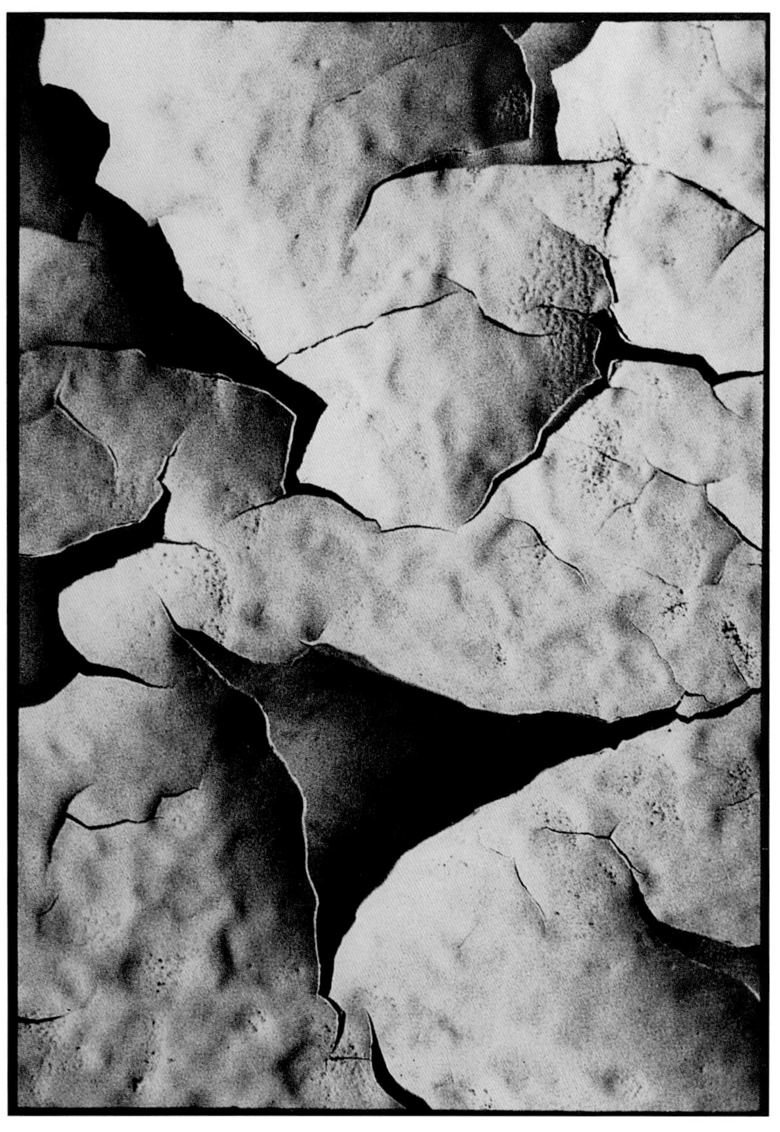

WILLIAM MCNEIL

83.

Elegy, 1993

Black-and-white photograph

9" x 6"

David Driskell's patronage of young photographer and former student William McNeil is a testament to his dedication to the support of emerging artists. William McNeil believes that he is at a stage of development where he is trying to become conscious of what he has within himself and to express those discoveries within his art. His 1993 photograph *Elegy* represents part of this extremely personal journey. *Elegy,* McNeil's visual testament of sorrow, was created in memory of his father.

As part of his series *Echoes of Passage, Elegy* represents a stylistic shift in McNeil's work from primarily representational photographs to images of nonobjective subjects.   T. F.

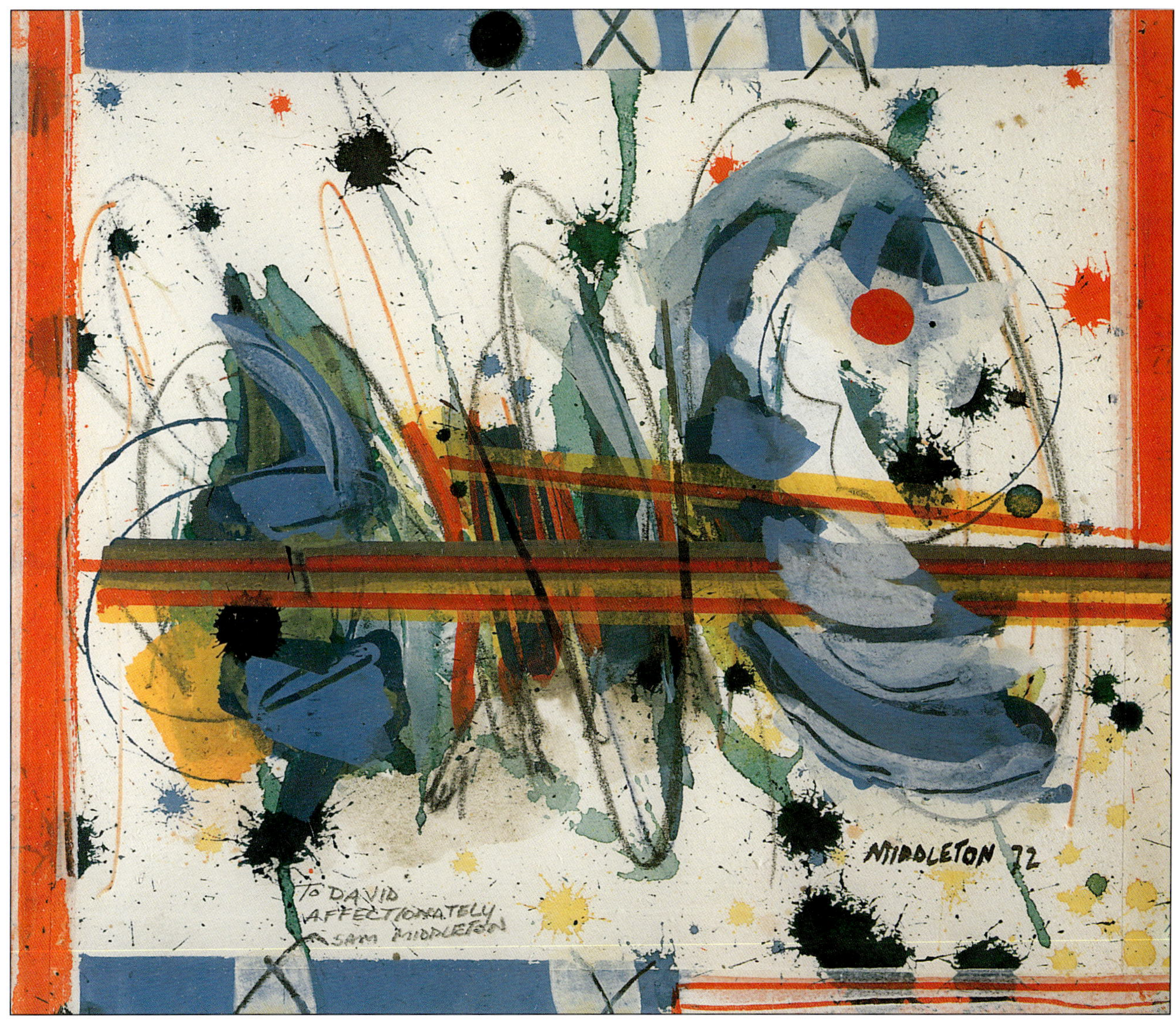

SAM MIDDLETON

84.

Untitled, 1972

Watercolor on paper

9" x 10"

The life and artistry of Sam Middleton truly embody the notion of global arts. As a young man Middleton embarked on a journey as a merchant marine crewman that led him virtually around the world. In 1962, Middleton decided to settle in Amsterdam, where, after establishing an international reputation as an artist, he came to be considered a Dutch painter. Middleton's collages, paintings, and lithographs use the universal language of abstraction, a tool that has bridged cultural gaps worldwide since the beginning of the century. Middleton's 1972 water-color *Untitled* emerges from an era when many African American painters were fully invested in the abstract movement. Deeply inspired by jazz music, Middleton utilized improvisational brush strokes and splashes of color in his melodic compositions.   A. L. C.

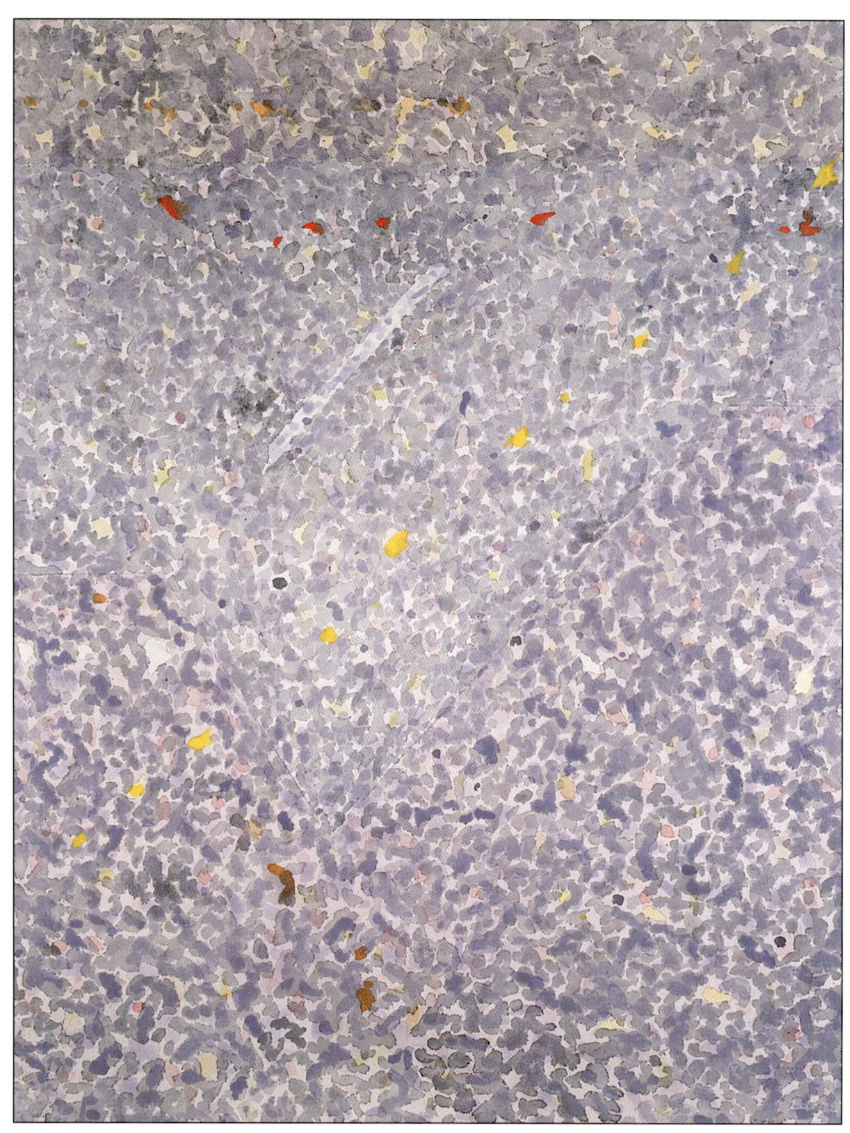

KEITH MORRISON

85.

Nightrane, 1981

Watercolor on paper

30" x 22"

In his quest to create his personal style, Keith Morrison fluctuates between Abstract Expressionist–inspired formal compositions and a narrative, richly figurative style. In such pieces as *Nightrane,* Morrison works through issues of color, pattern, rhythm, and design in a non-objective setting. These brightly painted canvases are inspired by bold African and Jamaican textile prints that hold aesthetic and spiritual dimensions. "In every case the source of the patterns is a fascination with its emotional and sensual power….This use of pattern is also very much a part of folk art in Jamaica and other parts of South and Central America where I got my first interest. Further, I have always liked the 'funky' quality of the patterns of the clothes and decoration of poor people in Jamaica."   K. A. K.

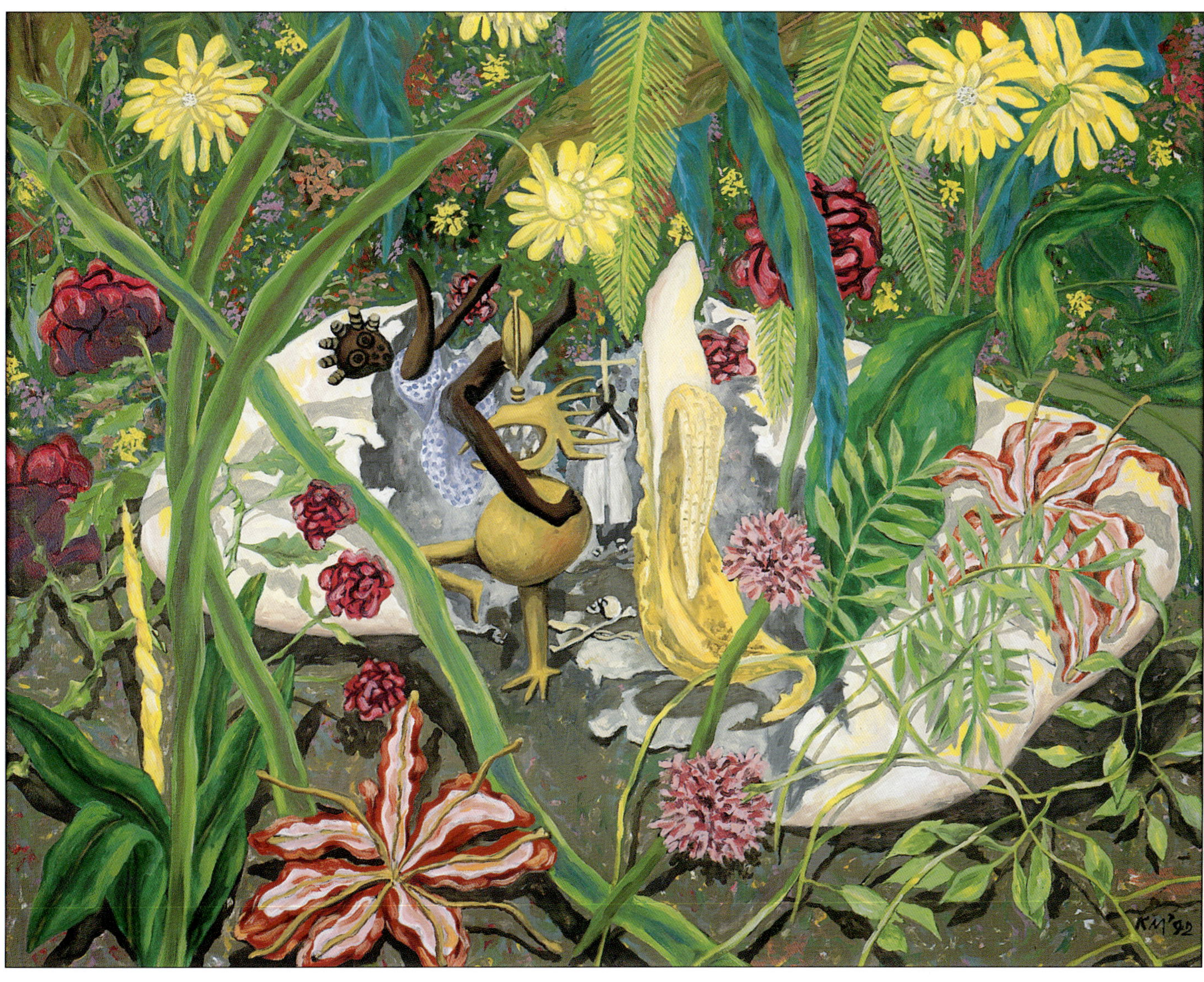

KEITH MORRISON

86.

Night Food, 1992

Oil on canvas

26.5" x 32"

Born in Jamaica and educated in the United States, Keith Morrison combines African, Caribbean, and American influences in the creation of his colorful signature style. Schooled in Abstract Expressionism, Morrison found that the abstract style was not fulfilling his creative needs as an African/Caribbean/American artist and turned to a personalized style of the abstract-figurative. His source of inspiration is his childhood spent in the Caribbean, which was laden with folk tales, legends, religion, family life, and community.

Night Food pays homage to a mixture of African and Caribbean traditions, embracing voodoo and Christianity. Imagery from both spiritual sects intermingle among exoticized flowers, animals, and fruit. Symbols of life, death, and resurrection are brought to life with Morrison's crowded picture plane and use of vibrant colors. Through retrospective examination of childhood beliefs, Morrison has created a rich and imaginative oeuvre rooted in his involvement in multiple cultures.   K.A.K.

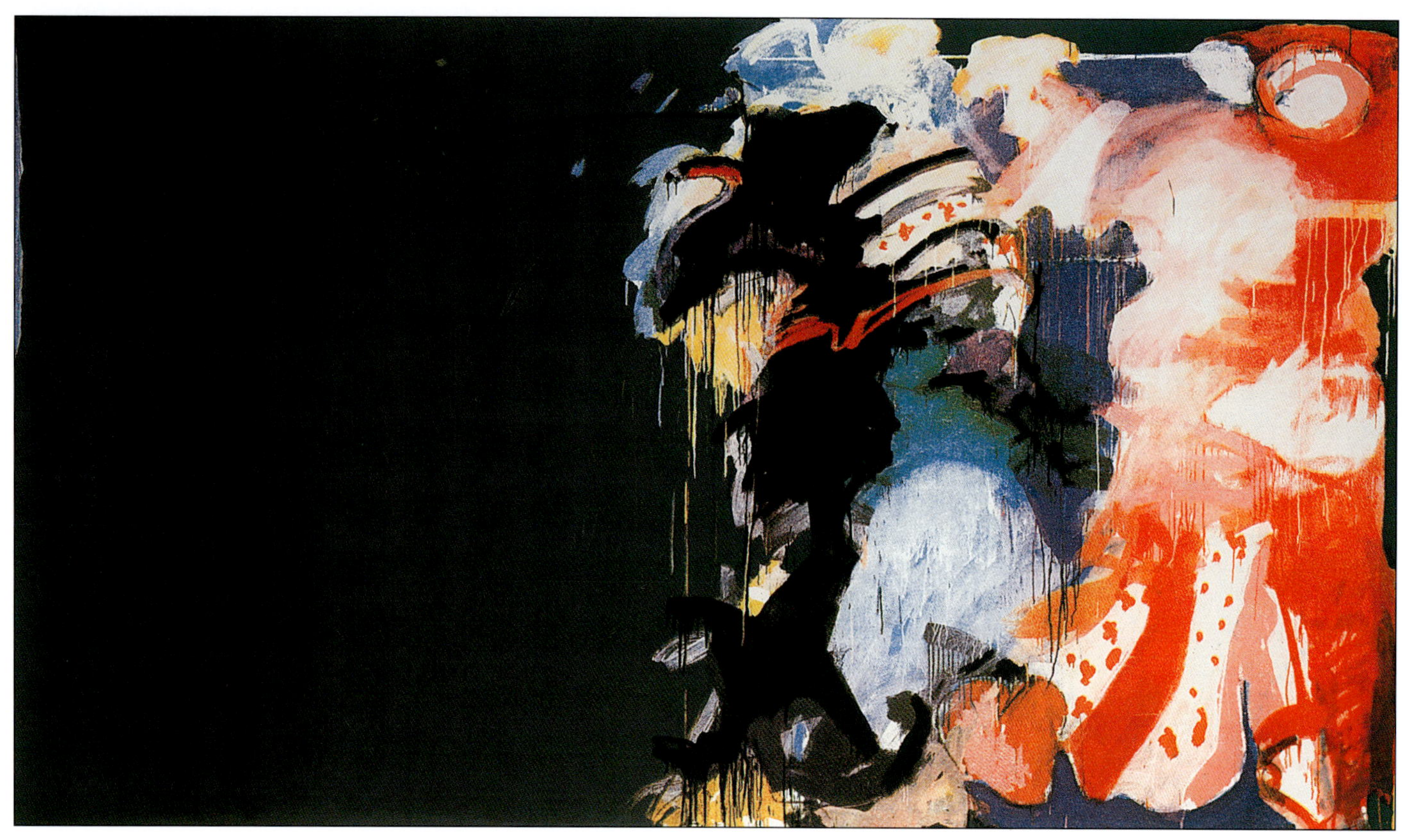

MARY LOVELACE
O'NEAL

87.

*Racism Is Like Rain, Either
It's Raining or It's Gathering
Somewhere,* 1993

Lithograph

13.25" x 22"

Mary Lovelace O'Neal utilizes high abstraction to give voice to her ephemeral artistic expressions of "intangible elements of the human spirit." Influenced by Abstract Expressionism and Minimalism, she has created highly abstracted compositions in which figurative elements are beyond or almost beyond recognition. Dreamlike shapes exist on the picture plane of her creations and almost come to life with vibrant coloration and wet-looking surface qualities. In her 1993 lithograph *Racism is Like Rain, Either It's Raining or It's Gathering Somewhere,* O'Neal departs from her usual subjects of the ethereal to address the omnipresent cloud of racism. O'Neal's piece was included in the California Afro-American Museum's 1992 exhibition "No Justice, No Peace? Resolutions," which was a direct response to the Rodney King verdict of 1992 and the ensuing riots and racial tensions that stratified the city during that period.

O'Neal addresses aesthetic and political concerns of the dark medium, exploring aesthetic qualities of black while also addressing literal symbology of blackness. Colorful abstracted forms work against themselves and the imposing gray and black masses to create a dynamic effect of push and pull, call and response. O'Neal's unique style gleans both aesthetic and political concerns into a provocative composition.   K.A.K.

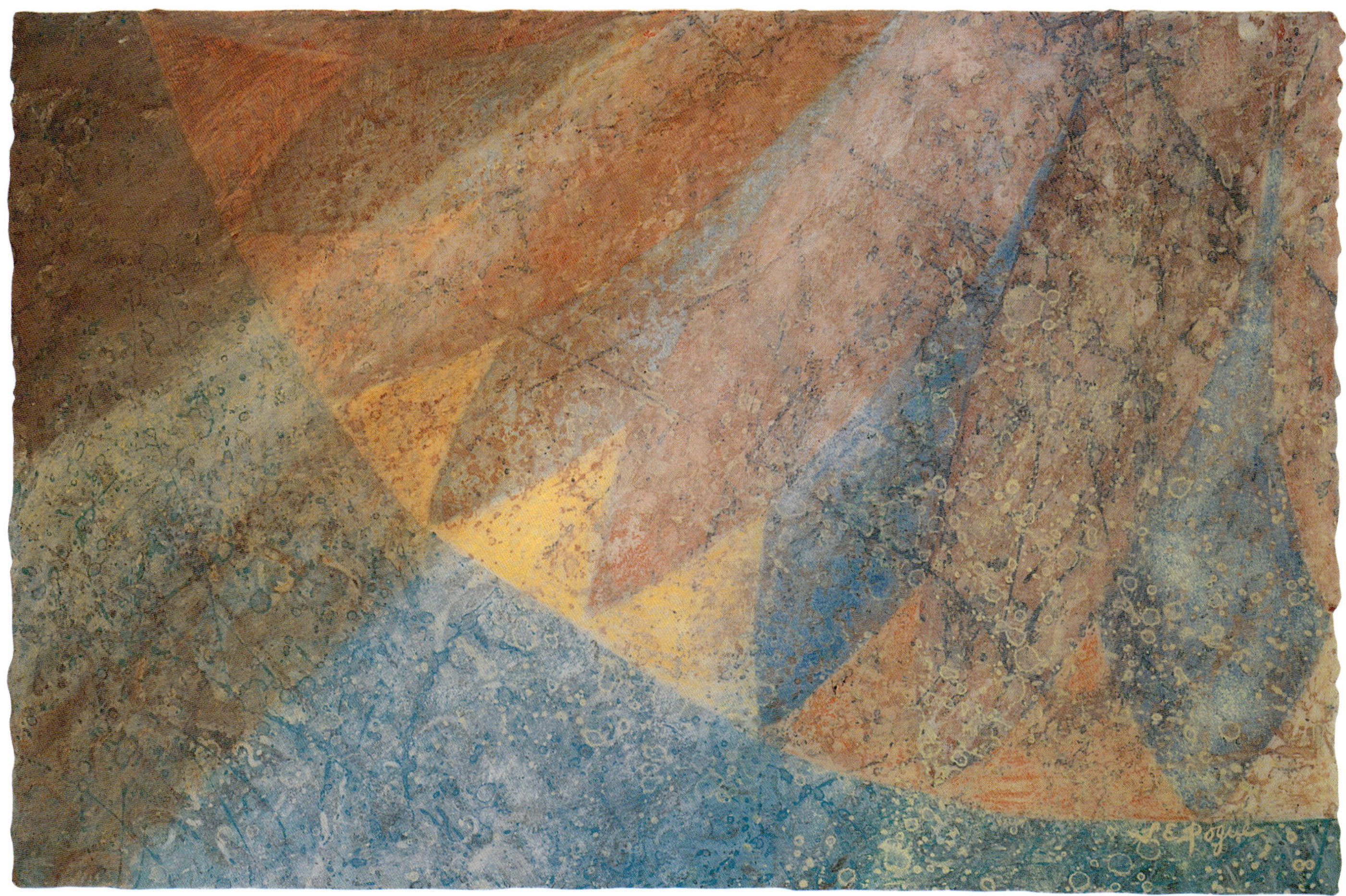

STEPHANIE POGUE

88.

India Pattern – Pattern of India,
1986

From *The Fan Series*

Mixed media on paper

15" x 22.5"

In 1981, printmaker and art instructor Stephanie Pogue participated in a group Fulbright-Hayes Fellowship to travel throughout India for the purpose of studying the country's architecture and sculpture. During a 1985 interview with Jacqueline Bontemps, Pogue fondly recalled her experience as the "most exciting experience I have had—one is constantly bombarded by the lift of the bright sun, exotic sights and sounds, and breathtaking vistas of ancient temples."

Upon her return to the United States, Pogue began to shift the aesthetic basis of her work from linear landscapes, figurative, and graphic compositions toward a more organic style emphasizing elements of texture, muted color, and universal motifs. Even though five years had passed since she had traveled in India, Pogue remained inspired by the seductive beauty and vitality of Indian architectural aesthetics. In 1986 she created the mixed media on paper worked entitled *India Pattern – Pattern of India*. Pogue states that the lyrical rhythmic patterns and colors of *India Pattern – Pattern of India* were based upon the lotus blossom design in the marble floor of a palace she saw during her travels. Pogue's version was not meant to duplicate the image on the floor but rather to recall, through her subtle use of color, texture, and form, the muted images of the marble design under the shimmering layer of water used to cool Indian palaces during the heat of the day. T. F.

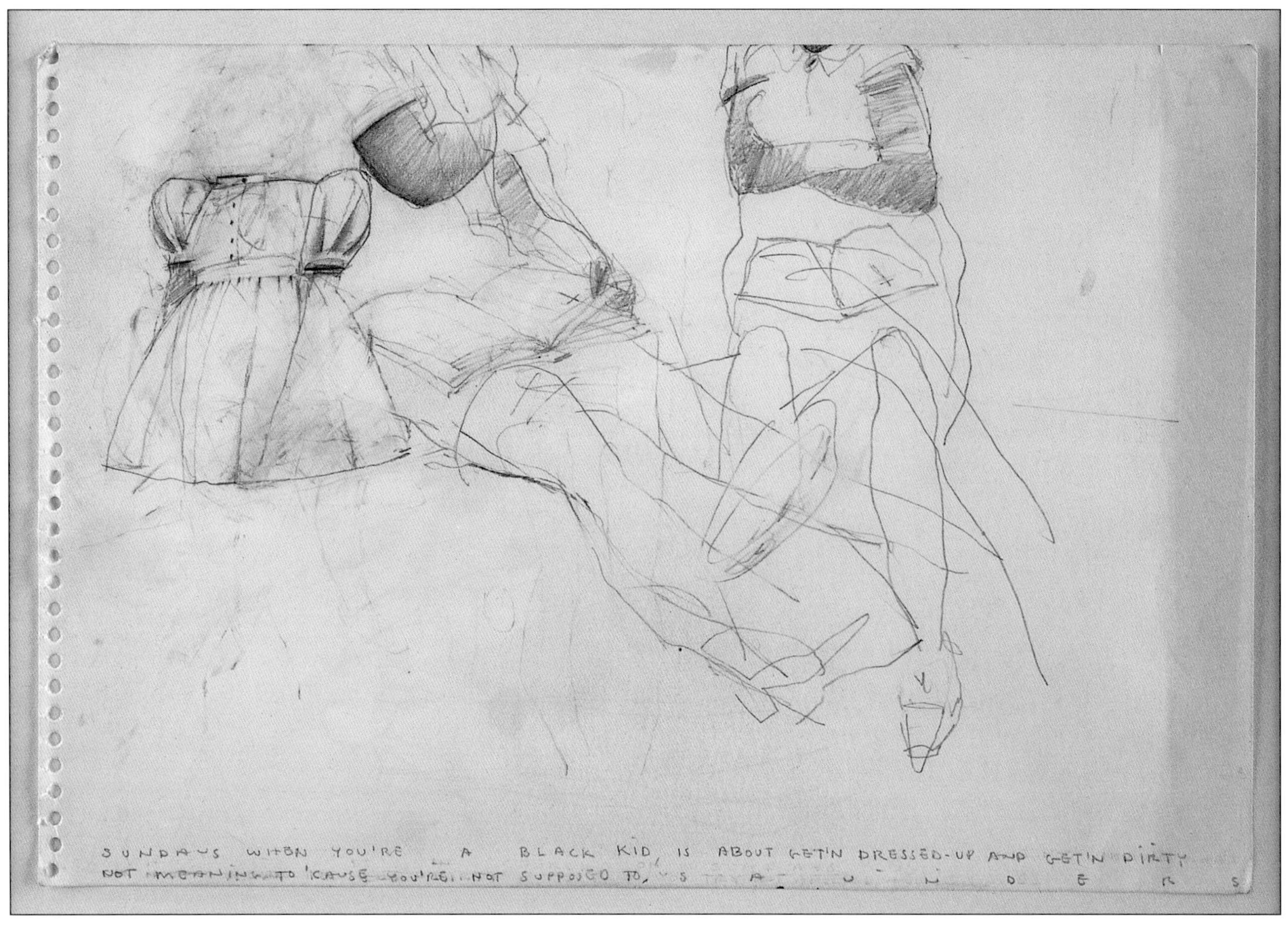

RAY SAUNDERS

89.

Untitled, n.d.

Pencil on paper

6" x 9"

California artist Ray Saunders has traveled to many parts of Europe, Africa, and Asia and has studios in Oakland, Paris, and Venice. Like his travels, his work is an eclectic assemblage of styles, techniques, and references. Personal references and, through those, references to African American history often predominate. Saunders gave *Untitled* to David Driskell as a gift; in its improvisational, sketch-like style and in the inclusion of text, it is similar to many of his larger multimedia works. In *Untitled,* a black girl who is effectively "erased" except for her detailed dress stands to the side of two seated, reading women. The pencil sketch suggests the importance of church and churchgoing to African American communities. The caption, "Sundays when you're a Black kid, is about get'n dressed-up and get'n dirty not meaning to 'cause you're not supposed to," also humorously refers to the restraints imposed on children who impatiently await Sunday's end.   J. S.

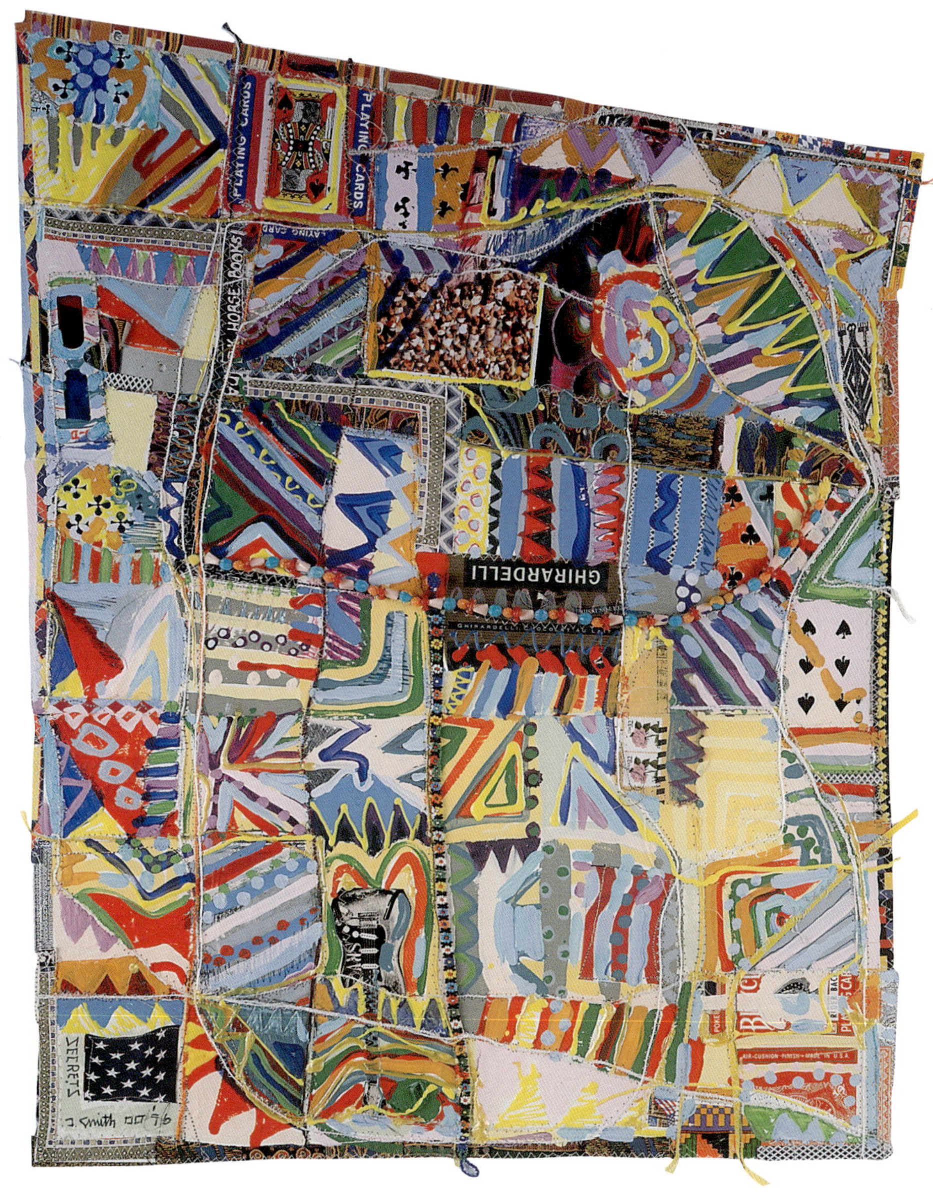

F RANK S MITH

90.

Improvisation from a Patch Quilt, 1986

Mixed media on canvas

36" x 21.5"

Frank Smith was attracted to paint texture and pattern as a young artist, seeking out a broad spectrum of European influences such as Van Gogh, Picasso, and Seurat. Raised in a family of musicians, Smith was especially attracted to Kandinsky's association of art and music through abstraction. By working on several pieces simultaneously, Smith combines disjointed rhythms and syncopated patterns of paint and mixed media by sewing the canvas together, using a sewing machine—though he does not deny the process or end product's resemblance to quilt-making.

Smith insists that the process comes out of necessity to sturdily adhere fabric together. *Improvisation from a Patch Quilt* (1986) is a colorful example of his assemblages. Bright zigzag stitching joins colorful patches of painted patterns and found objects. Smith's work simultaneously pays homage to his African heritage and African art education while serving as a vehicle for his own challenges as a contemporary abstract artist.   K. A. K.

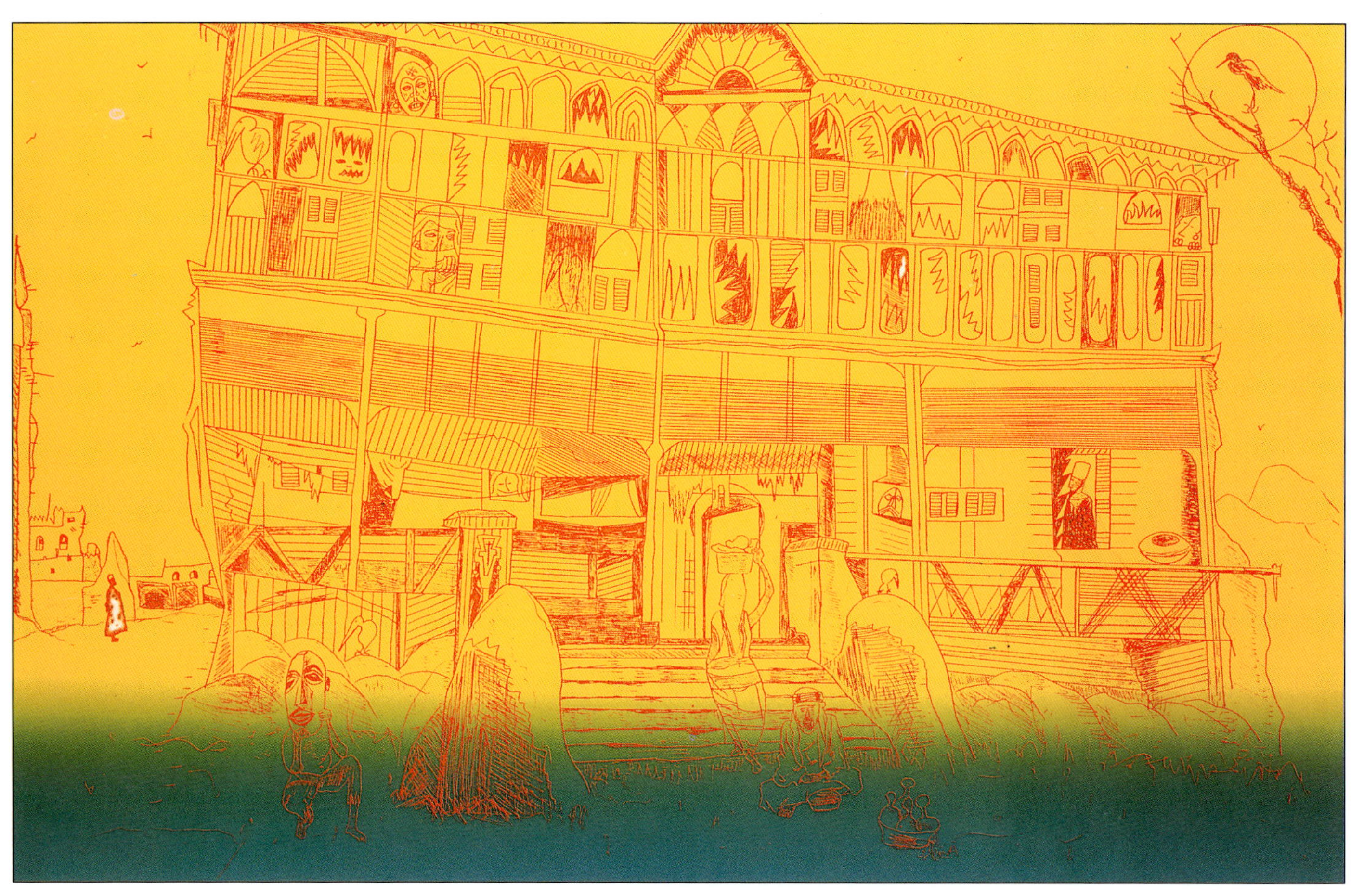

Vincent Smith's etching conveys many of his interests. Arthur Rimbaud, a French symbolist poet who died in 1891 at the age of thirty-seven, spent the last ten years of his life as a trader and gunrunner along the North African coast. His poetry profoundly influenced the Beat poets, whom Smith admired. Smith's interest and participation in New York's 1950s and 1960s literary scene, which included poets such as LeRoi Jones, extended to earlier poets and their works. In *Arthur Rimbaud's House in Harar,* Smith expressionistically conveys the creativity, decadence, and instability that characterized Rimbaud's life. The combination of yellow-orange and green tones imparts a feeling of delirium to the composition; the ornamented house with sagging features suggests both richness and decay. Smith emphasizes both a sense of place (Ethiopia) and Rimbaud's vitality through the African-derived masks that are present throughout the facade. In his works, Smith often explores his own heritage, particularly concentrating on jazz imagery and African-inspired masks and figures. *Arthur Rimbaud's House in Harar* shows his interest in African imagery while simultaneously suggesting that European history and figures are of no less interest to an African American artist.   J. S.

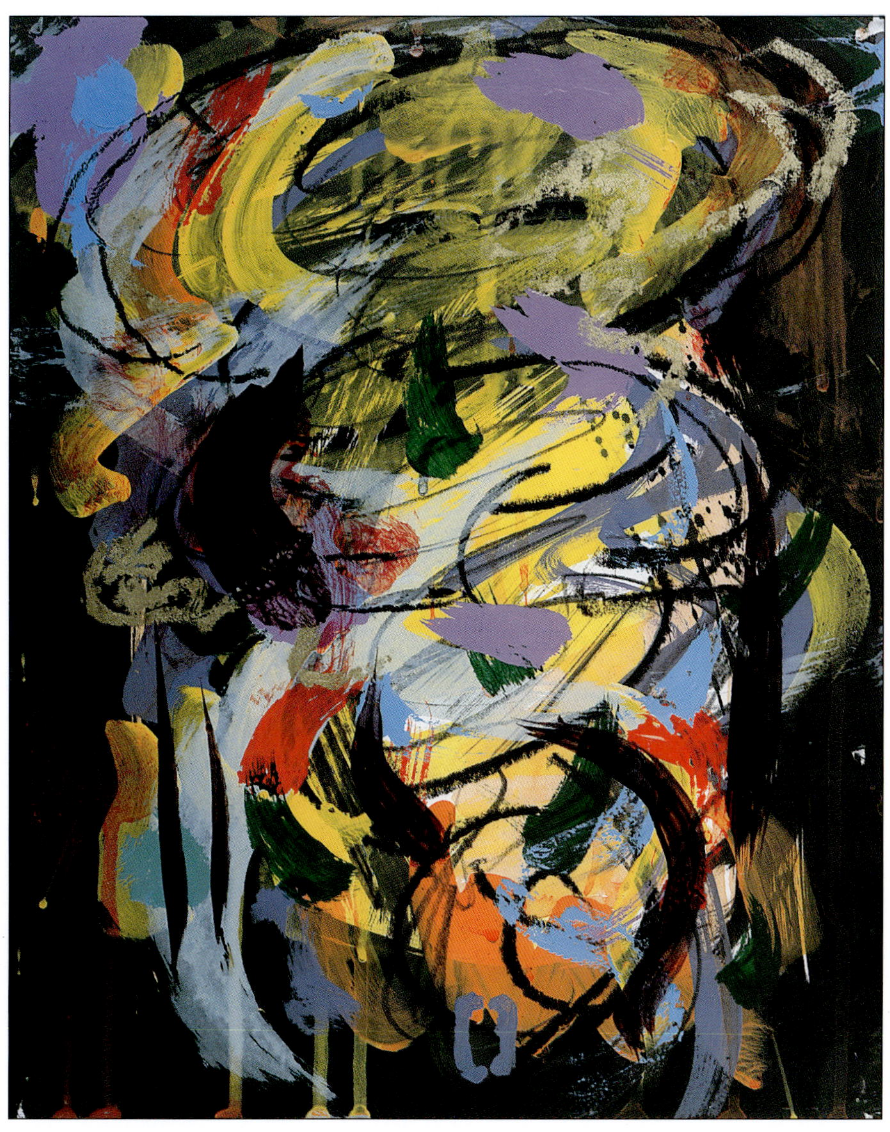

GILDA SNOWDEN

92.

Tornado, 1991

Mixed media on paper

14" x 11"

Gilda Snowden's works reflect the many influences on her artistic development: the urban environment of Detroit, where she continues to work; the loss of her parents in 1987, which forced her to consider the unpredictable nature of life; and a broad knowledge, acquired through her studies of American art history. Her works are often abstract representations of the forces and inner turmoil that drive humanity. *Tornado* is one of many images of tornadoes that she created in the late 1980s through the 1990s. Most often the tornadoes are depicted as swirling bands and bright slashes of color, with suggestions of objects caught in the storm; at times, Snowden's self-portrait is included in the fray. *Tornado* conveys the violence of a storm and implies the emotional upheavals and instability that life offers.   J. S.

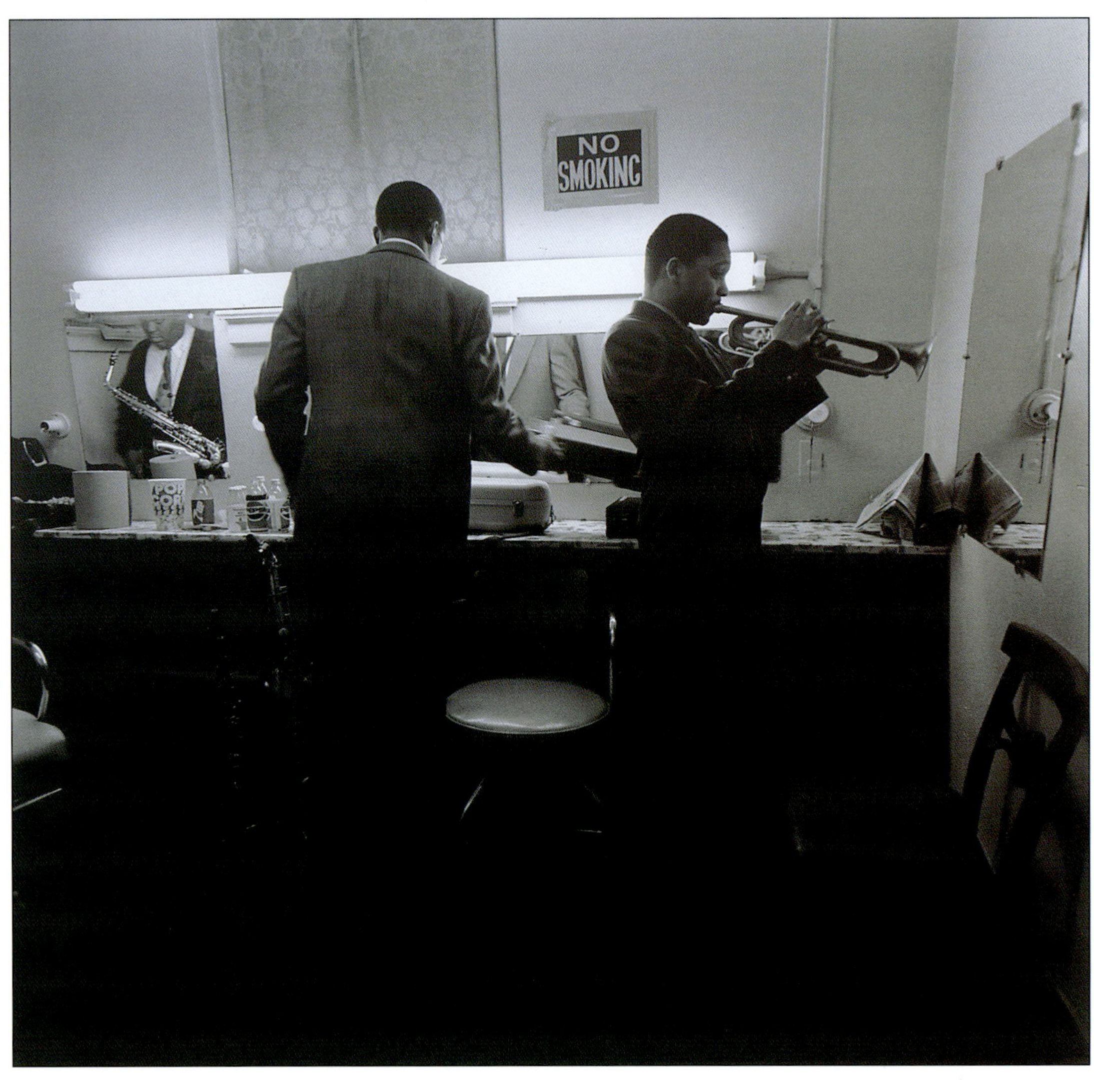

F R A N K   S T E W A R T

93.

Wynton Marsalis, 1991

From the *Sweet Swing Series*

Black-and-white photograph

15" x 15"

Harlem is a favorite subject of photographer, photojournalist, and curator Frank Stewart. In a tradition similar to that of Harlem Renaissance photographer James VanDerZee, Stewart's lens captures the variety of Harlem's residents—young and old, rich and poor.

In 1991, as part of his *Sweet Swing Series,* Stewart photographed jazz trumpet master Wynton Marsalis. Stewart's image of Marsalis both recalls the history of Harlem as America's great jazz mecca and captures an intimate glimpse of this renowned contemporary musician preparing himself and his instrument before a performance.   T. F.

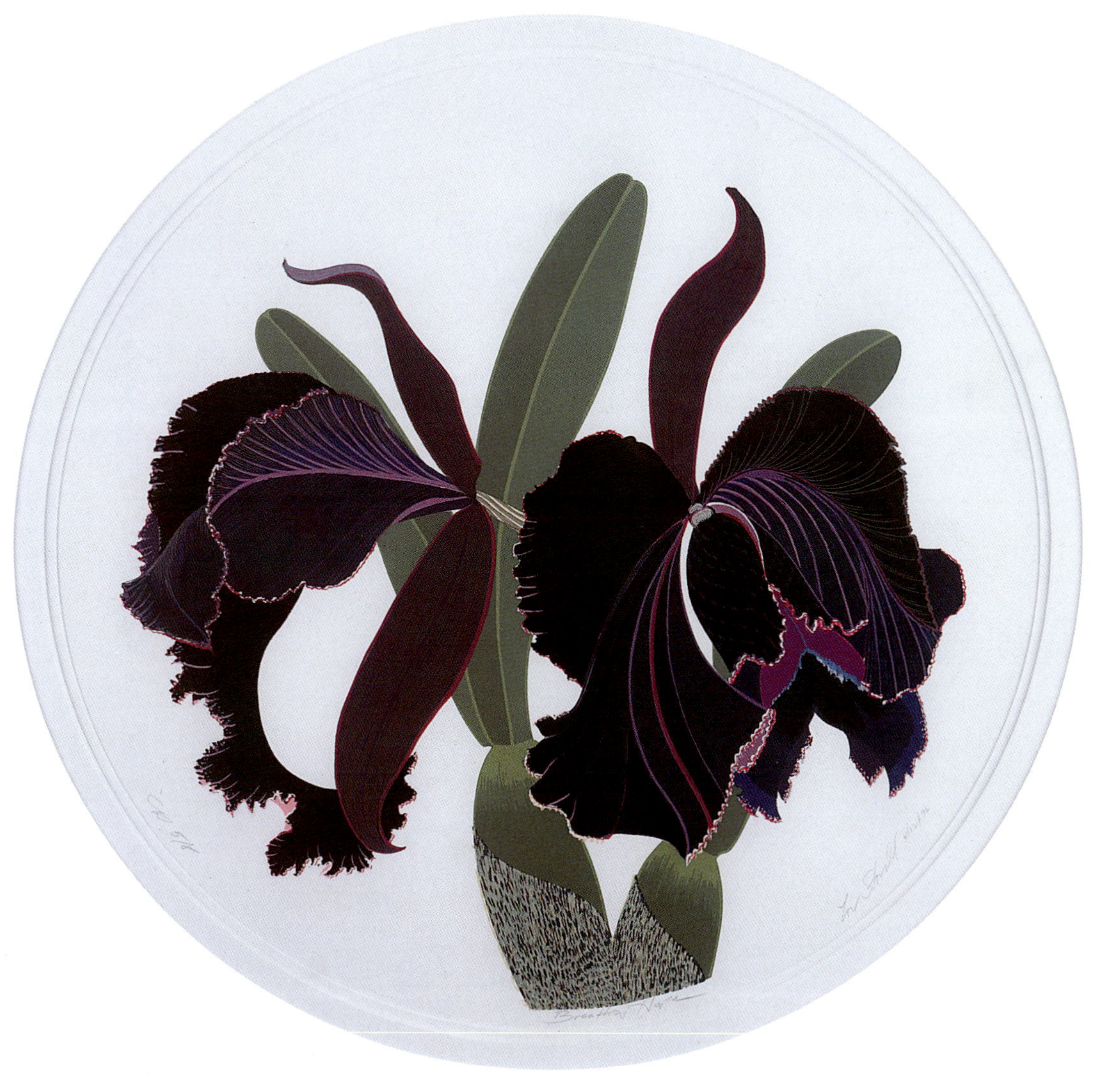

LOU STOVALL

94.

Breathing Hope, 1996

Silk-screen on paper

14.5" x 14.5"

Breathing Hope is an original silk-screen print of a black orchid created by master printmaker, craftsman, and poet Lou Stovall to commemorate the inauguration of Howard University's fifteenth president, H. Patrick Swyggert. Stovall chose the image of the perennial black orchid to symbolize the leadership, resurgence, and revitalization of Swyggert's presidency.

Stovall learned the value of printmaking from his mentor, Howard art professor and printmaker James Lesesne Wells. He states, "Wells knew more about making prints than anyone—more than books, I would say, and he was the most patient man that I have ever known." In addition to Wells, Stovall also cites Loïs Jones, Jacob Lawrence, James A. Porter, and David C. Driskell as influential mentors.

Since 1966, Stovall's passion for printmaking and his innovative techniques have attracted innumerable commissions to print works from a number of artists such as Josef Albers, Alexander Calder, Elizabeth Catlett, Jeff Donaldson, David C. Driskell, Sam Gilliam, Jacob Lawrence, and James Lesesne Wells. Over the years Stovall has not only benefited from the influence and knowledge of his mentors and peers but also has given much back. *Breathing Hope* is only one of many prints created by Stovall to commemorate important events within the African American community. Like his mentors who came before him, Stovall values the concept of giving back to the community and sharing his knowledge and wisdom through his own example and through apprenticeships to young artists in his Washington, D. C.–based studio, Workshop, Inc., established in 1968.   T. F.

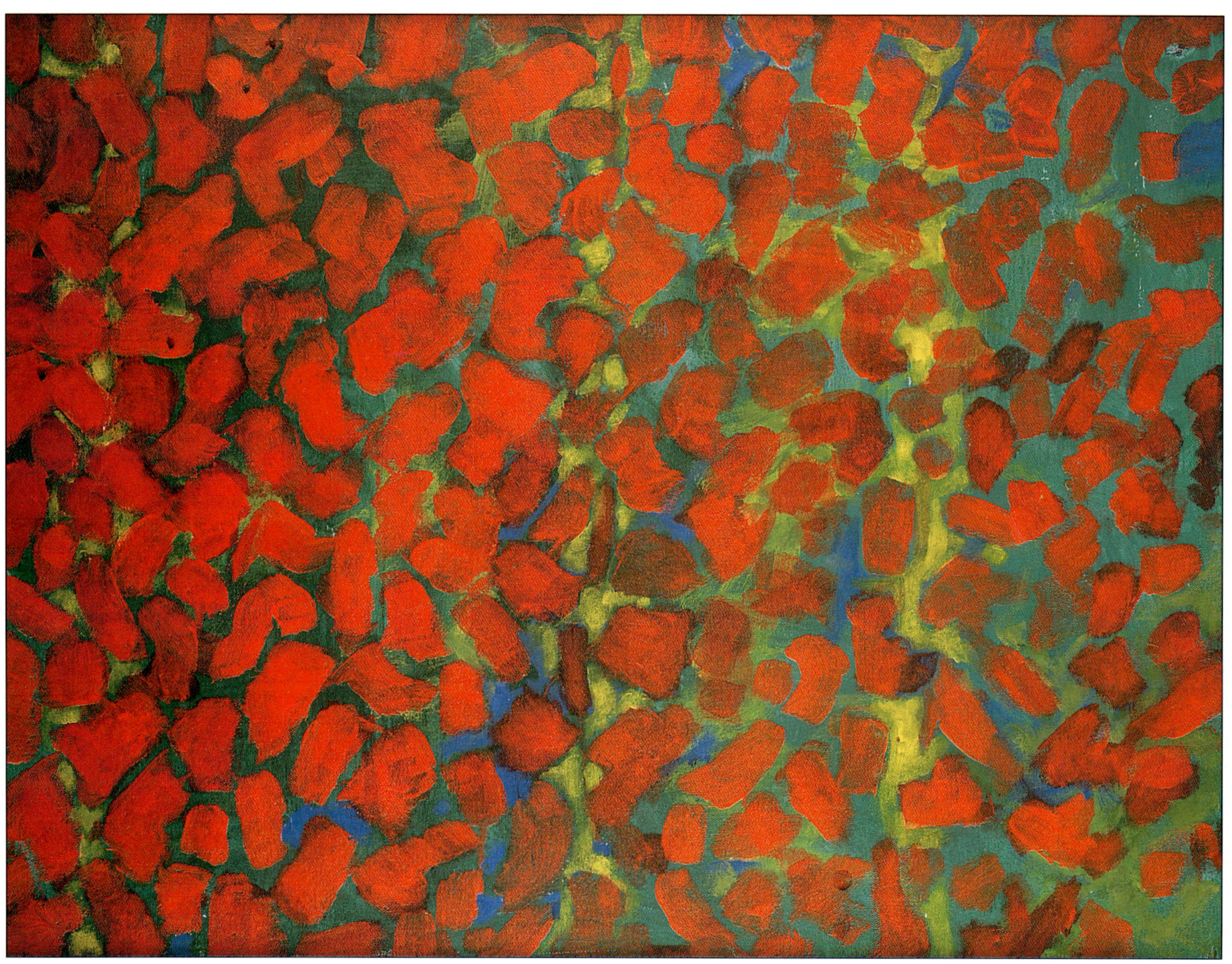

ALMA THOMAS

95.

*Falling Leaves Love Wind
Orchestra,* n.d.

Acrylic on canvas

21.5" x 27.5"

96.

Blue Abstraction, 1965

Oil on canvas

39.75" x 31.5"

Through her art, Alma Thomas contradicted assumptions about appropriate subject matter and styles for African American artists. She rejected suggestions that she paint "black" subjects and instead experimented with theories that were more national and international in scope. In Washington, D. C., Thomas was associated with the Color Field artists. However, as witnessed in the two works in this exhibition, Thomas's paintings incorporate a fluidity and a lack of structured boundaries unlike the works of other Color Field artists. In both *Blue Abstraction* and *Falling Leaves Love Wind Orchestra,* her colors possess a vibrant, organic quality that relates to the natural world. In the latter painting, the brilliant red, irregularly shaped leaves both create a pleasing pattern and evoke the "dance" of falling leaves. Thomas possessed a lifelong interest in observing nature, beginning with memories of the fields and trees of her childhood home in Georgia, and extending to the various seasons in Washington and the appearance of the earth as viewed from an airplane. Through her paintings, Thomas established a global identity that transcended perceived notions of what it meant to be both African American and an artist; although her works relate to her personal experience and observations, they are also a result of her intellectual interest in color theory and her exploration of abstraction.   J. S.

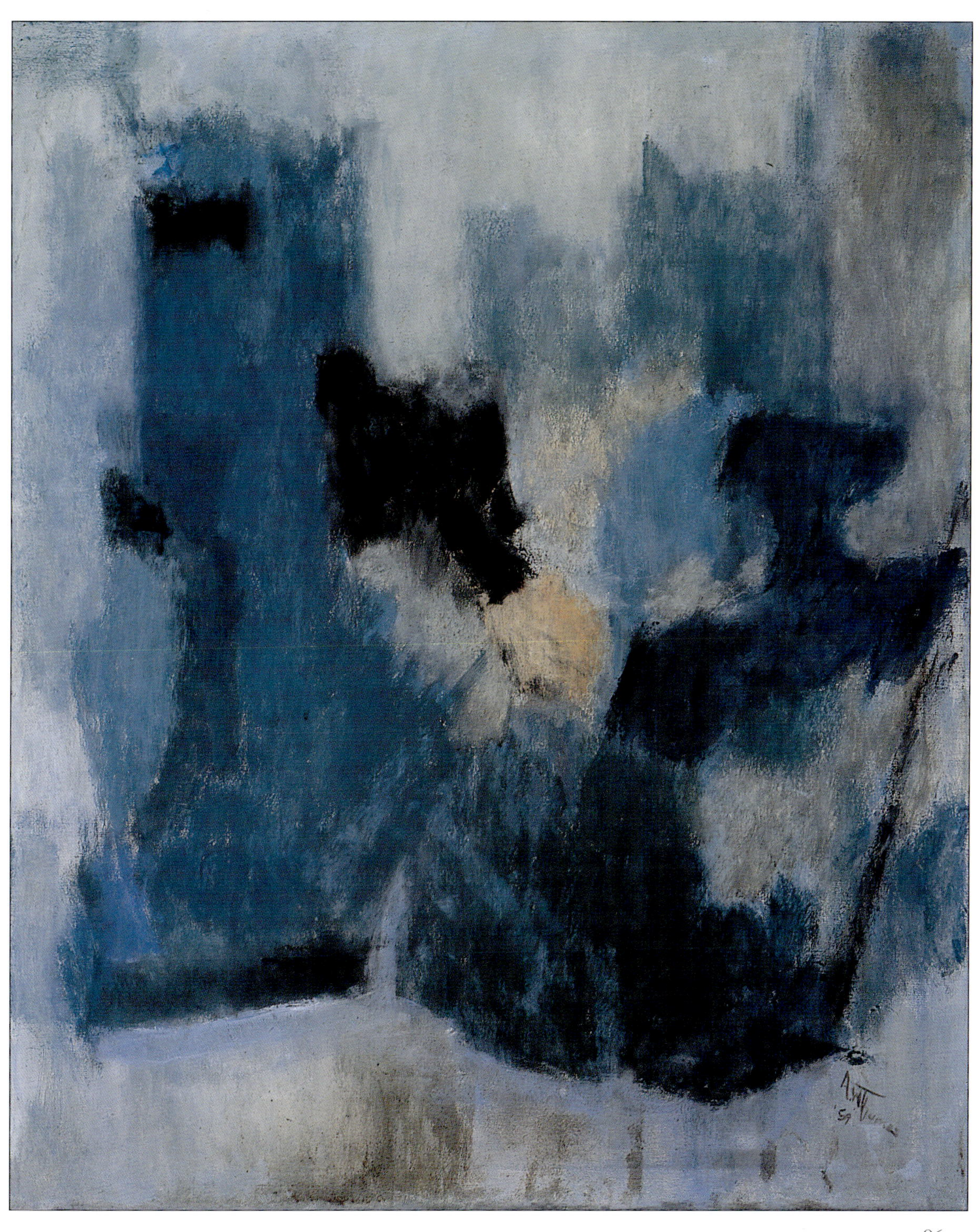

96.

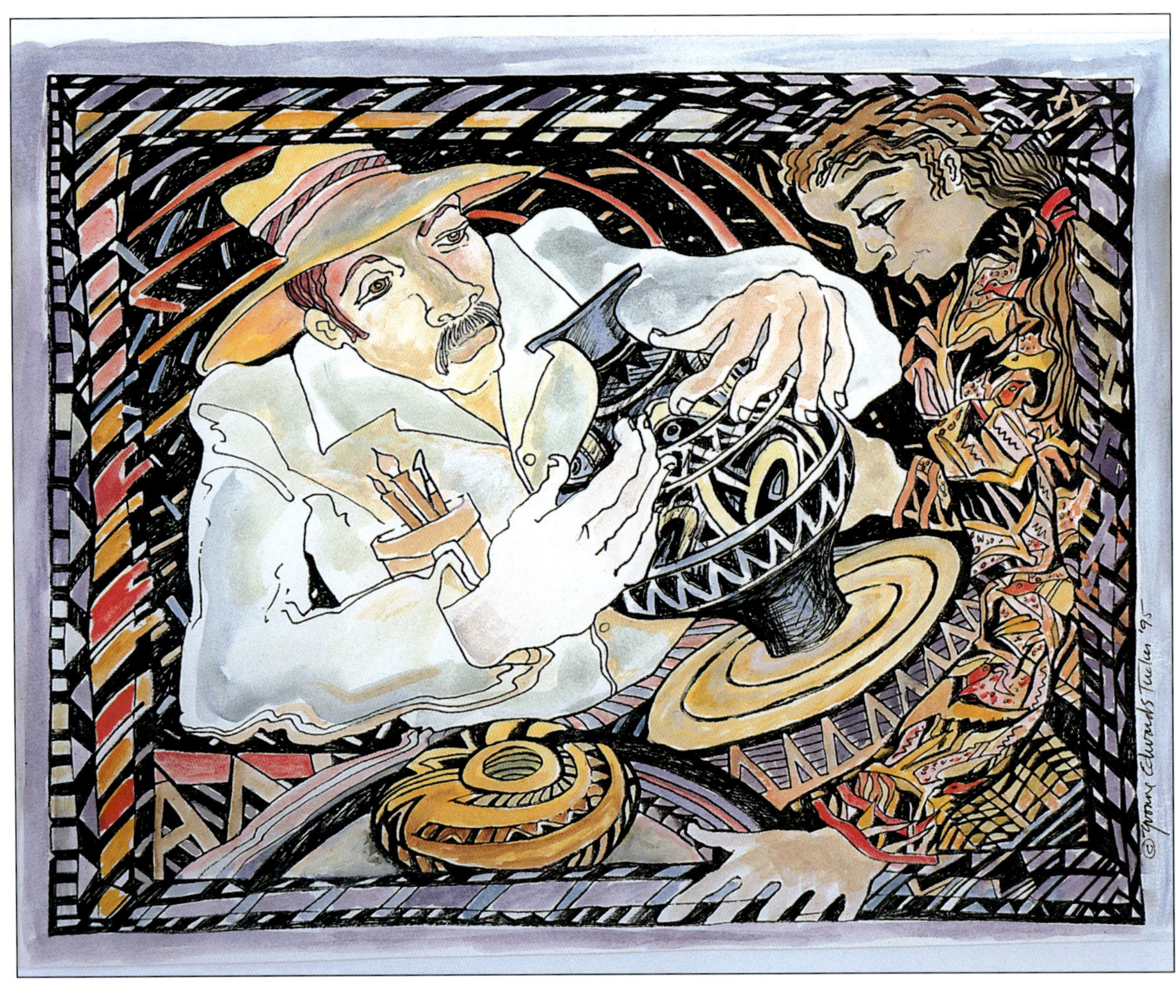

Yvonne Edwards Tucker's interest in the complexity of the artistic process is reflected in her mixed-media work *The Potter's House.* According to art historian Michael Harris, before turning to ceramics Tucker originally had thought of herself as a painter. As this work indicates, she never abandoned this first love and would often incorporate elements of painting into her sculptures.

The Potter's House is an autobiographical image of Yvonne Edwards Tucker and her late husband, ceramicist Curtis Tucker, working together on one of their many collaborative projects. The raku ceramic decorated with drawings (central to the Tuckers' compositions) represents one of the couple's signature works. To create such a vessel, Curtis Tucker would first throw the pot; the work would then be fired, using a technique they developed together derived from African, Native American, and Eastern ceramics called "Afro-Raku"; and finally, after glazing and burnishing, Yvonne Tucker would incise the pots with freehand, semiabstract drawings. Although the design of the pot in *The Potter's House* appears fully abstracted, Tucker's vessel designs often vary in content and form to reflect her interests in Zen, African spiritualism, and anthropomorphic forms.

Tucker describes her interest in the process of making ceramics as follows: "When throwing or hand building, I often hold my breath while centering myself in the moment in order to dance in partnership with my silent teacher, clay. It is then that I often feel my hands and mind becoming a conduit for greater forces from the inner realm of the spirit." Tucker's choice to represent herself and her husband, simultaneously touching the clay before them and creating what she describes as "the intangible quality of soul force," is an eloquent testament regarding the importance of the artistic process for the Tuckers.   T. F.

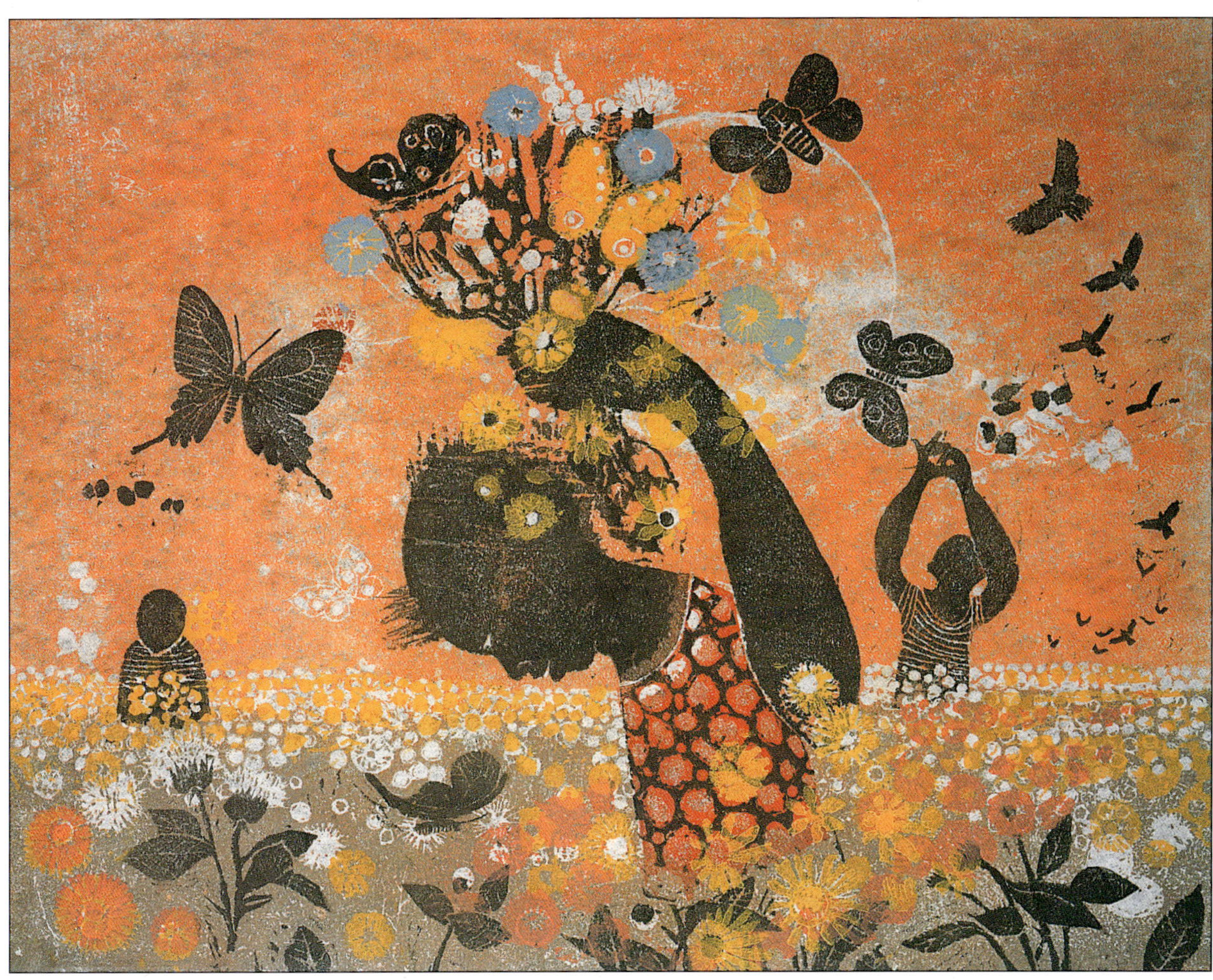

Painter and printmaker Walter Williams did not begin his career as an artist until relatively late in his life. During his thirties, after the second World War, the GI Bill enabled Williams to study art at the Brooklyn Museum's school. In 1951, Williams enrolled in the school's four-year program, where he worked with artists Ben Shahn, Gregorio Prestopine, and Ruben Tam. Upon graduation, Williams was awarded a John Hay Whitney fellowship, which he used to travel to Mexico.

According to Bearden's and Henderson's *History of African-American Artists,* after four years of living in Mexico's racially liberal environment, Williams "felt that freedom from racial prejudice was essential for his further development…" Thus, since 1959, Williams spent the majority of his time in Copenhagen and in 1979 officially became a Danish citizen.

While residing in Copenhagen, Williams's style shifted from realistic images of southern landscapes and cockfights such as the 1959 color woodcut *Fighting Cock* to idealized, surreal sunny landscapes depicting black children, butterflies, and flowers found in such works as *Butterflies #2.* In 1967, after visiting Williams in Europe, Driskell stated that Williams's new style represents a "dream world where the mind is at peace with nature and self."   T. F.

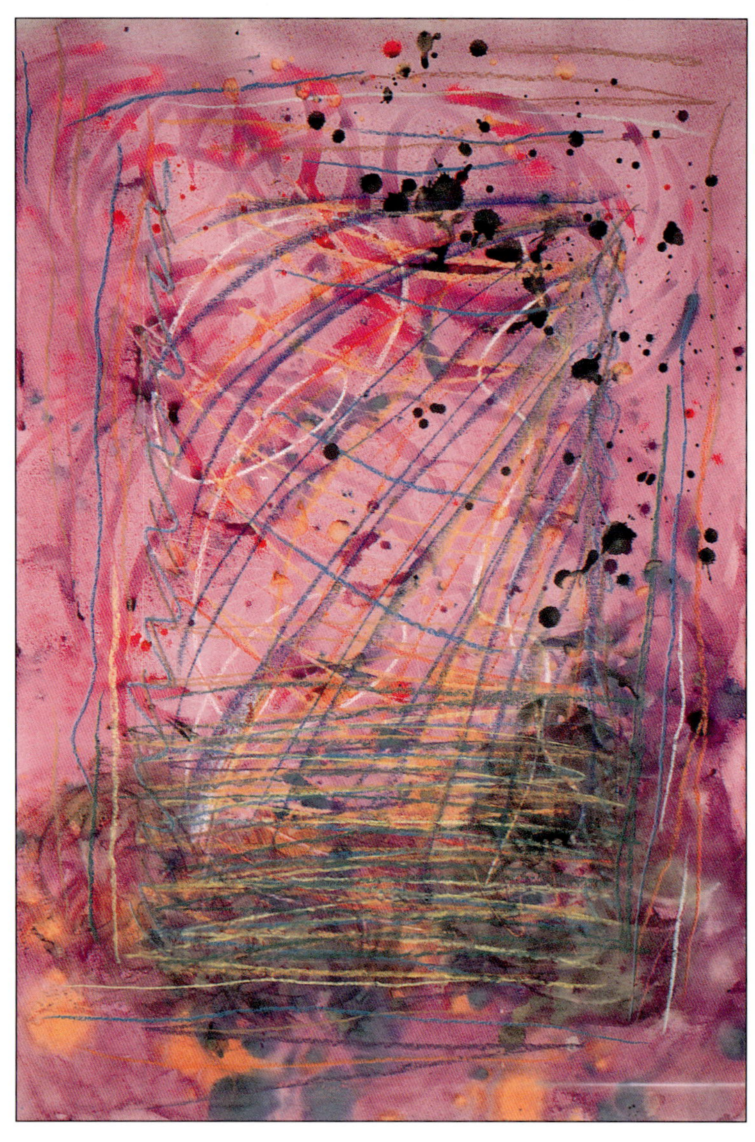

WILLIAM T.
WILLIAMS

99.

Untitled, c. 1973

Mixed media on paper

35" x 23"

Color Field painter, professor, and printmaker William T. Williams's interest in color began when he was a student during the 1960s. According to Driskell, "Color was greatly impressed upon his [Williams's] mind as the mechanism through which the structure of a painting is built." Williams took those lessons to heart and during the 1960s and 1970s searched for new ways of structuring color to create spatial volume.

Since the 1970s, Williams's work has generally been concerned with large-scale abstract imagery in combination with geometric and organic forms. In his 1973 untitled mixed-media-on-paper work, Williams sporadically overlays color in washes, splashes, and crayon pastels on a flat background of violet.   T. F.

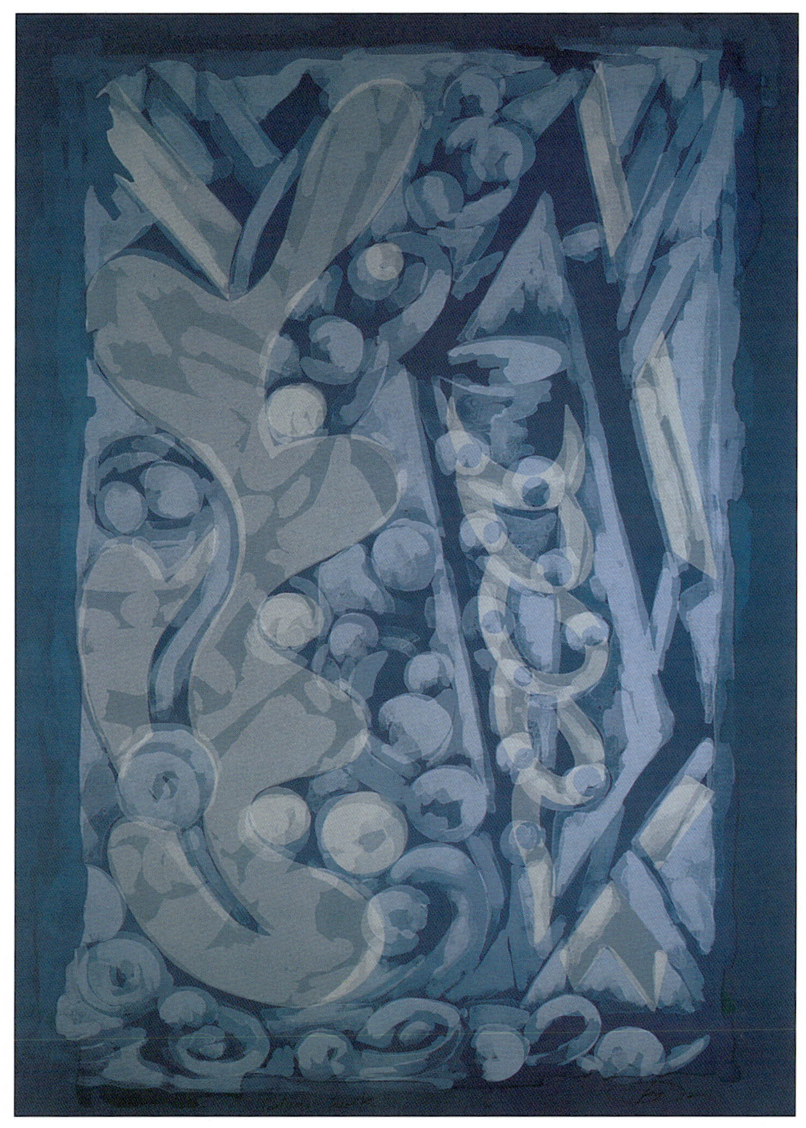

William T.
Williams

100.

Blue Walk, c. 1991

Color lithograph

41" x 29"

In the 1990s, Williams created a series of lithographs in which he pays homage to black jazz musicians and many of their popular tunes. *Blue Walk* is an actively conceived study in shades of blue that captures the quiet mood of this popular jazz tune. Here an effervescent flow of baroque-like forms moves in and out of Williams's spiraling compositional boundary like dancing figures on a ballroom floor. Instead of depicting the physical appearance of the dancer, Williams leaves us with the thought of a monochromatic poem that invites quiet reflection.

An avid lover of jazz music, Williams has set about renewing jazz themes in his art, much of which helped sustain the avowed interest he now has in collecting music from the great jazz era.   T. F.

Terry Adkins
Born Washington, D.C., 1953
B.S., Fisk University, Nashville, Tennessee, 1975
M.S., Illinois State University, Normal, 1977
M.F.A., University of Kentucky, Lexington, 1979
Instructor, Kentucky State University, Frankfort, 1977
Associate Professor, SUNY New Paltz, New York, 1996
Major Exhibitions:
Project Binz 39, Zurich, 1986
Salama-Caro Gallery, London, 1987
Whitney Museum of American Art at Philip Morris, New York,
     1995
International Gallery, Smithsonian Institution, Washington, D.C.,
     1997

Edward Mitchell Bannister
Born St. Andrews, New Brunswick, Canada, c. 1826
Emigrated to Boston, c. 1848
Attended anatomy classes with Dr. William Brimmer, early 1860s
Photographer, daguerreotypist, 1863–1865
Portrait painter, 1863–1872
Moved to Providence, Rhode Island, 1869
Bronze Medal in Art, Philadelphia Centennial Exhibition, 1876
Founder, Providence Art Club, 1872
Board of Directors, Rhode Island School of Design, Providence,
     Rhode Island
Died 1901
Major Exhibitions:
Boston Art Club juried annual exhibitions
Hall of Fine Arts, Philadelphia Centennial Exposition, 1876
Retrospective, Providence Art Club, Rhode Island 1891
Sharing Traditions: Five Black Artists in Nineteenth-Century America,
     National Museum of American Art, Washington, D.C., 1985
Newport Art Museum, New Jersey, 1990
Edward Mitchell Bannister 1828–1901, Kenkeleba House,
     New York, 1992

Richmond Barthé
Born Bay St. Louis, Mississippi, 1901
Chicago Art Institute, 1924–1928
Art Students League, New York, 1931
M.A., Xavier University, New Orleans, 1934
A.F.D., St. Francis College, Brooklyn, New York, 1947
Died 1989
Major Exhibitions:
Delphic Studios, New York, 1925
Caz–Delbos Gallery, New York, 1933
Whitney Museum of American Art, New York, 1933, 1935, 1939
World's Fair, New York, 1947

Romare Bearden
Born Charlotte, North Carolina, 1914
B.S., New York University, 1935
Studied at Art Students League, New York, 1936–1937
Case Worker, Department of Social Services, 1938–1966
     (intermittently)
Studied philosophy at Sorbonne, Paris, 1950
Began to work primarily in collage, 1963/1964
Died 1988

Major Exhibitions:
New Names in American Art, Baltimore Museum, Maryland, 1944
Samuel M. Kootz Gallery, New York, 1945
Cordier & Warren Gallery, New York, 1961
Projections, Corcoran Gallery of Art, Washington, D.C., 1965
Romare Bearden: The Prevalence of Ritual, Museum of Modern Art,
     New York, 1971
Memory and Metaphor: The Art of Romare Bearden, 1940–1987, Studio
     Museum in Harlem, 1991

John Biggers
Born Gastonia, North Carolina, 1924
Entered Hampton Institute, 1941
M.S., Pennsylvania State University, University Park, 1948
Ph.D., Pennyslvania State University, 1954
Joined staff at Texas Southern University, 1949
First trip to Africa, 1957
Retired as head of art department, Texas Southern University, 1983
Major Exhibitions:
Drawings and Paintings by John Biggers and Jack Boynton, The Museum
     of Fine Arts, Houston, Texas, 1954
Drawings of West Africa: Dr. John Biggers, The Museum of Fine Arts,
     Houston, 1962
*The Web of Life in Africa: An Exhibition of Drawings and Paintings by
     John T. Biggers,* African-American Cultural Center, Dallas 1978
John Biggers: Bridges, California Museum of Afro-American
     History and Culture, Los Angeles, 1983
Five Decades: John Biggers and the Hampton Art Tradition, Hampton
     University Museum, Hampton, Virginia, 1990
The Art of John Biggers: View from the Upper Room, The Museum
     of Fine Arts, Houston, and Hampton University Museum,
     Hampton, Virginia, 1995

Grafton Tyler Brown
Born Harrisburg, Pennsylvania, 1841
Moved to California, mid-1850s
Formed G.T. Brown & Co., 1867
Moved to Canada, 1882
Moved to Portland, 1886
Member of Portland Art Club, 1886–1890
Moved to St. Paul, Minnesota, 1892
Died 1918
Major Exhibitions:
The Oakland Museum, California, 1972
Two Centuries of Black American Art, Los Angeles County
     Museum, 1976
The Harmon and Harriet Kelley Collection of African American Art,
     San Antonio Museum of Art, 1994

Elizabeth Catlett
Born Washington, D.C., 1915
B.A., Howard University, Washington, D.C., 1937
Instructor, Hampton Institute, Hampton, Virginia, 1942–1943
Moved to Mexico, 1949
Member of Taller de Gráfica Popular, 1946–1966
Chairman, Sculpture Department, School of Fine Arts, National
     Autonomous University of Mexico, 1959

Major Exhibitions:
Solo Exhibition, New Orleans Museum of Art, 1983
Solo Exhibition, Hampton University, 1993
*Three Generations of African American Women Sculptors: A Study
    in Paradox,* Afro-American Historical and Cultural Museum,
    Philadelphia, 1996–1998
Bearing Witness, Spelman College, Atlanta, Georgia, 1996

Claude Clark

Born Rickingham, Georgia, 1915
Studied at the Philadelphia Museum School of Art, Philadelphia,
    1935–1939
WPA, Philadelphia, Pennsylvania, 1939–1942
Barnes Foundation Fellow, 1939–1944
Instructor, art department, Talladega College, 1948–1955
M.A., University of California at Berkeley, 1962
Instructor, Merritt College, Oakland, California, 1968–1981
Major Exhibitions:
A Retrospective Exhibition, 1937–1971, Paintings by Claude Clark,
    Fisk University, Nashville, Tennessee, 1972
*Claude Clark: On My Journey Now: A Selection of Paintings from
    1940–1986,* The Apex Museum, Atlanta, Georgia, 1996

Robert Colescott

Born Oakland, California, 1925
Studied with Fernand Léger, Paris, 1949–1950
B.A., University of California, Berkeley, 1949
M.A., University of California, Berkeley, 1952
Professor of art history, American College, Paris, 1967–1969
Instructor of painting and drawing, San Francisco Art Institute,
    1976–1985
Professor of art, University of Arizona, Tucson, 1985 to present
Major Exhibitions
Robert Colescott: A Retrospective, 1975–1986, San Jose Museum
    of Art, 1989
Katonah Museum of Art, Westchester County, New York, 1995
Brooklyn Museum, New York, 1993
Corcoran Gallery of Art, Washington, D.C., 1994

Eldzier Cortor

Born Richmond, Virginia, 1916
Art Institute of Chicago, 1936
WPA, Chicago, 1940
Studied in Sea Islands, Georgia, on Rosenwald Fellowship,
    1944–1945
Studied in Jamaica, Cuba, and Haiti on Guggenheim Fellowship,
    1949
Teacher, Centre d'Art, Port-au-Prince, Haiti, 1949–1951
Major Exhibitions:
*Three Masters: Eldzier Cortor, Hughie Lee-Smith and Archibald
    John Motley, Jr.,* Kenkeleba Gallery, New York, 1988

Allan Rohan Crite

Born Plainfield, New Jersey, 1910
One of the few African American artists to work briefly for the
    Federal Arts Project (FAP), 1930s
Studied at School of the Museum of Fine Arts Boston, 1939
A.B., Harvard University Extension School, 1968
Lives and works in Boston
Major Exhibitions:
Widely exhibited since the 1920s
Harmon Foundation Exhibitions, 1930s
Museum of Modern Art, New York, 1936
Corcoran Gallery of Art, Washington, D.C., 1939
Boston Museum of Fine Arts, 1978
Allan Crite's Boston, The Boston Athenaeum, 1997

Roy DeCarava

Born New York, 1919
Cooper Union Art School, 1938–1940
Harlem Art Center, New York, 1944–1945
Founder and Director, *A Photographer's Gallery,* New York,
    1954–1956
Freelance photographer, New York, 1959–1968 and since 1975
Professor of art, Cooper Union Institute, New York, 1969–1972
    and 1975–1988
Distinguished Professor of Art, Hunter College, New York, since
    1988
Major Exhibitions:
Always the Young Strangers, Museum of Modern Art, New York, 1953
Through Black Eyes, Studio Museum in Harlem, New York, 1969
The Nation's Capitol in Photographs, Corcoran Gallery of Art,
    Washington, D.C., 1976
Jazz pa Fotografiska, Fotografiska Museet, Stockholm, 1986
Recent Photographs, Witkin Gallery, New York, 1990
Roy DeCarava: A Retrospective, Los Angeles County Museum
    of Art, 1997

Beauford Delaney

Born Knoxville, Tennessee, 1901
Studied at the Massachusetts Normal School, 1924
Moved to New York City, 1929
Moved to Paris, 1953
Died 1979
Major Exhibitions:
Vendome Gallery, Artists' Gallery, New York, 1940s
RoKo Gallery, New York, 1940s
Gallerie Paul Fachetti, 1960
Black Master, Studio Museum in Harlem, 1978

Aaron Douglas

Born Topeka, Kansas, 1899
B.F.A., University of Nebraska, Lincoln, 1922
Studied under Winold Reiss in New York, 1924–1927
L'Académie Scandinave, Paris, 1931
M.A., Columbia University Teachers College, New York, 1944
Founder/Chair of art department, Fisk University, Nashville,
    Tennessee, 1937–1966
Died 1979
Major Exhibitions:
D'Caz-Delbo Gallery, New York, 1934
Howard University, Washington, D.C., 1937
Fisk University, Nashville, Tennessee, 1948, 1952, 1953
Newark Museum, New Jersey, 1971
Studio Museum in Harlem, New York, 1982

Robert Scott Duncanson

Born New York state, 1821
Moved to Cincinnati, Ohio, 1840
First traveled to Europe, 1853
Sought exile in Canada, 1863–1865
Traveled to England and Scotland and exhibited major works, 1866
Returned to Cincinnati, 1867
Died 1872
Major Exhibitions:
Two Centuries of Black American Art, Los Angeles County
    Museum of Art, 1976
Sharing Traditions: Five Artists in Nineteenth-Century America,
    National Museum of American Art, 1985
*Free Within Ourselves: African-American Artists in the Collection of
    the National Museum of American Art,* National Museum
    of American Art, 1992

Melvin Edwards
Born Houston, 1937
B.F. A., University of Southern California
Assistant Professor, University of Connecticut, Storrs, 1970–1972
Assistant Professor, Rutgers University, New Brunswick, New Jersey,
    1972 to present
Major Exhibitions:
Arts as Advocate, Museum of Modern Art, New York, 1971
Tradition and Conflict: Images of a Turbulent Decade, 1963–1973,
    Studio Museum in Harlem, New York, 1985
Lynch Fragment Series, Robeson Center Gallery, Rutgers University,
    New Brunswick, New Jersey, 1985
Melvin Edwards Sculpture: A Thirty-Year Retrospective 1963–1993,
    Newerger Museum of Art, State University of New York at
    Purchase, 1993
*Sources: Multicultural Influences on Contemporary African American
    Sculptors,* The Art Gallery, University of Maryland, College
    Park, 1994
Twentieth-Century American Sculpture at the White House, First Ladies'
    Garden, the White House, Washington, D.C., 1996

Minnie Evans
Born Long Creek, North Carolina, 1892
Died 1987
Major Exhibitions:
Retrospective Exhibition, Church of the Epiphany, New York, 1966
Solo Exhibition, Whitney Museum of American Art, New York,
    1975
North Carolina Museum of Art, Raleigh, 1986

Meta Warrick Fuller
Born Philadelphia, 1877
Attended Pennsylvania Museum and School for the Industrial Arts,
    1894–1899
Attended L'École des Beaux Arts and Académie Colarossi, Paris,
    1899
Died 1968
Major Exhibitions:
Annual exhibitions at the Pennsylvania Academy of Fine Arts, 1906,
    1908, 1920, 1923
Making of America Exhibition, New York, 1931
Harmon Foundation, 1931
Exposition of the Art of the American Negro, 1851–1940
Tanner Art Galleries, Chicago, 1940
Howard University, Washington, D.C., 1961
*Three Generations of African American Women Sculptors: A Study in
    Paradox,* Afro-American Historical and Cultural Museum,
    Philadelphia, 1996–1998

Sam Gilliam
Born Tupelo, Mississippi, 1933
M.S., University of Louisville, 1961
L.H.D., University of Louisville, 1980
L.H.D., Northwestern University, 1990
Relinquished figurative style for Washington Color Field, 1963
Relinquished narrative in compositions, c. 1982
Major Exhibitions:
Gilliam/Krebs/McGowin, Corcoran Gallery of Art, Washington,
    D.C., 1969
Gilliam/Edwards/Williams: Extensions, Wadsworth Atheneum,
    Hartford, Connecticut, 1974
Modern Painters at the Corcoran: Sam Gilliam, Corcoran Gallery of Art,
    Washington, D.C., 1983
African American Art from the Collection, Philadelphia Museum of Art,
    Philadelphia, 1990

Golden Windows Inside Gold, Whitney Museum of American Art,
    New York, 1993–1995
Forty-Fourth Biennial Exhibition of Contemporary American Painting,
    Corcoran Gallery of Art, Washington, D.C.

Michael D. Harris
Born Cleveland, Ohio, 1948
M.F.A., Howard University, Washington, D.C., 1979
M.A., Yale University, New Haven, Connecticut, 1991
M. Phil., Yale University, 1991
Ph.D., Yale University, 1991
Assistant Professor, Morehouse College, Atlanta, Georgia, 1981–1993
Georgia State University, 1993–1995
Assistant Professor, University of North Carolina at Chapel Hill,
    1995 to present
Major Exhibitions:
Howard University, Washington, D.C., 1979
AfriCobra: The First Twenty Years, Southern Arts Federation, 1990
University of Massachusetts at Boston, 1991
Nexus Gallery, Chastain Park, Atlanta, Georgia, 1994

James V. Herring
Born Clio, South Carolina, 1887
Studied at Syracuse University, Columbia University, and Harvard
    University
Instructor, Howard University, Washington, D.C., 1921
Chairman, Art Department, Howard University, 1931–1952
Opened Barnett-Aden Gallery, Washington, D.C., 1943
Died 1969
Major Exhibitions:
Two Centuries of Black American Art, Los Angeles County
    Museum of Art, 1976
*Reflections of a Southern Heritage: Twentieth-Century Black Artists
    of the Southeast,* Gibbes Art Gallery, Washington, D.C., 1979

Earl J. Hooks
Born 1927
B.A., Howard University, Washington, D.C., 1945–1949
Catholic University, Washington, D.C., 1949–1951
Graduate certificate, Rochester Institute of Technology, Rochester,
    New York, 1954
Certificate in ceramics, School of American Craftsman, New York,
    1954–1955
Professor/Chair of art department, Fisk University, Nashville,
    Tennessee, 1961–1967
Indiana University Northwest Campus, 1954–1961
Major Exhibitions:
Fisk University, Nashville, Tennessee, 1966
Carl Van Vechten Gallery of Fine Arts, Fisk University, Nashville,
    Tennessee, 1985
Smithsonian Institution, Washington, D.C., 1954, 1957, 1963
Art Institute of Chicago, 1967
Lagos, Nigeria, 1977

Margo Humphrey
Born Oakland, California, 1942
B.A., California College of Arts and Crafts, Oakland, California,
    1972
M.A., Stanford University, Palo Alto, California, 1974
Resident, Tamarind Institute, New Mexico, 1977
Associate Professor of art, University of Maryland, College Park,
    1989 to present
Major Exhibitions
New Perspectives, Oakland Museum, California, 1968
Herstory, Oakland Museum, California, 1990

Through Sisters' Eyes: Children's Books Illustrated by African-American Artists, National Museum of Women in the Arts Library and Research Center, Washington, D.C., 1992
Brody's Gallery, Washington, D.C., 1992

Clementine Hunter

Born Cloutierville, Louisiana, c. 1887
Began as domestic, Melrose Plantation, Natchitoches, Louisiana, 1925
Began painting, 1940
Began to exhibit, 1945
Died 1988
Major Exhibitions:
Clementine Hunter: Primitive Painter, Northwestern State University, Natchitoches, Louisiana, 1955
Solo Exhibition, Delgado Museum, 1955
La Jolla Museum of Contemporary Art, California,1970
Forever Free: Art by African American Women 1862–1980, Illinois State University, Normal, 1981
A Centennial Salute to Clementine Hunter, New Orleans Museum of Art, 1985
Clementine Hunter, American Folk Artist: A Retrospective Exhibition, Museum of African American Life and Culture, Dallas, 1993

Wilmer Jennings

Born Atlanta, Georgia, 1910
B.S., Morehouse College, Atlanta, Georgia, 1933
Rhode Island School of Design, Providence, Rhode Island, 1940s
Jewelry Designer, Imperial Pearl, Rhode Island, 1948–1979
Died 1990
Major Exhibitions
Black Printmakers and the W.P.A., The Lehman College Art Gallery, Bronx, New York, 1989
Against the Odds: African-American Artists and the Harmon Foundation, Newark Museum, New Jersey, 1989
Alone in a Crowd: Prints of the 1930s by African-American Artists; From the Collection of Reba and Dave Williams, American Federation of the Arts, 1993

William H. Johnson

Born Florence, South Carolina, 1901
National Academy of Design, New York, 1921–1926
Moved to Paris, 1926
Traveled to Tunisia, North Africa, 1932
Returned to New York, 1938
Teacher, Harlem Community Arts Center, WPA, 1939–1943
Died 1970
Major Exhibitions:
Harmon Foundation Exhibitions, 1930–1937
Paintings by William H. Johnson, Alma Reed Galleries, New York, 1941
American Negro Art: Contemporary Painting and Sculpture, Newark Museum, New Jersey, 1944
William H. Johnson: A Retrospective Exhibit, Countee Cullen Branch, New York Public Library, 1956–1957
Harlem Renaissance: Art of Black America, Studio Museum in Harlem, New York, 1987
The Blues Aesthetic: Black Culture and Modernism, Washington Project for the Arts, Washington, D.C., 1989
Homecoming: William H. Johnson and Afro-Americana, 1938–1946, National Museum of American Art, Washington, D.C., 1991

Loïs Mailou Jones

Born Boston, Massachusetts, 1905
Designers Art School of Boston, 1927–1928
Académie Julian, Paris, 1937–1938
A.B., Howard University, Washington, D.C., 1945
Académie de la Grande Chaumière, Paris, 1962
Chair, Palmer Memorial Institute, Sedalia, North Carolina, 1928–1930
Professor, Howard University, Washington, D.C., 1930–1977
Died 1998
Major Exhibitions:
Atlanta University Annual Exhibition, Georgia, 1949
Centre d'Art, Port-au-Prince, Haiti, 1954
Société des Artistes Français, Grand-Palais, France, 1966
Boston Museum of Fine Arts (retrospective), 1973
Corcoran Gallery of Art, Washington, D.C., 1994

Jacob Lawrence

Born Atlantic City, New Jersey, 1917
Harlem Art Workshop, New York, 1932–1939
American Artists School, New York 1937–1939
Instructor, Skowhegan School of Painting and Sculpture, Maine, Summers, 1954, 1968–1972
Instructor, Pratt Institute, Brooklyn, New York, 1955–1970
Instructor, Five Towns Music and Art Foundation, Cedarhurst, Long Island, 1955–1962 and 1966–1968
Full Professor, University of Washington, Seattle, 1970
Major Exhibitions:
Whitney Museum of American Art, New York, 1974
Midtown Payson Galleries, New York. 1993
Jacob Lawrence Gallery, University of Washington, Seattle, 1994
Art Institute of Chicago, 1995
Whitney Museum of American Art, New York, 1996
National Academy of Design, New York, 1996

Norman Lewis

Born New York, 1909
Columbia University, New York
Instructor, Savage Studio, New York, 1935–1937
Harlem Art Center, General Art Project, New York, 1936–1939
Art Students League, New York, 1972–1977
Died 1979
Major Exhibitions:
Willard Gallery, New York, 1949, 1950–1954, 1957
Museum of Modern Art, New York, 1951
Art Institute of Chicago, 1956
Whitney Museum of American Art, New York, 1958
Robeson Center Gallery, Newark, New Jersey, 1985
Kenkeleba Gallery, New York, 1989

Richard Mayhew

Born Amityville, New York, 1924
Columbia University, New York, 1953–1957
Art Students League, New York, 1956–1957
Spiral member, 1963
Instructor, Brooklyn Museum Art School, 1963–1968
Art Students League, New York, 1965–1971
Instructor, Smith College, Northampton, Massachusetts, 1971–1975
Professor, Pennsylvania State University, University Park, beginning 1977
Major Exhibitions:
Brooklyn Museum, New York, 1955
Minneapolis Institute of Arts, Minnesota, 1968
High Museum of Art, Atlanta, Georgia, 1969
Newark Museum, New Jersey, 1971
Studio Museum in Harlem, New York, 1978

William McNeil
Born Los Angeles, 1967
B.A., University of Maryland, College Park, 1996
J. Paul Getty Museum, Los Angeles, 1997
Major Exhibitions:
The James McLaughlin Memorial Staff Show, The Phillips Collection,
    Washington, D.C., 1994–1996

Jerome Meadows
Born Bronx, New York, 1951
B.F.A., Rhode Island School of Design, Providence, Rhode Island,
    1973
M.F.A., University of Maryland, College Park, 1981
Instructor, North Adams State College, Massachusetts, 1974–1975
Department Chair, Gallery Director, Baltimore School for the Arts,
    Maryland, 1982–1985
Assistant Professor, College of Fine Arts, Howard University,
    Washington, D.C., 1988–1992
Major Exhibitions:
Public Sculptures:
Carry the Rainbow on Your Shoulders, Unity Park, Washington, D.C.
Martin Luther King Living Memorial, Anchorage, Alaska
Truths that Rise from the Roots Remembered, African American
    Heritage Park, Alexandria, Virginia
To Create the Beloved Community, Martin Luther King, Jr. Memorial,
    Albuquerque, New Mexico

Sam Middleton
Born New York, 1927
Studied at the Instituto Allende, Mexico, 1956
Currently lives and works in Amsterdam
Major Exhibitions:
Excelsior Gallery, Mexico City, Mexico, 1957
Gallery Silo, Madrid, Spain, 1960
Contemporary Arts, New York, 1962
South Yarra Gallery, Melbourne, Australia, 1964
Muzik van nu, Stedlijk Museum, Amsterdam, Netherlands, 1966

Keith Morrison
Born Jamaica, 1942
M.A., Art Institute of Chicago, 1965
Began teaching career that included positions at Fisk University,
    DePaul University, University of Illinois, University of Chicago,
    University of Maryland, Maryland Institute College of Art,
    and University of Michigan, Ann Arbor, 1967
Relinquished Abstract Expressionist style for African and Caribbean
    figural themes, c. 1975
International Award for Painting, Organization for African Unity,
    Monrovia, Liberia, 1978
Major Exhibitions:
Contemporary Visual Expressions, Anacostia Museum, Washington,
    D.C., 1987
*Introspectives: Contemporary Art by Americans and Brazilians
    of African Descent,* California Afro-American Museum,
    Los Angeles, 1989
New Jamaican Painting, Smithsonian Institution, Washington, D.C.,
    1997

Mary Lovelace O'Neal
Born Jackson, Mississippi, 1942
B.F.A., Howard University, Washington, D.C., 1964
M.F.A., Columbia University, New York, 1969
Began teaching career that included positions at San Francisco Art
    Institute; University of California, Berkeley; California College
    of Arts and Crafts; and Humboldt State University, 1970
Began current career at University of California, Berkeley, 1979
Biennale Internationale des Arts Award, Dakar, Senegal, 1993–1994

Major Exhibitions:
*Introspectives: Contemporary Art by Americans and Brazilians
    of African Descent,* California Afro-American Museum,
    Los Angeles, 1989
Museum of Asilah, Morocco, 1989
Mary Lovelace O'Neal: Paintings and Prints, de Saisset Museum, Santa
    Clara University, Santa Clara, California, 1990
Mary Lovelace O'Neal, Institute Chileno Norte Americano de
    Cultura, Santigo, Chile, 1991
No Justice, No Peace? Resolutions…, California Afro-American
    Museum, Los Angeles, 1993
Berkeley Art Center, Berkeley, California, 1995

James Phillips
Born Brooklyn, New York, 1945
Philadelphia College of Art, 1964–1965
Artist-in-residence, Studio Museum in Harlem, New York,
    1971–1972
Howard University, Washington, D.C., 1973–1977
Major Exhibitions:
Weusi Numba Ya sanaa Gallery, New York, 1970
Pennsylvania Academy of Fine Arts, Philadelphia, 1972
Howard University, Washington, D.C., 1972
Corcoran Gallery of Art, Washington, D.C., 1973
American Center, Tokyo, 1981
Kenkeleba House, New York, 1983
Studio Museum in Harlem, New York, 1985

Stephanie Pogue
Born Shelby, North Carolina, 1944
Syracuse University, New York, 1962–1963
B.F.A., Howard University, Washington, D.C., 1963–1966
M.F.A., Cranbrook Academy of Art, Bloomfield Hills, Michigan,
    1968
Assistant/Associate/Chair/Gallery director, Fisk University,
    Nashville, Tennessee, 1968–1981
Professor/Chair, University of Maryland, College Park, 1981 to
    present
Major Exhibitions:
El Museo de Arte Moderna La Tertulia, Cali, Colombia, 1976
Cinque Gallery, New York, 1977
City Museum of Fine Arts, Taipei, Taiwan, 1983
Centre d'Art de Rouge-Cloitre, Brussels, Belgium, 1988
Museo do Gravura, Curitiba, Brazil, 1991
Fisk University, Nashville, Tennessee, 1966
Metropolitan Museum of Art, New York, 1975
James V. Herring Art Gallery, Howard University, Washington, D.C.,
    1992
Bearing Witness: Contemporary Works by African American Women Artists,
    Spelman College, Atlanta, Georgia, 1996

P. H. Polk
Born Bessemer, Alabama, 1898
Tuskegee Institute, Alabama, 1916–1920
Correspondence course in photography, 1922
Apprenticed with Fred Jensen, Chicago, 1922–1926
Owned and operated a private portrait studio in Tuskegee, Alabama,
    1927
Tuskegee Institute, Alabama, 1928–1938 and 1933–1984
Owned and operated a private portrait studio in Atlanta, Georgia,
    1938
Died 1984
Major Exhibitions:
Art Institute of Pittsburgh, n.d.
Corcoran Gallery of Art, Washington, D.C., 1981
New York Museum of National History, n.d.
Washington Gallery of Photography, n.d.

Charles Ethan Porter
Born Hartford, Connecticut, 1847
Began study at National Academy of Design, New York, 1869
Traveled to Europe, 1881–1884
Opened studio in Rockville, Connecticut, 1890
Became charter member of Connecticut Academy of Fine Arts, 1910
Died 1923
Major Exhibitions:
National Academy of Design, New York 1871, 1876, 1885
Vorce's Gallery, Hartford, Connecticut, 1889
Hartford Decorative Arts Society, Hartford, Connecticut, n.d.

James A. Porter
Born Baltimore, Maryland, 1905
B.A., Howard University, Washington, D.C., 1927
Institute of Art and Archeology, University of Paris, Certificat de
	Préséance, 1935
M.A., New York University, 1937
Head of Department of Art, Howard University, Washington, D.C.,
	beginning in 1953
Died 1970
Major Exhibitions:
Harmon Foundation, 1928
Smithsonian Institution, Washington, D.C., 1929
American Watercolor Society, 1932
Howard University, Washington, D.C., 1937, 1939, 1945, 1965
American Negro Exposition, Chicago, 1940
James A. Porter Gallery, 1970
James A. Porter, Artist and Historian: The Memory of the Legacy, Howard
	University Gallery of Art, 1993

Martin Puryear
Born Washington, D.C., 1941
B. A., Catholic University of America, Washington, D. C., 1959–1963
Swedish Royal Academy of Art, Stockholm, 1966–1968
M.F.A., Yale University, New Haven, Connecticut, 1969–1971
Teacher, Peace Corps, Sierra Leone, West Africa, 1964–1966
Assistant Professor of art, Fisk University, Nashville, Tennessee,
	1971–1973; University of Maryland, College Park, 1974–1978
Designer, SCAN, Scandinavia, 1968
Major Exhibitions:
Solomon R. Guggenheim Museum, New York, 1978 and 1985
Whitney Museum of American Art, New York, 1979 and 1981
Museum of Contemporary Art, Chicago, 1980
Art Institute of Chicago, 1991
Hirshhorn Museum and Sculpture Garden, Washington, D. C., 1992

Ray Saunders
Born Pittsburgh, Pennsylvania, 1934
B.F.A., Carnegie Institute of Technology, 1960
M.F.A., California College of Arts and Crafts, 1961
Lives and works primarily in Oakland, California
Major Exhibitions:
Stephen Wirz Gallery, San Francisco, 1980
Albright-Knox Art Gallery, Buffalo, New York, group exhibit, 1989
Pennsylvania Academy of the Fine Arts, Philadelphia, 1990
Studio Museum in Harlem, New York, group exhibit
Metropolitan Museum of Art, New York, group exhibit, 1995

Augusta Savage
Born Green Cove Springs, Florida, 1892
Tallahassee State Normal School (now Florida A&M), 1915
Cooper Union, New York, 1921
Académie de la Grande Chaumière, Paris, c. 1929
Founded Savage Studio of Arts and Crafts, New York, 1932

Assistant supervisor, Works Progress Administration (WPA)
	Federal Art Project (FAP), beginning 1936
Commissioned portrait artist
Died New York, 1962
Major Exhibitions:
Académie de la Grande Chaumière, Paris, c. 1929
Argent Gallery, New York, 1932
Anderson Art Gallery, New York, 1932

Charles Sebree
Born Kentucky, 1914
Studied at the Art Institute of Chicago
WPA, Illinois, 1936–1938
Died 1985
Major Exhibitions:
American Negro Exhibition, 1940
South Side Community Arts Center, Chicago, 1941
Institute of Modern Art, Boston, 1943
RoKo Gallery, New York, 1949
Retrospective Exhibition, Evans-Tibbs Collection, Washington,
	D.C., 1984

Frank Smith
Born Chicago, 1939
B.F.A., University of Illinois, Chicago, 1958
Began teaching career in Chicago Public Schools, 1959
Began career at Howard University, Washington, D.C., 1970
Joined African Commune of Bad Relevant Artists (AfriCobra), 1970
M.F.A., Howard University, Washington, D.C., 1972
Diaspora-3 Award, Paramaraibo, Suriname, 1982
Major Exhibitions:
Since the Harlem Renaissance: 50 Years of Afro-American Art, Bucknell
	Center Gallery, Bucknell University, Lewisburg, Pennsylvania,
	1985
National Museum of Fine Arts, Kinshasa, Zaire, 1988
AfriCobra: The First Twenty Years, Nexus Contemporary Art
	Center, Atlanta, Georgia, 1990
Norman Parish Gallery, Washington, D.C., 1993
Japan Information and Cultural Center, Washington, D.C., 1995

Vincent Smith
Born New York, 1929
Studied at Brooklyn Museum Art School, 1954–1956
M.E., Skowhegan School of Painting, Maine
Empire State College, 1953–1956
Studied at State University of New York, Saratoga, 1980
Major Exhibitions:
Studio Museum in Harlem, New York, 1974
Portland Museum of Art, Maine, 1974
Cooper Square Gallery, New York, 1979
Journey to the Source, Spectrum IV Gallery, New Rochelle,
	New York, 1982
Spiral Gallery, Brooklyn, New York, 1988
Anderson Gallery, Virginia Commonwealth University, Richmond,
	1990
Milwaukee Art Museum, Wisconsin, 1990
Robeson Gallery, Rutgers University, New Brunswick, New Jersey,
	1994

Gilda Snowden
Born in Detroit, Michigan, 1954
B.F.A., Wayne State University, Detroit, Michigan, 1977
M.A., Wayne State University, Detroit, Michigan, 1978
M.F.A., Wayne State University, Detroit, Michigan, 1979
Continues to live and work in Detroit

Major Exhibitions:
Signature Images, Detroit Institute of Arts, group exhibit, 1990
Detroit Institute of Arts, group exhibit, 1991
Out of Sight, Out of Mind, Center for Creative Studies, Detroit,
    Michigan, 1995
A Detroit Tradition: Collecting African American Art, Community Arts
    Gallery, Wayne State University, group exhibit, 1996

Frank Stewart

Born Nashville, Tennessee, 1949
B.F.A., Cooper Union
Instructor, State University of New York, Purchase, New York
Instructor, Studio Museum in Harlem, New York
Artist-in-residence, Kenkeleba House, New York, 1987
Associate Director, Contemporary American Artists Series, Inc.
Major Exhibitions:
Corcoran Gallery, Washington, D.C., 1977
International Center of Photography, New York, 1979
Studio Museum in Harlem, New York, 1979
Gallery 62, National Urban League, New York, 1980
Allen Memorial Art Museum, Oberlin College, Ohio, 1983
Kenkeleba House Gallery, New York, 1986

Lou Stovall

Born Athens, Georgia, 1937
George Walter Vincent Smith Museum, Springfield, Massachusetts,
    1954–1956
Rhode Island School of Design, Providence, Rhode Island,
    1956–1957
B.F.A., Howard University, Washington, D.C., 1965
Owner and operator of Workshop, Inc., founded in 1968
Major Exhibitions:
The Phillips Collection, Washington, D.C., 1972
Baltimore Museum of Art, Maryland, 1975
El Museo de Arte Moderna La Tertulia, Cali, Colombia, 1976
Smithsonian Institution, Washington, D.C., 1980
The American Embassy, Moscow, U.S.S.R., 1984
The Corcoran Gallery of Art, Washington, D.C., 1992
Fondo Del Sol, Washington, D.C., 1996

Henry O. Tanner

Born Pittsburgh, Pennsylvania, 1859
Entered the Pennsylvania Academy of the Fine Arts, Philadelphia,
    1879
Moved to Paris, 1891
Included in World's Columbian Exposition in Chicago, 1893
Died 1936
Major Exhibitions:
Pennsylvania Academy of Fine Arts, Philadelphia, Pennsylvania, 1880
National Academy of Design, New York, 1885
World's Columbian Exposition, Chicago, 1893
Salon, Paris, 1894
Art Institute of Chicago, 1908
Solo Exhibition, American Art Galleries, New York, 1908
Solo Exhibition, Thurber Art Galleries, Chicago, 1913
Solo Exhibition, Grand Central Art Galleries, New York, 1924
Two Centuries of Black American Art, Los Angeles County Museum
    of Art, 1976
Sharing Traditions: Five Black Artists in Nineteenth-Century America,
    National Museum of American Art, Washington, D.C., 1985
Henry Ossawa Tanner, Philadelphia Museum of Art, 1991

Bill Taylor

Born Atlantic City, New Jersey, 1927
Washington Institute of Contemporary Art
Catholic University of America, Washington, D.C.
Major Exhibitions:
Howard University Gallery of Art, Washington, D.C., n.d.
Atlanta University, Georgia, n.d.
Fisk University, Nashville, Tennessee, n.d.
Los Angeles County Museum, n.d.
B'nai B'rith Klutznick National Jewish Museum, Washington,
    D.C., n.d.

Alma Thomas

Born Columbus, Georgia, 1896
B.S., Howard University, Washington, D.C., 1924
M.F.A., Columbia University, New York, 1934
American University, Washington, D.C., 1950–1960
Teacher, Shaw Junior High School, Washington, D.C., 1924–1960
Vice President, Barnett-Aden Gallery, Washington, D.C.
Died 1978
Major Exhibitions:
Howard University, Washington, D.C., 1966
Baltimore Museum, Maryland, 1970
State Armory, Wilmington, Delaware, 1971
Corcoran Gallery of Art, Washington, D.C., 1972
Whitney Museum of American Art, New York, 1972

Yvonne Edwards Tucker

Born Chicago, 1941
B.F.A. Otis Art Institute (now Otis/Parson's School of Design),
    Los Angeles, 1968
M.F.A. Otis Art Institute, Los Angeles, 1968
University of Miami, 1971–1972
Florida State University, 1979–1980
Assistant Professor, Miami-Dade Community College, South
    Campus, 1968–1973
Associate Professor, Florida A & M University, Tallahassee, since
    1973
Co-founder, Harambee Council of Tallahassee
Administrator and project director of folk and fine arts festivals
    annually from 1980–1990
Major Exhibitions:
Contemporary Gallery of Fine Arts, Dallas, 1969
Micanopy Gallery of Fine Arts, Florida, 1972
Morgan State College, Baltimore, Maryland, 1975
Malcolm Brown Gallery, Shaker Heights, Ohio, 1981
Contemporary Art Center, Kansas City, Missouri, 1989
Florida State University, Tallahassee, 1991

James VanDerZee

Born Massachusetts, 1886
Assistant Photographer, Gertz Department Store, Newark, New
    Jersey, 1915–1916
Owner, Guarantee Photos and GGG Photo Studio, Harlem,
    1916–1968
Metropolitan Museum of Art Life Fellowship Award, 1970
President's Living Legacy Award, Washington, D.C., 1978
Honorary Doctorate, Howard University, Washington, D.C., 1983
Died 1983
Major Exhibitions:
Harlem on My Mind: Cultural Capital of Black America 1900–1968,
    Metropolitan Museum of Art, New York, 1969
The Legacy of James VanDerZee: A Portrait of Black Americans,
    Alternative Center for International Arts, New York, 1979
VanDerZee Photographer: 1886–1983, National Portrait Gallery,
    Washington, D.C., 1993

Laura Wheeler Waring
Born Hartford, Connecticut, 1887
Pennsylvania Academy of Fine Arts, Philadelphia, 1907–1910
Harvard University Summer School, Cambridge, Massachusetts,
    1918
Columbia University Summer School, New York, 1920
Académie de la Grande Chaumière, Paris, 1924–1925
Instructor, Art Department, Cheyney State Teachers College,
    Cheyney, Pennsylvania, 1906–1925
Director, Art Department, Cheyney State Teachers College,
    Cheyney, Pennsylvania, 1925–1948
Died 1948
Major Exhibitions:
Galerie du Luxembourg, Paris, 1929
Howard University, Washington, D.C., 1940, 1949
National Portrait Gallery, Smithsonian Institution, Washington, D.C.,
    1944, 1997
Brooklyn Museum, New York, 1945
Newark Museum, New Jersey, 1989

James Lesesne Wells
Born Atlanta, Georgia, 1902
Moved to Harlem, New York, 1919
National Academy of Design, New York, 1924
Columbia University Teachers College, 1924–1928
Instructor of design, Howard University, Washington, D.C., 1929
Summer in Paris, 1937
Retired from Howard University as Professor Emeritus, 1969
Traveled to Africa, 1969
Died 1993
Major Exhibitions:
Paintings and Prints by James L. Wells, Carl Van Vechten Gallery
    of Art, Fisk University, Nashville, Tennessee, 1972/1973
James L. Wells: Retrospective of Prints and Paintings, Howard University,
    Washington, D.C., 1977
James Lesesne Wells: Sixty Years in Art, Washington Project for the
    Arts, Washington, D.C., 1986

Charles White
Born Chicago, 1918
Art Institute of Chicago, 1937
Art Students League, New York
Taller de Gráfica Popular, Mexico
Teacher, South Side Community Art Center, Chicago, 1939–1940
Artist-in-residence, Howard University, Washington, D.C., 1945
Teacher, Otis Art Institute (now Otis/Parson's School of Design),
    Los Angeles, until 1979
Died 1979
Major Exhibitions:
Howard University, Washington, D.C., 1939, 1967
Institute of Modern Art, Boston, 1943
First World Festival of Negro Arts, Dakar, Senegal, 1966
Pushkin Museum, Moscow, 1968
Whitney Museum of American Art, New York, 1968
Boston Museum of Fine Arts, 1969
La Jolla Museum of Art, California, 1970
Los Angeles County Museum of Art, 1971

Walter Williams
Born Brooklyn, New York, 1920
Brooklyn Museum School, n.d. (post-World War II)
Artist-in-residence, Fisk University, Nashville, Tennessee, 1968–1969
Whitney Museum Fellowship, 1955
Obrig Prize of the National Academy of Design, New York, 1972
Died 1998

Major Exhibitions:
RoKo Gallery, New York, 1954
Studio Museum in Harlem, New York, 1982

William T. Williams
Born Cross Creek, North Carolina, 1942
A.A.S., City University of New York, New York Community
    College, 1962
B.F.A., Pratt Institute, Brooklyn, New York, 1966
Skowhegan School of Painting and Sculpture, Maine 1965
M.F.A., Yale University, New Haven, Connecticut, 1968
Professor/Instructor of art, Pratt Institute, Brooklyn, New York, 1970
School of Visual Arts, 1970
Professor of art, City University of New York, Brooklyn College,
    since 1971
Major Exhibitions:
American Embassy, Moscow, 1969
Museum of Modern Art, New York, 1969
Foundation Maeght, St. Paul, France, 1970
Kolner Konstmarkt, Cologne, Germany, 1971
Whitney Museum of American Art, New York, 1971
Indianapolis Museum of Art, Indiana, 1972
Contemporary Visual Expressions, Anacostia Museum, Washington,
    D.C., 1987
Montclair Art Museum, New Jersey, 1991

Ellis Wilson
Born Mayfield, Kentucky, 1899
Studied at the Art Institute of Chicago, early 1920s
WPA, New York, 1930s
Guggenheim Fellowship, 1944
Traveled to Haiti, 1950s
Died 1977
Major Exhibitions:
Retrospective Exhibition, Fisk University, Nashville, Tennessee, 1971

Hale Woodruff
Born Cairo, Illinois, 1900
John Herron Art Institute, Indianapolis, Indiana, c. 1918
Fogg Art Museum, Cambridge, Massachusetts
Académie Scandinavia, Paris
Académie Moderne, Paris
Worked on frescoes with Diego Rivera in Mexico, 1936
Professor, Atlanta University, Georgia, 1931–1945
Instructor/Professor Emeritus, New York University, 1947–1970
Initiated annual art shows for black artists, Atlanta University,
    Georgia, 1941
Died 1980
Major Exhibitions:
Howard University, Washington, D.C., 1967
Museum of Fine Arts, Boston, 1967
San Diego Art Museum, 1967
Los Angeles County Museum of Art, 1967, 1976
Newark Museum, New Jersey, 1971
Bellevue Art Museum and the Art Museum Association
    of America, 1985

Notes

The Color of Art:
African American Artistic Identities
in the Twentieth Century

1. The phenomenon of the African American artist as both artist and scholar received consideration in a recent Smithsonian Institution exhibition entitled *In the Balance: The African American Artist/Scholar,* curated by Deborah Willis-Kennedy. David Driskell was featured in this exhibition in a selection of artists that included Floyd Coleman, Michael Harris, and James Porter, among others.

2. Letter from Frederick Douglass to Harriet Beecher Stowe (Rochester, March 8, 1853), read at the 1853 Colored National Convention in Rochester, New York, in Howard Holman Bell, ed., *Minutes of the Proceedings of the National Negro Conventions, 1830–1864* (New York: Arno Press), p. 38.

3. See chapter five, "Leaders and Community Activists," in James Oliver and Lois E. Horton, *Black Bostonians, Family Life and Community Struggle in the Antebellum North* (New York: Holmes & Meier, 1979), pp. 53–66; also Benjamin Quarles's 1969 study of both black antislavery leadership and the rank and file: *Black Abolitionists* (New York: Oxford Univ. Press, 1969).

4. Horatio Greenough, "Remarks on American Art, 1843," in John W. McCoubrey, ed., *American Art 1700–1960: Sources and Documents in the History of Art Series* (Englewood Cliffs, N.J.: Prentice-Hall, 1965), pp. 125–132.

5. For the most recent scholarship on these two artists, see Lynda Roscoe Hartigan's *Sharing Traditions: Five Black Artists of the Nineteenth Century;* Joseph Ketner's *The Emergence of the African American artist Robert S. Duncanson;* and the author's dissertation, *Co-Workers in the Kingdom of Culture: Edward Mitchell Bannister and the Boston Community of African American Artists, 1848–1901,* Columbia University and University Microfilm, 1997.

6. Booker T. Washington, Fannie Barrier Williams, and N. B. Wood, *A New Negro for a New Century: An Accurate and Up-To-Date Record of the Upward Struggles of the Negro Race* (Chicago: American Publishing House, 1899).

7. David Levering Lewis, *When Harlem Was In Vogue,* p. 91.

8. George Schuyler, "Black Genesis," *The Modern Quarterly,* 5 (Spring 1929), pp. 571–572.

9. African American newspapers gave detailed coverage to Haiti's revolution, and Toussaint L'Ouverture appears in numerous nineteenth-century compilations and descriptions of African American heroes, written by contemporary black writers.

10. For a more complete discussion of African American artists' participation in Harmon Foundation exhibitions, see the exhibition catalog *Against the Odds: African American Artists and the Harmon Foundation* by Gary A. Reynolds and Beryl Wright (Newark: The Newark Museum, 1989).

11. Reynolds and Wright, *Against the Odds: African American Artists and the Harmon Foundation,* p. 41.

12. Romare Bearden and Harry Henderson, *A History of African-American Artists, From 1972 to the Present* (New York: Pantheon, 1993); *Harlem Renaissance: Art of Black America* (New York: Studio Museum in Harlem & Harry N. Abrams, Inc., 1987), pp. 111–112.

13. Beryl J. Wright, "The Harmon Foundation in Context: Early Exhibitions and Alain Locke's Concept of a Racial Idiom of Expression" in *Against the Odds: African-American Artists and the Harmon Foundation,* pp. 16–17.

14. Wright, p. 18.

15. Juanita Holland, "Augusta Christine Savage: A Chronology of her Art and Life 1892–1962," *Augusta Savage and the Art Schools of Harlem,* exhibition catalogue (New York: Schomburg Center for Research in Black Culture, 1988), p. 14.

16. Wright, p. 14. After his graduation from Columbia University Teachers College, printmaker James Lesesne Wells had illustrations accepted in the periodicals *Survey Graphic* and *Opportunity,* and in a book entitled *Plays and Pageants of Negro Life.*

17. Savage was one of the founders of the Vanguard, a political organization of black artists and intellectuals interested in communist and socialist ideas.

18. Holland, pp.16–18. The exhibitors included Norman Lewis, Meta Fuller, Richmond Barthé, Robert Pious, Rex Gorleigh, Morgan Smith, Gwendolyn Knight, Beauford Delaney, Georgette Seabrooke, Marvin Smith, William Farrow, Loïs Mailou Jones, Selma Burke, Ernest Crichlow, James Lesesne Wells, and Ellis Wilson.

19. Bearden and Henderson, pp. 392–393.

20. Deirdre Bibby, "Augusta Savage and the Art Schools of Harlem," *Augusta Savage and the Art Schools of Harlem,* exhibition catalogue (New York: Schomburg Center for Research in Black Culture, 1988), p. 8.

21. Quoted from Bibby, p. 9.

22. Bibby, p.10.

23. Bearden and Henderson, p. 393.

24. Bearden and Henderson, p. 338. Quotation taken from p. 338.

25 Bearden and Henderson, p. 339.

26. Exhibitions include the 1966 *Contemporary Art of the American Negro* and the 1967 show *The Evolution of Afro-American Artists: 1800–1950* at City College, New York City. His contributions to scholarship include the 1972 *Six Black Masters of American Art* and the 1995 *History of African American Artists,* which he co-authored with Harry Henderson.

A History of Collecting African American Art

1. Ivan Karp, Christine Mullen Kreamer, and Steven D. Lavine, eds., *Museums and Communities: The Politics of Public Culture* (Washington, D.C.: Smithsonian Inst. Press, 1992), p. 24.

2. Quoted in James Porter, *Modern Negro Art* (1943; reprint, Washington D.C.: Howard Univ. Press, 1992), p. 40.

3. Juanita Holland, "Reaching Through the Veil: African American Artist Edward Mitchell Bannister" in *Edward Mitchell Bannister* (New York: Kenkeleba House, 1992), pp. 17–20, 25.; Steven Jones, "A Keen Sense of the Artistic," *International Review of African American Art,* vol. 12, no. 2, pp. 4–29.

4. Gladys-Marie Fry, "Harriet Powers: Portrait of an African American Quilter" in *Stitched from the Soul: Slave Quilts from the Ante-Bellum South* (New York: Dutton Books, 1990), p. 86.

5. Karp, *Museums and Communities,* p. 25.

6. Edmund Barry Gaither, "Hey! That's Mine: Thoughts on Pluralism and American Museums" in Karp, *Museums and Communities,* pp. 61–62.

7. Susan M. Pierce, *On Collecting: An Investigation into Collecting in the European Tradition* (London and New York: Routledge, 1995), p. 5.

8. Benny Andrews, "The Decade of the Black Artist," *International Review of African American Art,* vol. 14, no. 2:15.

9. Amei Wallach, "The Contemporary Collector's Art," *The New York Times Magazine* (Oct. 26, 1997), p. 43.

10. Regenia Perry, "The Frenzy Over Black Folk Art," *International Review of African American Art,* vol. 14, no. 2:24.

11. Pierce, *On Collecting,* pp. 149–151.

12. John Elsner and Roger Cardinal, eds., "Introduction" in *The Culture of Collecting* (Cambridge, Mass.: Harvard Univ. Press, 1994), p. 3.

13. Ibid., p. 5.

14. W. O. Evans, Foreword, *Walter O. Evans Collection of African American Art,* (Detroit, 1991), pp. 9–11.

15. Jean Baudrillard, "The System of Collecting" in Elsner and Cardinal, *The Culture of Collecting,* p. 12.

The David Driskell Motives

1. The quotations are from an exhibition brochure of a David Driskell solo exhibit titled *Two Worlds: One of Sight, One of Vision* at the Bomani Gallery, San Francisco, November 7–December 27, 1997. In this same brochure, Keith Morrison, Dean of the College of Creative Arts, San Francisco State University, said that Driskell "...documents the vernacular history of his environment...."

2. If works of art can be enlarged by other works of art created by other artists, then it is suggested that Driskell's "chair" series owes some small measure to Vincent van Gogh. It should be noted that the chair also symbolically relates to the "seated figure," the "altar," the "hearth," and the "throne." See J. E. Circlot, *A Dictionary of Symbols,* trans. Jack Sage (New York: Charles Scribner's Sons, 1959).

3. Kenneth Clark, *Landscape Into Art* (1949; reprint, New York: Harper & Row, 1976).

4. In a private conversation, Driskell once facetiously described his more abstract paintings as being a stylistic synthesis of Alma Thomas and Mark Toby.

5. George S. Schuyler (1895–1977) was a journalist who was considered to be one of the best working. He went from being what has been described as a "radical socialist" to an "arch conservative." Schuyler was also a novelist and, coincidentally, the father of the piano prodigy, Phillipa Schuyler. His essay "The Negro-Art Hokum" was published in *The Nation* (June 16, 1926) and was responsible for Langston Hughes's rebuttal, "The Negro Artist and the Racial Mountain." These two essays established polar positions on the discussion of a racial school of black art.

6. This article was also published in *The Nation* the same year following Schuyler's essay. In it, Hughes insisted that the reason a black art had not been developed was that black artists were, like Schuyler, more intent on being like white Americans rather than seeing and knowing that they were "black and beautiful." Hughes felt that when a black art was developed, it would be because the black artist realized the validity of his or her own unique experiences.

7. This essay was first published by Alain Locke, ed., *The New Negro* (1925; reprint, New York: Atheneum, 1968), p. 254.

Selected Bibliography

Adams, Brooks. "Tanner's Odyssey." *Art in America* (June 1991): 108–113.

Adams, Clinton. "Art as a Testament: A Conversation with Margo Humphrey." *The Tamarind Papers* 9 (Spring 1986): 16–26.

Allen, Jane Addams. "Letting Go." *Art in America* (Jan. 1986): 98–147.

Andre, Linda. "Alma Thomas: Evening Glow," exhibition brochure. Baltimore: The Baltimore Museum of Art, 1996.

Baigell, Matthew. *A Concise History of American Painting and Sculpture*. New York: Harper & Row, 1984.

Belk, Russell W. *Collecting in a Consumer Society*. London/New York: Routledge, 1995.

Bearden, Romare, and Harry Henderson. *A History of African-American Artists from 1972 to the Present*. New York: Pantheon Books, 1993.

Benjamin, Tritobia H. *The World of Loïs Mailou Jones*. Washington, D.C.: Meridian House International, 1990.

Bennet, Lerone, Jr. *Before the Mayflower: A History of Black America*. Chicago: Johnson Publishing Company, Inc., 1988.

Bier, Justus. "Ellis Wilson: Kentucky Negro Artist." *The Courier-Journal Magazine* (April 30, 1950): 36–37.

Bishop, Robert, and Jacqueline M. Atkins. *Folk Art in American Life*. New York: Penguin Books, 1995.

Boime, Albert. "Henry Ossawa Tanner's Subversion of Genre." *The Art Bulletin* 75.3 (1993): 415–442.

Bond, Fred F. *A One-Man Exhibition: Prints and Paintings by James L. Wells*. Nashville: Van Vechten Gallery, Fisk University, 1973.

Broadway, Bill. "Pictures at an Exhibition Paint Black Point of View." *The Washington Post* (Aug. 30, 1997): B6.

Brunson, Jamie. "Improvisation in the Realm of Memory." *Artweek* 20 (May 27, 1989): 1.

Byrd, Rudolph P., ed. *Generations in Black and White: Photographs by Carl Van Vechten from the James Weldon Johnson Memorial Collection*. Athens, Ga.: The University of Georgia Press, 1993.

Campbell, Mary Schmidt, et al. *Harlem Renaissance: Art of Black America*. New York: Harry N. Abrams, Inc., 1987.

Campbell, Mary Schmidt, and Sharon F. Patton. *Memory and Metaphor: The Art of Romare Bearden 1940–1987*. New York: Oxford University Press, 1991.

Carrier, David. "Raymond Saunders/Carnegie Museum of Art/Pittsburgh Center for the Arts." *Artforum International* 35 (Oct. 1996): 122.

Cederholm, Theresa Dickason, ed. *Afro-American Artists: A Bio-Bibliographical Directory*. Boston: Trustees of the Boston Public Library, 1973.

Cohen, Jean Lawlor. "Sam Gilliam." *ARTnews* (May 1993): 145.

Cohn, Terri. "Raymond Saunders—*Malcolm X: Talking Pictures* at Stephen Wirtz Gallery." *Artweek* 25 (Oct. 20, 1994): 17.

Coker, Gilbert, and Corrine Jennings. *The Harmon and Harriet Kelley Collection of African American Art*. San Antonio: San Antonio Museum of Art, 1994.

Conwill, Kinshasha Holman. "In Search of an 'Authentic' Vision: Decoding the Appeal of the Self-Taught African-American Artist." *American Art* 5.4 (1991): 2–8.

Crite, Allan Rohan. *An Autobiographical Sketch*. Unpublished manuscript. Boston: Suffolk University archives, donated 1984.

Dallas Museum of Art. *Black Art Ancestral Legacy: The African Impulse in African-American Art*. New York: Harry N. Abrams, Inc., 1989.

Davis, Tonya Bolden. "Collecting Black Art." *Black Enterprise* (Dec. 1986): 85–86.

Davis, Tonya Bolden, and Devin D. Thompson. "Going Once…Going Twice…Sold." *Black Enterprise* (Dec. 1988): 73–76.

Donaldson, Jeff Richardson. "Generation '306' Harlem, New York." Dissertation. Northwestern University, 1975.

Douglas, Robert L. "Robert Colescott's Searing Stereotypes." *New Art Examiner* (June 1989): 34–37.

Driskell, David C., ed. *African American Visual Aesthetics: A Postmodern View*. Washington, D.C.: Smithsonian Institution Press, 1995.

Driskell, David C. *Contemporary Visual Expressions*. Washington, D.C.: Smithsonian Institution Press, 1987.

Driskell, David C. *Earl J. Hooks*. Nashville: The Art Gallery, Fisk University, 1966.

Driskell, David C. *Hidden Heritage: Afro-American Art 1800–1950*. San Francisco: The Art Museum Association of America, 1985.

Driskell, David C. "James Lesesne Wells 1902–1993." *Washington Review* 18.6 (1993): 22.

Driskell, David C. *Two Centuries of Black American Art*. New York: Alfred A. Knopf, 1976.

Driskell, David C., and Gladys E. Rodgers. *Claude Clark: On My Journey Now*. Atlanta: The Apex Museum, 1996.

Ebony, David. "Richmond Barthé and Richard Hunt at the Anacostia Museum." *Art in America* (July 1993): 109.

Elsner, John, and Roger Cardinal, eds. *The Cultures of Collecting*. Cambridge, Mass.: Harvard University Press, 1994.

Ferris, William, ed. *Afro-American Folk Art and Crafts*. Jackson: University Press of Mississippi, 1983.

Fifty Years of Paintings by Georgia Artist Claude Clark. Atlanta: Hammonds House Galleries and Resource Center for African American Art, 1990.

Fusscas, Helen K. "The Paintings of Charles Ethan Porter." *Charles Ethan Porter*. Marlborough, CT: The Connecticut Gallery, Inc., 1987.

Gaither, Edmund Barry. *Massachusetts Masters: African American Artists*. Boston: Museum of Fine Arts, 1988.

Gibson, Eric. "William H. Johnson" (review). *ARTnews* (Dec. 1995): 141.

Gilliam, Sam. *Small Drape Paintings 1970–1973*. Washington, D.C.: Middendorf Gallery, 1990.

Glueck, Grace. "Richmond Barthé, Sculptor, Dies." *The New York Times* (March 16, 1989).

Gonzalez, Michel. "Notre Lois Jones." *Pot Pourri* 7 no. 4 (27 July 1978): 6–7.

Greene, Carroll Jr., ed. *American Visions: Afro-American Art—1986*. Washington, D.C.: The Visions Foundation, 1987.

Harlem Renaissance Art of Black America. The Studio Museum in Harlem. New York: Harry N. Abrams, Inc., 1987.

Harley, Sharon. *The Timetables of African-American History*. New York: Simon & Schuster, 1995.

Hartigan, Lynda Roscoe. *Sharing Traditions: Five Black Artists in Nineteenth-Century America*. Washington, D.C.: National Museum of American Art, Smithsonian Institution Press, 1985.

Hedgepeth, Chester M., Jr., *Twentieth-Century African American Writers and Artists*. Chicago: American Library Association, 1991.

Heller, Jules, and Nancy G. Heller. *North American Women Artists of the Twentieth Century: A Biographical Dictionary*. New York: Garland Publishing, Inc., 1995.

Henkes, Robert. *The Art of Black American Women: Works of Twenty-Four Artists of the Twentieth Century*. North Carolina: McFarland & Company, Inc., 1993.

Henry, Gerrit. "A Metaphor for Human Being: New Paintings by Sam Gilliam." *Arts Magazine* 59.6 (Feb. 1985): 78–79.

Herzog, Melanie. "Elizabeth Catlett in Mexico: Identity and Cross-Cultural Intersections in the Production of Artistic Meaning." *The International Review of African American Art* 11.3 (1994): 19–25.

Hirsch, Faye. "L'École de Paris is Burning." *Arts Magazine* 66 (Sept. 1991): 52–57.

Holland, Juanita Marie. *Edward Mitchell Bannister 1828–1901*. New York: Kenkeleba House, 1992.

Howard University. *James A. Porter: Artist and Art Historian: The Memory of the Legacy*. Washington, D.C.: Howard University Gallery of Art, 1992.

Howard University. *Lois Mailou Jones and Her Former Students: An American Legacy*. Washington, D.C.: Department of Art, Howard University, 1995.

Hulick, Diana Emery. "James VanDerZee's Harlem Book of the Dead: A Study in Cultural Relationships." *History of Photography* 17.3 (1993): 277–283.

Igoe, Lynn Moody, and James Igoe. *250 Years of Afro-American Art: An Annotated Bibliography*. New York: R. R. Bowker Company, 1981.

Impressions/Expressions: Black American Graphics. New York: The Studio Museum in Harlem, 1980.

Intimations of Immortality. Washington, D.C.: The B'nai B'rith Klutznick National Jewish Museum, 1997.

Introspectives: Contemporary Art by Americans and Brazilians of African Descent. Los Angeles: California Afro-American Museum Foundation, 1989.

James, Curtis. "Richmond Barthé, Richard Hunt." *ARTnews* (March 1994): 146–147.

Johnson, Ken. "Colescott on Black and White." *Art in America* (June 1989): 148–153ff.

Jones, Loïs Mailou. *Peintures 1937–1951*. Tourcoing, France: Georges Frère, 1952.

Karp, Ivan, Christine Mullen Kreamer, and Steven D. Lavine, eds. *Museums and Communities: The Politics of Public Culture*. Washington, D.C.: Smithsonian Institution Press, 1992.

Kenkeleba Gallery. *Norman Lewis: From the Harlem Renaissance to Abstraction*. New York: Kenkeleba House, Inc., 1989.

Ketner, Joseph D. *The Emergence of the African American Artist: Robert S. Duncanson 1821–1872*. Columbia: University of Missouri Press, 1993.

Ketner, Joseph D. "Robert S. Duncanson (1821–1872): The Late Literary Landscape Paintings." *The American Art Journal* 15.1 (1983): 35–47.

King-Hammond, Leslie. *Black Printmakers and the W.P.A.* New York: Lehman College Art Gallery, 1989.

King-Hammond, Leslie. *Gumbo Ya Ya: Anthology of Contemporary African American Women Artists*. New York: Midmarch Arts Press, 1995.

Kirschke, Amy Helene. *Aaron Douglas: Art, Race, and the Harlem Renaissance*. Jackson: University Press of Mississippi, 1995.

Koota, Sharon D. "Cosmograms and Cryptic Writings: 'Africanisms.'" *The Clarion* 16.2 (1991): 48–52.

Kozloff, Max. "Time Stands Still: The Photographs of Roy DeCarava." *Artforum* 34.9 (1996): 78–83.

LeFalle-Collins, Lizzetta. "Grafton Tyler Brown: Selling the Promise of the West." *The International Review of African American Art* 12.1 (1995): 27–44.

LeFalle-Collins, Lizzetta, and Shifra M. Goldman. *In the Spirit of Resistance: African American Modernists and the Mexican Muralist School*. New York: The American Federation of Arts, 1996.

Lehman College Art Gallery. *Black Printmakers and the W.P.A.* New York: The City University of New York, 1989.

Lewis, David Levering. *When Harlem Was in Vogue*. New York: Oxford University Press, 1982.

Lewis, David Levering, ed. *The Portable Harlem Renaissance Reader*. New York: Viking Press, 1994.

Lewis, Samella. *African American Art and Artists*. Berkeley: University of California Press, 1990.

Lewis, Samella. *Art: African American*. Los Angeles: Hancraft Studios, 1990.

Lippard, Lucy R. "Crossing into Uncommon Grounds." *The Artist Outsider: Creativity and the Boundaries of Culture*. Ed. Michael D. Hall and Eugene W. Metcalf, Jr. Washington, D.C.: Smithsonian Institution Press, 1994.

Livingston, Jane, and John Beardsley. *Black Folk Art in America 1930–1980*. Jackson: University of Mississippi, 1982.

Locke, Alain, ed. *The New Negro*. Atheneum Edition ed. New York: Atheneum, 1925.

Main Gallery of Art. *"Resonance": Williams/Edwards/Gilliam*. Baltimore: Morgan State University, 1976.

Matthews, Lydia. "Kate Delos and Margo Humphrey, an *Artweek* Interview," *Artweek* 22 (Feb. 14, 1991): 16–17.

McElroy, Guy C., Richard Powell, and Sharon F. Patton. *African-American Artists 1889–1987: Selections from the Evans-Tibbs Collection*. Seattle: University of Washington Press, 1989.

McManus, Michael. "Recognition for the Invisible Man." *Artweek* 18.1 (1987): 1–3.

McWillie, Judith, John Mason, and Robert Farris Thompson. *Another Face of the Diamond: Pathways through the Black Atlantic South*. New York: INTAR Latin American Gallery, 1989.

Metcalf, Eugene W. "Black Art, Folk Art, and Social Control." *Winterthur Portfolio* 18.4 (1983): 271–289.

Mhire, Herman. *Baking in the Sun: Visionary Images from the South*. Lafayette: University Art Museum, 1987.

Miller, Henry. *The Amazing and Invariable Beauford Delaney*. New York: The Alicat Book Shop, 1945.

Minnie Evans: Artist. Greenville, N.C.: Wellington B. Gray Gallery, 1993.

Montclair Art Museum. *Fourteen Paintings: William T. Williams*. Monclair, N.J.: The Monclair Art Museum, 1991.

Morrison, Keith. *Art in Washington and Its Afro-American Presence: 1940–1970*. Washington, D.C.: Washington Project for the Arts, 1985.

Mosby, Dewey F. *Henry Ossawa Tanner*. New York: Rizzoli International Publications, Inc., 1991.

National Afro-American Museum and Cultural Center. *Uncommon Beauty in Common Objects: The Legacy of African American Craft Art*. Wilberforce, Ohio: National Afro-American Museum and Cultural Center, 1993.

No Justice, No Peace? Resolutions… Los Angeles: The California Afro-American Museum Foundation, 1993.

Pearce, Susan M. *On Collecting: An Investigation into Collecting in the European Tradition*. London/New York: Routledge, 1995.

Perry, Regenia A. "Contemporary African American Folk Art: An Overview." *The International Review of African American Art* 11.1 (1993): 5–29.

Perry, Regenia A. *Free within Ourselves: African American Artists in the Collection of the National Museum of American Art*. Washington, D.C.: National Museum of American Art in association with Pomegranate Artbooks, 1992.

Porter, James A. *Modern Negro Art*. Washington, D.C.: Howard University Press, 1992.

Powell, Richard J. *Black Art and Culture in the 20th Century*. London: Thames and Hudson, 1997.

Powell, Richard J. "Talking with James Lesesne Wells." *Print Review* 9 (1979): 65–75.

Powell, Richard J., and Jock Reynolds. *James Lesesne Wells: Sixty Years in Art*. Washington, D.C.: Washington Project for the Arts, 1986.

Raboteau, Albert J. "African Americans, Exodus, and the American Israel." *Religion and American Culture*. Ed. David G. Hackett. New York: Routledge, 1995.

Reflections of a Southern Heritage: 20th Century Black Artists of the Southeast. Charleston, S.C.: Carolina Art Association, 1979.

"Resonance" The Gallery of Art. Baltimore: Morgan State University, 1976.

A Retrospective Exhibition 1937–1971. Nashville: The Carl Van Vechten Gallery of Fine Arts, Fisk University, 1972.

Reynolds, Gary A., and Beryl J. Wright. *Against The Odds: African American Artists and the Harmon Foundation*. Newark: The Newark Museum, 1989.

Rhapsodies in Black: Art of the Harlem Renaissance. Berkeley: Hayward Gallery, Institute of International Visual Arts, University of California Press, 1997.

Riggs, Thomas, ed. *St. James Guide to Black Artists*. Detroit: Schomburg Center for Research in Black Culture, 1997.

"Rimbaud, (Jean Nicholas) Arthur." CD-ROM. Encarta 1994. Redmond, Wash.: Microsoft, 1994.

Roche, Paul. *The Bible's Greatest Stories*. New York: Mentor, 1990.

Romare Bearden: Paintings and Projections. Albany, New York: The Art Gallery, State University of New York, 1968.

Romare Bearden: The Prevalence of Ritual. New York: The Museum of Modern Art, 1971.

Sam Gilliam: Extensions Part One. Anderson Gallery. Richmond: Virginia Commonwealth University, 1978.

Since the Harlem Renaissance: 50 Years of Afro-American Art. Lewisburg, Pa.: The Center Gallery of Bucknell University, 1985.

Spelman College. *Bearing Witness*. New York: Spelman College and Rizzoli International Publications, Inc., 1996.

Stange, Maren. "Shadow and Substance." *Art in America* 84.3 (1996): 35–39.

Studio Museum in Harlem. *Harlem Renaissance: Art of Black America.* New York: Harry N. Abrams, Inc., 1987.

Terry Adkins. Richmond, Va.: Anderson Gallery at the Virginia Commonwealth University, 1991.

Tesfagiorgis, Freida High W. "Afrofemcentrism and its Fruition in the Art of Elizabeth Catlett and Faith Ringgold." *The Expanding Discourse: Feminism and Art History.* Ed. Norma Broude and Mary D. Garrard. New York: HarperCollins, 1992.

Thompson, Robert Farris. *Flash of the Spirit: African and Afro-American Art and Philosophy.* New York: Vintage Books, 1984.

Three Masters: Cortor, Lee-Smith, Motley. New York: Kenkelba House, Inc., 1988.

Traditions and Transformations: Contemporary Afro-American Sculpture. New York: The Bronx Museum of the Arts, 1989.

Trechsel, Gail Andrews, ed. *Pictured in My Mind: Contemporary American Self-Taught Art from the Collection of Dr. Kurt Gitter and Alice Rae Yelen.* Birmingham, Ala.: Birmingham Museum of Art, 1995.

Turner, Nannette. "Barthé: A Giant Returns Home." *Neworld* no. 7 (1978): 29–35.

Wallach, Amei. "The Contemporary Collector's Art." *The New York Times Magazine* (Oct. 26, 1997), 42–46.

Walter O. Evans Collection of African American Art. Savannah, Ga.: Beach Institute, 1991.

Wardlaw, Alvia J. *The Art of John Biggers: View from the Upper Room.* New York: Harry N. Abrams, Inc. in association with The Museum of Fine Arts, Houston, 1995.

Wayne, Cynthia. *Dreams, Lies and Exaggerations: Photomontage in America.* College Park: The Art Gallery, University of Maryland at College Park, 1991.

Wheat, Ellen Harkins. *Jacob Lawrence: American Painter.* Seattle: University of Washington Press, 1986.

Williams, Reba, and Dave Williams, eds. *Alone in a Crowd: Prints of the 1930's–40's by African American Artists.* Reba and Dave Williams, 1993.

Willis-Braithwaite, Deborah. *VanDerZee, Photographer 1886–1983.* New York: Harry N. Abrams, Inc., 1993.

Willis-Thomas, Deborah. *An Illustrated Bio-Bibliography of Black Photographers 1940–1988.* New York: Garland Publishing, 1989.

Wilson, James L. *Clementine Hunter: American Folk Artist.* Gretna, La: Pelican Publishing Company, 1990.

Wolf, Conradin, and Jacqueline Battle. *Terry Adkins: Arbeit/Work, 1986–1987.* Zurich: Galerie Emmerich-Baumann, 1987.

Yelen, Alice Rae. *Passionate Visions of the American South.* New Orleans: New Orleans Museum of Art, 1993.

Yolles, Sandra. "Gilda Snowden." *ARTnews* 87 (Dec. 1988): 169.

I. Strategic Subversions: Cultural Emancipation, Assimilation, and African American Identity

1. Bannister, Edward Mitchell
Untitled (Landscape with Cows), n.d.
Watercolor on paper
6.75 x 10
Acquired 1988

2. Bannister, Edward Mitchell
Untitled (Landscape with Pond),
c. 1876
Oil on canvas
7.75 x 11.75
Acquired 1983

3. Brown, Grafton Tyler
Mt. Hood from John Day's Station,
1884–1885
Oil on canvas
15.5 x 25.5
Acquired 1998

4. Duncanson, Robert Scott (attribution)
Scottish Landscape, c. 1870
Oil on canvas
15 x 21
Acquired 1979

5. Fuller, Meta Warrick
Pietà, c. 1930
Bronze, wood stand
6 x 5 x 5
Acquired 1983

6. Herring, James V.
Newport Scene, n.d.
Watercolor on paper
7 x 5
Acquired 1980

7. Porter, Charles Ethan (attribution)
Untitled (Still Life: Mums in a Bowl),
n.d.
Oil on canvas
11.75 x 19.5
Acquired 1987

8. Tanner, Henry O.
Gate at Tangier, 1910
Etching on paper
9.5 x 7
Acquired 1996

9. VanDerZee, James
VanDerZee Boys, c. 1900
Black-and-white photograph
7 x 9.5
Acquired 1993

10. VanDerZee, James
*Portrait of First Wife and Daughter
(In the Woods),* n.d.
(also known as *Kate and Rachel*)
Black-and-white photograph
10 x 8
Acquired 1993

II. Emergence: The New Negro Movement and Definitions of Race

11. Barthé, Richmond
Untitled (Head of a Man), c. 1935
Terra cotta
4 x 1 x 1
Acquired 1978

12. Barthé, Richmond
Head of Dancer (Harold Kreutzberg),
1930s
Bronze and concrete
12 x 7.5 x 6.5
Acquired 1985

13. Douglas, Aaron
*Aspects of Negro Life: An Idyll of the
Deep South* (study), late 1930s
Tempera on paper
9.75 x 42
Acquired 1977

14. Douglas, Aaron
Go Down Death, 1934
Oil on Masonite
48 x 36
Acquired 1977

15. Johnson, William H.
Seated Woman, c. 1939
Hand-colored linocut on paper
18 x 12
Acquired 1976

16. Johnson, William H.
I Baptize Thee (study), n.d.
Watercolor on paper
8 x 8
Acquired 1976

17. Jones, Loïs Mailou
Ethiopian Boy, 1948
Tempera on paper
7.75 x 5.75
Acquired 1960

18. Jones, Loïs Mailou
Notre-Dame de Paris, 1936
Oil on canvas
14.25 x 17.25
Acquired 1977

19. Lawrence, Jacob
General Toussaint, 1986
From the *Toussaint L'Ouverture Series*
Silk-screen on paper
29.5 x 18.5
Acquired 1989

20. Polk, P. H.
Portrait of Aaron Douglas, c. 1933
Black-and-white photograph
10 x 8
Acquired 1992

21. Savage, Augusta
Gamin, 1929
Bronze
9 x 5.5 x 3.5
Acquired 1992

22. VanDerZee, James
Roberts and Johnson, 1932
(also known as *Looking Backward*)
Black-and-white photograph
10 x 8
Acquired 1993

23. VanDerZee, James
Barefoot Prophet, 1929
Black-and-white photograph
10 x 8
Acquired 1993

24. VanDerZee, James
Undeclared War, 1929
(also known as *Just Before the Battle*)
Black-and-white photograph
10 x 8
Acquired 1993

25. VanDerZee, James
Couple in Raccoon Coats, 1932
Black-and-white photograph
8 x 10
Acquired 1993

26. Wells, James Lesesne
Escape of the Spies from Canaan, 1932
Woodblock engraving
9 x 12
Acquired 1976

27. Wells, James Lesesne
Sisters, 1929
Linocut on paper
8.5 x 6.75
Acquired 1976

28. Woodruff, Hale
Trusty on a Mule, 1939
Woodblock print on paper
8 x 10
Acquired 1990

III. The Black Academy: Teachers, Mentors, and Institutional Patronage

29. Bearden, Romare
Morning, 1975
Collage on paper
13.5 x 17.75
Acquired 1980

30. Bearden, Romare
Woman and Child Reading, 1977
Lithograph
25.5 x 18.5
Acquired 1984

31. Bearden, Romare
Untitled (Verso), 1977
Lithograph
25.5 x 18
Acquired 1984

32. Catlett, Elizabeth
Harriet, 1975
Linocut on paper
12.25 x 10
Acquired 1983

33. Crite, Allan Rohan
Last Station: Suggestion for the Station of the Cross, 1935
Ink on paper
18 x 15
Acquired 1976

34. DeCarava, Roy
Portrait of Paul Robeson, 1950
Black-and-white photograph
11 x 8
Acquired 1995

35. Douglas, Aaron
The Junk Man, n.d.
Etching on paper
9 x 7.25
Acquired 1975

36. Driskell, David C.
Boy with Birds, 1953
Oil on canvas
23.5 x 29.5

37. Herring, James V.
Campus Landscape, 1922
Oil on canvas
9.5 x 7.5
Acquired 1961

38. Jennings, Wilmer
Still Life, 1939
(also known as *Still Life with Fetish*)
Wood engraving on paper
10 x 8
Acquired 1976

39. Johnson, William H.
Children Playing London Bridge, c. 1942
Watercolor on paper
12 x 10.5
Acquired 1976

40. Pogue, Stephanie
Aaron's Meadow, 1977
Color viscosity etching on paper
15 x 21
Acquired 1978

41. Porter, James A.
Playground, n.d.
Oil on canvas
10 x 8
Acquired 1989

42. Savage, Augusta
Boy on a Stump, 1930s
Bronze
30 x 13 x 13
Acquired 1994

43. Sebree, Charles
Untitled (Head), 1952
Pastel and gouache
13.5 x 9.75
Acquired 1977

44. Taylor, Bill
Torso, c. 1965
Stone, wood stand
15 x 5.5 x 3
Acquired 1965

45. Waring, Laura Wheeler
Rose of Sharon, n.d.
Oil on canvas
19.25 x 15.25
Acquired 1977

46. Wells, James Lesesne
Primitive Girl, 1929
Linocut on paper
7.5 x 7
Acquired 1976

47. White, Charles
Awaiting His Return, 1945
Lithograph
16.25 x 12.75
Acquired 1979

48. Wilson, Ellis
Untitled (Fish in Net), n. d.
Oil on Masonite
9 x 12
Acquired 1978

49. Woodruff, Hale
Two Figures in a Mexican Landscape, c. 1934
Oil on canvas
22 x 18
Acquired 1992

IV. Radical Politics, Protest, and Art

50. Bearden, Romare
Urban Street Scene, early 1970s
Collage on paper
11.75 x 9.75
Acquired 1988

51. Biggers, John
Quilting Party, 1981
From the *Shotgun Series*
Lithograph
22.25 x 15
Acquired 1983

52. Catlett, Elizabeth
Sharecropper, 1968
Linocut on paper
17.5 x 16.5
Acquired 1973

53. Catlett, Elizabeth
The Black Woman Speaks, 1970
Polychromed wood
15.75 x 7.5 x 15.25
Acquired 1973

54. Clark, Claude
Slave Lynching, 1946
Oil on canvas
13.25 x 16.5
Acquired 1980

55. Cortor, Eldzier
Cuban Souvenir, n.d.
Oil on canvas
8 x 10
Acquired 1989

56. Driskell, David C.
Behold Thy Son, 1956
Oil on canvas
40 x 30

57. Edwards, Melvin
Sippi Eye, c. 1988
From the *Lynch Fragment Series*
Welded and forged steel
13 x 11 x 8
Acquired 1998

58. Hooks, Earl
Maternal Family, 1974
Ceramic
16 x 10 x 6
Acquired 1974

59. Lawrence, Jacob
We Declare Ourselves Independent, 1955
From the *Struggle Series*
Egg tempera on cardboard
16 x 12
Acquired 1979

60. Lawrence, Jacob
The Travelers, 1961
Egg tempera on Masonite
11.5 x 8.5
Acquired 1980

61. Lawrence, Jacob
Carpenters, 1977
Silk-screen print
18 x 22
Acquired 1978

62. Meadows, Jerome
Bound Between, 1994
Mixed media
10 x 19.5
Acquired 1995

63. Phillips, James
The Dealer, 1966
From the *Junkie in the
Twilight Zone Series*
Oil on canvas
20 x 16
Acquired 1975

64. White, Charles
Wanted Poster Series, 1970
Lithograph
21.5 x 29.25
Acquired 1993

65. White, Charles
The Prophet, 1975–1976
Lithograph
27 x 36.5
Acquired 1976

V. Diaspora Identities/Global Arts

66. Adkins, Terry
Budo, 1993
Wood
33.5 (h)
Acquired 1995

67. Adkins, Terry
Untitled #1, 1986
Collage on paper
19 x 24
Acquired 1987

68. Puryear, Martin
Gbows Gård, 1967
Aquatint, engraving, and etching
13 x 19.25
Acquired 1998

69. Catlett, Elizabeth
Seated Mother and Child, 1982
Bronze
15.5 x 7 x 7
Acquired 1984

70. Colescott, Robert
I Love You Forever, 1993
Woodblock engraving
22 x 14
Acquired 1998

71. Cortor, Eldzier
Jewels/Theme V, c. 1980
Etching on paper
23 x 16.75
Acquired 1989

72. Delaney, Beauford
Untitled, c. 1965
Oil on canvas
25.5 x 21.25
Acquired 1988

73. Douglas, Aaron
City Scape, 1956
Watercolor on paper
14.5 x 19.5
Acquired 1977

74. Evans, Minnie
Face of a Man, n.d.
Crayon and watercolor on paper
12 x 9
Acquired 1993

75. Harris, Michael D.
Mothers and the Presence of Myth, 1997
Lithograph
30 x 21.5
Acquired 1997

76. Humphrey, Margo
The Last Bar-B-Que, 1989
Lithograph
26 x 38.5
Acquired 1994

77. Hunter, Clementine
Baptism, c. 1964
Oil on canvas
15.5 x 19.5
Acquired 1994

78. Gilliam, Sam
From *The D Series,* 1982
Mixed media on canvas
32 x 42
Acquired 1983

79. Lawrence, Jacob
Lawyer and Clients, 1994
Silk-screen print
30 x 22
Acquired 1997

80. Lewis, Norman
Good Morning, 1960
Oil on canvas
42 x 50
Acquired 1995

81. Lewis, Norman
The Red Umbrella, n.d.
Etching on paper
11.75 x 15.75
Acquired 1995

82. Mayhew, Richard
Landscape, n.d.
Watercolor on paper
11 x 14
Acquired 1996

83. McNeil, William
Elegy, 1993
Black-and-white photograph
9 x 6
Acquired 1994

84. Middleton, Sam
Untitled, 1972
Watercolor on paper
9 x 10
Acquired 1972

85. Morrison, Keith
Nightrane, 1981
Watercolor on paper
30 x 22
Acquired 1985

86. Morrison, Keith
Night Food, 1992
Oil on canvas
26.5 x 32
Acquired 1997

87. O'Neal, Mary Lovelace
Racism is Like Rain, Either It's Raining
  or It's Gathering Somewhere, 1993
Lithograph
13.25 x 22
Acquired 1994

88. Pogue, Stephanie
India Pattern–Pattern of India, 1986
From *The Fan Series*
Mixed media on paper
15 x 22.5
Acquired 1989

89. Saunders, Ray
Untitled, n .d.
Pencil on paper
6 x 9
Acquired 1976

90. Smith, Frank
Improvisation from a Patch Quilt, 1986
Mixed media on canvas
36 x 21.5
Acquired 1997

91. Smith, Vincent
Arthur Rimbaud's House in Harar, 1975
Etching on paper
14.75 x 22.25
Acquired 1976

92. Snowden, Gilda
Tornado, 1991
Mixed media on paper
14 x 11
Acquired 1996

93. Stewart, Frank
Wynton Marsalis, 1991
From the *Sweet Swing Series*
Black-and-white photograph
15 x 15
Acquired 1993

94. Stovall, Lou
Breathing Hope, 1996
Silk-screen on paper
14.5 x 14.5
Acquired 1996

95. Thomas, Alma
Falling Leaves Love Wind Orchestra,
  n .d.
Acrylic on canvas
21.5 x 27.5
Acquired 1977

96. Thomas, Alma
Blue Abstraction, 1965
Oil on canvas
39.75 x 31.5
Acquired 1977

97. Tucker, Yvonne Edwards
The Potter's House, 1995
Mixed media on paper
11 x 14
Acquired 1996

98. Williams, Walter
Butterflies #2, 1977
Color woodcut on paper
20.25 x 25
Acquired 1978

99. Williams, William T.
Untitled, c. 1973
Mixed media on paper
35 x 23
Acquired 1974

100. Williams, William T.
Blue Walk, c. 1991
Color lithograph
41 x 29
Acquired 1992

Photography Credits

All photographs of objects from the collection were taken by Greg Staley with the exception of object entries #42, #66, and #80, which were taken by Frank Stewart, and object entry #68, which is printed courtesy of The Art Institute of Chicago.

All credits for photographs other than those accompanying objects in the collection are noted in their accompanying captions.

M. Colleen Chapman, project coordinator for the Driskell exhibition, is a graduate student in the Department of English at the University of Maryland, focusing on African American Literature. She has created and taught museum courses in African American art and culture for elementary and middle school students. As a feature writer for Gannet Newspapers, Chapman wrote extensively on the urban world as seen through the eyes of inner-city children. She received her B.A. in religion and classics from the University of Rochester and is currently completing a master's thesis on the representation of African American and Caribbean writers in the *Oxford English Dictionary*.

Adrienne L. Childs, assistant curator for the Driskell project, is a graduate student in the Department of Art History and Archaeology at the University of Maryland. Childs earned an M.B.A. from Howard University and a B.A. in art history from Georgetown University. She has held positions at the African American Museums Association, the Charles Sumner School Museum and Archives, and the DuSable Museum of African American History. As curator for the Sumner Museum and Archives, Childs organized an exhibition of Driskell's work in 1988.

Tuliza Fleming, assistant curator for the Driskell project, is a Ph.D. student in the Department of Art History and Archaeology at the University of Maryland. She received her M.A. in art history from Maryland and a B.A. in art history and art studio from Spelman College. Fleming has served in numerous professional research and curatorial positions, including that of guest curator for *Breaking Racial Barriers: African Americans in the Harmon Foundation Collection* at the National Portrait Gallery in Washington, D.C. Her most recent publication is *Breaking Racial Barriers: African Americans in the Harmon Foundation Collection*, a Smithsonian exhibition catalogue.

Terry Gips is director of The Art Gallery and associate professor of art at the University of Maryland. In addition to "The David C. Driskell Collection" exhibition, Gips has overseen the production of several major exhibitions and catalogues at The Art Gallery, including *Sources: Multicultural Influences on African American Sculptors; Significant Losses: Artists Who Have Died From AIDS;* and *Terra Firma*, an exhibition of contemporary women's art on the body. Gips also writes on women in the arts and the relationship of technology to art.

Allan M. Gordon, retired professor emeritus in Art History at the California State University in Sacramento, has previously published on Driskell's work. A well-known scholar and critic in the field of African American aesthetics, Gordon has authored numerous essays on black aesthetics and culture, African American women artists, and links between black art and music. He has served as contributing editor for *Artweek* since 1991.

Juanita M. Holland, curator for the exhibition and assistant professor in the Department of Art History and Archaeology at the University of Maryland at College Park, is a specialist in the arts of the African Diaspora. She pursued her Ph.D. in African American art history from Columbia University. Holland was guest editor and contributor for the *International Review of African American Art* for three issues, focusing on nineteenth-century African American art. She helped organize the largest Edward Mitchell Bannister retrospective since 1901 and was principal author for the accompanying catalogue, *Edward Mitchell Bannister 1828–1901*. Holland writes, lectures, and teaches about how the arts of people of African descent engage and reflect issues of assimilation and the construction of ethnic and artistic identity in North and South American and Caribbean cultures.

Keith Morrison is the dean of the College of Creative Arts, San Francisco State University. An artist, writer, curator, and educator, he has exhibited internationally, including at the Art Institute of Chicago; the Museum of Modern Art, Monterrey, Mexico; the National Museum of American Art; the Corcoran Gallery of Art; The National Collection of Fine Arts; the Pennsylvania Academy of the Fine Arts; and the Caribbean Biennale. He has published numerous articles and catalogues and has taught or lectured in many universities, art schools, and cultural institutions around the world.

Sharon F. Patton, an art historian and curator, is director of the Center for Afro-American and African Studies at the University of Michigan, where she is an associate professor in the Department of the History of Art. Patton received her Ph.D. in art history from Northwestern University. She has served in various curatorial positions, including that of chief curator for *Traditional Forms and Modern Africa: West African Art at the University of Maryland* (1983). She formerly held the position of chief curator of the Studio Museum in Harlem, where she coordinated numerous major exhibitions, including *The Decade Show: Frameworks of Identity in the 1980s* and *Memory and Metaphor: The Art of Romare Bearden*. She has contributed work to various journals and compilations, including *African American Artists 1880–1987*.

Richard J. Powell, chair of the Department of Art and Art History at Duke University, has written extensively on African American art. His most recent publication, *Black Art and Culture in the Twentieth Century*, was released earlier this year. Powell has authored numerous essays in journals and edited collections and exhibition catalogues. His major publications include *The Blues Aesthetic: Black Culture and Modernism* (1989) and *Homecoming: The Art and Life of William H. Johnson* (1991). He is also a noted curator, having coordinated exhibitions for the Smithsonian Institution, the Studio Museum in Harlem, and the Washington Project for the Arts. He received his Ph.D. in art history from Yale University.

Index

Page numbers in boldface indicate color plates; page numbers in italics indicate black-and-white photographs.

A History of African-American Artists from 1792 to the Present 66, 79, 97, 113, 148, 165, 177nn. 12, 19, 23–25; 179
A New Negro for a New Century 27, 177n.6
Aaron's Meadow (Pogue) 37, 106, **106,** 173, 184
Adkins, Terry 20, 42, 134, **134,** 185
African American Art and Artists 66, 181
African American Artists 1880–1987, Selections from the Evans-Tibbs Collection 52
African American Visual Aesthetics 10
Alfred Stieglitz Collection 18–19
Allen, Billie 49
Alone in a Crowd: Prints of the 1930s–1940s by African-American Artists 48
Alston, Charles 30, 33, 34, 35, 38, 48, 49
Alston, Peg 52
An Exhibition by Young Negro Artists (exhibition) 32
Anacostia Museum, Washington, D.C. 14
Andrews, Benny 50, 178col.1, n.8
Angel with Trumpet (Driskell) 60
Archibald Motley 43, 47, 48
Art Gallery, The (University of Maryland) 4, 8, 9, 12, 13, 187
Artists and Models Exhibition (exhibition) 33
Arthur Rimbaud's House in Harar (Smith) 43, 158, **158,** 186
Artis, William 33
Ascent of Ethiopia, The (Jones) 84
Aspects of Negro Life: An Idyll of the Deep South (study) (Douglas) 29–30, 80, **80,** 101, 106, 183
Atlanta University 35, 36, 49, 55, 94
Awaiting His Return (White) 35, 39, 113, **113,** 184

Ball, James P. 46
Baltimore Museum of Art 11, 86
Bannard, Henry W. 35
Bannister, Edward Mitchell 21, 26, 46, 51, 68, **68,** 69, **69,** 169, 183, 187
Baptism (Hunter) 43, 144, **144,** 185
Barefoot Prophet (VanDerZee) 30, 90, *91,* 183
Barjon, Dutreuil 53
Barnes, Albert 17, 20
Barnett-Aden Gallery, Washington, D.C. 17, *17, 34, 37,* 49, *52,* 57, 103
Barr, Alfred H., Jr. 49
Barthé, Richmond 29, 37, 49, 78, **78,** 79, **79,** 169, 177n.18, 183
Baudrillard, Jean 54, 178col.1, n.15
Beard, Derrick 53
Bearden, Romare 4, 17, 19, 21, 31–32, 35, *38,* 38, 40, 48, 49, 55, 56, 66, 94, 96, **96,** 97, **97,** 117, **117,** 169, 177nn.12, 19, 23–25, 26; 179, 181
Behold Thy Son (Driskell) 123, **123,** 185
Belafonte, Harry 49
Benjamin, Tritobia 20, 84, 179
Biggers, John 35, 39, 118, **118,** 169, 184

Birmingham Museum of Art 11
Black Artists on Art 55
Black Enterprise 51
Black Folk Art in America 52
Black Madonna (Barthé) 78
Black Madonna (Williams) 21
Black Woman Speaks, The (Catlett) **22,** 40, 119, **120,** 185
Blackburn, Robert 35
Blue Abstraction (Thomas) 162, **163,** 186
Blue Walk (Williams) 167, **167,** 186
Bocour, Leonard 18
Bomani, Asake 52
Bontemps, Arna Alexander *55*
Bontemps, Jacqueline 20, 155
Boss, The (Polk) 31
Bound Between (Meadows) 129, **129,** 185
Boxer (Barthé) 78
Boy on a Stump (Savage) 33, 108, **108,** 184
Boy with Birds (Driskell) 36, 102, **102,** 184
Bradley, Tom *41*
Brady, Mary Beattie 12, 19, 20, 48, *48*
Braxton, William E. 32
Breaking Racial Barriers: African Americans in the Harmon Foundation Collection 187
Breathing Hope (Stovall) 161, **161,** 186
Brown, Evelyn S. 18
Brown, Grafton Tyler 26, 70, **70,** 169, 183
Brown, Richard Lonsdale 32
Budo (Adkins) 42, 134, **134,** 185
Builders (Lawrence) 128
Burke, Selma 35, 177n.18
Burrell, Thomas J. 51
Burroughs, Margaret 20, 50, 109
Burwell, Ann *37*
Butterflies # 2 (Williams) 42, 165, **165,** 186

Campbell, Mary Schmidt 20, 45, 179
Campus Landscape (Herring) 36, 103, **103,** 184
Canada Lee 35
Carl Van Vechten Collection 18
Carmichael, Stokely 20
Carpenters (Lawrence) 128, **128,** 185
Catholic University of America 10
Catlett, Elizabeth 13, 19, 21, **22,** 35, *40, 55,* 98, **98,** 119, **119, 120,** 136, **136,** 161, 169, 184, 185
Center for African American Decorative Arts 53
Cheyney State Teacher's College 35
Chieftain's Chair (Driskell) **59,** 60
Children Playing London Bridge (Johnson) 105, **105,** 184
Cinque Gallery 50
City Quartet (Driskell) 102
City Scape (Douglas) 42, 101, 140, **140,** 185

Clark, Claude 10, 19, 39, *39,* 121, **121,** 170, 185

Clark, Kenneth 61

Colby College Museum of Art, Maine 4, 9, 14

Colescott, Robert 43, 137, **137,** 170, 185

Collecting African American Art: A Detroit Tradition (exhibition) 52

Collins, Samuel O, 32

Color Field school 145, 162

Confrontation at the Bridge (Lawrence) 21

Conover, James Francis 46

Contemporary African Art (exhibit) 18

Corcoran Gallery of Art 11, 52

Cortor, Eldzier 39, 43, 49, 109, 122, **122,** 138, **138,** 170, 185

Cosby, Camille and William 10, 51

Couple in Raccoon Coats (VanDerZee) 29, 90, *91,* 184

Crichlow, Ernest 33, 35, 177n.18

Crisis, The (periodical) 33, 47, 92

Crite, Allan Rohan 38, 99, **99,** 170, 179, 184

Crosby, Caresse 49

Cuban Souvenir (Cortor) 39, 122, **122,** 185

Cullen, Countee 35

D Series, The (Gilliam) 21, 42, 145, **145,** 185

Dancing Angel (Driskell) 60, **60**

Dave the Potter 56

David C. Driskell Collection 8, 13, 20, 24, 26, 31, 66

De Villis, Clinton J., 32

Dealer, The (Phillips) 40, 130, **130,** 185

Decade Show: Frameworks of Identity in the 1980s, The (exhibition) 52, 187

DeCarava, Roy 40, 100, *100,* 170, 184

DeGrasse, John V. 46

Delaney, Beauford 31, 42, 139, **139,** 170, 177n.18, 185

Delaney, Joseph 31

Dodd, Lois 18

Douglas, Aaron **frontispiece,** 4, 12, *16,* 19, 29, 30, 32, 33, 35, 36, 37, 42, 47, 48, *55,* 80, **80,** 81, **81,** 88, *88,* 101, **101,** 106, 140, **140,** 170, 183, 185

Douglass, Frederick 26, 177n.2

Douglass, Robert, Jr., 46

Downtown Gallery 48

Driskell, David C. 14, 24, 51, 55, 66, 79, 80, 85, 86, 89, 97, 102, **102,** 103, 106, 107, 112, 121,123, **123,** 150, 156, 161, 165, 166, 177n.1, 178col.2, nn.1, 2, 4; 179, 184, 185

    antecedents 10

    artist 9, 10, 59–61

    associations 12

    awards 10

    collector 16, 20–21, 57

    cultural values 20–21, 59

    curator 7, 12, 18–21, 56

    education 17–18

    educator 16, 20

    exhibitions 8–9, 11

    and the Harmon Foundation 56–57

    home life 11, 13

    lecturer 57

    mentor/mentee 12, 20, 36–37, 57

    publications 10

    travel 57

   photographs

      1953, as a young artist *63*

      1964, with Loïs Mailou Jones and others at Howard University *58*

      1968, letter from artist Georgia O'Keeffe *19*

      1973, with Aaron Douglas and others at Fisk University *55*

      1974, with Keith Morrison and others at Fisk University *16*

      1975, with Romare Bearden at Fisk University *38*

      1975, with Claude Clark at Fisk University *39*

      1976, with Mayor Tom Bradley and Charles White at Los Angeles County Museum of Art *41*

      1977, with Mary Beattie Brady at her residence *48*

      1995, portrait *8*

      1997, with Tritobia Hayes Benjamin and others at Smithsonian Institution *57*

      1998 with Elizabeth Catlett at June Kelly Gallery *40*

      1998, with Thelma Driskell at their Hyattsville, Md. residence *11*

   works

    Angel with Trumpet 60

    Behold Thy Son 123, **123,** 185

    Boy with Birds 36, 102, **102,** 184

    Chieftain's Chair **59,** 60

    City Quartet 102

    Dancing Angel 60, **60**

    Earth Angels 60

    Flowing Like a River **62**

    Guardian Angels 60

    Nocturne 61

    Pines at Falmouth **61**

    Self Portrait **18**

Driskell, Thelma G. DeLoatch 11, *11,* 13, *52*

Du Bois, W. E. B. 28, 29, 40, 47, 88

Du Sable Museum, Chicago 50

Dunbar, Paul Lawrence 32

Duncanson, Robert Scott 26, 46, 51, 71, **71,** 170, 183

Earth Angels (Driskell) 60

Echoes: The Art of David C. Driskell 1955–1997 (exhibition) 9

Edmundson, William 53

Edwards, Melvin 124, **124,** 171, 185

Elegy (McNeil) 42, 150, *150,* 186

Ellington, Duke 49

Ellison, Ralph 35, 49, 56

Escape of the Spies from Canaan (Wells) 30, 31, 92, **92,** 184

Ethiopia Awakening (Fuller) 28

Ethiopian Boy (Jones) 29, 84, **84,** 183

Evans, Minnie 43, 141, **141,** 171, 185

Evans, Walter O. 20, 53, 178col.1, n.14

Evans-Tibbs, Thurlow 52

Evanti, Lillian 52, *52*

Face of a Man (Evans) 43, 141, **141,** 185

Falling Leaves Love Wind Orchestra (Thomas) 21, 42, 162, **162,** 186

Fan Series (Pogue) 155, **155,** 186

Farrow, William McKnight 37, 177n.18

Father Vincent ("the Painting Priest") 19

Fauset, Jessie 28

Federal Arts Project (FAP) (1935–1943) 31, 34, 35, 48, 49, 80, 104, 108, 114

Fighting Cock (Williams) 165
Fine Arts Museums of San Francisco 4, 9, 14
Fish, Janet 18
Fisk University 7, 10, 16, 18, 19, 20, 36, *38, 39,* 49, *55,* 125
Flowing Like a River (Driskell) **62**
Franklin, John Hope *57*
Freeman, Roland L. 52
Fuller, Meta Warrick 27–28, 30, 32, 33, 72, **72,** 171, 177n.18, 183

G Place Gallery 49
Gaither, Edmund Barry 50, 178col.1, n.6; 180
Gamin (Savage) 21, 31, 89, **89,** 183
Garvey, Marcus 28
Gate at Tangier (Tanner) 27, 75, **75,** 183
Gbows Gård (Puryear) 135, **135,** 185
General Toussaint (Lawrence) 30, 86, **87,** 183
Giampietro, Alexander 110
Gilliam, Sam 21, 42, 54, 145. **145,** 161, 171, 180, 185
Go Down Death (Douglas) **frontispiece** 4, 30, 81, **81,** 183
God's Trombones Series (Douglas) 81
Good Morning (Lewis) 42, 147, **147,** 185
Greene, Carroll 51, 180
Greenough, Horatio 26, 177n.4
Guardian Angels (Driskell) 60

Halpert, Edith 48
Hammons, David 52
Hampton University 35, 49, 98
Harlem Community Art Center 35, 108
Harlem Renaissance 17, 25, 28, 29, 32, 33, 34, 40, 56, 72, 80, 88,
    90, 92, 100, 104, 106
Harleston, Edwin 33
Harmon, William E. 17, 19, 48, 56
Harmon and Harriet Kelley Collection of African American Art, The 52
Harriet (Catlett) 35, 98, **98,** 184
Harris, Michael D. 142, **142,** 164, 171, 177n.1, 185
Hartzell, Joseph Crane 47
Harvey, William (Bill) 20
Hayden, Palmer 19, 34
Head of Dancer (Barthé) 79, **79,** 183
Henderson, Harry 66, 79, 113, 148, 165, 177nn. 12, 19, 23–25,
    26
Herring, James V. 17, 18, 36, *36,* 49, 73, **73,** 98, 103, **103,** 171
Hidden Heritage: Afro-American Art, 1800–1950 (exhibition) 51
High Museum of Art, Atlanta 4, 9, 14, 35
Hines, Watson 51
Hirshhorn, Joseph 49
Hirshhorn Museum and Sculpture Garden, Washington, D.C., 49
Historically Black Colleges and Universities 32, 35–37, 48–49
Holland, Juanita M. 13, 20, 23, 47, 66, 89, 177n.15, 178col.1, n.3;
    180, 187
Hooks, Earl J. *16, 19, 55,* 125, **125,** 171, 185
Howard University, 7, 10, 16–17, 18, *33, 36,* 47, 49, 56, 57, *58,*
    73, 84, 98, 102, 112, 161, 180, 181, 187
Hughes, Langston 32, 35, 178col.2, nn.5–6
Humphrey, Margo 42, 143, **143,** 171, 185
Hunt, Richard 19
Hunter, Clementine 43, 144, **144,** 172, 185
Hunter, Sam 20
Hurston, Zora Neale 32

I Baptize Thee (study) (Johnson) 21, 30, 83, **83,** 183
identity, artistic/cultural 9, 12, 15, 24, 25, 26–31, 34, 37, 38, 39,
    40, 41–42, 43–44,
45, 47, 52, 53–54, 94, 104, 112, 147, 162
I Love You Forever (Colescott) 43, 137, **137,** 185
Improvisation from a Patch Quilt (Smith) 157, **157,** 186
India Pattern–Pattern of India (Pogue) 42, 155, **155,** 186
Indiana, Robert 18
Invisible Man 56
Invisible Man Among the Scholars (Lawrence) 127

Jackson, May Howard 32
Jennings, Wilmer 35, 104, **104,** 172, 184
Jewels / Theme V (Cortor) 43, 138, **138,** 185
Johnson, Charles 28
Johnson, James Weldon 30, 34, 81
Johnson, Robert 49
Johnson, William H. 19, 21, 29, 48, 57, 82, **82,** 83, **83,** 105, **105,**
    172, 187
Johnston, Joshua 51
Jones, Loïs Mailou 13, 17, 19, 29, 31, 33, *33,* 36, 55, 56, *58,* 84,
    84, 85, **85,** 98, 102, 161, 172, 177n.18, 180, 183
Jones, Steven 47, 178col.1, n.3
June Kelly Gallery, New York 50
Junk Man, The (Douglas) 36, 101, **101,** 184
Junkie in the Twilight Zone Series (Phillips) 40, 130, **130,** 185
Just Before the Battle (aka *Undeclared War)* (VanDerZee) 31, 90, *91,*
    183

Karamu House 49
Karp, Ivan 45, 178col.1, nn.1, 5
Kate and Rachel (aka *Portrait of First Wife and Daughter [In the
    Woods]*) (VanDerZee) 76, *76,* 183
Kedebe, Alitash 52
Kelley, Harmon and Harriet 52
Kenkeleba Gallery 50, 180
King, Martin Luther, Jr. 41
King-Hammond, Leslie 20
Knight, Gwendolyn 34 , 35, 177n.18

Lam, Wilfredo 17
Landreau, Eleanor 19
Landscape (Mayhew) 42, 149, **149,** 186
Last Bar-B-Que, The (Humphrey) 42, 143, **143,** 185
Last Station: Suggestion for the Station of the Cross (Crite) 38, 99,
    99, 184
Lawrence, Jacob 12, 18, 19, 30, 34, 35, 40, 44, 48, 49, 56, 86, **87,**
    126, **126,** 127, **127,** 128, **128,** 146, **146,** 161, 172, 183, 185
Lawyer and Clients (Lawrence) 146, **146,** 185
Lee, Canada 35
Lee-Smith, Hughie 54, 132
Les Fétiches (Jones) 84
Levine, Jack 17, 102, 123
Lewis, Edmonia M. 46, 51, 56
Lewis, Elma 50
Lewis, Norman 34, 147, **147,** 148, **148,** 172, 177n.18
Lewis, Reginald F. 51
Lewis, Samella 20, 55, 181
Lightfoot, Elba 35
Locke, Alain 17, 28, 29, 37, 47, 48, 63, 84, 88, 108, 178col.2, n.7;
    181

Loïs Mailou Jones: Peintures 1937–1951 85, 180
Looking Backward (aka *Roberts and Johnson*) (VanDerZee) 30, 90, *91,* 183
Los Angeles County Museum of Art 10, *41*
Loving, Alvin 54
Lynch Fragment Series (Edwards) 124, **124,** 185

McElroy, Guy 20, 181
McKay, Claude 35
McMillen Gallery, New York City 49
McNeil, William 42, 150, *150,* 173, 186
Malcolm X Speaks for Us (Catlett) 40
Mary Turner: A Silent Protest Against Mob Violence (Fuller) 28
Masai (Barthé) 78
Mason, Charlotte 32
Maternal Family (Hooks) 125, **125,** 185
Mayhew, Richard 42, 54, 149, **149,** 172, 186
Meadows, Jerome 129, **129,** 173, 185
Memory and Metaphor: The Art of Romare Bearden (exhibition) 187
Middleton, Sam 42, 151, **151,** 173, 186
Midtown Payson Galleries, New York 11
Migration of the New Negro Series (Lawrence) 48
Modern Negro Art 36
Morning (Bearden) **cover,** 4, 21, 38, 96, **96,** 184
Morrison, Keith 14, 16, *16,* 18, 19, 43, 152, **152,** 153, **153,** 173, 186, 187
Moss, Carlton 20
Mothers and the Presence of Myth (Harris) 142, **142,** 185
Motley, Archibald 43, 47, 48
Mt. Hood from John Day's Station (Brown) 26, 70, **70,** 183
Murray, Albert 49
Museum of African American Art and Culture 20
Museum of African-American Life and Culture 53
Museum of the National Center of Afro-American Art 21, 50

N'namdi, George 52
NAACP 32, 47
National Endowment for the Humanities 56
National Museum of African Art 51
National Museum of American Art 51, 69, 187
National Portrait Gallery 48, 187
National Urban League 33, 47
Negro Art: Past and Present 37
New Negro movement 27, 47, 62, 90, 177n.6
Newark Museum 4, 9, 14
Newport Scene (Herring) 27, 73, **73,** 183
Nigger Heaven (Van Vechten) 29
Night Food (Morrison) 43, 153, **153,** 186
Nightrane (Morrison) 152, **152,** 186
No Justice, No Peace? Resolutions (exhibition) 173
Nocturne (Driskell) 61
Norton, Peter and Eileen 52, 53
Notre-Dame de Paris (Jones) 31, 36, 85, **85,** 183

O'Keeffe, Georgia 12, 18, 19, *19,* 55
O'Neal, Mary Lovelace 20, 42, 154, **154,** 173, 186
One Hundred Fifty Years of Afro-American Art (exhibit) 18
Opal Magazine (periodical) 33
Opportunity (periodical) 33, 47, 92, 177n.16
Ordeal of Alice, The (Lawrence) 127
Other Side of Color: The African American Collection of

Camille O. and William H. Cosby, Jr., The 10
Palmer Memorial Institute 36
Paul Robeson as Othello (Barthé) 78
Perry, Regenia 52, 178col.1, n.10; 181
Phillips, Duncan 17, 49
Phillips, James 130, **130,** 173, 185
Pierce, Joseph and Aaronetta 51
Pietà (Fuller) 27, 72, **72,** 183
Pines at Falmouth (Driskell) **61**
Pious, Robert Savon 35, 177n.18
Pippin, Horace 37, 53
Playground (Porter) 36, 107, **107,** 184
Pogue, Stephanie E. 14, 19, 37, 42, 106, **106,** 155, **155,** 173, 184, 186
Polk, P. H. 29, 31, 88, *88,* 173, 183
Poor, Henry Varnum 18
Porter, Charles Ethan 27, 74, **74,** 174, 183
Porter, Constance *57*
Porter, James A. 10, 12, 13, 17, 18, 20, 36, *37, 52,* 56, 92, 98, 102, 107, **107,** 161, 174, 177n.1, 178col.1, n.2; 181, 184
Porter-Wesley, Dorothy *52,* 107
Portinari, Candido 17
Portrait of Aaron Douglas (Polk) 29, 88, *88,* 183
Portrait of First Wife and Daughter (In the Woods) (aka *Kate and Rachel*) (VanDerZee) 76, *76,* 183
Portrait of Paul Robeson (DeCarava) 100, *100,* 184
Potter's House, The (Tucker) 43, 164, **164,** 186
Powell, Richard J. 20, 55–56, 181, 187
Powers, Harriet 47, 178col.1, n.4
Prestopine, Gregorio 165
Primitive Girl (Wells) 34, 112, **112,** 184
Prophet, The (White) 41, 132, **132,** 185
Puryear, Martin 19, 20, 135, **135,** 174, 185

Quilting Party (Biggers) 118, **118,** 184

Rabb, Madeline 52
Racism is Like Rain, Either It's Raining or It's Gathering Somewhere (O'Neal) 42, 154, **154,** 186
Reason, Patrick H. 46–47
Red Umbrella, The (Lewis) 42, 148, **148,** 185
Rinksbureau voor Kunsthistorisches Documental den Haag 18
Robbins, Warren 51
Roberts and Johnson (aka *Looking Backward*) (VanDerZee) 30, 90, *91,* 183
Robertson, Eric 52
Robeson, Paul 40, 78, 100, *100*
Robinson, Leo *58*
Rockefeller Foundation 57
Rose of Sharon (Waring) 35, 111, **111,** 184

St. James Guide to Black Artists 66
Saunders, Ray 42, 156, **156,** 174, 186
Savage, Augusta 21, 31, 32, 33–34, 35, 89, **89,** 108, **108,** 147, 174, 177nn.17, 20; 183, 184
Schomburg, Arthur 32, 34
Schomburg Center for Research in Black Culture 32
Schuyler, George 29, 62, 177n.8; 178col.2, n.5
Scott, William E. 33, 47
Scottish Landscape (Duncanson) 26, 71, **71,** 183
Seabrooke, Georgette 34, 177n.18

Seated Mother and Child (Catlett) 136, **136,** 185
Seated Woman (Johnson) 29, 82, **82,** 183
Sebree, Charles 109, **109,** 174, 184
Self Portrait (Driskell) **18**
Shahn, Ben 165
Sharecropper (Catlett) 119, **119,** 184
Sharing Tradition, Five Black Artists in Nineteenth Century America 51
Shotgun Series (Biggers) 118, **118,** 184
Significant Losses: Artists Who Have Died From AIDS (exhibition) 187
Simmons, Johnny 20
Simmons, Gary 52
Simon, Sidney 18
Simpson, Lorna 52
Sippi Eye (Edwards) 124, **124,** 185
Sisters (Wells) 29, 92, **93,** 184
Skowhegan School of Painting and Sculpture, Maine 10, 17–18, 102, 123
Slave Lynching (Clark) 39, 121, **121,** 185
Smith, Albert A. 33
Smith, Frank 157, **157,** 174, 186
Smith, Marvin 33, 34, 49, 177n.18
Smith, Morgan 49, 177n.18
Smith, Vincent 19, 43, 158, **158,** 174, 186
Smithsonian Institution, Washington, D.C. 14, 47, *57,* 177n.1
Snowden, Gilda 42, 159, **159,** 174, 186
Sources: Multicultural Influences on African American Sculptors (exhibition) 187
Spelman College 35, 49, 94, 181, 187
Spencer, Ella 32
Spiral 38, 97
Stamos, Theodoros 17
Stephens, David *58*
Stewart, Frank 43, 160, *160,* 175, 186
Still Life (aka *Still Life with Fetish*) (Jennings) 104, **104,** 184
Stovall, Lou *58,* 86, 161, **161,** 175, 186
Stowe, Hariet Beecher 47, 177n.2
Struggle Series (Lawrence) 126, **126,** 185
Sweet Swing Series (Stewart) 43, 160, *160,* 186
Survey Graphic (periodical) 47, 86, 177n.16

Talladega College 7, 10, 36, 102, 121
Tam, Ruben 165
Tanner, Henry O. 27, 28, 32, 46, 47, 51, 55, 56, 75, **75,** 78, 85, 175, 183
Target Practice (Catlett) 40
Taylor, Bill 110, **110,** 175, 184
Terra Firma (exhibition) 187
Third Ward (Biggers) 39
Thirty Contemporary Black Artists (exhibition) 51
Thomas, Alma 21, 42, 110, 162, **162, 163,** 175, 186
Thompson, W. O. 32
Thrash, Dox 48
Thurman, Wallace 32
Tornado (Snowden) 42, 159, **159,** 186
Torso (Taylor) 110, **110,** 184
Toussaint L'Ouverture Series (Lawrence) 30, 86, **87,** 183
Travelers, The (Lawrence) 40, 127, **127,** 185
Trusty on a Mule (Woodruff) 31, 94, **94,** 184
Tucker, Curtis 164

Tucker, Yvonne Edwards 43, 164, **164,** 175, 186
Two Centuries of Black American Art (exhibition) 10, 51, 56–57, 66
Two Figures in a Mexican Landscape (Woodruff) 35, **64,** 115, **115,** 184
Two Worlds: One of Sight, One of Vision 178col.2, n.1

Uncle Tom and Little Eva (Duncanson) 46
Undeclared War (aka *Just Before the Battle*) (VanDerZee) 31, 90, *91,* 183
Under the Oaks (Bannister) 46, 69
University of Maryland 4, 7, 8, 9, 10, 11, 12, 13, 14, 36, 37, 58, 187
Untitled (Delaney) 42, 139, **139,** 185
Untitled (Middleton) 42, 151, **151,** 186
Untitled (Saunders) 42, 156, **156,** 186
Untitled (Williams) 42, 166, **166,** 186
Untitled (Fish in Net) (Wilson) 21, 31, 37, 114, **114,** 184
Untitled (Head) (Sebree) 109, **109,** 184
Untitled (Head of a Man) (Barthé) 29, 78, **78,** 183
Untitled (Landscape with Cows) (Bannister) 26, 68, **68,** 183
Untitled (Landscape with Pond) (Bannister) 26, 69, **69,** 183
Untitled #1 (Adkins) 134, **134,** 185
Untitled (Still Life: Mums in a Bowl) (Porter) 27, 74, **74,** 183
Untitled (Verso) (Bearden) 38, 97, **97,** 184
Urban Street Scene (Bearden) 40, 117, **117,** 184
Uzelac, Constance Porter 57

Van Vechten, Carl 17, 18, 29, 40
Van Vechten Collection 18
Van Vechten Gallery, Fisk University *16, 39*
VanDerZee, James 27, 29, 30, 31, 40, 76, *76,* 90, *91,* 160, 175, 183, 184
VanDerZee Boys (VanDerZee) 27, 76, *76,* 183

Waddy, Ruth 55
Walker, A'Lelia 47
Walker, Kara 52
Walker, Madame C. J. 47
Wallach, Amei 52, 178col.1 n.9; 182
Walter O. Evans Collection of African American Art 52, 182
Wanted Poster Series (White) 40, 131, **131,** 185
Waring, Laura Wheeler 32, 35, 47, 111, **111,** 176, 184
Washington, Sherry 52
We Declare Ourselves Independent (Lawrence) 126, **126,** 185
Weems, Carrie Mae 52
Wells, James Lesesne 7, 29, 30, 31, 33, 34, *34,* 36, 37, *37,* 55, 56, *58,* 92, **92, 93,** 112, **112,** 161, 176, 177n.18, 184
White, Charles 35, 39, 40, 41, 49, 113, **113,** 131, **131,** 132, **132,** 176, 184, 185
Whitney Museum 49, 51
William E. Harmon Foundation 12, 19, 25, 31, 36, 56, 114
Williams, Reba and Dave 48, 182
Williams, Walter 19, 21, 42, 165, **165,** 176, 186
Williams, William T. 12, 18, 19, 42, 54, 166, **166,** 167, **167,** 176, 186
Wilson, Ellis 19, 21, 31, 37, 114, **114,** 176, 177n.18, 184
Woman and Child Reading (Bearden) 38, 97, **97,** 184
Woodruff, Hale A. 30, 31, 35–36, 49, 94, **94,** 115, **115,** 176, 184
WPA Federal Arts Project. *See* Federal Arts Project
Wright, Richard 35
Wynton Marsalis (Stewart) 43, 160, *160,* 186